AF737818

THE THIRD STATISTICAL ACCOUNT
OF SCOTLAND

THE COUNTY OF

BERWICK

Plate 1a. A game of bowls at Eyemouth, 1930s.

Plate 1b. Fish sale, Eyemouth, 1930s.

Plate 1c. Fish curing, Eyemouth, 1930s.

THE THIRD STATISTICAL ACCOUNT
OF SCOTLAND

THE COUNTY OF
BERWICK

EDITED BY

JOHN HERDMAN

SCOTTISH ACADEMIC PRESS
EDINBURGH
1992

Published by
Scottish Academic Press Ltd,
56 Hanover Street, Edinburgh EH2 2DX

SBN 0 7073 0608 6

© 1992 Scottish Council for Community and Voluntary Organisations

All rights reserved. No part of this publication may be reproduced,
stored in a retrieval system, or transmitted, in any form, or
by any means, electronic, mechanical, photocopying, recording
or otherwise, without the prior permission of the
Scottish Council for Community and Voluntary Organisations,
19 Claremont Crescent, Edinburgh.

Typeset by Trinity Typesetting, Edinburgh.
Printed by Martin's of Berwick Ltd.

CONTENTS

ILLUSTRATIONS

Plates

FOREWORD

It gives me great pleasure to welcome the publication of this volume about the County of Berwickshire.

In accordance with the general principles of The Third Statistical Account of Scotland the area concerned is that of the county as it was before the re-organisation of local government in Scotland in 1975.

When he composed and edited The First Statistical Account of Scotland in 1791-1795 Sir John Sinclair discovered the merit of allowing the views and personalities of the contributors to illuminate the catalogue of facts which he had asked them to compile. The original parish accounts for this volume were written by local ministers and others in the period shortly after the Second World War; they present a fascinating picture, made all the more striking by the recent and careful editing of the manuscripts.

In commending this volume it gives me special pleasure to record the gratitude of the Scottish Council for Voluntary Organisations to the original contributors, many of whom alas are no longer with us, and particularly to Lady Brigid McEwen for her early help with the editing and to Dr John Herdman, the ultimate editor, for undertaking the difficult task of bringing this enterprise to its successful conclusion.

This volume could not be published without the generous financial support of many individuals and institutions. I should like specifically to thank the Robertson Trust, the Binks Trust, the Berwickshire District Council, the Borders Regional Council and the Tweeddale Press, and for their advice and encouragement the Lords Lieutenant, the late Sir William Swan KCVO CBE TD and Sir John Swinton KCVO OBE DL.

Alexander Law
Honorary Vice-President
Scottish Council for Voluntary Organisations

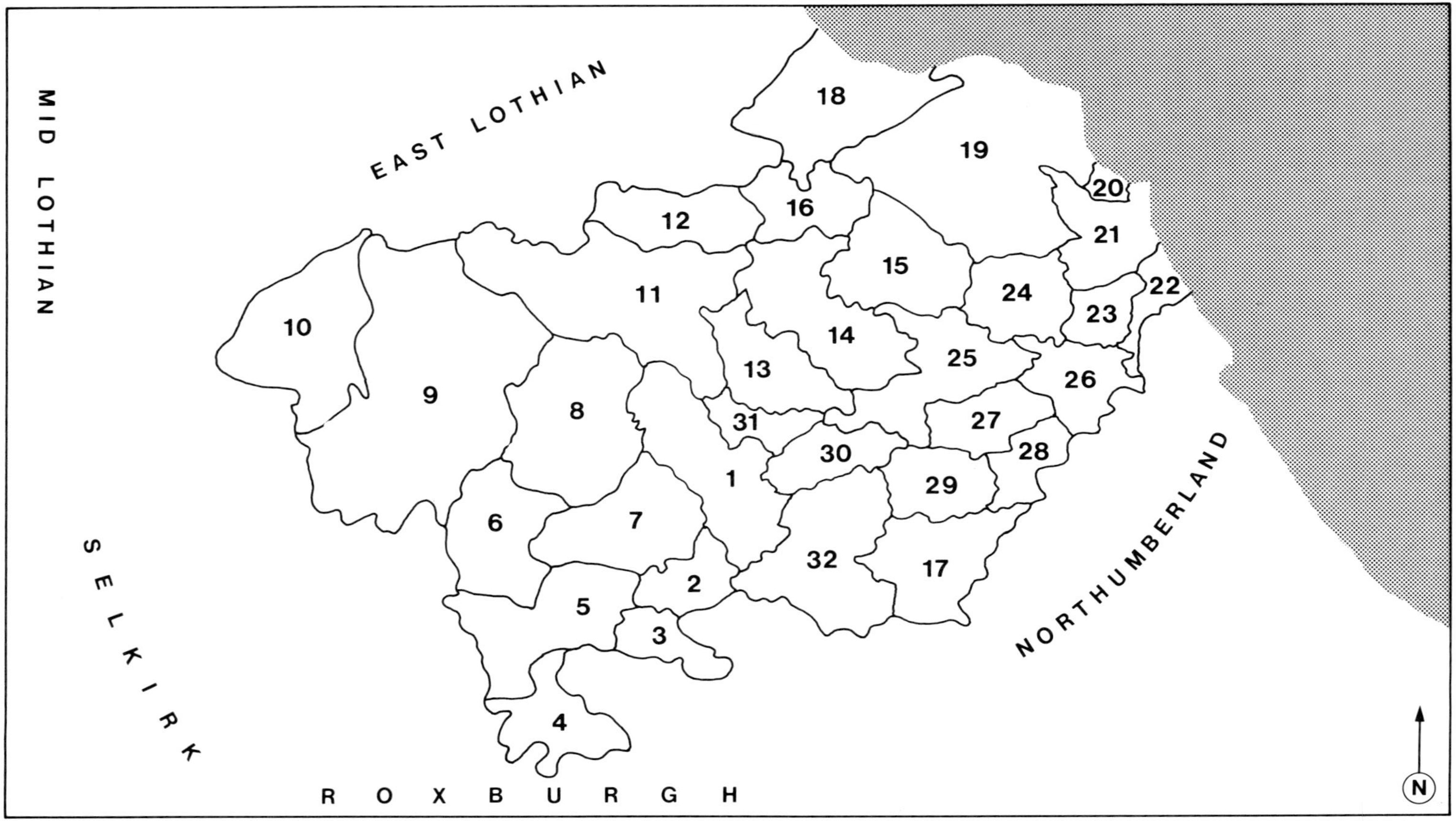
MID LOTHIAN
EAST LOTHIAN
SELKIRK
ROXBURGH
NORTHUMBERLAND
N
1
2
3
4
5
6
7
8
9
10
11
12
13
14
15
16
17
18
19
20
21
22
23
24
25
26
27
28
29
30
31
32

County of Berwick
Key to Parishes

1 Greenlaw
2 Hume
3 Nenthorn
4 Merton
5 Earlston
6 Legerwood
7 Gordon
8 Westruther
9 Lauder
10 Channelkirk
11 Longformacus
12 Cranshaws
13 Langton
14 Duns
15 Bunkle and Preston
16 Abbey St. Bathans
17 Coldstream
18 Cockburnspath
19 Coldingham
20 Eyemouth
21 Ayton
22 Mordington
23 Foulden
24 Chirnside
25 Edrom
26 Hutton
27 Whitsome
28 Ladykirk
29 Swinton and Simprim
30 Fogo
31 Polwarth
32 Eccles

PREFACE

Work on the present volume of the Third Statistical Account of Scotland began in the early 1950s under the auspices of Edinburgh University, and at that time accounts of the social, economic, cultural and religious life of the parishes of Berwickshire were completed (mostly, but not exclusively, by parish ministers) for all but six of the parish units: Ayton, Earlston, Edrom, Greenlaw, Hume and Nenthorn. In the early 1980s, The Scottish Council for Voluntary Organisations having assumed responsibility, the project was resuscitated; but as the intervening thirty years had been a time of unprecedentedly rapid change, it was considered appropriate to obtain supplementary, somewhat shorter essays to bring the picture up to date, while retaining the 1950s account which fulfilled the original intention of reflecting the condition of the country at mid-century.

In fact, even some of the later accounts have now been overtaken by the rapid march of events. Most of the original contributors were deceased by 1980; the only 1950s author to update his previous account in the later decade has been the Earl Haig (Mertoun Parish), and his new article subsumes his earlier work. The six parishes previously untreated have now been covered.

While many of the later accounts have again been contributed by parish ministers, the range of authorship now reflects a much wider occupational spectrum. All contributors, however, are expert in their local knowledge, and their affection and enthusiasm for their parishes and their inhabitants are happily apparent in their writing. The contributions are gratifyingly varied in style, approach and in the degree of detail with which particular topics have been treated; this variety has been encouraged, since Berwickshire is a remarkably homogeneous county, and too rigid a uniformity of approach might have issued in monotony and repetition. Editorial intervention has been kept to a minimum, but some accounts have unavoidably been subject to some shortening. Berwickshire is a small county but it has an unusually large number of parishes, and with two accounts for most of them, this volume has turned out considerably longer than originally envisaged.

Berwickshire remains overwhelmingly a farming county, with a substantial fishing industry centred on Eyemouth. Apart from C. H. Dexter's paper mill at Chirnside and a small industrial estate at Duns, there are few employment opportunities outside agriculture and fishing. The story of the county is very much the story of its individual parishes writ large, and it was felt, therefore, that an overview of the county as a whole, such as has been included in some previous volumes of the Third Statistical Account, would in this case be redundant.

Economically and socially the most important change affecting all the parishes during the period covered by the present Account have been the linked phenomena of agricultural mechanisation and rural depopulation. The remarkable improvements in services, facilities and living conditions welcomed or eagerly anticipated by the writers of the 1950s have unhappily not sufficed to halt the decline in population (see Table of Census figures). Many of the 1980s writers comment, too, on the decline in religious observance which has accelerated during the past thirty years, and this is surely a major change in the way of life of the people of Berwickshire.

It is possible that future social historians will underline the importance of a further trend which has become increasingly visible (and audible) in recent years. Thirty-five years ago the vast majority of people in every parish had been born in Berwickshire (though not necessarily in the parish of their present residence, since agricultural workers tended to move around within a restricted orbit); and in most cases so had their forebears been for generations. The proportion of whom this is true is now very much less. The number of incomers has risen steeply; mainly retired people, holiday home owners, and people travelling to work outside the county, although a number have found employment within the immediate area. These new residents of Berwickshire come from both sides of the Border, but probably more of them from the southern side of it, and their presence and contribution will modify, for good or ill, the traditional life of the county in ways which cannot yet be foreseen.

The Berwickshire District of Borders Region, created by the reform of Local Government in Scotland in 1975, is not identical with the old county. The latter, however, is the unit covered by the present volume in continuing the descriptive scheme initiated by Sir John Sinclair, Bart., in his First Statistical Account of Scotland, published during the 1790s.

The gathering of the contributions from the 1980s, with many onerous attendant duties, has been the work of Lady McEwen of Marchmont. The present Editor took over at a late stage when much of the spadework had been accomplished; and as a recent and transient resident of Berwickshire, he has relied greatly and gratefully on her continued interest and help and on her vastly superior knowledge of the county and its people. Berwickshire, because of its strategic position on the Border, has a rich and fascinating history which has been linked with and has contributed much to the wider history of Scotland. To Lady McEwen and to all the contributors from the two separated decades, the thanks of future students and friends of the county will be due for the insights which we hope that this volume will offer on the present chapter of its history.

January 1992

COUNTY OF BERWICK — POPULATION FIGURES FOR SELECTED CENSUS YEARS 1980-1981

Parish	1801	1851	1861	1871	1881	1891	1901	1911	1921	1931	1951	1961	1971	1981	
														Present	*Resident*
Abbey St Bathans	138	155	179	195	250	193	213*	229	203	169	149	125	109	86	81
Ayton	1453	1959	2014	1983	2040	1827	1629	1577	1521	1413	1483	1769	1956	1880	1821
Bunkle and Preston	674	715	756	764	726	672	629	562	542	507	417	343	324	261	258
Channelkirk (E&L)	640	728	671	705	607	545	568	478	499	418	413	357	339	306	293
Chirnside	1147	1384	1502	1413	1516	1459	1580	1508	1402	1414	1218	1111	1101	1459	1457
Cockburnspath	930	1196	1194	1133	1130	1112	982*	997	941	876	761	635	513	568	505
Coldingham	2391	3188	3241	3093	3173	2946	2813*	2749	2830	2398	2302	2031	1742	1751	1692
Coldstream	2269	3245	2823	2619	2561	2388	2281	2192	2013	1922	1840	1693	1601	1931	1901
Cranshaws	166	127	134	142	106	85	159*	125	97	119	116	98	84	82	71
Duns	3163	3407	3595	3602	3353	3137	3199	3042	2818	2677	2877	2495	2383	2674	2639
Earlston (E&L)	1478	1819	1825	1977	1767	1784	1677*	1749	1643	1689	1761	1831	1770	1907	1867
Eccles	1682	1892	1861	1780	1546	1446	1433	1449	1245	1182	1023	972	836	715	712
Edrom	1355	1474	1592	1513	1514	1361	1290	1269	1119	1015	861	747	487	375	361
Eyemouth	899	1488	1804	2372	2935	2670	2487*	2561	2573	2321	1999	1518	1611	2587	2573
Fogo	507	604	559	502	468	420	445	389	383	369	425	256	202	138	137
Foulden	393	430	431	425	393	351	386	313	253	306	294	317	261	246	250
Gordon	802	983	931	876	832	843	791	711	719	702	673	643	561	523	505
Greenlaw	1270	1378	1370	1381	1245	1110	1015	941	909	889	831	777	794	770	746
Hume	415	406	420	460	407	366	311*	298	258	259	246	234	171	184	188
Hutton	955	1102	1067	1077	962	815	750	682	655	614	556	482	408	439	444
Ladykirk	516	561	564	518	438	339	316	315	338	305	261	201	181	160	161
Langton	428	484	502	548	505	417	398	408	385	363	386	307	277	242	233
Lauder (E&L)	1760	2154	2198	2120	1940	1588	1461*	1336	1369	1214	1190	975	948	1102	1065
Legerwood	495	587	599	525	549	475	431	401	379	332	295	257	197	184	176
Longformacus	406	411	448	452	385	378	281*	263	250	259	320	240	208	176	161
Mertoun (E&L)	535	692	729	734	682	622	576*	532	463	522	460	398	364	270	251
Mordington	330	427	377	402	367	324	284	292	299	319	247	221	181	139	141
Nenthorn (Rox)	395	441	461	434	454	400	416*	356	363	349	279	213	178	116	112
Polwarth	291	331	251	249	227	203	203	197	167	160	115	94	65	41	42
Swinton	875	994	964	996	964	847	791	727	689	676	571	503	442	367	369
Westruther	779	791	786	784	671	615	504	503	448	421	395	316	265	287	258
Whitsome	560	612	640	608	560	573	525	492	473	433	304	278	222	192	193

(E&L) = now in Ettrick and Lauderdale District (Rox) = now in Roxburgh District * Change in parish boundary in intercensal period.

THE PARISH OF ABBEY ST BATHANS AND CRANSHAWS

by The Rev. Crichton S. Eddy, M.A.

BOUNDARIES

ABBEY ST BATHANS

The detached portion of Longformacus at Blakerston was incorporated in Abbey St Bathans about 50 years ago.

CRANSHAWS

The detached portion of Cranshaws was incorporated in Longformacus about 50 years ago, and part of Longformacus was included in Cranshaws to give the present boundaries.

GENERAL

The population of Abbey St Bathans and Cranshaws has not fluctuated greatly in the last 150 years mainly because the type of farming has not changed except in method, but the population is constantly changing, as farm workers do not nowadays care to live in the comparative isolation of the hills without the full amenities of urban life. Added to that is the fact that opportunities are not forthcoming for boys leaving school to be employed in the farms. There are, for instance, no boys learning to herd sheep. On the whole the population tends to be an aging one. Girls find no attraction in domestic service, preferring low paid jobs in towns as typists and shop girls. There are, of course, not many opportunities for entering agriculture, but no girl seems keen. The policy of removing children from the rural areas to central Junior Secondary Schools does not help them in fixing on agriculture for their livelihood, nor does National Service help young men to settle. Few can do the varied, skilled work that an older generation of farm labourers could do. Tractor driving being an end in itself, young men do not want to learn all the aspects of the farm labourer's craft.

No tradesmen or craftsmen live in either parish, with the exception of a blacksmith at Cranshaws, whose main work lies outside the parish, at horse-racing stables at Grantshouse.

CRANSHAWS

HISTORY

The parish of Cranshaws is very ancient. The original church was dedicated to St Ninian in the 7th century, and there still exist ruins in the old churchyard of a church, built prior to the 17th century. It was replaced in 1739 by a new church on a new site. This, in turn, was replaced in 1899 by a modern building of a beautiful nature, by Andrew Smith of Cranshaws and Whitchester, then principal heritor, and uncle of the present proprietor. There was in the old church, opposite the pulpit, a Royal coat of arms, placed there by James V to remind the minister to pray for him. It was placed in the 1739 building, and again in the 1899 church.

The Lands of Cranshaws were once the property of the Swintons of that Ilk and have, through many changes, come into the possession of S. E. A. Landale, Esq., of Cranshaws and Whitchester.

Cranshaws Castle, c. 1500, is in excellent repair and is still occupied. There is, in the Castle Gardens, an ancient burial ground of the Swintons.

At Ellemford are the remains of the ancient Parish Church of Ellem, and a few gravestones from about 1600. In Ellem Church James IV held a Council of War before proceeding to Flodden. Here also the Douglas refused to accompany James IV further as they were not given the place of honour in the battle line. There was until c. 1750 a separate parish of Ellem, but it was then united with Longformacus. Ellemford is now in Cranshaws parish. In the lease of Ellemford Farm, there is a clause which gave to the minister the right to graze sheep on Ellemford Moor; now, however, the landlord pays, to the General Trustees of the Church of Scotland, a fixed annual sum in lieu. There was, at one time, a Corn Mill in the Mill Hough, but only a few stones now mark the site.

BOUNDARIES

The parish of Cranshaws is the most northerly in Berwickshire and is situated in the valley of the Whiteadder. It is roughly the shape of the continent of Australia, being about four miles east to west — and one mile north to south. There are six farms:

1. Cranshaws: 2,100 acres — of which 1,200 are rough grazing; 700 acres arable; 200 woodland and waste.
2. Fellcleugh: 400 acres arable.
3. Ellemford: Approximately 2,100 acres — of which 1,200 are rough grazing; 300 marginal; 600 arable.
4. Cranshaws Smithy: 12 acres arable.
5. Craig's Windshiel: Approximately 600 acres is a hirsel on Harehead Farm, which lies in Innerwick Parish.
6. Smiddyhill: 200 acres. (Principal Proprietor of 1-4 is S. E. A. Landale, Esq., who also farms Cranshaws and Ellemford.)

The larger farms came into being in the course of the 19th century by swallowing up small farms, crofts and hirsels: e.g. "Cranshaws" comprises Howbog, Bountree, Cowie Haugh and the original Cranshaws.

Fellcleugh is let to a tenant.

Smiddyhill is farmed by the owner, T. Miller, who also is a trapper and dealer in rabbits.

SHEEP

The rough ground is grazed by black-faced sheep of which there will be about 100 score ewes in the parish. There are also a considerable number of Cheviot — or cross-bred ewes — about 60 score ewes. Each farm keeps a stock of cross-bred cattle. The principal crops are mainly for feeding and are hay, oats and turnips. There are three pairs of work horses in the parish and about ten tractors of varying types. Poultry and pigs are kept on a domestic scale. There is no dairying but most of the shepherds are required to keep a cow. There is one hunter kept in the parish. All the farmers own cars.

LABOUR

All the adult male population is engaged in agriculture or its ancillaries, viz:

4 Shepherds
2 Farm Managers
20 Other farm workers
2 Gamekeepers
2 Rabbit-trappers

The farmers also employ a varying number of Irish labourers for seasonal work. These Irishmen form a kind of hidden population. They take no part in the life of the community. Living in bothies, they fend for themselves — often under poor living conditions.

CHURCH AND SCHOOL

There is a primary school with one female teacher. Scholars number 16. Older children are transported night and morning, to and from Duns. None of the children leaving school in the last four years have found an opportunity to enter agriculture. School meals are provided from Duns. The Primary children, living more than one mile from the school, are transported morning and night, to school. (The cost for Berwickshire, per annum, for school transport, is more than £1 per head per annum of the total population.)

CHURCH

The Congregational Roll is 86 and represents the total adult population of the Parish and landward parts of neighbouring parishes. There are no other religious sects or denominations. There is a Kirk Session, jointly, with Abbey St Bathans. Four of the Elders reside at Cranshaws, as does the Minister.

ORGANISATIONS

Woman's Guild:	24
Carpet Bowling Club:	15
Fishing Club:	20

CRANSHAWS HALL

Built 1922 — partly endowed by the late Mrs Smith of Whitchester and maintained by the people of the parish.

HOUSES

All modernised except for electricity.

4 Orlits — built 1951

2 Farm cottages built at Ellemford in 1951

1 Small mansion 1937

There is no County water supply. Each farm has a local supply. Some of the farms have privately-owned electric installations.

POPULATION

This numbers 121 — none are natives of the parish beyond one generation, except one shepherd at Cranshaws, whose father and grandfather were also shepherds there.

TRANSPORT

Bus twice weekly (once daily) to Duns.

POST OFFICE, Etc.

There is a Sub-Post Office. There are no shops but there is an adequate service of all types of provisions and merchandise, by vans daily from Duns.

BEQUEST

The Hon. John Watson of Saughton, a former owner of Cranshaws, in 1833, bequeathed £1,000 sterling for the poor of the parish. This bequest is now administered by the County Council.

STIPEND

Tiends and Endowments £447
Glebe — about £3

ECCLESIASTICAL PARISH

United with Abbey St Bathans, in 1927.

1950s

CRANSHAWS

by Sheila McKinnon

GENERAL

The area of Cranshaws is the most northerly of Berwickshire, which is now part of Borders Region, though it is still largely administered by Berwickshire District Council. It has lately (1986) been increased in size by a Lothian-Borders Boundary Review, which extends it to the North to include the Bothwell and Monynut valleys, an area of some 20 square miles. The Church of Scotland does not appear to have made any adjustment to the parish size, and this creates difficulty in making accurate comparison between the Cranshaws Parish of previous Statistical Accounts and the Cranshaws area of today. It also appears to create difficulty in bureaucratic systems; a recent road wash-out within the new sector was at first declared by the Berwickshire District Council office in Duns to be "a Lothians problem" until they were reminded of the new boundary.

The population, in common with that of most agricultural areas, fluctuates, but basically is on the decline, owing to changes in farming methods and to certain other factors in the type of land use. In a society in which unemployment is at this time very high, particularly among young people, there is an even greater tendency than before for these young people to leave the area to seek work in the towns and cities, and the fact that they attend the High School in Duns from the age of 12 onwards seems to hasten this movement.

The district is one of great natural beauty and its status now as an "Area of Greater Landscape Value" has enabled the worst eyesores, such as electricity pylons, to be avoided. It is also, unfortunately, an area where very low flying for training purposes is permitted, and this constitutes a great nuisance, giving rise to fear in both animals and humans, the latter dreading crashes, some of which have already occurred at no great distance; protests and appeals by many, including the local M.P., to the Ministry of Defence and the R.A.F. have so far had no effect in reducing the number of planes which zoom over.

Several picnic sites and some new motor roads of a quiet type bring visitors to the district in fine weather, and there are some holiday-makers who stay in caravans, bed-and-breakfast houses and other types of accommodation, but in general tourism has little effect on the local economy.

HISTORY

According to the records, the parish is a very old one, but it has few buildings of great historical interest.

Cranshaws Castle (c. 1500) is still occupied and in good repair. The ancient burial ground of the Swinton family is, however, in a state of some neglect.

The present church (built 1899) still has the Royal coat-of-arms, reputed to have been gifted to the old church by James V, and this is now maintained as an Ancient Monument. The church is of a fine design and has recently been extensively repaired and re-decorated. Under the terms of a bequest, it is floodlit during the hours of darkness, to provide guidance for anyone lost in snow or the mist which is so frequent and dangerous in the Lammermuirs.

The largest farms in this almost totally agricultural area are:

Cranshaws Farm

1500 acres rough grazing
300 acres improved grazing
700 acres arable

This is farmed by a tenant farmer.

Fellcleugh
400 acres arable
This is run by a tenant farmer and his son.

Craigs Windshiel
550 acres rough grazing
50 acres arable
This is worked by a farm manager.

Smiddyhill
200 acres rough grazing
This is all let to neighbouring farmers.

Ellemford
2,100 acres
Much of this is now under forest.

In the area from Lothians Region which is now included are:
Bothwell Farm
1,330 acres rough and improved grazing
300 acres arable
This is run on traditional lines by the owner and 2 men.

Crichness
2,300 acres
About 2,000 acres of this are now under trees, and run by a consortium.

There are also small holdings at Friars' Dykes and Belton Dodds, but these are not yet permanently occupied and the small amounts of arable land and livestock are managed with part-time help from local farm workers.

Cranshaws Smiddy is also now run virtually as a small holding, with about 20 sheep. A racehorse is also kept there, and there are some caravans available for holiday-makers.

AGRICULTURAL CHANGES

The most important and noticeable change in the agriculture of the area is the increase in forestry. The bulk of this in Cranshaws Parish is owned by the Landale family (based in, and living in, Cranshaws House) and administered through the Estate of Whitchester, along with woodlands in Longformacus and, to a lesser extent, Duns parishes.

Approximately 750 acres of woodland belong to Whitchester Estate, mostly in small plantations of less than 20 acres, with some larger blocks. Shelter is a prime purpose of many of the smaller woods, with finished production and sporting uses (for pheasant covers) as further important purposes of management. The sawmill, central to the enterprise, lies just outside the Cranshaws boundary, but employs several people who live within it. It produces fencing materials, gates, firewood and boiler fuel in the form of woodchips, which latter supplies four households on the estate. Much of the hill ground in the area is now covered by trees, mostly conifers, and managed by several consortia, much in the way just described, though without the adjacent sawmill.

A further very noticeable change in the countryside is the introduction of oil-seed rape — a profitable crop, and outstanding with its brilliant yellow blossom. It is not without its critics, because it appears to accentuate hay fever symptoms, and even to cause them in those who did not have them before; the connection has not yet been proved, but official investigations are now taking place, after a spate of complaints.

Eye-catching also is the amount of winter wheat which is now grown, as this produces a green haze over many fields, much earlier in the year than most of us have been accustomed to see it.

LIVESTOCK

Much of the rough ground is still grazed by blackface sheep, of which there are about 6,000. There are also about 1,000 Cheviot and crossbred sheep.

Each farm still has a stock of cross-bred cattle, amounting to between 300 and 350 in the area. The main change in these in the last few years has been the introduction of Charolais and other European breeds to improve beef production and to achieve calves which mature earlier.

There are no longer any work horses in Cranshaws, although there is one racehorse and several riding horses and ponies. To do the work formerly done by the big horses there are now some 16 tractors, three combine harvesters and two or three other large machines. In some cases, contractors are employed to do seasonal work; in this connection it is perhaps worth mentioning that these contractors, who come to the area for a few hours, or days at most, have completely replaced the groups of itinerant (mainly Irish) workers who have been mentioned in previous accounts.

Poultry is still kept on a domestic scale, but not pigs, though from time to time one sees a few goats tethered. There is no dairying, nor do any shepherds keep cows; the area is largely dependent for milk on a thrice-weekly delivery from Duns.

LABOUR

Still almost all the adult males are employed in agricultural pursuits. There are:

3 shepherds
12 general farm workers (including farmers and tenant farmers)
1 farm manager
2 woodcutters
2 sawmill workers
2 gamekeepers
1 estate manager
1 Water Board attendant

Some others live in the area but travel by car to work elsewhere — e.g. a teacher.

Few women in the district are in full-time employment — the school teacher, the school bus driver and the estate secretary — though some have part-time domestic employment, and some others, as in the case of men, travel to work in Duns, Dunbar, etc.

CHURCH

The only church represented in the community is the Church of Scotland.

In 1983, the Parish of Cranshaws, which had already been joined under one minister to that of Abbey St Bathans, was further amalgamated with the Parish of Longformacus. These three now form the Kirk of Lammermuir, of which the Congregational Roll is 144. It will be obvious that no direct comparison of numbers with those of previous accounts is possible.

The present incumbent of the Kirk of Lammermuir, the Rev. A. Slorach, is also responsible for the joint Parishes of Langton and Polwarth, so that the Sunday services must be spaced out; basically, Cranshaws and Longformacus alternate in having the 12 noon service, with Abbey St Bathans having its service in the evening, except for a Family Service if there is a fifth Sunday in the month.

The minister and two of the elders live in Cranshaws, where there are active Prayer Meetings and a Bible Study group for women. The only other organisation in the community is the Woman's Guild, now also under the aegis of the Kirk of Lammermuir, which has 20 members.

SCHOOL

There is a primary school in the village with one teacher and numbers of pupils fluctuating from 10 to 15. Recent attempts by the Education Committee to close the school in pursuance of its policy of centralisation have been fought by the Community Council on the grounds that the children come from such scattered parts (some even from places technically in Lothian Region) that the journey to Duns would make the day too long for young ones, and also on the grounds that bad weather can cut off isolated farms in a very short time. It now seems as if the threat of closure has been lifted for the next few years.

The school bus which transports pupils morning and evening is also used to take them to Duns for swimming and some other sporting activities, and for educational outings; it no longer brings the school meals, however, and the pupils carry their own packed lunches.

Secondary pupils attend the Berwickshire High School in Duns.

AMENITIES

The Village Hall still exists and is used for some social functions. It is now being renovated and it is hoped that this will encourage people to make more use of it.

The Sub-Post Office no longer exists, and the building has been converted to a private house. This loss can make things difficult, particularly for old or disabled people, who sometimes find it hard to get to Duns to collect pensions.

The buses referred to in the last Account no longer run; the school bus to Duns runs on weekdays during term-time, but that is all. The daily vans mentioned no longer call; there is the thrice-weekly milk delivery to farm road-ends, and a van with fish and fruit comes once a week. The County Library van calls fortnightly. Most people have their newspapers delivered by post.

The lack of vans is attributed to the high cost of fuel and relatively low sales. The low sales, in turn, have been attributed to the fact that owing to the lack of public transport virtually every family must have a car: with a car, and a freezer (which, again, almost every family has), people can get to supermarkets and stock up with enough provisions for several weeks. Thus the vans were only used for odd items that had been overlooked. But as the number of vans declined over several years, the relation of cause and effect is in doubt. Incidentally, the increased use of freezers also helps to explain why shepherds are no longer 'required' to keep a cow; the cow's milk used to be necessary to feed orphan lambs, but it has now been replaced by readily available supplies of frozen colostrum, and by easily stored powdered milk.

WILD LIFE

Despite fears about pollution and habitat destruction, the wild life around Cranshaws appears to be thriving. After myxomatosis the rabbits have returned in vast numbers, though some infected ones do appear. Weasels and stoats are always about, as are hedgehogs — many, unfortunately, killed by traffic, but nevertheless many healthy and active. Grey squirrels are fairly plentiful, and the recent appearance of a pair of red ones near the river close to Cranshaws village gives hope that they may breed. Roe deer may be glimpsed quite often crossing the roads or in the forestry plantations, and foxes are still about in the hills. Recently, pest control men had to be called in to deal with mink in the village itself near the school, and one pet cat was thought to have been killed by them. They have not been seen now for some months, but it is, of course, possible that they may re-appear.

As regards birds, the herons or 'cranes' which give the area its name are to be seen, but only rarely. Pheasants, as has been mentioned, are bred, and partridges are also here, together with some grouse. Most of the common species — robins, chaffinches, tits, starlings, wagtails, swallows, cuckoos, owls, house martins, the crow family, seagulls, etc. — are still plentiful, though the experts note that the house sparrow appears to have declined in numbers. On the other hand, a kingfisher has been seen by the Whiteadder, though, sadly, on very few occasions.

Fishermen continue in quite large numbers to use the Whiteadder and smaller burns, and seem to be satisfied with their catches, which would suggest that the pollution level here is not high enough to damage the stock.

SUMMMARY

In brief, Cranshaws area is like most other rural areas in Scotland in that the number of people living and working there is declining and the population is aging. Increase in mechanisation means that fewer workers are needed on the land, so the young people are forced to seek work elsewhere, and they seldom return.

No houses have been built since the last Account, though all existing ones have been modernised and have electricity. But, as elsewhere, many are now occupied only as holiday homes, or by retired people. It seems that this trend may well continue; it is very difficult for any rural area to go against the general tendency of the whole country.

1986

ABBEY ST BATHANS

by Rev. Crichton S. Eddy, M.A.

HISTORY

The parish of Abbey St Bathans is of very ancient origin. There are records of a religious foundation here as early as the 6th century. In the Chapel Field, there are enclosed, parts of the foundations of a very ancient church. Excavation work was done here in the early 19th century but nothing of importance was found. A stone cist found on the Abbey Hill was placed in the enclosure, a long number of years ago.

The present church occupies part of the site of the old conventical buildings and is not noteworthy as a piece of architecture, though it incorporates some parts of the walls of the 15th century Abbey. The

Abbey was founded in the 12th century and belonged to the order of Cistercian nuns. It was never of any great size or importance. Inside the present church there is, in a niche, a stone recumbent female figure, reputed to represent Ada, the first abbess or prioress.

Abbey St Bathans incorporates another small parish — Strafontain where there was a leper hospital and a burial ground. All traces of religious buildings at Strafontain have long since disappeared. Godscroft Farm was apparently a grange, attached to Strafontain and it was the birthplace of David Hume, 1563-1630, who is best remembered for his *History of the House of Wedderburn*. The *Dictionary of National Biography* has a full notice of him as well as his daughter Anna who published her father's *History of the House of Douglas and Angus*.

On Cockburn Law there is the famous Edin's Hall Broch of which full details can be found in the Proceedings of the Berwickshire Naturalists Club, 1830-1950.

At Blakerston there is a house known as 'The Retreat' and presently used as the farmhouse. The Retreat is a bottle-shaped house, and was built circa 1782 by the then Earl of Wemyss, as a shooting-lodge.

After the Reformation the lands of Abbey St Bathans became the property of the Humes but in the 19th century, by successive purchases, became the property of a family named Turnbull. They were succeeded in the estate by the Gillons. The present laird is Stair Agnew Gillon, lately Sheriff-substitute at Newton Stewart.

BOUNDARIES

Abbey St Bathans is contiguous to Cranshaws and is roughly the same shape and size. Like Cranshaws, it is traversed by the river Whiteadder and comprises the farms of:

1. Barnside
2. Shannobank
3. Part of Godscroft
4. Part of Whiteburn
5. Part of Quixwood
6. Part of Cockburn
7. Blakerston
8. Abbey St Bathans

These comprise an area of about 6,000 acres and are marginal farms, devoted to sheep and cattle, with cropping of oats, hay and turnips, mainly for winter feeding. The larger farms owe their extent to the absorption in the 19th century of smaller places: e.g. Abbey St Bathans comprises: Frampeth, Hard Hissels, as well as the original Abbey St Bathans.

Shannobank comprises Bankend and Strafontain with the original Shannobank.

There was a Meal Mill at Strafontain but this is now ruinous.

LABOUR

There are no tradesmen or craftsmen resident at Abbey St Bathans. Most of the adult male population are engaged in agriculture, forestry or their ancillaries. During the 1939-45 war there were extensive woods cut down. These are now to be replanted under the Forestry Commission's Dedication Scheme. The Forestry Commission have built two houses — one for a forester and one for a Vermin Exterminator. The total population is about 120. There are none native beyond one generation.

CHURCH AND SCHOOL

There is a primary school with 23 scholars aged 5-11 years, with one female teacher. Older pupils are transported to Duns, daily.

The Congregational Roll is 80, which is the total adult population of the parish and neighbourhood.

The Parishes of Abbey St Bathans and Cranshaws were united ecclesiastically in 1927. The Abbey St Bathans manse was sold. There are four elders of the Kirk Session resident at Abbey St Bathans.

ORGANISATIONS

Woman's Guild	24
Carpet Bowling Club	25
Fishing Club	25

1950s

ABBEY ST BATHANS

by William S. J. Dobie

TOPOGRAPHY AND LANDSCAPE

Abbey St Bathans parish lies in the foothills of the Lammermuirs to the north of Duns. It covers about 5,500 acres and lies between 500 and 900 feet above sea level. The main impression is of a beautiful secluded valley. The River Whiteadder runs through the middle of the parish and is joined by the tributaries of the Weirburn and the Monynut. The land rises from fertile river haughs, and most of the steeper ground is wooded. Some of this is ancient oak woodland and has been designated a site of special scientific interest because of its wildlife interest. The rest consist of larch and pine plantations established since the last war. The higher ground is open farmland with a blend of pasture grazed by sheep and cattle, cultivated land and scattered shelter belts. There is some heather moorland but most of this has been reclaimed within the last 20 years.

HISTORY

Evidence of past occupation dates back to pre-history. A bronze dagger of the Middle Period Bronze Age (1500-1200BC) was unearthed in 1962 in the Camps Field above Shannobank. In the same field can be seen the outlines of an Iron Age fort. Christianity came early, no doubt drawn by the peaceful seclusion, and in the Chapel Field lies the site of a Christian settlement founded by St Bothans in the 7th century. At the end of the 12th century a Cistercian Priory with 12 nuns and a Prioress was founded in the valley by Ada, wife of the Earl of Dunbar. The Priory was destroyed by the English army in 1543, but the north wall and east gable were incorporated in the present parish church. On the east side of the river stands the Retreat, built in 1784 by the Earl of Wemyss as a hunting lodge. It is of special architectural interest, being circular in design with a central chimney stack. Likewise Abbey St Bathans House is an interesting example of Victorian architecture. It was originally a thatched cottage and reached its present size in 1880. In the past Strafountain was a distinct settlement, but virtually all traces of church, graveyard and mill have vanished. Godscroft is associated with David Hume, the 17th century scholar and poet.

POPULATION

There are 59 adults and 20 children under the age of 15. Apart from a square of six cottages opposite the church there is no distinct village, with the population scattered round the parish in individual house and on farms. Only five of the adults were born in the parish, which reflects a frequently changing population. The school closed over 20 years ago and the children are taken by minibus to schools in Duns. There are no shops or pubs and Duns is the local centre. Berwick and Dunbar are also important shopping centres with their large supermarkets. Milk and groceries are delivered by van. There is no public transport and most families own cars.

ECONOMY

Agriculture is still the mainstay of the local economy. There has been little fundamental change over the last 200 years. The land is still devoted mainly to the raising of sheep and cattle, with the better ground under rotation growing crops of barley, swedes and rape to feed the livestock during the winter. The recent trend towards more intensive cultivation with crops such as potatoes and oil seed rape has been reversed, and over 400 acres of cultivated land are now under a government set-aside scheme. The greatest source of change has been mechanisation, which means much less labour is required and the land supports fewer families. Four farms give full time employment to 13 men.

However, the community still thrives as new opportunities have arisen to allow a more diverse economy. The trees planted in the 1950s are providing a flow of thinnings which are sent to chipboard factories in Stirling and Hexham or are processed into fencing materials in the estate sawmill. The parish provides good quality shooting, particularly of pheasants from the steeper woods, and there is a game farm raising pheasant to supplement the wild stock and for resale. The river is well known for its trout fishing, and thanks to a new fish ladder at the Chirnside Paper Mill, sea trout and salmon are now present again. The old mill lade which used to drive a sawmill has provided an ideal source of water for a fish farm which rears trout for the table and for restocking rivers and reservoirs.

Visitors are attracted by the beauty of the valley and tourism is a welcome new source of employment and income. By the fish farm there is a tea room and interpretive centre. The old school house is a pottery and the school room serves as a gallery. Houses which are no longer needed for agricultural workers are now being let as self-catering holiday accommodation. The Southern Upland Way, a long distance coast to coast footpath from Portpatrick to Cockburnspath, runs through the parish, and redundant farm buildings have been converted into a rest house providing low cost accommodation for walkers and other visitors.

CHURCH AND COMMUNITY LIFE

The parish is now united with Cranshaws and Longformacus to form the Kirk of Lammermuir, which in turn is linked to Langton and Polwarth. The minister lives in Cranshaws and there is a service most Sunday evenings attended by 10-20 people. There is a regular Sunday School during term-time and there is a united Woman's Guild with Cranshaws. The Community Council is active and is joined with Bonkyl and Preston. The village hall provides another focus for community life and there is a thriving bowling club. Other community activities are the S.W.R.I. and the Playbus, a converted double-decker bus which provides a mobile playgroup service for isolated areas. In general Abbey St Bathans looks set to enter the next millenium as a small but distinct and vibrant community.

1980s

THE PARISH OF AYTON

by Robert A. H. Robinson

TOPOGRAPHY AND NATURAL HISTORY

The River Eye — or Eye Water as it is known locally — roughly bisects the parish, running from north-west to south-east through the low lying lands of the Eye Valley, turning in a northerly direction to join the North Sea at Eyemouth Harbour. The Ale Water, the principal tributary of the Eye, likewise flows from north-west to south-east, joining the Eye at Millbank. These two rivers, with the various burns and drains, form the main watershed of the parish, the principal burns being the Horn Burn, Biglawburn, Cocklaw Burn and Hill Burn. The Eye and the Ale pass through the fertile lands to the north-west where low banks and grasslands predominate, then on and through the deep, tree- and scrub-lined gorges nearer the sea, east of Ayton village and at Millbank, Ale Water Banks and Netherbyres.

The parish is approximately four miles from north to south, and about the same west to east, giving an approximate area of 13 square miles. To the north the parish is bordered by Coldingham Parish, to the east by Eyemouth and the North Sea, while to the south and west the bounds are Mordington, Foulden, Chirnside and part of Coldingham. The coast line extends from the village of Burnmouth to Eyemouth, a distance of about three miles. At the southern end of the parish the ground rises to form a sloping ridge inclining sharply towards the sea south of Burnmouth at Greystonelees, and extending south-westerly towards Foulden and Chirnside, the highest point being Ayton Hill (660 feet). Precipitous cliffs form the coast line, being less high and rugged towards Eyemouth, with small inlets at Burnmouth and along the coast nearer Eyemouth. The remainder of the terrain within the parish is undulating, with minor elevations between the valley of the Ale and Eyemouth, and between the Eye Water and Millerton Hill.

Except within the grounds of Ayton Castle Estate, and at Netherbyres and Ale Water Banks, very few hardwood trees have survived, and of these practically all the elms have been felled, killed off by 'Dutch Elm Disease' which renders the timber fit only for firewood and posts. The predominant trees are soft-woods — fires, pines and larches — mostly sited in man-made plantations providing timber when mature for pulping, chipboards and posts. Scots pine, Norway and Sitka spruce

Plate 2. Ayton Castle.

Plate 3. The High Street, Ayton, in the 1950s.

and larch predominate, with smaller plantings of less common types of soft-woods, sometimes bordered by silver birch and the more decorative hard-woods. The main hard-woods of the area are oak, ash, beech, sycamore, willow, alder, chestnut, rowan and gean. There is a sawmill at Littledean, for Ayton Castle Estate.

The frequency and thickness of the soft-wood plantations has not greatly enhanced the wild-life of the area, for few birds utilise the woods before they are thinned. Some birds nest in the plantations and others roost there, but generally the more common woodland species are not attracted to this man-made habitat. This is not so for red squirrel and roe deer, both species of which are found locally and appear to be on the increase. Fox and badger seek sanctuary in the plantations, together with some smaller mammals. Since mink were introduced to the area in the 1930s, when it was popular to raise these animals in captivity for their fur, there have been frequent sightings of the survivors of the many escapees, which thrive and have multiplied in the seemingly ideal habitat to which they were introduced. These ferocious mammals can, and do, cause havoc to fish stocks, nesting birds and small mammals, and are a menace to the natural wild-life; so much so that they are regarded as pests and rigorously hunted and trapped.

On the coastal strip of the parish sea-birds such as eider, razor bill, guillemot, oyster catcher, turnstone, red shank, knot, most species of gulls, kittiwake, shag and rock dove frequent the inlets, cliffs and waters. On the lower fields and grasslands can be found sparrow-hawk, kestrel, owls, heron, collared dove, wood pigeon, pied wagtail, chaffinch, blue tit, tree creeper, goldcrest, blackbird, thrush, redwing, moorhen, mallard, dipper, robin, mistle thrush, wheatear, warblers, dunnock, rook, jackdaw, crow, pheasant, partridge, to name but a few. On the uplands red grouse, curlew, common sandpiper, skylark, lapwing, meadowpipit, wheatear and grey wagtail predominate. In April 1986 a little auk was blown ashore at Fairnieside where snow buntings were also found, and a hoopoe was seen near Hallydown.

The more common mammals are fox, hedgehog, rabbit, brown hare, red squirrel, long tailed field mouse, voles, shrews, weasel, stoat, water voles, brown rat, house mouse, roe deer, badger, and bats — the pipistrelle being the most common. On the rocks and off shore grey seal are frequently seen, while of the fish and reptiles brown trout, sea trout, salmon, frogs and toads predominate.

HISTORICAL SKETCH

Ayton — or Eitun as it was previously spelt — takes its name from the Eye Water, and between 1098 and 1107 was a dependency of Coldingham Priory, together with another small village known as Nether Ayton, which stood to the east of the present churchyard on the south side of the Eye Water and contiguous to the Roman road which extended from

Newcastle to St Abbs Head. It is possible that a third small hamlet, known as Hornford or Horford, existed near the site of the present Jubilee Bridge over the Eye Water south-west of Ayton Village, or where the Horn Burn joins Eye Water about quarter of a mile further south.

The first recorded settlers in Eitun, a hundred years after the Norman Conquest, were a Norman family by the name of De Vesci, who formed a settlement on the banks of the Eye, and built a castle or defensive tower for the protection of the family and vassals. Similar small towers were built at Huldie and on the site of the present Wall Tower field. The De Vescis changed their name to de Eitun and gained considerable power in the area. In 1472 the lands were granted to the Homes of Dunglass, but in 1716 the estates were forfeited by the then Earl of Home because of his support for the Jacobite cause and passed to the Crown. The lands were eventually purchased by John Fordyce, who was Commissioner for Lands and Forests of Scotland. In 1834 the lands — the present Ayton Castle Estate and much of the land about Ayton — were sold to William Mitchell-Innes who built the present Ayton Castle in 1846. In 1888 the estate of Ayton Castle was bought by the forbears of the present owner, David Liddell-Grainger, who resides in the Castle today.

Meanwhile, the settlement of Ayton grew to a village about the estate and to its present extent. In the old and original part of the village — to this day known as the Old Town — the only known hostelry existed. This inn, the King's Arms, had adequate accommodation and a large assembly room and undoubtedly served as shelter for travellers on the direct route between Scotland and England which passed through the village. Agriculture, albeit primitive by today's standards, became established throughout the parish, with some sea fishing from the hamlet and harbour of Burnmouth leading to further expansion of population and accommodation. A fair was held twice yearly in Ayton village until 1832. Later a monthly cattle market was established, with dealers from Berwick and surrounds coming to buy and trade horses and cattle. There were four mills in the parish providing flour, oatmeal and barley, and the village and parish became more or less self-sufficient and expanded further. Approximately sixty years ago the population was reckoned to be between 500 and 600 in Ayton village and 1200 and 1400 in the remainder of the parish. There were no fewer than 70 tenemented properties in the village and about 120 men and women were actually employed within the village while today there will be no more than 40. The largest employer in that time was the now disused and converted Bleachfield Paper Mill which was originally a cloth mill but converted to paper making about 1845, and worked in conjunction with the paper mill at Millbank until it was burned down in 1866.

The second major centre of habitation in the parish is at the small fishing village of Burnmouth. The small bay is an ideal haven for small boats and sea fishing has occurred there for many centuries. The harbour's foundation stone was laid in 1831 and the work was completed one year later, at the cost of £2,000. In 1877 an addition was made bringing the structure to its present state. There have been many changes since the beginning of this century; the composition of the village has been completely altered and it is difficult today to picture it as it was in the 'olden days'. There are still three groups of houses within Ayton parish at the foot of the hill at the harbour side. These are Cowdrait, Lower Burnmouth and Partanhall, Upper Burnmouth being the habitation at the top of the hill adjacent to the A1 road. Originally, the houses were of low single-storied 'but and ben' type. Although there was not much accommodation in these houses many held large families. Between the wars Cowdrait and Lower Burnmouth were entirely rebuilt and the picturesqueness of the village was lost. The houses at Partanhall have not been dramatically altered but only two are inhabited throughout the year, the remainder being used as holiday homes.

When the new houses were built at the foot of the braes they were inhabited by young fishermen and their families. However, between the wars the first council houses were built in Upper Burnmouth and gradually the fishermen moved away from the lower houses and today only three families remain there, most of the other houses being occupied by pensioners. Before the introduction of council houses Upper Burnmouth was a very small community; it was however the 'business centre' of the village, Lyall Terrace consisting of four houses and the post office, which looked across to the busy main line railway station and the school. Further up the road was (and still is) the busy inn known as the Flemington Inn. In Lower Burnmouth there were smoke houses and other buildings where fish was cured. It was imperative that such buildings were in close proximity to the harbour. There were also two shops and a ship chandlers business, with another shop in the small community of Ross, which is in Mordington Parish, although situated in Lower Burnmouth.

The fishing industry of Burnmouth has also seen many changes: at the beginning of the century there was a fleet of at least a dozen 'big boats' of up to 60 feet in length, relying on sail power, operating out of Burnmouth Harbour. From May until August these boats fished for herring from Eyemouth, Berwick and North Shields, occasionally venturing through the Forth and Clyde Canal to the West coast and Southern Ireland. In September their nets were overhauled before the boats moved on to Great Yarmouth, to fish off there until November. A successful Great Yarmouth fishing was a boon to the village. After Great Yarmouth the Burnmouth fishermen commenced fishing, with lines, from their own harbour. For this type of fishing they used smaller yawls or cobbles of about 30 feet in length, with a crew of four, each crewman having a line of 11 hundred hooks which had been baited the previous night by their womenfolk. The tedious business of shelling and baiting the hooks with mussels was undertaken by the womenfolk in addition to their home-keeping functions.

During the First World War only two of the 'big boats' were merchandised and a fleet of motor yawls was introduced. Each yawl had a crew of four and in addition to the line fishing the crew turned to creel fishing, for lobster and crab: until then the fishing had mostly been part-time. New fishing grounds were found in Goswick Bay, south of Berwick, and big catches of up to 400 lobsters were landed. At that time Burnmouth Railway Station was a hive of industry, with large quantities of crab and lobster being loaded on the London bound trains to arrive early the next morning fresh for the London market. Incidentally, the mussels for the line-fishing were brought by rail from Morecambe, Lancs. to Burnmouth Station, then transported to the harbour by horse and cart to be tipped into the sea in the rocky area nearby, to multiply and keep fresh for gathering later as bait. Crab and lobsters were transported to the station in the same horse-drawn carts, with two pair of horses to overcome the steep brae. In 1922 net fishing was introduced and some of the younger fishermen went over to this type of fishing. Larger boats were accordingly necessary and gradually these boats and their crews moved to the larger and nearby port of Eyemouth: this new era sounded the death knell for the line fishing and no-one, especially the womenfolk, was sorry for its passing. Those who preferred to stay in Burnmouth went over to full-time creel fishing, but this too has its drawbacks and the amount of shellfish landed during the past few years has fallen dramatically, perhaps from over-fishing. Fortunately, the market price for lobster and crab has risen sharply but today this industry in Burnmouth provides a precarious livelihood. Looking to the future it seems that creel fishing will revert to part-time, along with the salmon-netting (presently a lucrative trade) and become second to tourism and the provision of holiday accommodation.

Four buildings in the village appear much as they did one hundred years ago: the Church, half-way up the hill between Lower and Upper Burnmouth, has a service every Sunday officiated by the Rev. Hebenton, of Ayton Parish Church, but the congregations are considerably smaller than 50 years ago. The school, at the top of the hill, has a roll of some 25 pupils and a staff of two, whereas in earlier days it catered for 120, with likewise a staff of two. The post office is in the same premises today as it was originally, having moved four times throughout the village according to the residence of the presiding post master. The hostelry, the Flemington Inn, is in its original location and relies much on passing traffic as does the adjacent licensed restaurant, the Gull's Nest. There is a village hall and a public telephone in the village and there are public toilets. Several houses give bed and breakfast facilities, and in Upper Burnmouth there is a site offering holiday accommodation in chalets. All tourism is by passing trade, pre-booked accommodation or permanently owned holiday homes, the A1 road being the dominant factor as the railway station on the main London/Edinburgh line, and branch line to Eyemouth, closed in 1962. The population today is approximately 250, having fallen by about 100 over the past 50 years.

A character of note in the village is Robert Johnston of Cowdrait, who is a hale and hearty 103 years of age! (1986).

AGRICULTURE

Many far-reaching changes have occurred in land management and agriculture during the century, with mechanisation perhaps being the main factor, followed by changes in methods and demand. The number of persons obtaining their livelihood from the land has altered correspondingly, as has the type of crops grown and breeds of stock maintained. The following are details of the farms in Ayton Parish showing the present situation, with comparisons where applicable:

AYTON CASTLE ESTATE

The history of the Estate has been given under Historical Sketch: the lands were purchased by the forebears of the present owner — David Liddell-Grainger — in 1888. The estate, including the grounds about Ayton Castle, encompass the farms of Littledean, Redhall, Ayton Cocklaw, Whitfield and Linthill. Of the 3,500 acres of the original estate 400 acres were sold in 1984, the remainder being utilised as grasslands, arable and woodlands. Ayton Cocklaw and Redhall are tenanted farms and are recorded below. Emphasis is now on arable farming but formerly 'mixed farming' predominated. Today, 50 per cent of the arable land is wheat and barley, the remainder in oats, oil-seed rape and peas for human consumption (freezing and canning), and grasslands. Some 500 acres are in woodlands, mainly softwoods which are felled when mature for pulping, chipboards and posts. Some planting of hardwood is presently under way and softwood plantations are replanted once clear-felled. There is no resident forester, timber management being given to contractors. The shootings of the estate are let to syndicates. Formerly the estate employed four persons in the gardens, four in estate forestry, one in estate maintenance and nine in agriculture, with 45 as indoor staff of the Castle. Today five persons are employed for all aspects of agriculture, with no garden staff nor forestry personnel. One full-time cook and five part-time domestics form the staff today in the Castle. Therefore, within 50 years the workforce, mainly found from the locality, has fallen from 63 full-time to six full-time and five part-time.

Many years ago there were 32 mills situated on the Eye Water and today the remains of two can be found on Ayton Castle Estate. One mill — at Old Flemington — was buried by silt in the severe floods of 1948, but is presently being excavated with possible restoration in mind, for its historical interest. This mill was a corn mill while the other on the

Estate, Bleachfield Mill, started as a cloth mill before being converted to a paper mill and was the largest employer in Ayton and district. Although standing today it has long been disused and is now a substantial dwelling house.

The Castle and grounds are open to the public on Sunday, from May until October.

AYTON COCKLAW

A farm on Ayton Castle Estate, it is tenanted by Norman Steel whose family have farmed the lands since 1929. An ancient farm once standing beside the original road from Berwick-upon-Tweed to Ayton via Lamberton Moor, the lands are of 590 acres of mixed farming. Stock consists of 250 beef cattle, 100 cows and 400 sheep, with crops of wheat, barley, oil-seed rape, swedes, vining peas for canning and beans. The acres of grassland are for summer grazing and hay, while the cattle are wintered in large cattle courts in the farm steading.

Twenty years ago, 15 persons were employed full-time on the farm, with additional assistance at harvesting times provided by squads of itinerant workers. Today, but two full-time workers operate the farm. Eighteen years ago eight of the farm cottages which housed the farm workers were demolished and four new ones erected. At one time a forge was sited in the steading, for use by the visiting blacksmith who regularly called to attend to the ten or more horses.

The farm draws its water supply from a spring on Ayton Hill; there is a farm pond near the steading. Red squirrel have been seen near the farmhouse this year, an animal not previously noticed in the vicinity although there are some in Ayton Castle grounds lower down.

AYTON LAW

The farm was formerly part of Ayton Castle Estate but in 1984 part was purchased from the Estate by the present owners — R. H. and D. H. Allan — and is farmed as a unit in conjunction with farms situated outwith Ayton Parish. Of the original 700 acres of the farm 437 were acquired for the present farm lands while about 30 acres were purchased by the local authority as the site for housing in Lawfield Drive, Ayton.

Crops produced currently are wheat, barley (for stock feeding and as a cash crop), potatoes, protein peas for stock feeding, and vining peas for canning. Stock held at present are some 260 bullocks for fattening, which are wintered in covered cattle courts in the steading and graze in summer on the 55 acres of grasslands maintained for that purpose. About 250 Suffolk Down Cross ewes are also held. In 1947 stock consisted solely of 100 beef cattle. Silage has been made since 1961 and today the process is by 'high-dry matter' which ensures that when placed in the silage pits the grass is nearly moisture free. Some hay is made, for stock feeding. Two persons are permanently employed today, contrasting with 14 in 1947, in addition to itinerant workers — Irish labourers — who stayed in the farm bothy throughout the crop gathering seasons. The ten existing farm 'cottages' are all presently occupied, most being let to non-farm workers. The farm has its own stock transporters which may be hired to others when farm needs permit.

The water supply is via the mains and there are underground pipes to each field for irrigation, the water being drawn from the nearby Eye Water. In 1947 sowing of autumn cereal crops was 5 per cent of the total, while today it is 75 per cent; this increase is due mainly to the availability of better and hardier strains of winter barley giving a good yield, the seed being particularly suited to the gravelly soil of the area. The original farmhouse was some 15 yards from the present. A site of antiquity on the farm is recorded as a Roman hengiform ditch with rectangular post holes set in a 100 metre square.

BASTLERIDGE

During the 15th century this estate belonged to the Homes and there is a deed in which the Home of Bastleridge is styled as Bailiff of the Barony Peelwalls. Sometime prior to 1834 the farm was purchased by James Sherri, Merchant, of Leith. The farm is presently owned by William G. Cowan, who runs the farm together with his family and one full-time employee. Twenty years ago there were three full-time workers plus assistance from part-time squads as required.

The 317 acres are utilised mainly for crop growing — barley, wheat and protein peas — with 53 acres in grasslands, for grazing, and 11 acres in woodlands. Thirty beef cattle, of Hereford cross Frisian, are kept for fattening. There is no dairy herd. Until 22 years ago water was taken from a well on the farm but today it is from the mains supply. The original farmhouse still stands near the present which was built in 1962.

On a map dated 1645 reproduced in *Coldingham Parish and Priory* by A. Thomson, F.S.A., the house is marked under the name Bafleurigg, probably because the lands once formed part of the Lands of Fleurs, some of the extensive possessions of the Earls of Home. The ancient Roman Camp at Drumaw or Habchester is situated within the farm bounds. Recently, a peregrine falcon was seen taking pigeons near the farm.

CHESTERBANK

A former compiler of the Statistical Account for Ayton parish, in 1794, was one John Renton of Chesterbank, who appears to have been a person of some standing in the community. On the ancient map dated 1645 it is possible that the farm is marked under the name Crailfledd. In 1830/35 simple hand-mills, known as querns, believed to have been left behind by Leslie's army, were recovered on the farm lands.

The farm has been in the Wood family for very many years and is to this day in the hands of James Wood & Sons. Forty acres of the lands are presently set in wheat, mainly for stock feed, with 70 in spring barley, for malting. Stock consists of 300 head of beef cattle which are wintered in covered cattle courts. Fifty years ago there were six full-time workers on the farm, with casual workers hired as required; today the farm is worked by the owners (two persons) with contract labour utilised as necessary.

The farm includes that under East Flemington.

FAIRNIESIDE

Situated between Ayton and Burnmouth just east of the A1 road and with lands bordering the coast, this ancient habitation is shown on most maps dating back to 1645. It was undoubtedly a fortified dwelling and perhaps a smugglers' retreat. It is possible that the present farmhouse is not on the original site, which may be on a small hill to the north of the present house. It is also probably that the original name was Farndum but it is not known when this was changed to the present title. In 1876 a stone-age celt (a prehistoric cutting or cleaving instrument in stone or bronze) was found in Blaikies' Field on the farm, and in 1968 a stone-age grave containing the bones of an adult male, estimated to be 3,000 years old, were uncovered by a plough in Station Field. The present farmhouse and steading have beneath them the remains of a lade from the farm pond which at one time led water as power to turn a water wheel for a threshing mill. In 1981 the lands were acquired by the present owner, John Wilson & Son. They consist of 533 acres utilised for the growing of wheat, barley, oil-seed rape and potatoes, as cash crops but with some cereal retained as feed for the 300 head of beef cattle which are fattened for the meat market. The principal breed of cattle are Charolais cross Hereford, wintered in cattle courts in the steading. Stock feed is kept in silos with additional feeding from chopped straw enriched with molasses.

The present day staff of the farm consists of the farm manager and two full-time employees, with squads hired from contractors for harvesting potatoes. Fifty years ago there were at least ten full-time workers who resided in the adjacent farm cottages. There was a forge available for the visiting blacksmith who tended the ten pair of farm horses.

The coastline within the bounds of the farm is designated a nature reserve and in the winter of 1985/6 a little auk was found alive near the farm having been blown during a severe gale, a similar fate overtaking snow buntings seen at the same period.

WEST FLEMINGTON

This farm is owned by Ian Liddell-Grainger and managed in conjunction with Fairnieside. It is 155 acres and almost entirely arable, cropping wheat, barley and potatoes. It is one of the Flemingtons which feature in historical accounts and maps, seemingly taking the name from the Flemish weavers and merchants who established a community in the district. Their markets were known as redhalls, hence the name of the nearby farm of Redhall, also part of the Flemish settlement in the parish.

GREYSTONELEES

This farm is the most southerly in the parish and is adjacent to the A1 and thus was near to the old post road between Berwick-upon-Tweed and Edinburgh, passing over Lamberton Moor. It appears that it was once a coaching inn. The farmhouse and farm cottages are let and the farm lands of 130 acres are farmed in conjunction with two other farms outwith the parish, the owners being Andrew S. and John Davidson. Barley, wheat, protein peas and oil-seed rape are cropped. Sixty head of beef cattle are kept in two cattle courts. Three men are employed to work the combined farms, whereas in the past five were employed at Greystonelees alone. The farm takes its water from the mains supply, but formerly the supply was from a spring on Lamberton Moor. An additional 14 acres belonging to the farm form a coastal strip which is not grazed or cropped but is part of the nature reserve.

GUNSGREEN HILL

Farmed in conjunction with Redhall, this land of 200 acres is owned by Jean D. Glen and has been in her family for many years. Cropping barley, wheat, potatoes, swedes and hay, and with a beef herd of 80 cattle, it employs three persons today, whereas in 1940 the number was 20.

PEELWALLS FARM

Formerly part of Peelwalls Estate, the mansionhouse of which is on the opposite side of the B6355 Duns/Eyemouth road and is now used as a local authority home for the elderly. The farm was purchased from the estate by the Brown family in 1933 and is now farmed by Gordon Brown. The farm and estate are of ancient origin and shown on maps of 1645, when they formed part of the estates of the Homes.

Of 135 acres, the farm is mainly arable, with seed potatoes as a cash-crop and barley for feed for the Frisian herd held under 'intensive feeding', i.e. in covered cattle courts. The owner plus one full-time worker operate the farm, with contract labour as required. Fifty years ago there were five full-time and several part-time employees. There is no dairy herd.

The farm has its own water supply from a bore-hole of 100 feet, believed to tap into an underground river entering the sea near Burnmouth — but this is not confirmed.

PRENDERGUEST

Shown on a map dated 1645 as 'Plandergaist', this ancient farm land is steeped in history. It is referred to as part of the lands granted by Charter of Edgar, King of Scots, and thereafter belonged to Swain, priest of the ancient parish of Fishwick, who renounced his title in favour of the monks of Coldingham. A Charter of 1190-1200 is signed by Helio of Prenderguest, and Henry of Prendirgest, knight, subscribed to a Charter of 1276. In 1538 the lands, extending to 'fifteen husbandlands', were sold to William Hume of Lochthullo, and the lands thereafter appear to have remained in the hands of the Home family for centuries. The records of Lindisfarne Monastery show that in 1326 William de Prenderguest — being somewhat of a Border reiver — rendered himself notorious by plundering the brewhouse and bakehouse of that religious establishment. The present farmhouse of Prenderguest was the former mansionhouse, the original farmhouse being sited in the existing farm steading.

Today the farm is the property of Alastair W. Lindsay, whose forebears acquired the lands in 1915. Of 653 acres of which 60 are in grasslands, the principal crops are wheat, oats, barley, potatoes and vining peas (for canning). Stock is beef cattle — Simmental cross — the 110 head grazing the grasslands in summer and wintering in the covered and enclosed cattle courts in the farm steading. There are 35 acres of woodlands, mainly hardwoods. Present employees are three full-time, with part-timers engaged as necessary. In 1930 no less than 45 persons were dependent upon the farm for shelter and livelihood, ten being employees and the remainder their families, all of whom occupied the farm cottages on the farm. The bothy in the steading provided shelter for two itinerant Irish workers who came for the seasonal harvesting of crops and the singling of turnips. Water supply is from a spring on the farm and as the lands are mainly on sloping ground natural drainage occurs. The farm has its own silos and grain drier. The closing of the nearby Ayton Railway Station in October 1966 affected the farm in that the sidings were used for the loading of farm crops on to railway wagons for transport to markets, the system being that one or two empty wagons were allocated to the farm, into which sugar-beet, potatoes and other crops were loaded, for removal at a later date. Nowadays, contractors transport produce from the farm by motor lorry.

NETHERBYRES

Netherbyres was once the home of Captain Brown, the inventor of the suspension bridge. One of his first experiments was carried out across the Eye Water on his estate, but the most noticeable in the district is the Chain Bridge over the River Tweed at Horncliffe.

The estate was purchased by Sir Christopher Furness, Bt. in 1928, from Mr Hewat Pate, of Boston, U.S.A. Sir Christopher died in 1974 and the estate is now owned by his son, Lt. Col. S. J. Furness, who resides in Netherbyres House and maintains the very fine oval walled garden.

The estate is of 110 acres of which 50 are arable, 20 permanent grasslands and the remainder maturing woodlands and shelter belts. The arable is rotated between grass, for grass park lets, corn, potatoes, turnips and cabbage, let to a sub-contractor. Eyemouth Mill Farm, part of the estate, was once a dairy farm but ceased to be so about 15 years ago, and the farm buildings and steading are now used for storage. South Lodge, Netherbyres, is now derelict. The water supply is from a combination of mains and spring water from the estate.

Prior to 1939 the estate employed 14 workers, as inside and outside staff: today there are one permanent and four part-time.

REDHALL

Farmed together with Gunsgreen Hill, this farm is part of Ayton Castle Estate and is tenanted to Mrs Jean D. Glen. It is of 200 acres, with crops of barley, wheat, swedes and potatoes. Together with the Flemingtons it is believed to have inherited its name from a colony of Flemish weavers and merchants who established themselves in the district. Fifty years ago the farm cottages housed a work force of ten: today three persons manage the farm.

WHITERIG

Owned by James W. Scott & Sons, this ancient farmland is shown on maps dated 1645, under the name of 'Whyterigg'. It comprises today 601 acres which are utilised mainly in the growing of crops — malting barley, wheat and swedes. About 600 Cheviot sheep and 120 beef cattle are held on the farm, the latter wintering in enclosed cattle courts. There is a crop store (silo) and grain drier. Today four persons are engaged full-time on the farm, while in the 1970s ten such employees worked the lands. Formerly, itinerant work squads were engaged as necessary while today part-time workers are engaged from the locality.

No new woodlands have been planted. The farm takes its water supply from the mains.

AGRICULTURE (SUMMARY)

Once the principal employer of local labour in the parish, the farming industry has changed drastically: mechanisation has affected nearly all aspects with most 'manual' functions now done by machine, and consequently a more highly-skilled and technically-minded work-force is today found working the land. An analysis of present and previous numbers so employed is included in this summary. Traditional breeds of cattle have been practically replaced by cross-breeding with continental strains, giving faster-maturing and heavier stock. Fewer sheep graze the fields and no pigs are accommodated, nor are there any dairy herds. Hay is made, but silage predominates as stock feed, with molasses-enriched straw and grain, and protein peas forming additional winter diet. Apart from mechanisation other factors of change are the demand for new crops, and increased existing crops, by the home-food frozen vegetables and fruit industry, and E.E.C. requirement policies and subsidies.

Traditional crops of the parish consisted of sugar-beet, swedes and cereals, but with the closure of the sugar-beat processing plant in Cupar, Fife, in the 1960s local farmers looked to an alternative source of cash crops and land usage, hence the vegetable freezing and processing industry based in Eyemouth. The processing and freezing plants, at Ayton Mains within the parish, and at Eyemouth, are supplied with peas and beans, soft fruits, brussels sprouts, cauliflowers and cabbage, all grown in the Eastern Borders. Oil-seed rape is another 'new' crop, for stock feed and oil extraction. Much of the arable land in the parish is devoted to barley — for malting and stock feed — wheat, oats, turnips and potatoes. Cattle, mainly reared for fattening, are wintered in large, covered cattle courts, to be fed on protein-enriched silage/hay/straw/ cereals, and summered in the lush grasslands. When mature they are transported by road (previously by rail) to central markets and abattoirs. No longer are local butchers able to buy their fat stock 'on the hoof' in local markets or direct from the farmer, to slaughter them in their own killing-houses. Few poultry 'free range' the farm steadings and there are no deep-litter egg producers in the parish.

Many local farmers own their farm machinery and implements, grain driers, silos and stock transporters, and use powerful tractors which can be put to many functions, six or more sheared ploughs, and a variety of tilling, sowing, fertilising and harvesting implements. Gone are the hay rakes, threshing mills, byres, potato pits, large squads for singling turnips, potato-picking and root-crop harvesting. Several farms are managed as units in conjunction with other farms in the district, and few farm 'cottages' (new, all-modern houses with all facilities) are occupied by farm workers, the majority being let as accommodation to local residents or as holiday homes. At least two of the farmhouses, once the home of the farmer or landowner, are not occupied by people of the farming community.

The average wage for farm workers has increased from £66 in 1981 to over £100 today, and is enhanced by over-time — an unheard-of thing 50 years ago. Farm workers still enjoy an allocation of potatoes as in the past, or an allowance in lieu. It is interesting to note that perhaps the only aspect of farming which has not altered drastically over the centuries is that of the shepherd; flock husbandry and herding is still very much a 'man and dog' operation, the only differences possibly being that he may have a motor vehicle for transport instead of a horse or bicycle, and the increased use of preventative medicines and dips. There are no gamekeepers, drystane dykers, hedgers and ditchers, mole or rabbit trappers, thatchers or blacksmiths resident in the parish, trades and crafts which employed more than 15 persons in the past.

The following shows the decrease in agricultural employment (excluding associated industries).

Previous (50 years ago)	Present
130	35

INDUSTRY, COMMERCE AND TRADE

Fifty years ago the parish was a self-sufficient community boasting two doctors, a hospital at Millerton, a veterinary surgeon, police station and Justice of the Peace Court, two churches, a post office at both Ayton and Burnmouth, a school in both villages, a gas works, paper mill, two sawmills, a market garden, a lemonade factory, a railway station at Ayton and at Burnmouth, five dairies, three bakers, three grocers, two butchers, three sweet shops, one draper and dressmaker, one tailor, one barber, one watchmaker, one bootmaker/saddler/cooper, one newsagent, one wallpaper supplier, two cycle shops, three blacksmiths, one joiner, one stone mason, one slater, one plumber, one painter, one carter and coal merchant, one carter for hauling fish and coals, a thriving fishing industry in Burnmouth, and two banks in Ayton. The Royal Bank of Scotland was situated in Beanburn while the Commercial (later the National Commercial) occupied the building of the present Royal Bank of Scotland. In the 1970s the National Commercial and the Royal Bank of Scotland amalgamated, retaining the title Royal Bank of Scotland, and this bank occupies the building which has housed a bank in Ayton for 130 years or more. There was one hotel and public house in Ayton and one public house in Burnmouth. There was one solicitor's practice, and one chip shop. Today there is the one bank, a post office in both villages, local primary schools in Ayton and Burnmouth, a police station, automatic telephone exchange, one sawmill, one engineer and welder's, one precision engineer's, one upholsterer, two painters, two joiners (one undertaking welding), one plumber, one heating, plumbing and electrical engineer's, one toy maker, one hotel, one public house in both Ayton and Burnmouth, one licensed restaurant, two grocers in Ayton and one in Burnmouth (at the post office), one newsagent, one solicitor's practice, one fish and chip shop, two garages/petrol filling stations, one garage for sales and repairs, one vegetable processing plant at Ayton Mains, two transport firms, a small lobster/crab/white fishing industry at Burnmouth, and oil storage depots at Biglawburn and the former Ayton Railway Station, supplying domestic, agricultural and fishing fleet fuels. There is a small holiday complex in Burnmouth and several houses in the parish offer 'bed and breakfast'. There is no resident doctor or veterinary surgeon.

EMPLOYMENT

Factors adversely affecting employment in the parish include the closure of the main line and branch line railway stations, the decline in the fishing industry, the vast decline in agricultural workers, the closure of the paper mill at Bleachfield, and the general reduction of employment in the smaller trades and industries. On the plus side, the frozen and package vegetable, fruit and fish industry in Eyemouth employs considerable labour from the parish, as does the nuclear power station in Torness, various trades, industries and facilities in Berwick-upon-Tweed, the local authority roads depot at Peelwalls, shops and trades in Ayton, the fishing industry in Burnmouth, and the hotel, public house and holiday business. There is a small number on the Youth Training Scheme.

Despite current national trends of high unemployment the parish is fortunate in having three centres of employment close by (Berwick, Torness and Eyemouth), and consequently unemployment in the parish is minimal.

TRANSPORT AND COMMUNICATIONS

Much change has occurred in this area. The A1 road passes through the parish on a roughly north-south line, with the B6355 from Duns to Eyemouth bisecting the southern end of the parish. Via the A1 road travel is possible to Berwick-upon-Tweed (seven miles), Edinburgh (50 miles) and Newcastle (60 miles). With the closure of the railway stations at Ayton and Burnmouth in 1966 and 1962 respectively, the nearest railhead is Berwick-upon-Tweed, with airports at Edinburgh and Newcastle (60 miles both). Eastern Scottish Bus Company provides a regular service between Berwick and Edinburgh, Duns and Eyemouth, while a courier service links Ayton with Coldingham and St Abbs. A considerable proportion of the population have their own transport, enabling them to travel to larger centres for shopping and supplies. Ayton village, until the opening of the A1 by-pass in November 1981, suffered from the considerable volume of heavy traffic passing on the village main street; today it is much quieter and safer, but some trade has been lost from the reduction of through traffic.

There are two transport firms operating from within the parish, which is well served by the many supply vehicles and delivery vans calling daily — or frequently — to maintain supplies to all trades and businesses. Two taxi firms operate from Ayton.

Postal services are now centralised in Eyemouth, but sub-post offices remain in Ayton and Burnmouth, with mail collected from boxes within the parish, to be sorted and dispatched from Eyemouth, where all postmen are centred. The last resident postman in Ayton finished in October 1955, and the last mail from Ayton Post office bearing the franking of Ayton postmark was dated 29th April 1972. Ayton Post Office was once the head post office for the district. Four clerks, four or five postmen and a telegraph messenger were employed from Ayton, under a postmaster; mail for the outlying areas being delivered by pony and trap. There were three deliveries daily and the office was open for one hour on Sundays for collections. There was a manual telephone exchange with five operators, this facility remaining until the installation of the automatic exchange in Ayton in 1956. There are full dialling facilities today from the automatic exchange, which became digital in 1986/7.

MEDICAL SERVICES

There is no resident doctor in the parish, the last — Dr Duff — leaving in 1953. In Ayton there is a clinic provided by Borders Health Board which is used as a consulting room and surgery by two medical practices — Dr Aitken of Chirnside and Dr Nichol, of Eyemouth — each having consulting hours twice weekly. For hospital treatment and examinations Berwick Infirmary and Roodlands Hospital, Haddington are available. There is a dental clinic in Eyemouth and the area ambulance service is centred there. Ayton has a resident district nurse — Nurse Herald — and there are health visitors together with social workers, remedial and ancilliary medical services in Eyemouth. Borders Regional Council maintain Peelwalls House, Ayton, as a home for the elderly, with accommodation for 29 patients and a staff of 16, full-time and part-time.

EDUCATION

In the early 19th century there were no fewer than five private schools in the parish, each dependent upon school fees, and one supported by the Mitchell-Innes family. It is known that in the Parish School French, German and Latin were taught in addition to the normal school subjects. The school fees in 1830 were £84 per annum in the Parish School but were somewhat lower in the private schools.

Today there is a primary school in Ayton and another in Burnmouth. Education thereafter is continued in Eyemouth High School.

A headteacher and three teachers are in attendance in Ayton while at Burnmouth the staff consists of one headteacher and one teacher. 'Civilian' staff — full-time and part-time — are employed in both schools. No meals are provided in the schools, but pupils can bring their own mid-day meal.

The school hall of Ayton School is much used for functions and meetings (taking the place of the now demolished Volunteer Hall), and the surrounding and adjacent playing fields are available for outdoor activities and as the 'home' ground of Ayton Amateur Football Club. The school hall is set out for use as a badminton court.

Further education classes in various academic and vocational subjects are held during the winter in Eyemouth, Duns and Berwick-upon-Tweed. The former school in Ayton, used as a primary school until replaced by the present school in 1974, together with the old schoolhouse, is unoccupied and put to no useful purpose despite its central position in the village. Fifty years ago it was a thriving establishment with over 100 pupils and a staff similar to that of today. At present there are 78 pupils in Ayton School and 25 in Burnmouth: in 1930 the figures were 118 and 120 respectively.

CHURCHES

Ayton Parish Church stands at the foot of the village, on the north bank of the Eye Water. In the beginning of the 13th century records state that a chaplain was stationed in Ayton, but no details of the cell or chapel are on record, only that the chapel was dedicated to St Dionysius. The ruins still visible in the churchyard, are said to occupy the site of the nave of an earlier building whose chancel wall stood firm until well into the 19th century. It is possible that this was the church of the district within the walls of which John o' Gaunt met the Scottish Commissioners appointed by King Robert II and confirmed the prolongation of the truce between the two kingdoms in 1380. The English and Scottish representatives are said to have met again in Ayton Church in 1384.

The present church, the foundation of which was laid in 1864, is of Gothic structure. Seemingly, Ayton was blessed with two congregations, for as early as 1771 one such gathering — Ayton Springbank — was reputed to have worshipped in a 'disused carpet factory' in Ayton, but records of such a factory have not been unearthed. The second congregation — Ayton Summerhill — held services in a building which is now a large house in Beanburn, Ayton. The congregations combined in 1895 and held services in the present church. The minister is the Rev. Hebenton, who also officiates at Burnmouth, Reston, Houndwood and Grantshouse. Burnmouth Church is situated on the hill between Upper and Lower Burnmouth.

Plate 4. Blanerne Bridge, over the River Whiteadder.

Plate 5. The village of Birgham in the 1950s.

CLUBS AND FACILITIES

Ayton once boasted a nine-hole golf course in Ayton Law Haugh, had a cricket club at Ayton Castle, a quoiting club in the yard behind the Red Lion Hotel, a tennis club on the site where Mossman's Garage now stands, a football club which played in Ayton Law Field, a curling club using the pond at Littledean (winter conditions permitting), a reading and billiard room in the Beanburn, situated in what had been the hall and vestry of Ayton Summerhill Church, and held annual sports in the Garden Park, Ayton Castle, on almost professional lines. The annual flower show was a grand occasion, with an orchestra providing music throughout the day-long proceedings, held in the Volunteer Hall, with fine trophies and prizes to be won. After the 1914-18 war the Ex-Servicemen's Club was erected in the Old Town, which led to the decline of the reading and billiards room. Today the club is principally used for indoor bowling.

Ayton today has its football club, pigeon club, leek and onion clubs, indoor bowling club, darts teams, and a fine new outdoor bowling green which opened in 1985 after much effort on the part of local enthusiasts. The parish retains the annual flower show — still a fine event — and Ayton has its Civic Week, with numerous functions and activities. There are Scouts, Guides, Womens' Rural Institutes in Ayton and Burnmouth, Woman's Church Guilds in both villages, an Evergreen Club, Masons, and Community Councils in both Ayton and Burnmouth. Sea-fishing is available from Burnmouth and fresh-water angling is still much favoured in the Eye and Ale. The County Library van calls fortnightly and there are libraries in Eyemouth and Berwick-upon-Tweed.

There is no local roadman in the parish, attention being given from the local roads depot at Peelwalls. There are two refuse collections weekly and mains water supply is from the Watch Water Reservoir.

POLICE AND FIRE SERVICES

Ayton Parish comes under the Eyemouth Section of 'G' Division of Lothian and Borders Police, and is policed by officers from Eyemouth Section. Until regionalisation in 1975 it was under Berwickshire Division of Berwick, Roxburgh and Selkirk Constabulary. Ayton Police Station was built in 1939 and remains one of the two county stations in the Section, the other being at Coldingham. It is presently occupied by one of the sergeants of Eyemouth Section, and is the local station for Ayton and district although not providing 24 hour coverage.

Prior to regionalisation minor offences and court matters were dealt with by Ayton Justice of the Peace Court, which presided quarterly in the Court House at the Clock Tower, Ayton. Nowadays, such matters are dealt with by the District Court, or Sheriff Court at Duns.

Fire cover is by part-timers retained at Eyemouth. They form the Eyemouth Section of Lothian and Borders Fire Brigade, with back-up from appliances stationed at Duns, Coldstream and Galashiels.

POPULATION

Some factors affecting the fluctuations in population are family size, availability of and changes in employment, the health of the community and standards of living. All these plus two world wars may be reflected in the fluctuations depicted in the table given below. It has already been shown how considerable is the decrease in the numbers of agricultural workers in the parish, but this has not led to an overall decline in the population. Undoubtedly the size of families has decreased, from a norm of four to six children to an average of two today. To offset this people are generally healthier and live longer, and whereas 50 years ago a considerable proportion of the population of the parish was under 16 years of age today a corresponding proportion is over 60 years of age.

Census Year:												
1851	1861	1871	1881	1891	1901	1911	1921	1931	1951	1961	1971	1981
Numbers:												
1959	2014	1983	2040	1827	1629	1577	1521	1413	1483	1769	1956	1880

The figures for 1981, the latest census, show a reduction of 76 over the ten-year period; since 1971 Torness Power Station and other new industries have attracted people to the area and it is possible that the figure for today could be in the 1900s. There are 402 occupied properties (dwellings) in the parish.

OTHER OBSERVATIONS

It is a considerably more comfortable and healthier life in the parish today than it was 50 years ago. Houses are generally better constructed and designed, with damp-proofing, wall and ceiling insulation, double-glazing and central heating. Gas supply is now by pipeline, from the North Sea fields, and electricity has been in general use since 1936. Telephones are an accepted part of the home, as is the television set, video recorder, hi-fi system and radio, washing machine, dish-washer, and, more recently, home computer. Social and medical services are such that no person should be homeless, cold, hungry or uncared for, and there are facilities for the less fortunate, blind, handicapped and elderly provided by the local authority and the state. There is more leisure time and facilities, with swimming pools at Eyemouth and Berwick, squash courts, tennis courts, badminton, indoor games and fitness classes. Football, cricket, hockey, rugby are there for those wishing to participate — or spectate — and green bowls, horse riding, sub-aqua diving, sailing and many other competitive sports or pastimes are available. It is sad to record that despite the increase in facilities crime, vandalism and the spread of litter have not diminished. Nevertheless, there is still much community spirit and involvement and it is satisfying to find that village and rural life, although quicker nowadays in pace and style, has many benefits and much to offer.

1986

THE PARISH OF BUNKLE AND PRESTON

Prepared by R. G. Johnston, Esq., O.B.E., J.P.
formerly County Clerk of Berwickshire

BOUNDARIES

No change has taken place in the parish boundaries which are as stated in the second *Statistical Account*. The form of this united parish is very irregular. The greatest distance between the farthest points may be five or six miles; yet the mean length is only four and a half miles, and the mean breadth three and a quarter. It is bounded on the north and east by Abbey St Bathans and Coldingham; on the south-east by Chirnside; on the south and west by the river Whiteadder, which separates it from Edrom and Duns. Ecclesiastically the parish is called 'Bonkyl and Preston'.

POPULATION

Census Year	*Population of parish*
1801	674
1821	787 (maximum)
1851	715
1901	629
1911	562
1921	542
1931	507
1951	417 of which 211 were males and 206 females.

The main centre of population is at Preston with some 20 houses.

It will be seen that the population is steadily declining due to the exodus to towns where professions or occupations, sought as a result of the general availability of higher education, can be learnt, and pursued, and social and other amenities and greater facilities for pleasure are more easily obtained. It is possible also that the advent of the internal combustion engine, which has caused a considerable reduction in the number of pairs of horses working on the farms, is a contributory cause.

PHYSICAL CHANGES

The graveyard around the Church at Bunkle has been practically closed and a new one opened immediately to the south-west of and adjoining the old cemetery at Preston. It is a restful site facing south close to the Duns road and the River Whiteadder.

Many small holdings have disappeared, among which may be mentioned Billy Mill, Billy Hill, Little Billy, Ashfield, Buncle East Mains, Buncle West Mains and Lintlaw Mill.

The aspect of the parish has somewhat changed. Owing to the scarcity of timber in the First and Second World Wars, the famous Bonkyl Wood and many other woodland strips have disappeared under the woodman's axe. It is to be hoped that steps will be taken to replant these derelict areas, which are for the most part a bed of willowherb (Epilobium).

On 12th August 1948, when six and a half inches of rain fell in 24 hours, the Whiteadder overflowed its banks causing great damage to the Blanket Mill at Preston, and to the bridges. Vast quantities of gravel and debris were deposited on the haughs adjoining the river. The innumerable trees washed down formed a dam at Blanerne Bridge, and the water flowed over the parapet 29 feet above the river bed. Had not the earthen embankment on the south side given way, the inmates of the cottage about 200 yards west of the bridge, where the water flowed through the top storey, would have been drowned.

The Government undertook the restoration of the haughs; the repairs to the banks; and the cleansing of the river bed. All trees and bushes growing on the banks were pulled up, the river's course straightened, and its banks heightened, so that what was a picturesque river looks more like a canal.

The disturbance to the river bed has had a very detrimental effect on the fishing. Trout have almost ceased to exist.

Another feature which has disappeared is the giant hemlocks which grew profusely close to Blanerne Bridge, but it is hoped they will reappear, for when in flower, these plants of six feet 8 inches high were a fine sight.

INDUSTRIES

Agriculture is still the main industry. The farms — some 12 in number — absorb, save for small areas of woodland, the whole of the acreage (8,900 acres) of the parish. With the exception of parts of the upland, the land is in a high state of cultivation, and the rentals thereof, varying largely according to acreage, run from £90 to £1,200. The quality of the stock in the parish is high.

The internal combustion engine has revolutionised the methods of cultivation. The bulk of the ploughing, sowing, reaping, threshing and haulage is now carried out by tractor. In the last few years the 'combine' has made its appearance. This machine reaps and threshes the corn simultaneously. The straw is then gathered up and baled by another machine. The threshed corn requires to be dried almost at once — at least within 48 hours. One farm in the parish has installed an electrical drying apparatus for the purpose and also for the drying of grass for winter feeding. It remains to be seen whether these new methods encourage the growth of noxious weeds.

Electricity from the grid supply has been installed in some of the large farms and cottages, and would have been extended to almost all farms but for the reduction in capital expenditure ordered by Government. Most of the farm cottages have been improved structurally, and water and water closets installed where practicable.

There are smithies at Hammerhall, Crossgatehall and Preston, and a joiner's shop at Preston.

HABITS AND SOCIAL LIFE

The solitude of country life has undergone a great change with the coming of the bicycle, motor cycle, motor car and motor omnibus. For some years past the hours of work on farms have been 47, which allow for a free afternoon on Saturdays. Most folk make for the towns for shopping, football matches or visits to the cinema. On certain days of the week motor buses pass, which enable the housewife to shop in the neighbouring town, and also the motor vans of the butcher, baker and grocer call regularly. It follows that where there are no such conveniences it is becoming increasingly difficult to fill a vacancy for a rural worker when it occurs.

This ease of movement has also been detrimental to village summer games such as quoits. An excellent Parish Hall was erected at Preston a few years ago and is much used when outdoor pastimes and entertainments are not possible. Carpet bowling and dancing, including a revival of old Scottish Country Dances, are much in vogue. It is pleasing to note that the homing instinct amongst those who leave the neighbourhood for work elsewhere is strong and most spend their holidays in their old country homes.

There is an active branch of the Scottish Women's Rural Institute, which regularly meets in the Parish Hall.

It is worth recording that the majority of farm cottages have a wireless set.

CHURCH GOING

The parish church (157 on the roll) is at Bunkle, two miles from the village of Preston . There has been a decline in the attendance, probably owing to the ease of attending places of worship in adjoining parishes. The Woman's Guild numbers 33, and the Sunday School 17.

EDUCATION

There are two Primary Schools, one at Preston and the other at Lintlaw some three miles distant at the other end of the parish. Preston school has one teacher and 24 pupils; Lintlaw has one teacher and 31 pupils. The Secondary schools are at Chirnside and Duns. Pupils attending any of these schools outside the recognised distance are conveyed either by car or bus.

The educational methods of today have not affected the characteristics of the shepherd or the agricultural worker. They are highly skilled in their professions. The shepherd and the agricultural worker all show the same enthusiasm and pride in their work, which is second to none. They are a contented and very highly skilled body of men.

LANDOWNERS

The principal landowners are the Douglas and Angus Estates Ltd. (the family of the Earl of Home). The Dower House of Bonkyl with its policies has been sold. That portion of the Billie (modern spelling) Estate in the parish — Billie Mains — was sold to the occupying tenant and the estate of Blanerne has been entirely split up. Blanerne Castle and Bunkle Castle, or rather their ruins, still remain, but those of Billie Castle have disappeared.

There is a rhyme:

'Buncle, Billie and Blanerne,
Three Castles Strong as airn,
Built whan Davie was a bairn.
They'll a' gang doun
Wi' Scotland's Croon,
And ilka ane sall be a Cairn.'

Bunkle Castle ruins stand close to the road between Preston and Reston, a little to the north of Bunkle Church. The moat surrounding the walls can yet be traced. There is very little record of the Castle or its owners. The Earl of Angus wrote from it on 1st November 1524, to his wife Margaret Tudor, widow of King James IV (*State Papers*, Record Series, vol. iv, p. 217). A small hamlet or village at one time surrounded the ruins of the Castle, but not a vestige remains. It was chiefly inhabited by weavers, but there were also sutors and ale houses. Billie Castle stood about three miles east of Buncle, on the south bank of a small stream. Blanerne Castle ruins are near Blanerne House.

BIRD LIFE

The barn owl is now a *rara avis* due, it is said by experts, to a disease. There has also been a very noticeable decrease in the number of green plover (peewits) which can be attributed to the increase in the crow tribe and also to the herring and common gulls. The corn-crake, whose strident note was frequently heard throughout the parish during the late spring and early summer, no longer makes its visits, nor indeed to any other part of the county. A pair of buzzards has for the past year or two been seen in the upland parts of the parish for some months of the spring and summer. The goldfinch which disappeared altogether from the parish and the greater part at any rate of the remainder of the county for many years, is again frequently seen. The bullfinch and chaffinch are very noticeable. The magpie is now rarely seen.

ANTIQUITIES

A Norman apse, the ruins of which adjoin the eastern extremity of the former Church of Bunkle, was the burying place of the Billy family — the Homes. It is believed that the last person to be buried therein was Mrs Margaret Home, Lady Billy, murdered by Norman Ross at Linthill in 1751. There is still to be seen *in situ* a piscina in which it is understood the holy vessels were washed.

In the ruins of the old pre-Reformation Church at Preston churchyard there is also a piscina. At Preston, in the centre of the village, are the remains — base and part of the shaft — of the old Mercat Cross, the shaft apparently being the only part of the original Cross left.

These, together with various forts and defensive enclosures, are described and illustrated in *The Report on the County of Berwick* (1915), pp. 5-11, of the Royal Commission on the Ancient . . . Monuments . . . of Scotland.

Under the bridge, carrying the highway over a small stream, from Preston to Chirnside, and about 100 yards from the former village, there is formed by the greater part of the arch of the bridge what tradition has it was centuries ago a local jail. It is in good condition, showing the doorway, small window facing south and a small light slit to the north. In all probability it was used by the Baron Bailie of Preston for the reception of offenders within his jurisdiction. It is known locally as 'Cuddy's Jail' from the fact that an old Preston woman called Nell Logan many years ago stabled her cuddy (donkey) therein.

HISTORICAL INCIDENTS

Bunkle Wood at one time extended over and along the hill called Bunkle Edge, from near the Whiteadder on the west, to within a mile of Auchencrow on the east, nearly four miles in length and as much in breadth. It is said that about the year 1296, William Wallace, after the battle of Spot Moor, pursued Patrick, the 8th Earl of Dunbar, surnamed 'Black Beard', at that time an adherent of Edward I and Bishop Bek, on their flight to Norham-on-Tweed, and lay the first night in Bunkle Wood.

In July 1544, Sir George Bowes, Governor of Berwick, and his garrison, burnt Preston and Edrom, and took away five horses, nolt 200, sheep 600, 50 nags, etc.

About the feast of St George (23rd April) 1317, Edmund Fitzallan, Earl of Arundel, Guardian of the country between Trent and Roxburgh, and other noblemen, invaded Scotland with 30,000 men, while the Scots were waging war against Ireland, and advanced as far as Lintilee (Lintlaw), where Jacobus de Douglas was lying with a force of 200 men. Hearing of the approach of the invading force, Douglas fled, leaving the Englishmen in possession of the place. While they were enjoying themselves and carousing, Douglas returned with an enlarged force, routed the English and having laid hold of a clerk called Helias, a bard of renown, cut off his head and 'barbarously affixed it to his posteriors'.

RHYMES

The Laird o' Blanerne

You're like the Laird o' Blanerne — feared for a taed.

Origin unknown, but applied to abnormally timid people, particularly men.

The Ballad of Bunkle Castle

A better mason than Rankin ne'er builded wi' a stane,
He builded Bunkle Castle but payment he got nane.
Come gie tae me Earl Robert noo, come gie to me ma hire
Come gie to me Earl Robert, or I'll burn your hoose wi' fyre.

Earl Robert tae the huntin's gane
They steekit the doors; they steekit the yetts, up to the cheek and chin,
They steekit them a' but ae little wicket where Rankin he crep in,
Rankin nippit the bonnie bairn and high the fause nurse sang
Rankin nippit the bonnie bairn and high the red bluid sprang.

The mother hears —
O nursie, nursie, please my bairn
O please him with the keys
He winna be pleased o mistress mine
Tho' I gang doon on ma knees.
O nursie, nursie, please my bairn

O please him wi' the bell
He winna be pleased o mistress mine
Till ye come doon yersel.

Earl Robert comes home
But leddy nor heir
He never saw mair
Until the day he de'ed.
A monk there is in Coudenhame (Coldingham) ne'er looks upon the sun.

Tradition has it that Rankin was burned on Bunkle braeheid, but the nurse she was boiled in a cauldron of lead.

Other local rhymes will be found in George Henderson's *Popular Rhymes, Sayings, and Proverbs of the County of Berwick, with illustrative notes. (Newcastle-on-Tyne, 1856).*

1951

THE PARISH OF BUNKLE AND PRESTON

by The Rev. Peter Graham

Over the past 35 years since Mr Johnston prepared his entry there have been a considerable number of major changes in this parish.

Rural depopulation, the result of ever-increasing mechanisation on farms and even compulsory redundancies in agriculture, has continued to the point where there are now 227 adults resident in the parish.

The number of habitable houses has also gone down, some former farm cottages being demolished, others being converted into attractive homes by amalgamation. The original farm town of Preston has grown with the building of houses by the former Berwickshire County Council at a site to the west end of the hamlet. Originally these provided accommodation for workers retiring from the nearby Cumledge Mill, now closed and demolished. With few exceptions the standard of housing is good and most homes are furnished to a high level of comfort.

The changes in agriculture throughout Scotland have been reflected in the farming practised in this parish. All of the farms are now owned by their present occupants, several buying their farms from Douglas and Angus Estates, others from Whitburgh Estates who had purchased them from the Home family. Although barley (often sown in the autumn to stand over the winter) and potatoes continue to be the main crops, farmers have followed the fashion of growing rape for its seed which can be crushed to produce oil and at least two have produced vegetables for processing at Eyemouth, in a plant originally set up by a farmers, co-operative and subsequently taken over by the Salvesen Group. In addition one farmer has succeeded in growing soft fruits (strawberries, raspberries and blackcurrants) which are picked by squads of children as well as being sold direct to those willing to pick their own fruit. Fewer farms now keep breeding ewes, while cattle are often kept indoors throughout the winter months.

A former feature of the rural scene, the local smithy, has now disappeared completely with the retiral of the last blacksmith from his ancestral forge at Crossgatehall. The two others mentioned by Mr Johnston ceased to function a long time ago.

The two schools of the parish have also closed, the one at Preston in the late 1960s and that at Lintlaw in the early 1970s. Most of the children are transported free of charge to Duns Primary School, with some travelling to Chirnside. Certain families choose to have their children educated privately. The Berwickshire High School in Duns provides comprehensive secondary education for the area. There is a small pre-school playgroup which meets weekly in Preston Village Hall.

The steady decline in population has also affected membership of the Church of Scotland, which now has 92 communicants on the roll of Bonkyl & Preston Parish Church. After some six years without a minister, but with the services of a lay missionary, this congregation was linked with Reston in 1958 under the ministry of the Rev. J. Hutchison and of his successor the Rev. James Bremner. This linking was terminated in 1973 to allow re-adjustment, from which time the congregation has been linked with Chirnside under the ministry of the Rev. W. P. Graham.

1986

THE PARISH OF CHANNELKIRK

by The Rev. Ernest Lawson, M.A.

The parish of Channelkirk, sometimes spoken of as Upper Lauderdale, lies in the extreme north-west corner of Berwickshire. On the south-west, west and north-west the boundary of the parish is identical with that of the county. The Armet Water flows along the north-west and west boundary. The eastern boundary is marked by the Kelphope burn, which makes a natural and distinct dividing line. The bordering parishes are Stow on the west and south-west; Fala-Soutra and Humbie on the north-west, while on the east and south-east the bordering parish is Lauder. The length of the parish is fully six miles from north to south, the breadth from east to west about five miles and the area 14,196 acres. There are 1,909 acres under tillage, 5,189 acres under grass and 6,957 acres under rough grazing.

The road from Edinburgh to Jedburgh and over the border into England passes through the centre of the parish. On the top of Soutra Hill, at a height of fully a thousand feet, it crosses from the Lothians into Berwickshire and the parish of Channelkirk. The road at this point is desolate and windswept, while amid snow and ice and also on nights of fog it is highly dangerous as it winds through the wide stretches of open, unfenced moorland so characteristic of this northern part of the parish. On the whole the parish is one of hills and valleys and is well watered everywhere by many streams. Among its hills the river Leader takes its rise. The climate is cold but dry and very healthy, even though in winter the winds blow often with a bitter bite and the roads are frequently heavy with snow.

The parish offers the antiquarians a rich field. Many interesting discoveries have been made of stone implements, such as axes and hammers, also of flints, such as arrow-heads and knives. In the Scottish Museum of Antiquities a collection of these flints can be seen; they were found on the adjacent farms of Overhowden and Airhouse. There also remain traces of various camps and forts — Roman and native. Then, beside the farmhouse of Carfrae, there still stands a Border Peel, the only remaining one out of the many that must have been erected in the parish about four centuries ago.

Again there is the Girthgate, the road probably made by the monks of Melrose to give easier and quicker access to Soutra Aisle and Edinburgh, traces of which can be clearly seen near the farm of

Threeburnford. There is also the Well of the Holy Water Cleugh, frequently called St Cuthbert's Well, which lies some 400 yards from the church in a south-west direct. Where and when St Cuthbert was born is uncertain, but we are told that it was while he 'tended as a shepherd in the night his master's flocks on the side of the Leader' that he had the vision which led him to dedicate himself to the religious life. Straightway 'he resigned to his master the charge of his flocks and became a monk in the neighbouring monastery of Melrose'. The year was 651 A.D. A few years later he returned to blaze the trail of Christianity throughout Berwickshire. The church of the parish is dedicated to St Cuthbert and the original building was reared in his honour. The situation of the church, which is constantly remarked upon by visitors because of its remoteness and inaccessibility, especially in the storms of winter, may mark approximately the spot where Cuthbert the herd had the vision which changed his life.

The name Channelkirk is puzzling and considerable discussion has been aroused as to its meaning. This present name appears to have come into use late in the 18th century and prior to that time the name took many forms. One of the earliest was Chyldeschirchae — the child being of course Cuthbert — and Channelkirk would seem to be a curious example of popular distortion. The Rev. Archibald Allan, minister of the parish for many years, wrote a 'History of Channelkirk' which was published by James Thin of Edinburgh in 1900. It is written with very full detail and a whole chapter is devoted to the name.

Channelkirk of today is vastly different from the Channelkirk of the last statistical account. Changes have been swift and sweeping and may be said to date from the beginning of the present century, with the coming of the railway. Prior to 1901 the parish and the whole of Lauderdale were isolated. The main railway lines did not touch Lauderdale; the line from Edinburgh to Carlisle by way of Galashiels, constructed in 1847, was fully six miles away across hilly, moorland tracks with no direct road. The isolation was felt keenly. A clamant cry for the service of a railway arose but remained for long unanswered. At last, in 1899 on the 3rd day of June, the Countess of Lauderdale cut the first sod of the Lauder Light Railway which was designed to link Lauderdale with the main railway line at Fountainhall, and the second day of June 1901 was a red letter day in the dale for on that day the line which ran right through the parish of Channelkirk, with a station at Oxton, was opened for traffic. A few years later the petrol-driven bus appeared. 'In 1923 George Deans of Lauder operated one day per week from Lauder to Edinburgh, on one day per week from Lauder to Kelso and on Saturdays he operated from Lauder to Galashiels.' In the same year 'Messrs Brook and Amos operated two return journeys between Earlston and Lauder daily, which had the effect of linking up Lauder and Earlston, Melrose and Galashiels. In 1924 Mr John Turnbull of Kelso operated three journeys daily between Kelso and Edinburgh. In 1927 the S.M.T.

operated between Edinburgh and Jedburgh via Soutra. Towards the end of 1927 the S.M.T. took over the business of John Turnbull of Kelso and operated between Edinburgh and Kelso'. Not only was the bus the cheaper method of travel, it was also more convenient and quickly became so popular that the Lauder Light Railway was closed to passenger traffic in September 1942. The Scottish Motor Traction Company, under progressive and energetic management, has linked the parish and the whole of Lauderdale with all the Border towns and villages and for many years has run a frequent service to Edinburgh at a return fare of 3/6d. from Oxton. The journey occupies one hour. So the isolation in which the parish stood for so long was banished and the people were brought into close contact with the centres of activity and thought.

With the coming of the railway it was expected that the decline in population which had been going on steadily for years, would be arrested and it was hoped that more people might take up residence within the parish. This expectation was not realised. In the census year of 1801 the population was 640 and by 1831 had risen to 841, the highest recorded, while 20 years later it had fallen to 728. In 1901 — the year when the Lauder Light Railway was opened — the census figure was 568, in 1911 it was 478. In 1921 there was a slight increase to 499 but ten years later in 1931 the population had dropped to 418 — a very steep decline of 50 per cent in 100 years. The sexes were very evenly divided. In 1921 the males numbered 251 and the females 248, while in 1931 the sexes were equal with 209 males and 209 females. The present population continues at about the level of the 1931 census. The voters' roll of the parish in December 1949 contained 280 names and there are around 90 children from infants up to 15 years of age.

The population is affected very naturally by the work that is available and that work lacks variety. The parish is a purely farming one, consequently the sole employment is work directly on a farm or in occupations closely linked with the farms, such as those of blacksmith, fencer, rabbit trapper, transport driver. For many years farm work has been growing progressively less attractive. It is skilled work but very strenuous. Until recently the hours were unregulated and long, the wages low and the prospects far from bright. Now many of the younger people do not incline to farm work. Some want, as they say, 'a cleaner job', others seek work that will bring a larger monetary reward, while others again desire work that holds out better opportunities of promotion to higher and more responsible positions. Then the close link between country and town due to modern speedy transport has had its effect. The glitter of the towns with their more abundant social and recreational opportunities is preferred to life in the country with its comparative solitude, so the countryside has grown emptier year by year until now the steep decline in population has become alarming and the supply of skilled farm workers falls short of the demand.

OWNERSHIP OF LAND

Here a notable change has taken place and the land is no longer in the hands of a few owners but of 15. A new land-owning class has sprung into being, through the breaking up of the large estates whose owners have found it necessary to dispose of part of their land. The sale of farms has been greatly accelerated in the past ten years during which about half of the farms in the parish have changed hands. The Marquess of Tweeddale, until recently the largest landowner, has just sold the last of his farms. The purchasers in nearly every case have been the sitting tenants with the result that now half of the farms are owned by the occupying farmer. One or two are owned by farmers outwith the parish but who have a very intimate connection with it. One farmhouse has as tenant a manager who has been appointed to run the farm but the owner is comparatively near and is able to pay frequent visits. This change in ownership ought to be for the better as ownership tends towards a better upkeep of farm buildings and the much needed modernising of the farm cottages in order to make them more attractive to, and more comfortable for, the workers. This indeed is what is happening in some instances. The farmers are most efficient and take a full share in the work on the land.

FARMS

There are 21 farms within the parish. Nine of these are tenant-occupied, ten are owner-occupied and the remaining two are run by a manager for a nearby owner. They vary greatly in size. The larger ones are Hartside with 2,225 acres, Hillhouse with 1,716 acres, New Channelkirk and Glengelt with 1,681 acres, Carfrae with 1,080 acres and Kirktonhill with 920 acres. There are several medium-sized farms with from 500 to 800 acres. The smallest farms have acreages varying from 59 to round 180 acres. The rentals of the large farms with a very considerable acreage of rough pasture range from 4/- to 8/6d. per acre, while the rentals of the medium-sized and small farms, with comparatively little or no rough grazing, run at from 10/- to £1.5/- per acre. The average length of lease of the tenant-occupied farm is 14 years.

In an upland parish like Channelkirk where very nearly half the total acreage is rough grazing, sheep farming predominates. The land is ideal for it and the hills abound with blackfaced sheep. At the lower altitudes there is much good agricultural land where excellent crops of oats, barley and hay are harvested. Occasionally a field of wheat is seen. Potatoes, but much more extensively turnips, are grown. The turnips and the hay are used as winter feeding for the sheep. Farming within the parish has become more and more mechanised during the past decade or two, until today there is not a farm without one or more tractors. The horse is being crowded out. The petrol-driven lorry calls at the farm to collect and to deliver produce and livestock; this means a big saving in time and labour to the farmer and his workers. The expenses of the farmers have risen steeply and still continue to rise and there is a shortage of skilled workers.

The people are scattered throughout the parish and live in the cottages of the farms on which they work. These cottages are for the most part old and small, many of them being two-roomed. On the larger farms endeavours have been made to bring them more into line with modern standards. A hot water circulation has been installed in many and in some, baths, so necessary for workers on the land, have been added. The largest concentration of people is in Oxton village. An old writer speaks of it as 'a homely hamlet amid the healthy hills' — a description accurate and fitting still. The village consists of some 65 houses with a population around 200. Most of these houses are of the older type, more or less modernised as far as sanitary arrangements are concerned but fully half are without baths. Nearly all have gardens which are well cared for. About 17 years ago a block of four council houses was erected. These were three-roomed, with a rental of £2.2/- per month. In the present year 12 new houses have been completed — six blocks with two four-roomed houses in each block. These are for agricultural workers and the rental is £3.15/- per month. The number of houses which are owner-occupied is about 20. Up to the present the people have been dependent on oil lamps for light, while for cooking oil stoves are extensively used. Electricity is now being brought into the village which, with its so slender population, is in many ways remarkably fortunate.

It possesses a first-rate water supply, constructed in the opening years of the century. The railway station for goods traffic is beside the village, while several of the buses run into the village. There is a post office very efficiently run by the postmistress whose duties have been gradually growing greater through the payment of pensions, the sale of national insurance stamps and saving certificates. The parish postman, who retired last year after 28 years service and received the Imperial Service Medal, walked a distance of 16 miles a day. There are two collections and two deliveries of letters daily. There is a police station in the village and also the parish school with a new schoolhouse built in 1939. One of the biggest assets is a remarkably good hall which was erected as a war memorial and was opened in 1923. At the entrance to the hall is a small plaque built into the wall on which are engraved the names of 19 men who fell in the 1914-18 war, and recently the names of two who fell in the 1939-45 war were added. The hall is managed by a local committee and is kept in good repair.

The village is also a shopping centre for the parish though there are fewer shops than formerly. Within the past few years two have disappeared, the one a boot and shoe shop and the other a tailor's. These were carried on by two excellent craftsman who had a lifelong connec-

Plate 6. The coast near Burnmouth, with harvested corn in stooks.

Plate 7. Corn stooks at Burnmouth, 1950s.

tion with the village. There remain two most necessary shops, a baker's and a grocer's. These are well run by their respective owners, who give very good service to the whole parish with delivery vans which make weekly calls at the outlying farms. There are also two other shops — one at the Post Office where the daily papers, stationery and a wide variety of articles are sold; the other of a somewhat similar nature though on a smaller scale. Meat and fish are brought by vans from Lauder. The vans of the Scottish Co-operative Society also come into the parish but the majority of the people are loyal to the local shopkeepers. There is a small haulage contractor's business within the village which renders a much needed service, especially to the farming community. It possesses seven lorries and employs about nine men. The railway gives employment to nine. There is one blacksmith. There are two hotels within the parish; the one is the Tower Hotel in the centre of the village and the other is the well known and largely patronised Carfrae Mill Hotel on the main road. Within recent years this hotel has had several additions made to it and has been completely modernised. Both hotels have seven-day licences.

The people of the parish are dependent for medical services upon Lauder, where there are two doctors and two nurses. Serious cases are treated either at Peel Hospital near Galashiels or at one of the hospitals in Edinburgh. The majority of births take place in the maternity hospitals at Galashiels or Edinburgh. During the five years 1945 to 1949 there were registered within the parish 12 births, 11 marriages and 26 deaths.

The school is a primary one with two teachers — a headmaster and a lady assistant; the number of pupils on the register is slightly over 50. Very recently a small room in the school was fitted out as a kitchen; a cook and an assistant prepare dinners for the children. The youngest pupils and those who live at the more distant farms are conveyed to and from the school by motor cars, while the older ones, at the age of 12, travel by bus to Earlston. The few from the parish who desire higher education go to Duns.

Voluntary social services are not lacking; several societies exist. The oldest of these is the Oxton Bovial Society which held its first meeting on the 11th May 1839 and still functions. It was founded for 'mutual assistance in case any member should lose a cow by natural disease or accident'. A branch of the Women's Rural Institute was formed in 1924 and in 1949 had a membership of 86. Its monthly meetings are well attended; some are educational while others are social and recreational. A branch of the Woman's Guild of the Church was formed in 1929. Through its meetings comes knowledge of the wider work of the church at home and overseas and with the knowledge interest is quickened. The members — about 50 — give very loyal support to the church of the parish and do much to make the congregational socials and the sales of work the success they usually are. A small committee, in which church and school are closely linked, the Picnic and Christmas Tree Committee, arranges in summer for a picnic for all the children of the parish and in the winter for a Christmas Tree. Not a child is left out. This committee is most generously supported. There is, since 1932, a Badminton Club for the younger people, connected with the church. There is also a Bowling Club, run by the Committee of the War Memorial Hall. Very recently a Horticultural Society was formed; in September each year a Show is held when the display of vegetables, fruits and flowers would do credit to one of the big horticultural shows. Mention must be made of the Games Committee. Annually in summer the Oxton Professional Games take place. The money prizes attract professional athletes from considerable distances and the Games day ends with a dance in the Hall.

The church is unfortunate in its situation, about a mile and a half from the village of Oxton. It stands on one of the highest parts of the parish at an elevation of about 950 feet. The road to it is steep and exposed and during a severe winter is often impassable, consequently the church, for a number of years, has been closed during the first three months of the year and the service has been held in the War Memorial Hall at Oxton. This hall is used also for extra services and for meetings of the Woman's Guild, for congregational social meetings and for sales of work. The Sunday School meets in the Public School where, recently, the Bible Class also met. During my ministry services in the summer were also arranged at some of the more distant farms and these were usually well attended. The situation of the church is a very real difficulty and handicap to both minister and people. The present church was built in 1817 and is in good repair. Within the past 25 years the churchyard has been closed for burials and a cemetery has been opened near the village. The old manse beside the church has been sold and a new one has been erected beside the village, but proposals to erect a new church in Oxton have been stoutly resisted so far though the murmurings about the long, steep kirk road have been growing louder and more frequent. The membership is about 200 and the church of Channelkirk is one of the very few where the old ladles are still in use for receiving the offerings of the worshippers.

The people of the parish may still be called 'the hardy sons of rustic toil'. There is, however, a distinct difference. The social revolution, which has been moving during the past few years at a greatly quickened pace, has reached the agricultural workers in this and other sparsely populated districts. Two world wars, a dollar scarcity and a world shortage of food have caused them to be looked upon as essential to the life, the well-being and the stability of the nation, every whit as essential as the workers in the coal mines, the engineering factories and the shipyards. They themselves are very sensitive to this change; they know the work they do is of vital importance and that has given to it a dignity it never had before. As a class they are patriotic and are encouraged to do their utmost and by their work to serve their country. Their living and working conditions have improved very considerably and, with the advent of electric light and power on the farms, ought to improve still more. They are better housed on the whole, wages are more adequate and, with recent advances, now approximate more nearly to those of the workers in the large, industrial centres. Their hours of work are regulated and they have extra pay for overtime. There are none who lack the necessities of life. They have a share of the things beyond necessities. In almost every house there is a wireless set and into every house daily and weekly papers come. There is an air of comfort in their homes and a spirit of greater contentment. In the long, winter evenings many of them gather in the village hall for social intercourse and to play bowls, badminton or darts. Dances and whist drives are very numerous and very popular so the monotony and dullness of country life has been banished. They feel that their position is secure and that they can look forward to the future without the haunting fear of unemployment. As a class they are hardworking and thrifty without being mean; the parish has a reputation for its generosity in supporting all worthy objects. They take a keen and intelligent interest in politics, especially where agriculture is concerned.

The majority of the people are members of the church of the parish, or at least have some link binding them to it. Some who, before the union of the churches, were members of the United Free Church congregation at Lauder have naturally continued as members there but these are growing fewer with the passing of the years. The attendance at church services is disappointing. A liberal allowance must be made for the difficulties due to the long kirk road and also for the work that must be done on Sundays, especially at the lambing season, at seed-time and harvest; yet, when ever allowance is made, the attendance at church ought to be better; but at Communion seasons, at Harvest Thanksgiving and at Remembrance Day services the attendance is good.

The general standard of conduct is not low. The lives of the great majority are straight and clean. There is a wonderful kindliness and helpfulness to neighbours in distress, that speaks of a Christian spirit. Certainly something of the piety of a former generation has gone. The old religious strictness has disappeared; Sunday is for many a day for visiting their friends at a distance. There is no antagonism to religion, to the church and its message. Baptism is still sought and there is a growing tendency to bring infants to the church for the sacrament. The majority, with only few exceptions, seek the blessing of the church at their marriage. They want the service of the church in their darker hours and they welcome eagerly the comfort which it brings. One and another has been heard to say with emphasis 'The kirk must be kept up' and 'We canna dae without the kirk'. Some appear to be totally indifferent, some have lapsed into apathy, while some are frankly doubting and perplexed as they look out upon the world as it is, yet they all hover round the church with wistfulness and expectancy. Religion must be likened to a candle flickering in its socket, but it is not extinguished, and signs are not wanting that it may, sooner rather than later, burn up into a steady, clear flame.

THE PARISH OF CHANNELKIRK

by The Rev. Duncan J. McGregor

The Parish of Channelkirk is the most westerly of Berwickshire, and is situated in the upper district of Lauderdale. It lies on the southern slopes of the Lammermuir Hills, and the A68 Edinburgh to Jedburgh road traverses the parish, entering it from Soutra Hill. The north bounds with the parish of Fala, while to the east the boundary is marked by the Kelphope Burn forming a natural divide from the parish of Humbie. To the west lies the parish of Heriot and Stow and to the south-east, that of Lauder. Its general outline is triangular; its length from the north to Collielaw in the south, is nearly eight miles, and at its broadest, from east to west it is five miles. The total area is 14,202 acres, much of which is high ground, suitable only for grazing. Approximate acreage of rough grazing is 6,900, some 5,100 acres are under grass and 1900 acres are cultivated, 12 under water and some 100 in roads.

The parish consists of hills and valleys, with a small area of flat land to the south, forming the valley of the River Leader, the tributaries of which rise in the parish. The highest point is the Clints Hill in the south-west which rises to 1535 feet, while Soutra Hill at its highest is 1209 feet; the old coach road from the Lothians to Newcastle at its highest point on Soutra Hill is 1100 feet and traverses a desolate and windswept moor. Adverse wintry conditions of snow, ice and fog contribute to make it highly dangerous. The winter of 1962 saw the road blocked for several weeks by walls of snow some 20 feet high. Since then, milder winters and a gradual widening and straightening of the road on the southern slopes has enabled vehicular traffic to maintain higher speeds.

Parochial boundaries have not changed after the re-organisation of local Government, though the parish is now part of the District of Ettrick and Lauderdale, but they are at present subject to re-scrutiny by the Presbytery of Melrose and Peebles. Recent warm summers (especially that of 1989) resulted in a serious lack of water for neighbouring farms, on some of which bore-holes were sunk to produce water for farm stock. The climate is cold, generally dry, but very windy, especially in winter when the prevailing west wind is often bitterly cold.

The area is rich in antiquity with the old Roman road of Dere Street proceeding westwards through the parish from the camp near Newstead, Melrose, through Oxton and thence past the front door of Channelkirk Church and up over the moorland, west of Soutra on the way towards Cramond, west of Edinburgh.

Another ancient road, traces of which may be seen near Threeburnford Farm, is the Girthgate, which was probably made by the monks of Melrose in order to give easier access to Soutra Aisle and on to Edinburgh. Along the valley near the track of the former Lauder Light Railway which linked Lauder to Fountainhall (opened 3rd June 1899 and closed in 1953), is the Well of the Holy Water Cleugh. This lies some 400 yards south-west of the Church, it is sometimes called St Cuthbert's Well; the child Cuthbert was believed to have come from Ireland to assist his maternal uncle as a shepherd in the Lammermuir Hills. Legend has it that while he 'tended as a shepherd in the night his master's flocks on the side of the Leader' he had the vision which led him to dedicate his life to the Lord. He became a monk in the neighbouring monastery of Mailros in AD 651. Some years later, he returned to Channelkirk to spread Christianity throughout Berwickshire. The parish Church is dedicated to his name and it is believed that the original building was erected on the spot where he had the vision. The Church is roughly in the centre of the parish, but some one and a half miles from the only village, Oxton, formerly Augston, and stands about 950 feet above sea level. Little remains of the ancient hamlet of Channelkirk west of the former manse beside the Church, which remains open throughout the year.

Because of adverse wintry conditions, Sunday worship in conducted in the War Memorial Hall, Oxton, during the first three months of the year. The name Channelkirk has given rise to much discussion, for in earlier centuries it was variously called 'Chyldeschirche', 'Childenechirch' and 'Chinglechirche', but the many names have been corrupted by local dialect and their true origin of 'Child's Church', or from the name of the nearby Roman camp, 'Childin', is now obscure. The present building dates from 1817, and is subject to all the care and attention which befits the House of the Lord. The road to it is steep and exposed and during severe winters often impassable. As in many rural churches, there is no running water or toilet facilities. It can accommodate a congregation of three hundred, but in the last 30 years the numerical strength of the congregation has fallen from around 200 to 95 in 1989. While this is commensurate with the national trend, it is recognised that the local population has also decreased. This is also reflected in the numbers who worship on Sundays, though when the services are held in the War Memorial Hall, the average attendance is higher. At certain times of the agricultural year, the lambing season, seed time and harvest, the numbers are understandably lower. In recent years, suggestions to close the church and build one in the village have fortunately been rejected and the peaceful serenity of its setting is much appreciated by all who worship there. The glebe of nine acres bounds the church on three sides; on the fourth is the former manse which was sold after the Union of Churches in 1929. The burial ground was closed for interments in the 1930s and a new cemetery opened a quarter mile from the village, and near the second manse which in turn was sold some 20 years ago, and after a seven-year vacancy, the charge of Channelkirk was linked with Lauder in 1975. The allegiance to Scottish Ecclesiastical history is retained by the use of the Authorised Version of the Holy Bible and the long-handled offering ladles. Soon to be mounted on the west wall of the church is a relic of the 'body-snatching' days when graves were desecrated and bodies exhumed and stolen to be used in Edinburgh for medical research. A rare example of a Mort Safe, a heavy latticed iron framework which held the coffin secure prior to burial, is at present being repaired before being returned to the church where it was often in use.

Old British and Iron Age forts are visible on the hills, notably those at Carfrae and Addinston, and also the Roman camp at Channelkirk. Many arrowheads, knives and flints have been found and a fine collection may be seen in the Museum of Antiquities in Edinburgh. Additional material on the parish can be obtained by perusal of 'The History of Channelkirk' by the Rev. Archibald Allan, published by James Thin of Edinburgh in 1900.

As is the case with many rural areas throughout Scotland, the years since the last Statistical Account have seen the population of the parish change greatly. The increased mechanisation of agricultural equipment has reduced the necessity for numerous farm workers, many of whom have left the area or indeed their former occupation. Their homes, the farm cottages, now house people who are in other employment, or have been sold as holiday homes. This practice, while gaining for the owner-farmer additional capital, has meant that many of these former dwelling houses lie vacant for long periods of time or are occupied by those who commute to Edinburgh or to neighbouring Border towns. This infusion of newcomers regrettably has not increased the community spirit in the way which was envisaged, and Oxton, like many other villages has become a dormitory settlement. The trend recognised in other parts of Scotland of the selling of farms continues. Most farms sold in recent years have been to farmers from England, where land prices are higher, thus enabling those new to the area to offer higher prices. Another practice has been the selling of farms to an institution or pension scheme society and then the leasing back of the farm. The acreage of certain farms has altered, Hartside becoming smaller, Kirktonhill now one with New Channelkirk, Overhowden partly sold to Inchkeith. Huntershall, on top of Soutra, is now outwith the parish and the farmhouse uninhabited.

Access is either by private car or by bus (the Edinburgh to Kelso bus calls regularly each day and turns at the crossroads in the village). The cost of a return journey to Edinburgh is about £3.50 and the single journey takes about an hour to the city centre. Local friendships are strong so that those in hospital are regularly visited and those without private transport are frequently offered 'lifts'. Government action in the 1950s meant that the Lauder Railway lasted only 50 years and until recently, when ownership of a motor vehicle became more widespread, there was a feeling of isolation.

For medical treatment, people are dependent either on the new Medical Centre in Lauder, which also maintains a consulting room in the village, or on the practice in Pathhead six miles distant. The new Borders General Hospital at Huntlyburn, Melrose, admits the more serious cases and the majority of births now take place there.

The Channelkirk Primary School, built in 1939, was enlarged circa 1968 with new classrooms and a kitchen which provides food for the 31 local children at present on the roll. There are two teachers who give a good educational foundation to the children who proceed to secondary school at Earlston High School, to which there is a daily school bus service.

There is no gas supply to the village or environs, heating choice being portable Calor Gas or coal. Supplies of coal are regularly brought from Duns or Hawick. The former Station yard became a coal supply depot and is now used to sell garden huts and furniture. There is no Police Station, that service being operated by mobilised Lothians and Borders Police from Galashiels with a small station in Lauder. The nearest Fire Stations are based in Dalkeith and Galashiels.

The population has reduced drastically in the past 190 years. In 1801, it was 640; by 1831 it had risen to 841, the highest ever recorded, but by 1851 it had fallen to 728. In 1901, the year in which the Railway came to Oxton, the figure was 568. In 1911 it was 478, and ten years on it was 499; 251 of whom were males and 248 who were females, despite the loss of 19 men who died in the Great War. By 1931 it had fallen to 418 (209 males and 209 females), a decrease of 50 per cent in 100 years. This figure remained static until 1949 when there were 280 names on the voters' roll and about 90 children from infant to 15 years of age. The present population consists of 160 males and 150 females (including 80 children under 15); that of the village is 136. There are 58 houses in the village, most being owner-occupied; there are 12 council houses, the rent for which is about £15 per week.

There is one General Store, the owner of which provides an excellent van delivery service to outlying farms and houses. This is also a valued personal contact with elderly and housebound and is a necessary adjunct to rural life. The advent of super stores and large market shops in Edinburgh and Galashiels has affected local shopping habits. A Sub-Post Office counter is now maintained in the General Store. The Postal service, with local delivery of mail from the Lauder Post Office, allows for one daily delivery and there are two collections of mail each week day from collection boxes. There are now no other shops in the parish. The Tower Hotel in Oxton provides locals and travellers with sustenance as does the neighbouring old post house, the Carfraemill Hotel. Both these hostelries have changed ownership several times in recent years, though always providing excellent service and employment to those in the locality. There is no unemployment in the parish.

The former blacksmith's shop at Carfrae, which shod the 155 horses employed on farms in the 1930s, has been for many years a petrol filling station.

While the focal point of most villages is or used to be the church, the only public building is the War Memorial hall, which was opened in 1923 as a memorial to those in the area who gave their lives in World War One. At the entrance of the Hall there is a plaque on which are engraved the names of 19 men who fell in World War One and two who fell in the Second World War. The Hall is managed by a local committee and is lovingly cared for. The Hall is used for worship especially on Remembrance Sunday and for the first three months of each year, and for the various activities organised locally. The Woman's Guild, formed in 1929, comprises 12 active members, all enthusiastic in holding regular meetings to which speakers on all topics are invited, thus enabling the members to appreciate the wider work of the Church. For some years there has not been a Bible Class and the Sunday School also ceased some four years ago. Children have been encouraged to attend the Sunday School of the linked charge of Lauder, but this has met with little response.

The Hall is marked out for Badminton, that club being well supported though not attached to the Church. There is indoor bowling in winter months and the enthusiastic and well known Oxton Scottish Country Dance Society meets every week. The Oxton Horticultural Society is well supported locally and many gardens reveal the talents of the owners in colourful floral displays. The Annual Horticultural Show is held in September and fruit, flowers and vegetables are in great abundance, doing great credit to local enthusiasts.

The Women's Rural Institute was formed in 1924 and while membership at 35 is smaller now, it is enthusiastically supported at all meetings whether they be educational, recreational or social. A Christmas party for all the children in the parish is held annually in the Hall, and this is generously financed by sales of work organised during the year.

The Oxton Bovial Society, founded on 11th May 1839 for 'mutual assistance in case any member should lose a cow by material disease or accident', meets regularly in the Hall, as does the Games Committee which organises the popular Oxton Professional Games which are held each summer and which attract athletes from Scotland and the North of England.

Oxton and its environs is a peaceful area, and until the Assessed

Rent Local Authority rating system was abolished in favour of the Community tax, the lower rating of properties encouraged many to come to live in the district. Amongst all there exists a friendliness and neighbourliness which is shown in kindly gestures in times of stress. This reveals a Christian spirit which is not however reflected in Church membership. There is no antagonism towards the Church or religion and the sacrament of baptism is sought as also is the Church for the occasional village marriage. In recent years there have been few births, marriages or deaths in the parish, all of which are notified to the Registrar in the new Church Centre in Lauder.

The parish has rightly earned a reputation for generosity for 'good causes' outwith and within the area.

There is a possibility of more new houses being built in Oxton, the nearby town of Lauder having reached its quota of new houses until the mid 1990s. While all new residents will be welcomed into this community, it is to be hoped that they will contribute their time and talents to the social, ecclesiastical and recreational well-being of a small but supportive community which, while following the trend of population decline, could never be described as a dying community, for it is vibrant in its many social activities.

1980s

THE PARISH OF CHIRNSIDE

by The Rev. Alfred McKeachie M.A.

Chirnside is a small parish in East Berwickshire of an area of 5569 acres of which 16.5 are water. Whiteadder Water winding 6.25 miles eastward roughly traces all the southern boundary, whilst its affluent Billymire Burn rises in the north-west corner of the parish, and first striking one and a half miles east-north-east next flows two miles west-south-west along the northern, and one and three quarter miles south by west along the western, border.

The parish is nine miles from Berwick-on-Tweed, six from Duns and five from Ayton — its nearest point on the Great North Road. It slopes up some 350 feet from the River Whiteadder to the ridge on which the village stands and the highest point of which is 466 feet above sea level. From its prominent position it commands extensive views in every direction. The eye can range from the sea at Berwick-on-Tweed to the Lammermuirs, and south-west to the distant hills of Teviotdale and even Dumfriesshire on a very clear day. Southward one looks across the broad valley of Tweed and its tributaries to the Cheviots almost 20 miles away, while to the north one views the well cultivated slopes of Bunkle and Coldingham, and to the north-east one can catch a glimpse of ships as they pass to and fro on the North Sea.

Forty years ago the prospect was enriched by the many woods scattered over the Merse. As elsewhere these have had to be sacrificed to the demands of war, but groups of trees surrounding mansion houses and fringes of trees round the fields and along the roads still enhance the view.

The parish itself has been unfortunate in that it has lost beautiful woods that once adorned Whitehall and Ninewells. Woods were also cut down at Maines, Harelaw, Blackburn and Edington Hill and at these places, except Blackburn, land, formerly under timber, is now under cultivation. A particular loss is that of the splendid avenue which began at Chirnside Bridge and ran the whole length of Ninewells estate along the Duns-Berwick road. Age overtook some of the trees, others have been taken down for safety and a few still remain to the west of the village.

The work done in former years to confine the river to its present course has been so successful that even the great spate of 12th August 1948, has not changed its course. It should be noted that the river

Whiteadder is not the parish boundary along its whole course. Between 10 and 11 acres of Broomdykes are on the north side of the river, while some 16 acres of Whitehall Estate are south of the river. Again, west of the Allanton Bridge the boundary runs north-west through a field until it reaches the river again. It should be mentioned that 87 sheep in this field were drowned by the 1948 spate and that two suspension bridges, one at Bluestone Ford and the other at Edington Mills, were also swept away by it.

The population of the parish reached its height of 1580 in 1901, and since then it has steadily declined until 1951 when it was 1,218.* The decrease has been due to the drift from the country to the town, especially from the farms, and it would have been much greater had it not been that the local paper mill has flourished since the first World War. In 1914, at Old Castles, with eight cottages, the population was 42, of whom seven attended school and one was under school age. Today, with one cottage vacant, there are 21 people at the farm of whom only one is of school age or under. The population is scattered as follows:

Farms:	219
Mansions and Lodges:	31
Odd Cottages:	23
Station Area:	98

The rest live in the village.

The station area consists of three railway station houses, Chirnside Mill Farm, three private houses, the residence of the Manager of the paper mill and 29 paper mill houses. The actual buildings of the paper mill — Chirnside Bridgemills — are in Edrom Parish but of its 180 employees, 147 at present belong to the parish of Chirnside. Chirnside Bridgemills were founded in 1786 by Mr John Pitcairn who was joined four years later by his brother-in-law Mr Young Trotter. The mill was then at Broomhouse — some three miles further up the River Whiteadder — but it was transferred in 1842 to its present site. In 1887 the business was formed into a company under the name of Y. Trotter & Sons. Originally it was a one-machine mill but two other machines were added. Of these one was sold in 1942 owing to the difficulty of securing raw material.

The railway station is a mile from the village but is now only used for goods traffic. Passenger traffic ceased in August 1948 and, though resumed for a time, between Reston and Duns, has now stopped altogether.

There is only one 'A' road in the parish, that from Duns to Berwick. All the rest are second class roads and in good condition.

* There are 581 males and 637 females. Of the total population there are 224 under the age of 15 years.

Of the four mills once in the parish, only one — Edington Mill — is working now. It is still used as a meal mill and is the most modern and best equipped of its kind in the Borders. Improvements were in process when it was heavily damaged by the flood of August 1948, and it did not start work again till August 1949. The water wheel was kept to make white oats but all other kinds are made by electricity on modern plant. It produces brown oats, oat flakes, oat flour and all the various 'Cuts' of oatmeal. A silo, for bulk storage of grain, equipped with a grain drier and dressing plant, was included in the recent additions. It employs 16 men.

Chirnside Mill is entirely out of use. An octogenarian of the parish declares that neither he nor his father knew of meal being produced there, though, until a dozen years ago, it was used as a threshing mill and also to pump the village water supply. There were two mills on the river below Ninewells. The meal mill was in use until 1898 when it was burned down. The woollen mill (locally known as "The Creashie Mill") made yarn for blankets and tweed and had only two hand looms. It was modernised and heightened to two storeys in 1899 and work was about to be resumed when it too was burned down.

The property opposite the western entrance to the churchyard is still known as the Brewery Buildings although the brewing of ale there ceased about 60 years ago. Men are still alive who as boys took farm carts there in the harvest time for the harvest ale. Brewery House where the proprietor lived is now called Rhuallan.

A zeppelin dropped two bombs in April 1916 to the west of the village, one falling in a field at Ninewells Mains, the other doing damage to a house near the station. Another bomb was dropped by an aeroplane on a field at Old Castles in 1940, blowing in windows at the cottages and the farm house.

The last vestiges of the Castle or tower of Edington, close to the Berwick road, were removed last year. The only buildings left now on the Berwick road at Edington are four cottages and a smithy.

THE VILLAGE

Chirnside formerly consisted of a long main street running from east to west and another from the middle of the village south to the Old Church. Lately, however, large groups of houses have been built at the extreme west and it is there, obviously, that the village will extend in future. Nearly all the gaps in the Main Street have been filled and it is likely that the few remaining ones will disappear soon. In all, there are 277 houses (or rather householders) in the village and of these 59 are Council houses built since 1925. Most houses are of two storeys. Business people own their properties as do many others, and these are all modernised and have both electricity and inside sanitation. The paper mill owns a considerable number of houses; one block with two main doors has ten tenants. Several old houses have recently been taken down and more are condemned, at least six on the Crosshill — the two at the top next to the school, the next one further south, and three at Heughs Row.

'Duiks' (Ducks) Dub
Fiddler's Raw
Quarry Mains
And Image Raw.'

This jingle was handed down by the late Mr Peacock, formerly proprietor of the Waterloo Hotel, who on his retiral feued the Duiks' Dub from Ninewells Estate and built Auburn Cottage. His daughter afterwards bought the small cottage and large garden next to it in the corner of which stands the old Dovecot of Ninewells which has been kept by the Estate. No name or date is on this building but a string course half way up indicates that it is old. Tradition has it that the Laird of Ninewells, having fallen out with the Laird of Whitehall, built the Dovecot on the boundary of his estate in order that the pigeons might feed on the Whitehall fields. Fiddler's Row was in the triangle north of Auburn Cottage and Quarry Mains. Some houses standing in front of Image Row have long since disappeared. There were two Images which gave Image Row its name — one at each end of the Row. These were supposed to represent Adam and Eve. The one at the west end disappeared at least 20 years ago; the one at the east end was taken down 15 years ago.

Until the beginning of the century the sanitation of the village was deplorable, indeed non-existent. Water was supplied to a small part of the village from the Carter (Quatre) Well by means of a small engine but the majority were dependent for their water on wells and pumps. There are still 26 houses without water and many more without inside sanitation.

When it was decided to have a public supply nearly 50 years ago, three sources were examined, Ninewells, Blackhouse and the Boiling Springs one and a half miles west of the village, and the last was chosen. At first, the mill wheel at Chirnside Mill Farm was used to raise the water to the tank on Harelaw Hill, but later an oil engine became necessary and finally, in 1945, electric power was used. Since then, the supply has proved ample and water has been introduced into an increasing number of houses. Along with the public water supply a sewerage system was introduced and has proved satisfactory, the water, after purification, entering the Whiteadder at the Bluestone Ford.

Chirnside is surrounded by a wide agricultural district and has always been a busy shopping centre, catering for a public far beyond the parish bounds. The following list shows the trades, businesses and professions carried on in Chirnside:

Motor Garages (5)
Agricultural Engineers (2)

Grocers (4)
Co-operative Store
Grocer and Draper
Drapers (2)
Butchers (2)
Baker
Blacksmith
Ironmonger
Joiner and Undertaker
Slaters and Plasterers (3)
Builders (2)
Painter
Watchmaker and Jeweller
Plumber
Newsagent and Stationer
Tea Rooms (2)
Hairdresser
Shoe Repairers (2)
Fish and Chips
Firewood Merchant
Insurance Agent
Policeman
Chiropodist
Chemist
Nurse
Banker
Lawyer
Doctor
Hotels (2)

Messrs A. & T. Mabon, Grocers (established 1883) have two shops, employ 17 people and send out four vans and a mobile shop every day.

Messrs John McBain & Son, Agricultural Engineers, became a Limited Company in 1946. This firm, which employs (1952) 44 people, sends windmills to Argentina, Uruguay and Pakistan. They also make centrifugal pumps for raising water. These are for the home market. The business was founded by Mr John McBain in 1876 and was extended by his son and his grandson who is now Managing Director. He was a man of great piety and integrity and was held in high esteem in the community. He built a small Mission Hall in the village where he conducted a weekly religious service and a Sunday School. He is commemorated by The McBain Trust with an annual income of five pounds, used to promote Bible knowledge among children.

Mr Alexander Dippie is, at least, the fourth generation of Dippies who have been master-blacksmiths in the village. He, his father and grandfather have all been elders in the Parish Church.

There are two halls in the village. The Drill Hall, which is owned by a private company, is at present being offered for sale to the public. The future of the Comrades Hall is at present under consideration.

The village streets were not lighted until 1924 when lighting by single petrol lamps was used. Electricity was extended to Chirnside in 1938. Gas, manufactured by a private company, was supplied to private houses for lighting till about 1950.

With the coming of motor transport the last carrier and carter disappeared from village life — about 1912. Within living memory milk was supplied to the village from 27 cows kept by 15 individuals who rented pasture from Whitehall and Ninewells. It is now supplied from the farms of Ninewells (44 cows) and Chirnside Mill and by various milk vans from outside the parish.

Chirnside Fair, which was held on the last Thursday of November, fell into abeyance about 70 years ago. The last stall holder was 'Auld Wullie' Glen whose stance was at the gable end of the Cameronian Church, and who sold bickers, tubs, beetles and such like. The last persons to observe the fair were Miss Ailie Ferguson, who had a shop on the Crosshill, and the late Dr McVie who ordered specially made gingerbreads to be sent to his friends and to old people in the village on Fair Day.

At the beginning of the Fair a Proclamation was read by a representative of the Laird of Whitehall and the following is a copy of the Proclamation:

OYEZ! OYEZ! OYEZ!

> 'In Her Majesty's Name and Authority and in name and authority of Alexander Mitchell-Innes Esquire of Whitehall, Right Sole Proprietor of the Lands and Barony of Chirnside by the said name, power and authority I debar out of this said Fair all illegal characters such as thieves, swindlers, robbers etc. and all unlawful games or in a word whatever tends to disturb the lawful Merchandise Peace or Quiet of said Fair. I likewise prohibit Portioners, Feu-holders, Innkeepers or others from harbouring any of the aforesaid characters within their possessions. If any are found so doing they are liable to the penalty of Twenty Pounds.'

GOD SAVE THE QUEEN

The village streets are kept clean and tidy by County roadmen. The 'Crofts' path from the village to the school is fairly well kept and has recently been relaid. In the west end the right of way to McBain's is not so much used. The 'Dominie's Loan' from the Crosshill to the Reston Road near Harelaw is in fair condition.

There is an automatic telephone exchange in the village and there is a kiosk in the middle of the village. The Post Office is a Sub-Post Office under Duns. It is staffed by two people. There are two postal deliveries on weekdays and three despatches. There is also a despatch on Sunday. There is only one policeman on duty in Chirnside. The present Police Station has been condemned and a new one is to be built before long.

The trees in the old quarry at the Manse gate were cut down after the First World War. The trees in the Manse grounds include a fine old ilex, a walnut, a lime, common maples, hollies, and three gean trees in the glebe in front of the Manse. The village is almost denuded of trees.

CHURCHES

Until 1919 there were three congregations in the parish — two of the United Free Church of Scotland and one of the Parish Church, but in that year the first two were united under the Rev. William McDonald, M.A., later Minister of Palmerston Place Church, Edinburgh. Union between the Church of Scotland and the United Free Church took place in 1929, but the two congregations remained until 1st April 1952. The Minister of the North Church having been transferred to Elgin and the Minister of the Old Church having resigned after 42.5 years service, the question of Union was raised by the Presbytery. Efforts to unite the two congregations having proved futile, the question was referred to the General Assembly of the Church which appointed a Special Commission with powers, and this Commission united the two congregations on that date. The Communion Roll of the united congregations is 725 and there are 17 Elders and 40 Managers. Sunday School scholars number 91 and both Churches have had a Bible Class. They also have had strong branches of the Women's Guild and it is anticipated that when the new Minister, the Rev. J. B. Longmuir, T.D., M.A., B.L., is inducted to the new charge in September there will be a new era of Church life in the parish.

The United Presbyterian Church was built in 1837. In 1922 it was handed over by the North Church to the local branch of the British Legion which has now returned it to the Church of Scotland, having been unable to maintain it financially.

The North Church was originally a Cameronian Church and was built in 1783 — a thatched building with an earthen floor. Later the building was improved. The congregation ultimately joined the Free Church and a new building was erected in 1898.

After the Church Union of 1929 the Parish Church went by the name of the Old Church. Its history goes far back, at least to the 12th century. A definite date is 10th April 1242, when David de Bernham, Bishop of St Andrews, dedicated it. Though the Church has been built and rebuilt since then, the ancient South doorway has remained intact.* It narrowly escaped destruction in 1878 when the Presbytery decided to build a new church on a new site. The heritors maintained that the church could be repaired but the Presbytery adhered to their

* Scott's Fasti dates it from 1150.

Plate 8. The Duns–Berwick road near Chirnside.

Plate 9. The Parish Church, Chirnside.

decision. The heritors appealed to the Sheriff of Berwickshire and won their case. It was during this rebuilding that the vault of the Hume family was removed from below the East Gallery.

The church again underwent change when the present tower, hall and vestry were added by the second Lord Tweedmouth in memory of his wife Lady Fanny Tweedmouth (née Churchill), who died in 1904 and by her own wish was buried beside the church. She had been a regular worshipper when the family were tenants of Ninewells during the repair of Hutton Castle. A life-size sculpture of her in bas relief by Waldo Story was brought from Brook House, their London residence, and placed in the wall of the church above the Ninewells pews. Lord Tweedmouth died in 1909 and the following year his son, the third Lord Tweedmouth, bought and removed two houses west of the church which formed part of the churchyard boundary and on the ground thus made available erected in memory of his father a beautiful entrance gateway and the present delightful approach to the church and the churchyard.

The old stone with the inscription 'Helpe the Purue 1573' is still in its place on the inside of the south wall of the Church, while on the outside of it is the memorial tablet of the Rev. Dr Anderson who wrote the article on Chirnside for the First Statistical Account of Scotland. Two links are left of the Jougs in the south wall immediately east of the ancient doorway and on the south-west corner is the sundial with its inscription 'Hoc age dum lumen adest'. The tombstone of Henry Erskine and that of Laird Spence,** murdered by Sir George Lauder of Edington in 1700, are in good condition.

The Church is in excellent repair. It was redecorated in 1951 and a new heating system was then installed. The Communion table at present in use was presented to the Church in 1911 by Mrs John Blackadder, late of Ninewells Mains, who died in 1925 at the age of 96.

Of the three Manses in the parish that of the former Free Church was sold. The Manse of the North Church, formerly U.P. Manse, is to be the residence of the Minister of the parish while the Old Church Manse is life-rented to the recently retired Minister. Both Manses are in good repair and the question as to which will be the permanent Manse has been meantime postponed.

The tradition is still maintained in the parish that Mrs Erskine, wife of the Rev. Henry Erskine and mother of Ralph and Ebenezer Erskine, came to life again the night she was buried. The story is that the sexton opened her coffin in order to secure a valuable ring which she wore and in doing so cut her finger. Blood flowed and she recovered from the 'dwam' in which she was and she appeared at the Manse in her grave clothes and knocked at the door. The knock was heard by

** *vide* Carr's 'History of Coldingham', 1836, p. 162.

her husband who took her into her home again. Nearly three years ago a correspondence took place in *The Scotsman* in which a family claimed to be in possession of the ring.

The first clergyman on record is Symon, 'parsona de Chirnesyde' (about 1250), and his successor was William de Blida (Blythe) whose name is mentioned in 1296. Chirnside was made the Seat of the Presbytery in 1581, a privilege which it retained till 1929. The present incumbent is only the sixth minister of the parish since 1704 and the first appointed by popular election, his predecessor having been presented to the charge by William Mitchell-Innes, Esq., of Ayton Castle and Whitehall.

ESTATES

Until 1916 there were only five Heritors in the parish. The following list shows the present lands and their owners.

1. Whitehall (2,354 acres) was bought in 1844 from Sir John Hall of Whitehall and Dunglass by Mr William Mitchell-Innes of Ayton Castle, the great-great-grandfather of the present owner, Dr William Mitchell-Innes. The rental then was £4,347. The estate now consists of Nether Mains, 238 acres; Broadhaugh, 120 acres; the Nursery, 5 acres; the four fields, 72 acres; lying between the Berwick and Ayton road immediately south of the village, and the extensive home, parks and policies of Whitehall.

The following five farms were part of the Whitehall estate.

(1) Old Castles, 561 acres, was sold in 1920 to the tenant Mr Peter Cowe (d. 1925) who came with his father from Dowlaw, Coldingham, to Old Castles in 1848. It is still owned by his family and farmed by his grandson Mr Robert P. Cowe of Butterdean.

(2) Chirnside Mill, 68 acres, was sold in 1943 to Mr William Marshall.

(3) Harelaw, 512 acres, was sold in 1949 to the tenant Mr David Keir Swan.

(4) The Crofts, 94 acres, was sold in 1947 to the tenants Mr J. Aitken Scott and Mr Walter Scott whose great-grandfather became tenant of The Crofts 100 years ago.

(5) Causewaybank, 399 acres, was sold in 1950 to Mr Wilson, a Northumbrian, who sold it a year afterwards to Mr James M. Wilson, a farmer from Fife.

2. Ninewells has been the home of the Hume family for centuries and consists of Ninewells Mains, 414 acres; Ninewells Mill, 28 acres; and the parks and policies of the Mansion House which was burned down and rebuilt about 120 years ago. The house is at present empty, having been occupied during the war by British and Polish soldiers. The present owner is Mr Euan David Ross Hume. 'David Hoome of Ninewells' is

the name which heads the list of Elders of the Parish Church at the first meeting of the Kirk Session held by the Rev. Henry Erskine on 10th May 1691 after 'a time of disorder and confusion'. David Hume (1711-1776) the philosopher and historian also lived there, a fact commemorated in a plaque erected in 1976 by the Berwickshire Naturalists on the Ninewells wall fronting the main road.

3. Maines consists of Maines farm, 386 acres, and Oxward, about eight acres. The estate was bought from the Trustees of Mr Thomas Begbie, who died in 1847, by Dr Hood of Sunnyside in the parish of Coldingham. It remained in his family until 1945 when it was sold by the Trustees of his grand-daughter, Mrs Andrew H. Glegg (died 1942) to Colonel Trotter, brother of the Laird of Charterhall. The present mansion house was built by Mr Thomas Begbie about 1837-8 and replaced the former one which stood 120 yards further west. The farm is still popularly called Molle's Mains after Mr William Molle* who was proprietor and farmer 150 years ago.

4. Edington Mains, Edington Hill (together 1,242 acres) and Edington Mill formed part of the Hutton Castle estate. The third Lord Tweedmouth, in 1916, sold them to Mr Ralph Lawson, a Northumberland farmer, the tenants then being Mr William Lyal and Mr William H. Elliot who became sole tenant 1919-1942. In the latter year Mr James Clark, Kilmany, Fife, became tenant of the two farms and in 1944 bought them, along with Edington Mill, from Mr Lawson's son and almost immediately sold the Mill to Messrs R. F. Bell and Son Ltd., Leith.

Blackburn, 450 acres, forming part of Hutton Castle estate, was sold in 1916 to Sir William Burrell when he purchased Hutton Castle.

5. Westfield, 71 acres, consists of a number of fields at the west end of the village. It was bought by Mr Peter Scott, the tenant of Crofts, and is now owned and farmed, with the Crofts, by his two grandsons, Mr J. Aitken Scott and Mr Walter Scott, Whiterig, Ayton.

FARMS

The farms and their sizes are given above and almost without exception they are cultivated with great skill. All are engaged in mixed farming except Ninewells Mains and Chirnside Mill which have dairies. The soil is a rich loam except for a tract in the south-east where a rather stiff clay grows excellent wheat and in the north-east where some bog and marsh are not under the plough. The southern slopes of the parish are particularly rich and fertile, but the northern half is also splendid land and produces excellent results both in cropping and feeding. The usual rotation of crops is now five years — cereals, turnips, potatoes, mangold or sugar-beet, cereals undersown with grass seed and then two years grass, though some have two white crops following each other. The

* The name was originally Mow.

average yield of cereals per acre has been 5-6 quarters of wheat, 6-8 of barley and 7-10 of oats, but of late greater yields have been obtained. Agriculture research, more scientific management, the use of higher-yielding varieties of grain and a more liberal application of artificial fertilizers have had surprising results. In the better fields and with a favourable season, the yield has been 8 quarters of wheat, 10 of barley and 12 of oats.

Similar progress has been made in root crops. Potatoes, which have been increasingly grown in the parish since the first World War, produce an average of 10-12 tons and sugar-beet 10 tons.

On most farms, on average, three-fifths of the arable area is under crop and the remainder in grass. Of the area under cultivation, two-thirds is in grain and one-third in root crop.

The mechanisation of agriculture has completely changed farm life and methods, and even nomenclature. The word 'hind', used to designate a ploughman, and the word 'bondager', i.e. a woman bound to work on the farm for a year, are no longer in use, though ten years ago these words were quite common.

There are only 20 farm horses in the parish now — three or four farms have none. There are 46 tractors and 7 combine harvesters. One farmer (Causewaybank) has plant for drying his grain and, on most farms, straw is baled in the harvest field. Two farms — Harelaw and Ninewells Mains — are at present experimenting with silage in pits. Besides combine harvesters and balers, the following modern mechanical implements are used in the parish — reversible plough, self-lifting harrow, manure (farmyard and artificial) spreader, potato planter, elevator and digger and harvester, sprayer for corn and potatoes.

The farm houses are almost all large and commodious with electricity from the grid or generated by an engine. The farm cottages usually consist of three apartments and until recently were very poor. Some still are so, but general improvement has begun and is now spreading. All the cottages at six farms have electricity and water and at three there are bathrooms. It is expected that when the County Water Supply is introduced — probably in 1953 — all farm cottages will be modernised.

It is increasingly difficult to induce people to stay on the land. Men are not inclined to act as horsemen or cattlemen owing to the Sunday work involved, and even shepherds and tractormen are also scarce.

Fifty years ago most shepherds and stewards had a cow but that privilege has ceased. Most workers keep pigs and feed two to four each year. An allowance of 1,700 yards of potatoes used to be given as part of the wage but this was stopped when the wage was increased, to which was added one ton of potatoes. Working hours are now 48 hours a week in summer and an average of 44 in winter. A word of praise is due to the tillers of the soil. They are men of high character, most faithful and conscientious in their work and thoroughly reliable. More than once, local farmers have told the writer that better or more skilful workers are not to be found anywhere.

EDUCATION

There is now only one school in the parish. It is on the Berwick road immediately to the east of the Old Church and churchyard. The site extends to seven acres of which 4.5 acres are used as a playing field and the remaining 2.5 acres are occupied by the school playground, its vegetable and flower gardens and its approaches.

The school, costing £30,000, was opened in October 1940, and in 1947 became a Junior Secondary School. It is of the most modern type and is splendidly equipped in every way. There are eight classrooms, each capable of holding 30 children very comfortably and three large rooms for Science, Domestic Science and Technical subjects. There is also a large Gynmasium which can be used as a Hall.

The school is most capably managed by Mr Peter McDonald, M.A., Headmaster, who is assisted by a staff of seven teachers (four male and three female) and five visiting teachers (three male and two female).

The number on the Roll at present is 202 — 111 girls and 91 boys — of whom 130 come from the parish and the others travel by bus from the surrounding parishes. Twenty-two pupils from Chirnside attend the Berwickshire High School at Duns. Evening classes for practical subjects are held during the winter.

Excellent dinners, costing 7d., are provided every day and on an average these are taken by 120 pupils, while 92 daily partake of a third of a pint of milk which is provided free. The children are very healthy looking and the attendance is excellent. There is an annual medical inspection and periodic visits by specialists.

The teachers take a keen interest in the welfare of the children. School Sports are held annually and there is an annual Sale of Work which is generously supported by the public. In 1951 the sum of £112 was realised. This money is used to provide educational excursions, Christmas parties and special school equipment, e.g. a radiogram this year. The session closes with a prize-giving day which is attended by parents and friends.

A private school was built in 1851 by Miss Hume of Ninewells and was maintained by her until 1889, when the building was purchased by Mr Cleghorn whose family still occupy it.

The old school at the centre of the village on the Crosshill was often condemned by School Inspectors and by the County Medical Officer before it was closed in 1940. It has not been decided yet how the buildings will be used, but meantime part is used as a Cooking Centre by the County Council to prepare the school dinners for Chirnside, Foulden, Paxton, Hutton, Edrom and Bunkle.

RECREATIONS

There is an excellent Bowling Club in the village with 70 members including half a dozen ladies. It was founded in 1925 and has been very popular. The annual membership fee is 17/6.

There is a Tennis Club, a Badminton Club and a Football Club as well as a Curling Club, though its members play only in Edinburgh now.

Three years ago a Choral Society was started and has over 40 members.

With the Whiteadder and Blackadder rivers so near, splendid fishing was at one time available and very popular, but in late years the sport has not been so good and fewer indulge in it. Formerly it was free, but recently it has been confined to members of an Angling Association.

A Common-Good Association was formed six year ago and has purchased the field south of the Bowling Green with a view to its use for public recreation. A piece of ground at the Greenwell has been presented to the Association, but nothing so far has been done with it.

Unfortunately the local branch of the British Legion went, at least temporarily, out of existence last year (1951) and with it the Comrades' Club which offered splendid opportunity to the youth of the parish for inside recreations — reading, games, billiards and carpet bowling.

At one time, too, Girl Guides, Brownies and Boy Scouts had branches here, but they lapsed with the war. So also did a Literary and Debating Society, an Ornithological Club, which held its Annual Show on New Year's Day, and a Flower Show, which was held in August.

WAY OF LIFE

A Sunday newspaper recently described Chirnside as a dying village, but that is an exaggeration. Indeed so long as the paper mill exists and is prosperous the village will be prosperous. It must be admitted, however, that it does not pulse with life as it once did.

The advent and development of road transport, regular employment and high wages have changed the life and habits of the community in recent years. Forty-two years ago when the writer first knew Chirnside the village on Saturday nights was a gay scene. The streets were busy and the Crosshill was literally crowded with people from our own and surrounding parishes. It was a regular meeting place for country people, especially, and shops and the two hotels were open and busy till 10 o'clock. Nowadays it is quite different. Shops are closed at 6 or 7 o'clock and the village street is almost empty. The only places where there are signs of life are the Crosshill when the buses stop and in summer the nearby Bowling Green.

Every day a dozen buses pass through the village between Berwick and Duns and young and old take advantage of these to go shopping or on pleasure bent, especially on Wednesdays and Saturdays. No longer does the village rely on itself for its pleasure and amusements. Family life is different from what it was and the home is no longer the centre of social life, especially for the young who spend their leisure hours, and seek for pleasure, elsewhere. An increasing number of people have motor cars so that visits are no longer confined to neighbours and opportunity is taken in the evenings and at weekends to go much further afield.

Until the end of the First World War the shifts at the Mill were 12 hours a day, Saturdays included, and there was much Sunday work. Wages too were not large. In both respects things have greatly improved — shifts now being eight hours a day and wages so acceptable that the employees are very contented. The prosperity of the workers is reflected in better dress, more comfortable and well-furnished homes and the amount of money spent on pleasure, travel, and cigarettes by both men and women.

In almost every house there is a wireless set and in three television is already installed.

The Church is the chief unifying factor in the Community and it is hoped that the union of the Churches, which has just taken place, will have a reviving influence on the social life of the Parish. Apart from Church organisations there are others which provide opportunities for social fellowship. There is a branch of the W.R.I., with a membership of 120, presided over by Mrs John Hay, wife of the Manager and Director of the paper mill. It meets monthly and has public meetings in the winter and picnics in summer. There is also a Co-operative Guild which has regular meetings. Other Societies and Clubs have frequent Whist Drives, public and private, for various objects, and summer and winter treats for old people and children. Regular Sales of Work are regarded as social meetings attended by everyone and are always successful. The Old Church sale, for example, has realised £350 annually for many years. There is a strong Lodge of Freemasons — Whiteadder 1245.

There has been a decided influx of strangers during the past 10 years. Some have come as employees of the Agricultural Engineers. It should however be added that there is not the same coming and going between the country and village people as there used to be.

Chirnside possesses a sober and law-abiding community. There is little or no poverty or drunkenness, no serious crime, no child delinquency and no serious cases of difficult children, though it must be admitted that here, as elsewhere, home discipline and parental control are not what they could and should be. There is a fair amount of gambling on horses and dog racing, while most households have a small weekly stake in the football pools. The present generation of young men and women is well behaved. Most of them go once or twice a week to the pictures and while dances are not so popular and successful in Chirnside as formerly, many go weekly to dances elsewhere. Experience of two wars in successive generations has broadened men's knowledge and experience, their outlook and opinions. It has also broadened and intensified their use of bad language and it is only too obvious that a third and youthful generation is entering into the unfortunate heritage.

In 1941-42 the Polish soldiers who were billeted in Ninewells made many friends in the village and several marriages took place. Altogether about a dozen marriages took place during the war between the young people of this parish and those from alien countries.

There are two War Memorials in the parish — a Celtic Cross at the west entrance to the churchyard and a bronze tablet inside the church. The names recorded on the first War Memorial number 24, on the second War Memorial 16.

Comment on the social life of Chirnside since the beginning of the century would not be complete without reference to the great influence, the splendid example and the outstanding service of the three ladies from our Mansion Houses, Mrs James A. Ross Hume, Ninewells, Mrs Andrew H. Glegg, Maines, both of whom died recently, and Mrs Harold Mitchell-Innes, Whitehall, who is happily still with us, though now living in Edinburgh. They were ladies of gracious personality and true Christian character, leaders in every good work and highly esteemed by the whole community.

1952

PARISH OF CHIRNSIDE

by Rev. Peter Graham

Throughout the period of Mr McKeachie's ministry, from 1909 to 1952, and even up to the time of his death in 1958, the village of Chirnside was a service centre for the surrounding agricultural community. With the continuing depopulation of rural areas a result of mechanisation and the increasing mobility of those still living and working on farms, this role has declined. Shorter working hours and almost universal car ownership have permitted people to travel further on shopping expeditions to places where a greater range of goods is on offer, with more competition between traders; not only to traditional market towns such as Duns and Berwick but also to the cities of Newcastle and Edinburgh and the Sunday market held at East Fortune.

The downward trend in population noted by Mr McKeachie continued until the early 1970s. By then the firm of Young Trotter & Sons had gone into liquidation and the paper mill had ceased operating.

Skilled workers had moved away in search of employment. In 1971 the C. H. Dexter Division of the Dexter Corporation from Connecticut, U.S.A., formed a British subsidiary to purchase the inactive mill, to serve as a manufacturing basis for a range of wet-laid non-woven products including tea-bags, sausage casing, vacuum cleaner bags and surgical disposables. Although Dexter's employed a number of former workers at the old mill, many more workers had to be brought in from other areas where there was paper-making expertise. For the incoming workforce Berwickshire County Council erected new housing in Chirnside, naming one street 'Windsor Locks' in honour of the home town of the Dexter Corporation.

Since the official opening of the new mill by H.R.H. Princess Anne in 1973 there has been a steady expansion in production and in the numbers employed. In 1976 Dexter's received a Queen's Award for Export, reflecting its position as market-leader in the production of tea-bags for both the home and export market. New products are constantly under development, using the latest technology. The acquisition of manufacturing capacity in France and of a processing plant for raw materials in England enabled the Chirnside operation to improve its profitability, to the benefit of employer and employee alike. Industrial relations are excellent, with no official trade union activities within the mill. And the workers take a considerable pride in their safety record, which is above the average for the industry as a whole.

The present population of Chirnside is approaching 1,600, of whom 1,100 are adults of 18 or over. The school roll dropped when Chirnside ceased to be a Junior Secondary School, but rose to over 200 pupils aged between 5 and 11+ in the late 1970s. There are now 160 pupils, with six class teachers and a Head Teacher, as well as a Nursery Department with 40 children of pre-school age, a teacher and a nursery nurse, and a special class for mentally-handicapped children brought to Chirnside from all over Berwickshire. After Class P.7 the children attend the Berwickshire High School in Duns, a six-year comprehensive school serving the whole of central Berwickshire.

About half the population reside in Local Authority housing. The older properties have been renovated with the replacement of old windows, re-wiring and insulation. Newer houses are well-planned and many have central heating. Tenants can now purchase their homes from the District Council and those who have done so have very quickly demonstrated their pride in home-ownership by improvements to the property and their garden. Privately-built residences have been erected on gap sites within the village and 17 occupy sites at both sides of the road at the east end of the village, eight of them where Messrs Mabon previously traded as grocers.

In 1984 Kirk Care Housing Association opened a complex of 25 units to provide accommodation for 35 elderly and infirm tenants in 16 x 1 person, 8 x 2 person and 1 x 3 person flats. A considerable advantage of this development is that each flat is linked by an alarm system to the office and flat of the Resident Warden. This sheltered housing complex stands partly on the site formerly occupied by the Comrades Hall, which was demolished to make way for it.

From 1952 to 1973 the North Church was in regular use as a place of worship, but thereafter ceased to be used by the worshipping community. For nine years it was available for community use and provided a meeting place for various activities. In 1983 it was handed over to the Borders Regional Council to be developed as a Community Centre for the village. At the time of writing (1984) no funds are available for refurbishing the former church and the small hall beside it, but it is hoped that in 1985/86 and in subsequent years money will be set aside for this project.

In 1973 the congregation of Chirnside entered into a linking with the congregation of Bonkyl and Preston and this linking was enlarged in 1978 to include Edrom-Allanton, all three congregations now being served by one minister resident in the Old Church Manse at Chirnside.

In line with national trends the number of Communicant members, the numbers attending services, and the number of children attending Sunday School have dropped from the mid-1960s onwards. The factors at work are felt in the country just as much as in the towns and cities. No longer is the country-dweller insulated from the latest fashions of thought and culture. No longer is there a rigid distinction between the life-styles of the people living in the cities and those living in rural Scotland. All alike have access to the same consumer durables and have similar expectations for their standard of living.

In addition to the Church of Scotland there is in Chirnside a group of Brethren, known as 'Chirnside Evangelical Church', with premises at the Crosshill. A group organised by the Faith Mission also meet regularly for worship.

All homes are furnished well and comfortably. Most households have a coloured television set, while many have a video cassette recorder. Young people in particular have many pieces of electrical and electronic equipment in their homes. Home computers are becoming more evident, some for playing games, but some for more serious use.

Despite the growth in home entertainment provided by television there is much support for the clubs and organisations of Chirnside. Notable among them are the Bowling Club, with a much enlarged Clubhouse; a small but enthusiastic Ornithological Society, entering pigeons for races most weekends throughout the season; Chirnside Amateur Boxing Club, which has enjoyed some successes since its formation in 1981; the Horticultural Society with its annual Flower Show; the Common Good Association with its perennial concern for the improvement of village amenities; the Woman's Guild; the W.R.I.; and the Wednesday Club, which runs various social events for ladies on a fortnightly basis. Over the years uniformed organisations for young people have had mixed fortunes, the Scouts and Guides never flourishing for very long, whereas the Brownies and Cubs thrive. There is a unit of the Army Cadet Force based on the Drill Hall in the village. A junior youth club has had no difficulty in maintaining support, but work with older teenagers has been unrewarding.

Since 1979 there has been a Chirnside Civil Week, held towards the end of May, with the crowning of a Gala Queen at the beginning of the week and a wide range of events during the week itself, mainly, but not solely, of a sporting nature.

A significant change since the compilation of Mr McKeachie's entry has been the altered status of landowners. There is no longer any single person identifiable as Chirnside's 'Laird', exercising a beneficient influence over the village, its inhabitants and their activities. The nearest to this may be the District Councillor, who in his own person embodies some of the more acceptable functions of the 'lairds' of former generations.

To the world at large Chirnside is now best known as the home of the late Jim Clark, twice World Motor Racing champion, son of Mr and Mrs James Clark of Edington, who was killed in an accident at Hockenheim Circuit, Germany, in April 1968 and was buried in Chirnside Churchyard. He is commemorated with a clock in the middle of the village and by a room containing a collection of his trophies in Duns.

1984

THE PARISH OF COCKBURNSPATH

by The Rev. R. Keltie, M.A.

THE PHYSICAL BASIS

The name of the parish is a corruption of Colbrandspath, which is found in written records in the year 1128 (Chalmers, *Caledonia* Vol. II, p. 783. n.) and seems to have been called after one, Colbrand, a Dane, who is said to have performed feats of valour in the district and settled here in early days. The name is also found written in various ways such as 'Coldbrandspeth'; 'Coburnspeth'; 'Coppersmith'.

Aspect. Although in early times, much of the parish was covered in trees, it now presents, on the whole, a somewhat bare appearance of wide sweeping fields and rounded hills, intersected with deep gorges. Its boundaries now run as follows: From the Hirst rocks on the coast east of Redheugh, south-west including Penmanshiel and Blackburnrig to Whiteburn, north-west over Corse Law and Dod Hill, then north-east along the line of the Berwick Burn, which is also the County boundary.

Soil. The basis of the soil in the lower part of the parish belongs to the Lower Silurian Formation. Generally, the soil is light, and quick draining, and, owing to centuries of good husbandry, fairly fertile.

Climate. The rainfall is light, as the clouds seem to follow the line of the Lammermoors, depositing the rain on either side of the parish. The local inhabitants believe that the district has almost the lowest rainfall in Scotland, second only to the Fochabers district. Frequently in travelling from Cockburnspath, either north or south, one can see the line of wet on the road, showing that there has been rain on either side of the parish, and yet it has missed the village altogether. Thunder is rarely close — what there is, seems to roll round the hills inland. In the village, wireless reception is often not very good. The prevailing wind is west, which usually brings fair, but gusty weather. East winds from the sea are cold, but are far less violent and frequent.

Woods. There are not more than about 600 acres of woodland in the parish. Oak and sycamore are the natural woods but these tend to develop heart rot. Recently, many of the immense beeches of Dunglass, planted c. 1720 by Sir John Hall, were cut down, but nearly all were diseased. In Dunglass there are many interesting species — Cedrun Deodara, Pinus Ponderosa, Cedrus Libani, Wellingtonia, Sciadopitys Verticillata, and others, while in about 1850, the laird planted four Mediterranean 'umbrella' pines (Stone pines) between the East and West Lodges of Dunglass, in order to hide the new railway from Dunglass House. It used to be said that these were the only specimens north of the Thames. Dunglass is really in Oldhamstocks parish, however. The biggest area of timber in the parish is Aikieside Wood (or Penmanshiel Wood as it is sometimes called). Originally of oak, much timber was obtained from this wood by Robert the Bruce in 1317 to prepare his catapults and siege engines, for the siege of Berwick. For many centuries, this wood provided charcoal for smelting. Today, Aikieside is composed of fir and larch, planted between 1920 and 1926, to replace timber cut down during the 1914-1918 War. Larch is not a success, as the type of soil renders it liable to canker. During the 1939-45 War, much diseased wood was cut out by German P.O.W. labour, and there are fairly good prospects of preserving the rest. In the last five or six years, 30 acres have been planted, mainly spruce and scotch Fir, both of which do well in the district. The floor of the woodlands is composed of oxalis, asperula, sorrel, foxglove, willow herb, wood anemone, garlic and rushes. Nearly all the woodlands belong to the type 'Oxalis'.

Animal and Bird Life. Roe deer are not numerous, but are found mainly in Aikieside wood. Rabbits abound [1951] and against them ceaseless war is waged by shooting, snaring and gassing. Hares are numerous, and the red squirrel is common, especially in Dunglass Dene. Game such as pheasant, partridge, woodcock and grouse are numerous as previously reported, but there have been one or two interesting changes in other bird life, possibly due to the reduction in hardwood. Increases which are most noticeable are goldfinches and common redstarts, while unusual birds for the district such as the green woodpecker, the little owl, and the fulmar petrel have made their appearance in recent years. The peregrine falcon and raven are seen fairly often. There are marked decreases in the lesser redpoll which nests in the young larch plantations — a decrease possibly attributable to the larch thinning previously mentioned — and in the snipe and golden plover. The stonechat which used to nest commonly on the sea braes has entirely disappeared.

HISTORY OF THE LOCAL COMMUNITY

The lands of Cockburnspath came into the possession of the Earls of Dunbar in 1072, and were retained by them until their forfeiture in 1435. Thereafter, Cockburnspath became the property of the Crown, and was administered for 30 years by the Homes of Wedderburn. In 1465, the lands and Barony were gifted by James II to his infant son, Alexander, who was at the same time created Duke of Albany and Earl of March. After his forfeiture for rebellion, Parliament, in 1487, again annexed the property to the Crown. In 1503, it was bestowed by James IV on Margaret Tudor as part of her dowry. On her marriage in 1514, after James' death at Flodden, to Archibald, Sixth Earl of Angus, the lands were acquired in tenandry by the Angus family, Archibald, eighth Earl of Angus, and his kinsman, Sir George Douglas, being the last holders. Parliament, in 1581 and 1593, reaffirmed the Crown's possession.

James VI gave the lands and lordship of Cockburnspath to Sir John Arnot, Treasurer Depute of Scotland, in 1594, "for his guid, trew and thankfull service done to His Majestie," which consisted in paying the christening celebration expenses of the King's eldest son, Prince Henry, to the tune of £1,500; William Arnot, second son of Sir John, who succeeded, was forced to sell the estate in 1622, and it was acquired by Thomas Nicholson, advocate, Edinburgh. His son was Sir James Nicholson of Cockburnspath (d. 1690). The Nicholsons, no more fortunate than the Arnots, were compelled to sell in 1694, and the estate was purchased by Sir John Hall, Bt., of Dunglass, the highest creditor. Cockburnspath and Old Cambus remained in the possession of the Hall family until 1919, when they were sold to Frank J. Usher, Esq of Dunglass, whose son is now (1951) proprietor.

The lands of Old Cambus in the parish were given to the monks of Durham by King Edgar in 1098 (Raine, *North Durham* ,Append. 2) and passed to the Priory of Coldingham in superiority. Some names of the proprietors during the 13th and 14th centuries occur in the *North Durham Charters* until 1441, when John Walsingham, Prior of Coldingham, exchanged the lands for others in Houndwood and elsewhere with Sir Alexander Home of Dunglass and David Home of Wedderburn. The greater part of Old Cambus remained the property of the Homes until it was sold in 1682 to the above Sir John Hall. The Templars appear to have held land in Old Cambus in the 15th century, and Logan of Restalrig who held Fast Castle in the 16th, and Patrick Hepburn of Waughton (17th century) were other proprietors. The lands have been united with those of Cockburnspath in ownership since 1682.

The farms of Blackburn, Ecclaw and Edmondsdene, Bowshiel, Fulfordlees, Whiteburn and Hoprig are separate properties, and have all had fairly frequent changes of ownership in the last two or three centuries.

Local folklore, customs, etc. The custom of 'creeling' at marriages is still practised occasionally in the parish, whereby immediately after the ceremony at the door of the Church, a creel filled with stones is hung by a rope round the neck and over the back of the bridegroom. The bride is then given a knife with which she cuts the rope and lets the burden fall from her new spouse's shoulders. Pennant noted this custom elsewhere in 1775.

Among the fishermen in former times, the common fisher taboos and fancies lingered. Mischievous boys might nail a pig's or rabbit's tail to a boat to discomfit the finder. The names of those animals might not be uttered afloat. So far as is known, no vocabulary of alternative names of taboo objects was used by local fishermen, except 'His Majesty', or 'him o' the crave' (pigsty) for pig. Ministers were also regarded as unlucky, and some men, if they met the minister on their way to work, would turn back and stay off for that day. If taboo words were inadvertently used, or if the minister happened to meet them, cold iron was touched. Though one or two men still feel strongly on this subject, most now regard these old superstitions with amusement.

The local dialect is very broad, and the accent is soft and musical. Most people use the past tense 'comed' for 'came' regularly, and many soldiers serving on other than the local regiment had to change their speech to avoid ridicule by their comrades from other districts. Turnips are always known as 'Baigies'.

Historical Monuments etc. See Report and Inventory of Monuments, etc. in the County of Berwick pp. 22-34 (H.M. Stationery Office, Edin. 1915.)

(a) *Prehistoric.* (*Inventory* pp. 26. ff.) In *Proceedings of the Berwickshire Naturalists' Club* vol. 24, 1919-22, p. 179 are particulars of 34 urn and cist burials discovered in the parish. In the same volume, p. 160, a total of 84 Bronze Age burial sites is claimed for Cockburnspath. In *B.N.C.* volume 25,1923-25, pp. 317, 440, is noted the discovery of an extensive early Christian burial area at Dene Dykes near Kirklands, on Hoprig Farm. In the same volume is a note of an unrecorded fort at the east end of Clifton Hill field, Hoprig.

(b) *Old St Helen's Church.* This is the most ancient historical monument in the parish, having been built before 1200 (Raine, *North Durham,* Append. 469). In 1650, it was still furnished with a pulpit and seats, and marriages were celebrated in it at that time. It had a manse and glebe attached. Tradition says that it was used by Cromwell's soldiery, and it may have suffered such damage then as to render it unserviceable. About the year 1860, a gale destroyed the east gable and chancel arch. The surrounding churchyard fell into disuse by 1850. The sum of existing information regarding Old Cambus Church is contained in an article in the *Records of the Scottish Church History Society,*vol. 6, part 2, 1937, by Rev. W. E. K. Rankin, D.D.

(c) *Cockburnspath Church.* (*Inventory,* p. 22.) The early 16th century may be taken as the date of the oldest parts of the present building. It is remarkable for its round west tower, the walls of which are not more than 18 inches thick, and for the narrowness of its original plan. The tomb house at the east end of the church was built by William Arnot of Cockburnspath in 1611 (*P.S.A.S.* volume 12, 4th series, 1913-14 p. 227). The sundial on the south-west corner of the church has a counterpart at Oldhamstocks, but the pattern is not known elsewhere. The projecting stone lug, noted in the *Inventory,* forms the gnomon of a remarkable supplementary afternoon and evening dial, telling the hours from 3 p.m. onward. The lines on this dial are still discernible on close examination from a ladder.

(d) *Market Cross.* (*Inventory* p. 34.) The Cross may have been erected in 1612, when James VI erected the township of Cockburnspath into a free Burgh of Barony, with market rights, harbourage, yearly fair and market. (*R.M.S.* volume 1609-20, 756.)

(e) *Sundial in Village.* A 17th century sundial stands on top of a garden wall opposite the grocer's shop. It consists of a block of freestone 11 1/2 inches in cubic measurement, with one main and two subsidiary dials, occupying three faces. On the fourth face are the initials I.H., M.V., standing for John Hoome, who was postmaster at Cockburnspath from 1673 to 1689, and Margaret Vertie, his wife. This dial was probably removed from a house at Dunglass Mill, where the old post office used to be.

(f) *Tombstones in Churchyard.* There are several eighteenth century stones (but none distinguishable as older) with tools carved, showing the occupations of the persons commemorated, and with conventional mortuary symbols. A stone with a trumpeting angel incised is noted in *P.S.A.S.* volume 12, 4th series, 1913-14, p. 229. The tombstone of the Rev. David Cluny M.A., parish minister 1689-1700, lies opposite the Church tower, and as the inscription is now nearly illegible, it is given under: 'Sub hoc saxo corpus piisimi reverentissimi doctissimique Mri. Davidis Cluny in hos parochio per annos undecim pastoris fidelisimi (Coldbrandpath) in spe requiescit. Cessit fato 29 Novembris An. Dom. 1700 aetatis suae 48.' The tombstone of the Rev. Henry Shaw, parish minister 1702-1746, also stands in the church-yard.

(g) *The Deid Bell.* This bell, formerly used at the announcement of funerals, and rung at the head of funeral processions, is of the following dimensions: handle four and a half inches, bell five inches, diameter at base five and three quarter inches, weight five and three quarter pounds. It bears the inscription 'Gifted be John Henrie Bower in Edinburgh to the Sessions and Kirk of Cockburnspeth 1650'. Henrie was son to Adam Henrie living in Leith Wynd, was apprenticed to John Forrest, bowmaker, Edinburgh 1630, married Janet Wallace 1637, became a burgess of Edinburgh 1640, died 1658 and was buried in Greyfriars Kirkyard.

(h) *The Communion Plate.* The Communion Plate consists of three sets: The Old Parish Church set comprising two silver chalices inscribed: 'This cup belongs to the Church of Cockburnspath H.M.S. M. 1708.,' one silver chalice inscribed: 'This cup belongs to the Church of Cockburnspath 1908;' two pewter flagons inscribed 'Cockburnspeth Kirk 1782', and two pewter patens without inscription.

The Stockbridge Church set comprising three pewter chalices inscribed 'A:C: Stock Bridge. 1795,' two pewter flagons with same inscription, and two pewter patens inscribed: 'Stockbridge Associate Congregation 1822'. The Free Church set, comprising two pewter chalices, one pewter flagon, all inscribed: 'Co-path and Oldhamsks. Free Church 1843', and one pewter paten without inscription.

The Local Records. No full history of the parish has yet been pub-

Plate 10. Coldingham in the 1950s, with the Priory at right of photograph.

Plate 11. On the coast near Coldingham.

lished though the materials necessary have been gathered. Among MSS. materials available are the following, preserved in H.M. Register House, Edinburgh:

(a) *Registers of Births and Marriages*
Vol. 1 Births 1642-1700. Marriages 1660-1784.
Vol. 2 Births and Marriages 1783-1819. Deaths 1784-1815.
Vol. 3 Births and Marriages 1820-1854.
The marriages entry is blank from 1699-1709.

(b) *Register House Ecclesiastical Papers.* Nos. 73 and 94b. These relate to Church matters in the parish between 1644 and 1674 and belonged to Sir James Nicholson of Cockburnspath, who was an active Engager.

(c) *Register House Miscellaneous Papers,* Boxes 218 and 219. These are household and estate accounts of Sir James Nicholson, with miscellaneous matters interspersed. They are useful for domestic and social conditions of the period 1623-1685.

(d) *Dunglass Papers of Lady Helen Hall.* These deal with estate affairs in the latter half of the 18th century and contain information about important road making, including the Pease Bridge.

(e) *Heritors' Records for the parish from 1776.*

(f) *Acreage, livestock and produce returns, 1866-1911.*

The Kirk Session Records etc. are preserved in The Tolbooth, St John's Church, Edinburgh and consist of Associate Church Kirk Session Records 1795-1901; Parish Church Kirk Session Records 1844-1938; Cockburnspath and Oldhamstocks Free Church Records 1846-1937. The Minutes of the Presbytery of Dunbar extend from 1652 and are preserved in the same place.

POPULATION

According to the first Statistical Account the population was 919 in 1755 and 883 in 1793. According to the information from the Registrar General's Office the population of the parish was:

1801 — 930
1851 — 1196 (the highest ever recorded)
1891 — 1112
1901 — 982 (after a boundary change)
1911 — 997
1921 — 941
1931 — 877
1951 — 761

The steady decrease since the 1914-1918 war is due to the general tendency nowadays for people to leave the country and seek employment in the town. There is little work for young people in Cockburnspath, unless they are engaged in the farming industry, so when they leave school, they have also to leave the district. The drift to the towns, though perhaps not so marked here as in other districts, is serious because farming is already short of labour and because the community is thereby deprived of much young life.

This parish is not cursed with the continual flitting of the farm workers. There is a little, of course, but much less than elsewhere, because of the fact that the village is on the main road, and has a good school, and also because the farms are well run, and the workers well housed. There is a good nucleus of people who have been here all their lives, perhaps 40 per cent of the population, while a good proportion of the rest, perhaps 45 per cent, hail from Berwickshire, and have been a good while in the district. There are a number of Irish workers — possibly two dozen at the moment, but most of these are constantly changing. There are three European displaced persons who have married and settled down in the district, and several farms employ displaced persons from a neighbouring D.P. camp. In the last five years, one family has emigrated to Australia, and several other families are considering emigration, but so far no more have gone. The most common surnames in the parish are Fairbairn (fishermen), Gray (fishermen), Paxton and Cockburn. Several names such as Gordon and Torrie (both fishermen) give evidence of immigration from the north-east of Scotland. This occurred during salmon fishing seasons; salmon fishers later settling down and setting up their homes. In general, the population is fairly stable at present, though the lack of any secondary industry is almost certain to make further depopulation likely in the future.

PUBLIC AND SOCIAL SERVICES

Public. (a) *Water.* The water supply in the village is very good and comes from a spring at Oldhamstocks. This is a comparatively recent improvement, because at the beginning of the century, the only house supplied with running water was the manse, which was supplied from a spring quite close to the village. The villagers were able to use this supply also, but it frequently gave out. Early in 1920, the laird, Frank J. Usher, Esq., sponsored another scheme to bring water from Hoprig. This was satisfactory for a while, but gave little head of water. When the County Council built new houses in the village, in the early 1930s, this supply became quite inadequate, so the Oldhamstocks spring was piped, and now the system must be one of the best in the county. Many of the farms have their own springs, some of them good, and some of them very poor. This of course affects the installation of baths etc., in the farm cottages, for where the water supply is poor, baths and lavatories tend to become purely ornamental. In the village, nearly every house has hot and cold water laid on, and more and more of the farm cottages are beginning to share in the same amenity.

(b) *Electricity.* There is no public supply of electricity in the parish. Its advent has been eagerly awaited and yearly expected for the past 15 years. Many houses have been wired in preparation for nearly 20 years, but though the scheme is now only three miles distant, its arrival in Cockburnspath seems still to be several years away. There is much local amusement at this, as well as a good deal of irritation, especially when there have been such large sums spent on the erection of a television relay station in the next parish. It is almost certain that had the local population been less good humoured electricity would have been here long ago. Homes are lit by Tilley and Aladdin paraffin lamps, and many farm houses have their own private electricity plant. Some have a small dynamo driven by wind which charges a battery, but these have not proved very satisfactory. Cooking is done with paraffin stoves (as coal ovens are far too expensive in fuel) or with Rural gas, which though expensive, is very satisfactory — the cost is approximately £1 for a month in an average sized family.

(d) *Sewerage and Sewage Disposal.* There is a first class sewage system. The works are situated just below Burnside, about 500 yards from the village. It is possible to live for years in the village without having any idea of their whereabouts. At the beginning of the century, sewage was disposed of in the burn, which was most unpleasant and rats abounded. Then a septic tank was installed, which improved matters, and finally in the 1930s a sewage works was installed. They are attended to each morning, and the resulting compost is used on the land.

(e) *Roads, Cleansing, Street Lighting.* Three road bridges cross the Dunglass Burn at the northern entrance to the parish, each marking an advance in ease of journeying and denoting the development of means of transport. The oldest stands nearest the sea, and was built in the 17th century. Before its building, the Edinburgh road had to descend to the sea shore and cross the burn by a ford there. The second oldest bridge was built towards the end of the eighteenth century, and the modern concrete structure, with its direct approaches, was opened in 1933. Similarly, three bridges span the Tower Dene or Elmdene. Below the modern bridge, which was built in 1929, is that erected in 1786. The latter was built in conjunction with the Pease Bridge at a time when the Edinburgh-London road still used the Old Cambus route. Not until the middle of the 19th century was the present line to Grantshouse *via* Glenfin opened up. The third bridge at Elmdene might escape notice in summer, at least, when it is overhung by the vegetation of the river banks. It was a tiny foot and stock bridge leading to the park of Cockburnspath and its miniature single arch preserves a precarious existence. It rejoices in the name of 'Cromwell's Brig', but it ante-dates the Protector's invasion. The route by Glenfin, mentioned above, was never attempted in olden times because of the marshiness of the land at the southern end. In 1846, soon after the opening of the railway, catastrophic floods inundated the line at Penmanshiel, and similar floods recurred in 1948.

Twice a week, the Cleansing Department of the County Council sends round a dust van. Previously, rubbish and ashes were dumped in private middens, and emptied by a local contractor every few months.

Before the 1939-1945 war, the village streets were lit by paraffin lamps. This was discontinued during the black-out in the war, and has never been resumed. The village square is now lit by a single electric lamp outside the bakery, by arrangement between the Parish Council and the baker.

Transport services are now omnibus only, as the Railway Station was closed to passenger traffic in 1951 after operating for over a century. There is an hourly bus service north to Edinburgh and south to Berwick, some of the buses going as far as Newcastle. This is during the summer months only; during the winter, the service is usually halved. The return fare to Edinburgh is 5/4d. and to Berwick 3/6d (1951). This was both cheaper and more convenient than the train service, which latterly carried hardly any passengers. The goods trains still deliver coal and farm accessories, and collect fish and farm produce.

(f) *Education.* At the beginning of the century, there were two schools in the village. One was on the main road, beside the hotel, and was a free church school, and the other was the parish school, which was situated in the square. There were also schools at Ecclaw, and at Old Cambus. These outlying schools were the local centres of culture and entertainment, as well as the places of instruction; concerts were held in them, meetings, Church services and Sunday Schools. The Church school closed shortly after the opening of the century, while the outlying schools closed only a few years ago. Scholars from Ecclaw and beyond are brought to the village school by taxi, while scholars from Old Cambus are collected by bus, and the young children taken to Coldingham and the older ones to Eyemouth. These leave home about 8 a.m. and do not return much before 5 p.m. The village school has a headmaster and two assistant teachers, and has between 70 and 80 pupils. When they reach the age of about 12 years, they go on to Eyemouth, the Junior Secondary School, which involves a bus journey of about 40 minutes: if they wish to attend school to Leaving Certificate standard, they must go to Duns, which involves a bus journey of under an hour. Elementary education is provided at Renton school, Grantshouse, for those children who live at the southern end of the parish. Thus children of the parish attend five different schools. The Cockburnspath school provides an excellent midday meal for all children who wish it at a cost of 7d. a head per week. Adult education classes in history, horticulture, sewing etc. are organised by the local headmaster under the County Council. The present school was built in 1913.

(g) *Miscellaneous.* There is a Public Library in the school building which is well patronised. A police constable is stationed in the village, and he has to cover a wide area on a bicycle. The telephone has recently been fitted with an automatic exchange, which is a great benefit to all users, and to the hard-working local post office staff.

(h) *Health.* In the early part of this century, there was a resident doctor in the village, and the steep hill leading into Crofts Road, (originally known as Red or 'Randy' Row) is still known as 'Doctor's Brae,' being just outside the house which was occupied by the doctor. Latterly, he was unable to make a living, and left the district, since when the village and parish have been served by five doctors, who come from Dunbar, Duns and Coldingham. A district nurse resides in the village, and a mobile clinic comes once a month to advise and care for mothers and babies. The nearest chemist is at Dunbar. Hospital cases go to Dunbar, Haddington and Edinburgh, and occasionally to Duns and Galashiels — these last two being rather unpopular because of the difficulty of communications.

Social. (a) *The Church.* Prior to the Reformation, the village of Cockburnspath lay within the parish of Oldhamstocks, and the Church of Cockburnspath was but a chapel, or church extension, of that parish. Robert, chaplain of Cockburnspath, occurs as a witness in 1255 (Raine, *North Durham*, Appendix 190). In 1627, the Church is mentioned as having been 'of old a capella regia'. This designation probably refers to its situation in the Crown lands of Cockburnspath, when possibly its maintenance was a royal charge. The parish of Cockburnspath was erected in 1610 by one of the ecclesiastical commissions of James VI, which disjoined the lands of Old Cambus from Coldingham, Cockburnspath and Hoprig from Oldhamstocks, Blackburn and the adjacent hill lands from Abbey St Bathans to form a new parish *quoad omnia.* The account of the Commission's proceedings is lost.

The present building, described above under Historical Monuments, was narrow and uncomfortable in the 18th century, but the construction of end galleries in 1827, and the projection of an aisle to the north side in 1876, augmented its seating, and made it somewhat more comfortable. The last extensive repairs were carried out in 1922, and the building now seats 360. In 1951, the building was wired for electricity. At the Union of the Churches in 1929, the name of St Helen's, belonging originally to Old Cambus Church, was revived, and given for distinguishing purpose to the parish church.

The Secession of 1733 obtained a footing in the parish first at Old Cambus in 1775. The first meeting house was built, however, at Stockbridge, in 1790. This was enlarged in 1865 to become Stockbridge United Presbyterian Church, and a manse was built adjacent to it. In 1857, there were 312 communicants, representing the highest peak attained in point of numbers. The congregation was drawn from a wide area. An old Church road led over Ewieside hill and was used by persons from Blackburn, Grantshouse and beyond. The Church joined with the Free Church of Cockburnspath in 1901 to form the United Free Church of Cockburnspath and Stockbridge.

At the Disruption, the parish minister, the Rev. Andrew Baird, author of the *New Statistical Account,* came out with a proportion of parishioners and probably took the Old Parish Church records with him. These have never been traced. The Free congregation had a church built at Oldhamstocks since no site was allowed in Cockburnspath. At the beginning of this century, however, a Free Church and manse were built in the village and continued in use until 1937, when the congregation joined that of the Parish Church. The Free Church Building was latterly known as St John's, and at the union of the congregations, was turned into the Church Hall. It is an excellent hall, and is used by many organisations.

Since then, there has been a linking of the parish churches of Cockburnspath and Oldhamstocks under the one minister, so once more the churches are joined, though this time Oldhamstocks, which was originally the mother church of Cockburnspath, is now by far the smaller of the two. It may be said that the successive unions of churches in the parish, have not been unaccompanied by some loss, and while not the causes, may be considered the symptoms of a progressive weakening of former intense church sentiment and attachment.

The membership of the parish church has been around the 450 mark for some time. Thirty years or so ago, each farm had its own seats where sat the farmer, his family and staff, and attendances were said to be large, compared to present attendance which averages not more than 75 each Sunday, and seldom more than 250 at the half yearly Communions. There are 11 elders (1951) consisting of four farmers, a farm steward, a forester, a fisherman, a blacksmith, a baker, a retired schoolmaster, and the village schoolmaster, who is also Session Clerk. The Sunday School is fairly well attended by about 80 scholars, while there are 15 in the Junior and Senior Bible Classes. The Woman's Guild has about 66 members, who take an active and practical interest in the work of the Church at home and overseas. They also hold an annual Sale of Work in aid of the work of the Church.

The morning service is at 11.30. Until a few years ago, it was the custom to ring the bell at 8 a.m. as well as at the time of the service. This may have been a relic of the olden time ringing to the 'reader's service', which preceded the worship conducted by the minister. An evening service is held monthly in the church, attended by 25-40 worshippers, and on the other Sundays, evening services are held at Old Cambus W.R.I. Hall (25-35 worshippers), at Blackburn in a farm cottage (12-15 worshippers), and at Fulfordlees farm house (9-12 worshippers). The singing of the congregation is hearty, though at the moment there is no choir. Organ accompaniment was introduced in 1880, before which a precentor led the praise. The office of precentor was continued until quite recently.

The churchyard is now the care of the County Council, and is kept very well. There was an attempt to extend it recently, as it is now nearly full, but there were one or two objections, mainly on the grounds that the churchyard was too near to dwelling houses, so another site for a new cemetery was obtained at the railway bridge near the station. This site was universally disapproved of, and is in almost every way unsuitable, but it was apparently all that could be found. It is a dismal little place, but efforts are soon to be made to beautify it.

The habit of coming to church for baptism and for weddings is now re-established, though many still find it rather an ordeal.

There are three families in the parish who belong to the Roman Catholic Church, and there are two Episcopalians. Also in the parish are several families who belong to the Christian Brethren, a religious body who meet at least twice weekly for worship in each others' houses. They are Christians who prefer not to have a professional minister.

(b) There are a considerable number of social organisations in the village. Many of the youth organisations have fluctuated a good deal, and at present, owing to the rising youth population, are enjoying a boom. There are Girl Guides and Boy Scouts, with a membership of about 20 in each. There is a young men's club, with about 20 members, which meets in the church hall; carpet bowls and billiards are the main activities, and the club is a member of the local carpet bowling league, and has numerous fixtures during the winter. The Football Club has a membership of about 25. The team plays in the Berwickshire Amateur League, and arouses keen interest. The Horticultural Society has a large membership, and runs a first class show annually, in conjunction with a local Sports Day, when the young men of the district compete in athletics and football. There is a flourishing and successful Bowling Club, and a Curling Club of well over a hundred years' standing, with minutes going back to 1854. The curling pond at Ewieside is seldom in use, most of the curling being done in the Edinburgh ice rink. Very popular is the Flying Club for racing pigeons. This sport is gaining in popularity, and the club has upwards of 20 members. The Quoiting Club still arouses interest, though rather less than previously. There is an Angling Club with over a dozen members. Three big competitions are held every year, with a ceremonial weighing of fish at the Market Cross in the evening. The biggest organisation in the village is the Women's Rural Institute, with a membership of nearly 80 in the Cockburnspath Branch, founded in 1924, and about 20 in the Old Cambus Branch founded in 1928. Very active in all things of practical interest, the W.R.I. also hold socials, concerts, and Burns Suppers, which stimulate local and national feeling. The Cockburnspath Branch meet in the church hall once a month, while the Old Cambus Branch have recently had a hall of their own built in the Cambus district, which has become a centre for that small community.

The Foresters, a Friendly Society, once had a big membership in the parish. Now, however, there are comparatively few members, mostly older men. They own a hall which is widely used for entertainments of various kinds, and dances. During the war, a Common Good committee was set up, and a large sum of money was raised to help with local projects. This committee helps with things such as the purchase of cups and saucers for use at socials, extra educational, sporting and other equipment, and gives financial support to any object which is considered to further the common good of Cockburnspath and District. The committee are also empowered to make *ex gratia* payments in local cases of hardship, necessity or need. Private grants have been made in connection with the benevolent side of the fund on several occasions. The blacksmith is the Treasurer.

A Young Farmers' Club was started in Berwickshire some years ago, and the first President was the farmer of Fulfordlees. This club is popular with the young people of the area who are interested in farming topics. Several young men of the parish attend. A senior counterpart of this club, called The Merse Discussion Society, was also formed a short time ago, and ten farmers from the parish attended.

HOUSING

In the village, the County Council has built about 17 double houses in the last 20 years. This includes four of the Orlit type and seven of the bungalow type built in the last five years. Previously, many of the houses were small two-roomed cottages with characteristic grooved red tiles, which were so much part of the countryside. Few of these had running water in them, and were miserable dwellings compared to the modern houses, and yet big families were brought up in them. Most of the council houses which replaced these are good looking buildings, red tiled and comfortable, and blend with the countryside well, though four of them are double-storied ugly buildings, built without much imagination. The double-storied houses have three bedrooms, a sitting room and a scullery, as do the bungalow type and the Orlit type. All these houses have a bathroom. A feature of the Orlit type is the installation of the heat storage cooker; these are good and give plenty of hot water, but as they are in the scullery, a separate fire has to be lit in the sitting room. This is hard on fuel, and often the fire cannot be lit in the sitting room owing to shortage of fuel.

At the beginning of the century, nearly every house in the village belonged to Dunglass estate, but some time after the Hall family sold the estate to the Ushers and many of the villagers were given the opportunity of buying their houses, which most did. Now, only about six houses out of a total of about 75 belong to the estate. The County Council own about 35, and the rest are owner-occupied. Nearly every house in the village has a garden, in which a keen pride is taken by most householders.

In the community of Cove, the old type of house is still in use, nearly all owner-occupied. They are also red-tiled and originally two-roomed, without sanitation or water. Now the owners have nearly all installed water and have carried out various improvements.

In the rest of the parish, dwelling houses are the farm cottage type, and most belong to the estate. They are now mostly fitted, or are about to be fitted, with new grates, as well as hot and cold water, and new rooms are being added. The general policy of the country to try to eliminate the tied house, by building council houses for farm workers, has only been partially welcomed. Rents and rates are as high as a guinea a week in some of the recent houses, and though it is a benefit to the community as a whole to have the village increased by these new houses, the occupiers are sometimes hard put to it to find the rent, and some look back with regret to the days of no rent in the tied house. Dwelling houses in the village number 75, in Cove, 29 and in the rest of the parish 133.

The mansion house of Dunglass was renovated and improved after the First War at a cost, together with improvements to the policies, which was said to be over £40,000. During the last war, it was occupied by the Donaldson Deaf and Dumb School. At the end of the war, the laird was faced with considerable repairs, and as it took an immense amount of fuel to heat it, and an army of retainers to run it, he dismantled it and now lives in the converted coach houses.

Cockburnspath House, the seat of the old lairds of Cockburnspath, the Arnots and the Nicholsons, was until recently a tramps' lodging house. In the 1920s, as many as 3,000 tramps were accommodated during a year. It is locally known as Sparrow Castle. Parts of it have been used in the past as a Volunteer Hall, and a church Meeting House as well, but now it is a private dwelling again.

AGRICULTURE, INDUSTRY AND COMMERCE

(a) *Agriculture*

Statistics. The approximate acreages in the parish are as follows: Arable — 6,000; Pasture — 5,000; Woodland — 600. This shows an increase on the acreage given in the *New Statistical Report* (1843) which was Arable — 5,000; Pasture — 4,000; Woodland — 550.

The approximate number of stock carried by the parish varies considerably from season to season, but may be taken as roughly: Sheep — 9,000; Cattle — 1,000. This is approximately double what the parish carried at the time of the *First Statistical Report* (1791).

There are 16 farms and two crofts in the parish, of which 11 farms and the two crofts are on the Dunglass estate, one (Blackburn) is owned by a Glasgow firm, and the rest are owner-occupied. The size of farm varies from the croft in the village of about 18 acres, to the big farms such as Redheugh and Hoprig of over 1,000 acres, and Blackburn of 1,800 acres. Eight of the farms are of about 300 arable acres, two are under 250 arable acres, and six are 400 arable acres or over. On the lower farms, rental varies between £1 (or less) and £2-10-0 per acre at most.

Crops. At the beginning of the century, cropping rotation was universal — usually potatoes, wheat or barley, hay, oats, and fallow — a method which was regarded as essential to keep the land in good heart. Nowadays, however, there is no fixed rotation. The largest possible acreage is under the plough, owing to the stimulus of the war years. Most farms maintain that this does not harm the land, which is now treated with large quantities of manure, both natural and artificial, and grass leys are quite common. Seed barley and seed potatoes are grown, large quantities of sugar beet are sent to the factory at Cupar, Fife, and oats, barley, wheat, potatoes and turnips are also grown.

See end of this subsection for agricultural statistics at 4th June 1953.

Mechanisation. Since 1936, the tractor has gradually banished the horse. Tractors average four per farm, and the increased speed gives the workers more leisure at night and at the weekends, though most tractor men are expected to maintain their tractors themselves, and are paid slightly more on this account. There are many different kinds of labour-saving machines in use, all of which are extremely expensive to buy, and as they are being constantly improved, the farmer who is going to keep up to date in his machinery has a vast outlay on this item alone. There are three combine harvesters owned locally, and they serve seven farms. They are satisfactory up to a point, though the quality of grain tends to be inferior to that which is dried naturally in the stook. They make the use of selective weed killers essential as they return the weed seeds to the land, whereas before weeds were carried to the stacks along with the grain. Before the 1939-45 war, it was customary to bring all grain back to the stackyard and thresh it as required in the farm threshing machine, built into the steading, but this wasted a lot of valuable time, and now stacks are made in the fields, and threshed by travelling mills. This is still the commonest method of harvesting.

Labour. Shortage of labour is presenting a serious difficulty in Cockburnspath. Farm work still tends to be regarded as an inferior job, and the ambition of many, especially of mothers, is to see the family employed as tradesmen in towns, rather than see them go into farm work. The hiring fairs, or feeing markets, have disappeared, and now labour is advertised for in the Press. Wages for the male worker over 21 are now well over £5 per week minimum, whereas in the early 1900s, the usual ploughman's wage was 18/-. The average farm staff is about eight male workers and one woman worker, but of course these vary greatly, from two or three in pastoral farms such as Whiteburn, to 18 in combined arable and pasture farms such as Blackburn. The average weekly work is 48 hours as against 60 in the 1900s. Workers have Saturday afternoons and Sundays free, except for stock workers. There is no objection to overtime work, which is at fixed rates, but there is not usually any particular desire to work overtime. Most workers still dislike Sunday work, as do most farmers, though it is frequently done during harvest, etc. Yoking is usually at 7 a.m., and 'lowsing' at 5 p.m. with one and a quarter hours off for meals. Holidays are six days in the year, with New Year's Day in addition. All work on Christmas Day.

An interesting experiment has been tried by Messrs J. & B. Coats Ltd. of the cotton factories in Paisley, who send out batches of their workers to help in the harvest. These west coast factory workers have been, on the whole, a valuable labour force for farmers, and from the community point of view, their annual arrival is very popular with the country people. Their free and easy way is in marked contrast to the rather reticent and shy ways of the district, and has a good effect on the local population, while the fresh air and exercise, and the hospitality of the country people, act as a tonic to the factory workers.

Miscellaneous. It is believed that the names of the various fields of the farms are very ancient, e.g. on Redheugh — Makempare (Mak' 'em puir), Gildermare and Flares (Fleurs?), on Hoprig — Tod's Mill, Clifton's Hill and Law Shots.

Agricultural Statistics as at 4th June 1953 supplied by the Department of Agriculture for Scotland

Crops (acres)	
Wheat	134
Barley	1,239
Oats	907
Potatoes	282
Turnips and Swedes	568
Sugar Beet	88
Rape	115
Other Crops	128
Ryegrass and other Rotation Grasses and Clover for mowing	314
Ryegrass and other Rotation Grasses and clover not for mowing	2,570
Total Arable Acreage	6,345
Permanent Grass for mowing (hay)	50
Permanent Grass not for mowing	1,405
Total Acreage Crops and Grass	7,800
Rough Grazings	3,648

Livestock (numbers)	
Horses	31
Cows in milk and cows and heifers in-calf — Dairy	62
Other Dairy Cattle	18
Cows in milk and cows and heifers in-calf — beef	88
Other beef cattle	655
Sheep and Lambs	16,235
Pigs	335
Poultry	2,765
Labour (Numbers)	
Regular Workers	128
Casual Workers	51
Classification of Holdings	
Acreage (Crops and Grass)	No.
1+ to 5	1
5+ to 15	1
15+ to 30	1
30+ to 50	—
50+ to 75	1
75+ to 100	—
100+ to 150	1
150+ to 300	6
Over 300	11
TOTAL	22
No. rented	16

(b) *Fishing.* At the end of the 18th century, fishing was prosecuted from Bilsdean (really in Oldhamstocks parish), Old Cambus and Redheugh, but by the turn of the century those stations were practically abandoned and the Cove harbour alone remained in operation. The harbour there was completed, as it stands, by Sir John Hall in 1831, and was able, in favourable weather, to take in ships up to 60 tons burthen. In 1834, 14 families were dependent on the fishing industry, and the number rose to a maximum of 20 by the middle of the century. Near the harbour, a curing house was built, which dealt with whitefish and herring, and was used on a small scale for the manufacture of cod-liver oil. The last curer at the Cove left in 1870. About 1870, there were 12 herring boats at the harbour. Ten years later there were three large line boats, four or five herring boats and about nine small crab and lobster boats. This represented the strength of the fleet at the occurrence of the disaster of 1881, when 11 were lost out of 21 fishermen and four boats were wrecked. The fishing underwent continuous decline thereafter, the larger boats being given up, and crab and lobster fishing became the sole occupation. Fish became scarcer and scarcer, and, of late years, even bait for lobster pots has been imported. In 1945 the boats in use at the Cove were two small motor vessels, and two rowing boats, which is the present strength. In the summer months, salmon fishing takes place off Cove harbour, and fairly good catches are reported. The heavy expense incurred in fitting out boats, fuel and accessories, makes it certain that soon there will be no more fishing at the Cove. This one-time flourishing little village is gradually dwindling; 30 or 40 years ago, 50 children used to come up to Cockburnspath school — now there are only two. Inhabitants are mostly elderly, and it seems only a matter of time before most of the Cove houses are sold as weekend cottages for townspeople.

(c) *Commerce.* Since 1900, local craftsmen have steadily decreased in numbers. In those days there were six blacksmiths (five journeymen) in the village, and two at Old Cambus, a mason employing several men, bootmakers, slaters and plasterers, joiners, a plumber, three tailors and a dairy. Now, there are three blacksmiths (two journeymen); and at Old Cambus one blacksmith, two joiners and a journeyman, one tailor, and all the rest have disappeared. Tradesmens' services are obtained from Dunbar and Ayton.

There are two big family businesses — a baker and a grocer, employing nine and seven persons respectively, also a family butcher and a newsagent and fancy goods shop, and the Post Office. Recently, a long established 'sweetie' shop, where generations of children pressed their noses against the window, has had to close. The family grocer sells a very wide range of goods, including clothes, shoes, tools and lamps and the baker also sells groceries and miscellaneous household goods. A very high standard of service is maintained by all the shops in the village, in pleasing contrast to the tendencies observed elsewhere.

The railway and the whinstone quarry at Old Cambus employ the rest of the available labour; there are about a dozen men employed on the line, in signals, and at the station, and several more are employed in the quarry. There are three regular postmen, who cover a wide area. There is a licensed hotel, which has a large passing trade.

WAY OF LIFE

(a) *Attitude to Religion and Church going.* The attitude towards the Christian religion is universally respectful. Most little children are still taught to say their prayers every night, and though the habit of family worship has almost entirely died out, most people would still claim to be Christian, and to have some connection with the Church. The attitude towards the Church, especially of those whose connection, though claimed, is slight, is often critical, and even occasionally hostile. The need for regular attendance at public worship is being increasingly denied, though a majority of people in the parish agree that it is desirable. Even in these days of increased leisure, lack of time is one of the main difficulties mentioned. Others blame the times. While admitting that our forefathers set great store upon attendance at worship, and while recalling with pride the great distances covered by fathers and grandfathers in order to go to church, they say that times have now changed, and that no one in his senses would put out so much effort on something which is not recognised as absolutely vital. The attitude to the celebration of the Lord's Supper, however, is such that most people do make the effort to be present on at least one of the two occasions in the year. By and large, the sense of the urgency of the Gospel message has been lost. While the outward effect of this is not obvious in this generation, it may well have a very serious effect on the next.

(b) *Attitude to Politics.* At the end of the last century, and during the first decades of this, Cockburnspath was a Liberal stronghold, and there was keen and good-humoured interest in the elections. Even the dogs were decorated with the Party colours, and trained to bark at the opposition. In the first election after the 1939-1945 war, however, the farm and railway workers were mostly Labour, but again in 1950, there appeared to be a swing back to Liberal, possibly because a local farmer stood as Liberal candidate. There is still considerable interest in politics, and election meetings are well attended — the only public functions, beside football matches, where the men outnumber the women. The light-heartedness of elections seems to have gone.

(c) *Attitude to Work.* There is a great tradition of work in the village. Men recall proudly that they have 'wrocht' so many years without ever having been off work. It is still the great aim of the men in the district to work well and faithfully, and there is general dismay at, and contempt for, the poor standard of work displayed by those coming from the towns. On the whole, the younger men inherit this tradition, though in some cases it is noticeable that some younger men are distracted by football and cinema, and have not the same heart in their work as the older men.

(d) *Domestic Life.* Though wages have increased greatly since the early 1930s, it is doubtful if the people have any more money in their pockets. The standard of living has risen very sharply, however, and now most people are better clothed and fed than 20 years ago. The women have a great interest in keeping their homes well, and now take great trouble with their personal appearance. As late as the 1920s, it was quite common to see children going barefoot to school in the summer, and in the winter both boys and girls wore 'tackety' boots, which gave considerable wear. Now, no children are seen barefoot, and most wear shoes, often without tackets, which greatly increases expenditure on shoe leather. In the 1920s, jerseys and corduroys were the common garb for Cove children, who liked to dress like their fisher fathers, while villagers wore jackets and corduroys. This was practically a uniform, necessary to distinguish friend from foe, in the pitched battles which took place between the rival parties. During the summer time, 20 years and more ago, families would double up their rooms to enable them to take in summer visitors, who used to crowd the Cove and the village. With the rise in living standards, and the housing regulations, this would neither be endured nor allowed nowadays, and so the tourist trade has almost disappeared.

(e) *Leisure.* A minority of younger men take active part in various sports, and a majority prefer to watch sport rather than to engage in it. For many young men, Saturday afternoon is spent in Dunbar. The programme is usually — watch football match (either local or in Dunbar, or occasionally in Berwick or Edinburgh), tea, pictures, fish supper, a drink and home, an outing which costs approximately 10/-. On Sunday it is usual to enjoy an extra hour or two in bed, and the afternoon is spent in seeing friends or in meeting together. The public house is fairly well patronised, though there is very little drunkenness. When dances are held at the Foresters' Hall, it appears to be the custom to go first to the hotel, and then to visit the dance after 10 p.m. Consequently a dance, though billed to start at 8 p.m., is usually a small affair until 10 p.m. There are two three-man dance bands made up of local men. There is a considerable amount of gambling, mainly on football pools, though there is also interest in horse racing. There is comparatively little reading, except for the newspapers, and many homes have no books at all.

(f) *Outlook on Life.* Amongst thoughtful people, and there are quite a few in the community, there is a gradual realisation that happiness does not depend on the standard of living. Although it is often a case of distance lending enchantment to the view, many look back at the days of not so long ago when simple pleasures were enjoyed far more than the 'high-powered entertainment' of today. Many are beginning to feel that much of the restlessness and discontent of youth is caused by the fear of missing something which might be going on somewhere else. Many blame the closing of the country schools which has taken the local children to town centres away from the local interests, and which makes young people turn their attention from the land, and the more abiding satisfactions of life. It is noticeable now, that the old class distinction which used to exist between the village people and the farm workers has largely disappeared. Many farm stewards own cars, and are able to go away occasionally on Sundays. The farm workers dress smartly, and are a well set-up race of men, with far more ease and assurance than their fathers.

The Future

With the growing shortage of farm workers, it seems likely that their status will improve, as more efforts will have to be made to induce young people to take up this fine calling, which is one of the mainstays of the country. Even if all the farms in the parish were adequately staffed, however, there would still be a great need for another industry such as furniture making or a branch of the textile industry. There is a large child population, and with a new industry, these children would be assured of good employment in the district. Local feeling is still strong, and it seems certain that were such an enterprise taken up, the response would be quick and the effect enlivening. But it seems that the greatest need is for spiritual revival which would restore people's sense of values, and bring back to the life of the community the dignity, zest and sense of enduring purpose which seems now to be in danger.

1951

COCKBURNSPATH

by J. W. Cockburn

In overall appearance the village and parish have changed very little in the past 30 years. A local nineteenth century poet wrote:

Auld Cockburnspath,
Yon red-tiled clachan,
Round whaes lums
The kyes are flappin' . . . (Kyes: crows)

This picture is not now so true as it was a century ago but a few red-tiled houses are still to be seen, and in the woods to the north-east there are still rookeries. But the village has changed greatly in other respects. Where once there were two grocers' shops, a baker, a butcher, a shoemaker and a tailor, now there remain only one grocer, a newsagent-stationer, and a shoe shop. The Post Office and Hotel remain, though the former is threatened with closure.

The village and the little fishing village of the Cove are still picturesque. The Cove tunnel and harbour, the Dunglass Dean, the Tower Glen, the Pease Dean and the Pease Sands are still lovely. The top of Ewieside, an outcrop of the Lammermoors, has of recent years been cultivated. So fine is the scenery that towards the end of last century it attracted a group of Glasgow artists, the "Cockburnspath School", who came to the Cove every summer and took rooms in the fishermen's houses. Their work is well known and the subject of a recent book. The Cove itself has not (1983) changed very much. The houses, quite well constructed at the time, have all been renovated recently, with bigger windows and central heating put in. Some are three-bedroomed, others just big enough to house one person.

Plate 12. Coldingham before the First World War.

Plate 13. Bridge Street, Coldingham, before or during the First World War.

The reason for the disappearance of the shops and local services is not far to seek. Most families have a car and on Saturdays go to Dunbar or Berwick where chain stores supply cheaply what they were once content to find in their home village. Many other needs are brought to their door by motor vans, a situation common to most country villages nowadays. The coming of television too has caused great changes. The Village Hall, which at one time found ready bookings for dances, concerts, whist-drives and plays, is now little used except for the annual Flower Show, a few local committee meetings and the well patronised weekly bank.

At the top of the village stands what was formerly the United Free Church of Cockburnspath and Oldhamstocks, and behind it its one-time manse. These were completed in 1901, and it is worthy of note that these solid buildings were built by the contributions of a few of the tenant farmers but also by the pennies and sixpences of the farmworkers and fishermen. Doubtless the spirit of bigotry played a great part in all this, but when one remembers the low earnings at that time the effort was admirable. After the Union of the Churches in 1929, this church was closed in 1937. Since then it has been used as the church hall for the parish church. In the last three years it has been much improved by the installation of a false ceiling and its length divided into rooms by sliding partitions.

One of the greatest changes is at Pease Bay, which has acquired a popular caravan park. The whole area surrounding the sands is covered with permanent caravans, the occupants coming from as far away as Glasgow to spend holidays and weekends by the sea. It has its own communal wash-houses, showers and sewage system. There are also a shop, phone box and petrol pumps. A tarmac road runs from end to end of the camp. The site is managed by a warden and an assistant and is well maintained. The season runs from April to September. In 1977 another caravan camp was opened on the Neuk Farm, at the foot of Ewieside in the beautiful valley of the Heriot Water. This camp is an all-year one, with water and electricity in the larger caravans. Many Torness workers live here winter and summer.

Prior to the First World War Berwickshire was always said to have more mansion houses per square mile than any other county in Britain. But this parish has no mansion house within its boundaries. The only 'big house' of note is Sparrow Castle in the middle of the village. This still imposing house was built in 1547 by Sir George Douglas, the last of the kin of that Earl of Angus who, after the Battle of Flodden, married the widowed Queen of James IV to whom he had given Cockburnspath as a dowry. The Halls, who acquired the whole of Dunglass Estate in 1685, made Dunglass their residence, and in 1790 they removed the top storey from Sparrow Castle, which must have robbed it of much of its grandeur. During the last 20 years it has passed into private hands.

The Cross in the middle of the Square has been repaired recently, the second tier having become badly worn. By the generous subscription of the village people and the help of the Berwickshire Civic Society and other bodies the stones were replaced, and the appearance of this ancient monument improved. Cockburnspath Church has suffered many additions and alterations in its long history. At the end of the church is the Arnott Aisle, built in 1624 as a burial place for that family. Within is a tombstone bearing a coat of arms, 'argent, three shields gules,' for Lady Nicolson who was a Hay of the Tweeddale family and who died in 1642. Two years ago the church was redecorated, the ceiling repaired, and the wooded fronts of the two galleries stripped of varnish. They now show the attractive red pine to advantage.

Several ancient landmarks and other familiar features have suffered in the last few years. At the Mount the joiner's house and workshop have gone, and the red-tiled sawmill building has become a dangerous ruin. The pond has been filled in and a hall built on the site for the Homing Pigeon Society. The Tower Castle, that ancient stronghold given to its first owner by the King for having rid the Tower Glen of robbers, and whose walls defied the Tantallon Douglasses besieging the Cospatricks in olden days, now begins to look a little precarious in the remaining eastern wall. The west end was blown down in a gale in 1881, possibly that which caused the famous tragedy among the fisherfolk. The nearby 'Cromwell's Bridge' has only the abutments left to mark its place.

The Pease Mill, originally known as Old Cambus Mill, has disappeared, along with the miller's house and two cottages. It was an oatmeal mill and was certainly in use from the 18th century until 1937. Vandalism, the great flood of 1948 and the subsequent landslide have left scarcely a trace of where it stood.

Population. The population of Cockburnspath village and parish at the present time cannot be given with any accuracy because of the large and constantly changing workforce engaged in the erection of the Torness Nuclear Power Station three miles to the north on the A1. Every available house in the village and almost every empty farm cottage — of which there are many — is let at high rents, for these men are highly paid. The permanent population is approximately 505. This shows a very considerable decrease from 1951, but a glance at previous figures — 1921, 941; 1931, 877; 1951, 671 — shows a steady decline. At present the numbers may fluctuate from month to month.

There is of course no industry in the parish, but a breakdown of occupations may be of interest. The following details apply to the permanent residents of Cockburnspath only, male and female. (Many women also do part-time work in shops, in the hotel and as home helps.)

Workers at Torness, Dunbar	7
Portland Cement	25
Railway	4

Farm workers	35
Casual farm workers	10
Fishermen	6
Unemployed	1
Total	88

At first sight the population appears to be an ageing one as there are 29 retired men, 23 widows (householders), and at least 26 female pensioners; but to counter this there are 91 children of under school-leaving age. Taken over all the prospects for Cockburnspath are not bright. Within three years Torness may be complete, Portland Cement may have extracted all the available limestone, and agriculture will continue to require only a minimum of labour.

Transport. Cockburnspath has always had the good fortune to stand on the road and latterly the railway that was the shortest route from Edinburgh to London, but this parish must have given the civil engineers the hardest problems of any they had to solve. Approaching from the north, the Dunglass Dean with its very steep banks was the first great barrier. Before 1620, when Dunglass Mill Bridge is said to have been built, wheeled traffic had to descend to sea level at Bilsdean, ford the Dunglass burn and regain the land level by a road chiselled out of the rock on the south side. After the bridge was built another road was cut out of the rock on the north side, which turned left on to the bridge. From there the coach went up by Castle Dykes to the Cove, past the New Cove farmhouse where the road becomes quite narrow round the garden wall. Within another mile the coach would be descending the 1 in 5 gradient down the Pease Sands, to be followed by an equally heartbreaking pull up the other side. Little wonder horses were changed at Tommy Flint's Inn at Old Linhead and at Headchesters. The building of the Pease Bridge in 1796, followed immediately by the bridge at the Tower Castle, must have meant a tremendous saving in horses and to drivers. The coaches must have run to some sort of timetable, for the tenant of the Tower farm wrote in his diary on a day in 1808: 'Philip arrived by coach this morning; could not wait to finish his tea having to run to catch the Union.' The Mail and the Union were the two coach companies.

The years 1812 to 1816 saw the construction of the new road from Dunglass to Renton. This became part of the A1 as it is today, but the Cockburnspath section has been troublesome ever since. In 1929 a new concrete bridge was constructed some 50 or 60 yards higher up the Tower ravine. In 1932 a new concrete bridge was built over Dunglass Dean. In the early 1960s an entirely new road was built from the top of the Faugh Hill to Cockburnspath Station bridge by government order and against much local opinion. This has become notorious as an accident black-spot: eight people have been killed and there have been innumerable accidents. The matter of a new road has already been before Parliament and there is much talk of an entirely new route being built passing to the west of the village, partly because of doubts as to the capacity of the Tower and Dunglass concrete bridges to withstand the weight of the new 'juggernaut' lorries. This is likely to meet with considerable opposition too, because of the inevitable loss of much good farmland.

If the road engineers found this district difficult, however, it was certainly no easier for the North British Railway when they arrived in 1847. To cross Dunglass Dean they had to build a bridge 156 feet above the stream, the highest between London and Edinburgh. They had to construct a culvert over the Tower Burn and transfer thousands of tons of soil to bring it up to rail level and so cross the Tower Glen. A mile and a half further on they were faced with the Black Craig of Penmanshiel, a solid rock through which they had to drive a tunnel, the only one between London and Edinburgh. Lastly they had to contend with the steepest gradient between the two capitals in the 1 and 40 slope that runs from Innerwick to Grantshouse. But they conquered all these apparently insuperable problems.

Only two have since given them trouble. In 1847, soon after the line was completed and running, a great flood washed hundreds of tons of soil from off the top of the Tower Glen culvert. The other, and recent, disaster occurred in the tunnel. It was too low to allow the passing of the new 8 ft. 6 in. containers, and the easiest way to remedy this appeared to be by the lowering of the railway lines. On a March morning in 1979 two men were removing soil with tractor shovels when without warning the roof collapsed, burying them under hundreds of tons of debris. The rest of the roof was so precarious that not even a team of mine rescue men dare enter. No attempt to recover the bodies could be made; a small monument enclosed by a brick wall was erected to their memory on the top of the rock and the tunnel sealed for all time. A new line was cut round the end of the rock; unfortunately this has resulted in such a sharp bend that the express trains must drop their speed to 50 m.p.h. over this section.

As a means of local transport, the railway could not compete against the buses. Cockburnspath Station was closed to passenger traffic in 1947 and to goods in 1966. Now the buses are fighting the private motor car, for few households in the village are without one. The bus service to Edinburgh started in 1924 and for many years was well patronised. At first it was an hourly service both ways, and ran to great profit. It was cheap and convenient, picking up passengers anywhere on the road and dropping them off at their door. As the price of fuel mounted steadily so did fares. Now the return ticket to Dunbar costs £1.60, and the buses carry very few passengers. The service now runs at two-hourly intervals, the first bus for Edinburgh leaving at eight in the morning and the last one at seven at night. Private buses collect men each morning all the way from Berwick to Torness.

Education. Cockburnspath School, like most village schools, is now only a primary school, with a headteacher and one assistant teacher. Children are now collected from outwith the parish, but even so numbers amount to only between 40 and 50. At the beginning of the century 50 boys and girls came up from the Cove alone, and the total roll was 154. But then there were 21 families in the Cove and the farms were at the height of their employment. Also, at that time 90 per cent of the pupils remained until they were 14, only the brightest ones going on to a secondary school and higher education. Now, at about the age of 11 they pass on to Eyemouth Secondary School and are collected by school bus each morning. From Eyemouth they may go straight on to university entrance, and an increasing number do. Cockburnspath has always had a high academic record, and has been fortunate in having a succession of able and enthusiastic schoolmasters. They instilled into their pupils not only a wide outlook on life but also ambition and a desire to succeed in their chosen path.

Behaviour. It has been said that even the smallest towns have some small element of undesirables within them; but the smaller the community the higher the standards. In villages of the size of Cockburnspath the fact that everyone has known everyone else since childhood could be a considerable restraint, especially so amongst teenaged boys who through boredom and idleness might be inclined, to use an old-fashioned Scots expression, to 'work mischief'. By and large the people of this village are good, sympathetic, helpful, and loyal to their neighbours. They will drive their carless friend to visit a sick husband, wife or child in hospital night after night. When a death occurs everyone, men and women, turn out to show their affection and pay their last respects. Good neighbours, young and able, help those who are no longer so strong to dig and keep their gardens, trim their hedges or prune their roses. Amongst the shopkeepers friendliness is particularly noticeable; they provide not merely the necessities of life, but a service. Most of what crime there is appears to originate outside the parish.

Church Attendance. Cockburnspath is no exception to the rule of declining church attendance in rural communities. The average congregation is around 35 and these are mostly regular attenders. Even in this small number women are in the majority, and few young people are church-goers. There are many reasons for this fall-off in numbers, the greatest perhaps being the rise in material prosperity. Sunday papers arrive several hours before the church bell rings. It requires hard times, a threat of personal danger, perhaps a war, fear or deep anxiety for the future before men and women will begin to think of spiritual things. Yet there cannot be said to be any antipathy towards religion, for the minister is quite welcome in all the houses. Also, when the church has to issue a special appeal for funds people respond generously.

Recreation and Entertainment. Like all small country villages, Cockburnspath offers no great scope for recreation. There are of course no picture houses in the parish, but there is scarcely a house without its TV aerial. Summer evenings are better provided for now that the bowling green is open from May till September. The game is popular with slightly older people, but whereas at one time it used to be confined to men, there now seem to be even more women on the green. Weather permitting there is a crowd there every evening. Another sport holds great attraction for the people of Cockburnspath: looking round the gardens it is surprising to see the large number of pigeon lofts. Rivalry is keen; there are 12 doocots in the village and several others at landward farms. The pigeons are often flown from distant places in England, but for the race of the year, the pigeon 'Derby', they are taken to Rennes in France. To win this is the ambition of all Scottish fanciers, and a Cockburnspath bird was victorious a few years ago. One skilled sport has almost disappeared. This is the game of quoits, said to have come up from the Northumberland miners. Over the years it has gradually lost its hold; whereas it used to be played by the farmhands in their own stackyards in the summer evenings, it is now included in only a few of the local village sports.

The annual Flower Show still attracts a large entry. People can derive a deal of pleasure from their gardens at very small cost. The village Games are held on the same day and are very popular. There are few dances now in the Village Hall. About the time of the First World War the Foresters' Ball and the Old Year's Night Ball were occasions not to be missed. But now 'discos' are more in keeping with the times and the days of the fiddle, melodeon and piano have gone. Scottish country dancing, however, is in a healthy state. Women form almost three-quarters of the groups, but men come regularly, though in lesser numbers.

There is still the occasional whist-drive in aid of some local cause, but the concerts of the old days, which gave such scope to local talent, are no more. Cockburnspath still has its football team, but because very few of the players belong to the parish, enthusiasm for the team and pride in its prowess have dwindled away.

Services. The telephone came in the spring of 1924; there are now approximately 250 instruments. The greatest need of all was, of course, water. In the 19th century the village was dependent on a spring which rises in the Tod's Mill field on Hoprig. A reluctant laird of those days put in a half-inch lead pipe to serve the whole of the village. There were one or two take-off stand-pipes, but one can imagine the queues that must have formed in a morning! At that time there were neither baths nor lavatories in any of the houses. As civilisation spread and living standards rose the Tod's Mill supply became inadequate, and so, to gain height and a fuller flow, water was piped from a spring beside the Haystall Cottages in the valley beyond Oldhamstocks. This was a great step forward for the village, the farms mostly finding private supplies from others on higher ground. The Oldhamstocks supply was completed in the mid-1950s and was for a time a great success. Within ten years, however, the building of more houses and the coming of the Pease Bay caravan camp so greatly increased the demand that only by linking up with the Watch Water scheme at Longformacus could the supply be guaranteed. Many of the farms were also put onto this supply, but those on the higher ground were situated at too high a level for the water to rise to them, so still had to find their own springs and provide for themselves. The water from the Watch Reservoir is soft and excellent for most purposes.

Electricity came to the parish in 1953. Paraffin lamps were consigned to the attic and village chimneys sprouted television aerials within days. Washing machines, electric irons and finally refrigerators have followed quickly and added greatly to the joys of country life.

Local Government. The regionalisation of Scotland has wrought great changes in the countryside. Cockburnspath, like many other places, now has a Community Council instead of the old Parish Council. At its meetings this council discusses all the parish problems, and, having no powers of its own, passes its findings on to the District or Regional Councils. The system appears to be working effectively.

Police. Like everything else the village policeman's life has changed greatly in the 20th century. In the early years of the century, he had to walk or cycle round all the outlying places on his beat at least once a month. Arriving at a farm, he would ask the first person he met to sign his book to prove that he had been on his rounds. The Cockburnspath 'beat' included Abbey St Bathans, Grantshouse and all their remote farms. In those days much of his work was the enforcement of sheep dipping orders: he had personally to see the sheep dipped. These were men of character respected by everyone from childhood upwards, and some of them were stationed so long in Cockburnspath that they almost became part of the landscape. These men were just and generous and were remembered with considerable affection long after they had been moved on. Yet in their work they were quietly efficient, knew everything that was done, and, most important of all, who did it. This simple old Berwickshire Constabulary is now linked to the Lothian force. Car accidents and motoring offences provide much of their work. Few of those crimes that do occur go undetected. The entire force is linked by radio and no matter what the emergency, they are ready.

Fishing. That fishermen lived in the parish two and a half centuries ago is quite certain. But as to where their dwellings were and from where they fished there is no exact information. There was a boatbuilder on Dunglass Beach early in the 19th century. It is said that fishermen lived on the side of the road that runs steeply down from Castle Dykes to Dunglass Mill Bridge. If they did live there it is more than likely that they fished from the Pan harbour. No doubt some sort of fishing must have been carried on from the Cove, though it must be borne in mind that the main interest of that village prior to 1752 was in the local coal mine. Mining was abandoned in that year, for the coal was hard to get and was of inferior quality to the East Lothian product.

If they did fish from the Cove before 1740 they may have used those boat channels still plainly visible, cut through the rocks just south of the Wishing Well. In 1753 Sir John Hall started to build a full protective harbour wall, but in one night a north-east storm washed away all that had been built and no further attempt was made at that time. It was not until 1831 that another Sir John, grandson to the above, completed the present harbour.

It would appear that a long time of comparative prosperity followed. There are several instances of Cockburnspath tradesmen in need of capital going to sea as a member of a boat's crew for one or two seasons. It was quite possible to earn as much as £70, which was a large sum in those days. One of the most profitable but unpredictable lines was the herring fishing. This activity was at its height as the herring shoals moved north about the middle of June. In times of a glut the sea off the Cove would be dotted with boats coming from as far afield as Eyemouth and the Fife coast. The coming of the steam trawlers must have put an end to this for in the early 1920s they ceased to come. In the summer there was the salmon fishing, but as this was let to a company it did not affect the Cove fishermen to any great extent.

Line fishing was the great stand-by. In this the fishermen's wives had a great deal of hard work. Mussels for bait came from either Newhaven or Morecambe. The women had to go 'down the brae' and pull quantities of long grass. They had to open the mussels, bait the hooks, ten to a 100-yard line, coil the baited line neatly round in a large, shallow basket called a 'swull', lay a line of coarse grass between each coil to prevent the hooks from fouling one another, and have everything ready for their men to carry down to the harbour in the early morning. When far enough out to sea the fishermen 'shot' these lines, a float having been attached to both ends. Leaving them for an hour or so, they hauled them in and as a rule had a fair catch. But even this is not what it used to be and the three boats (where there used to be 21) now get a living from crabs and lobsters. These can be caught all the year round, though they are at their best in August. Only six men now put to sea.

Exactly when the decline in fishing set in, no one seems to know. The Cove was a cheerful place. On a summer's morning the men used to sit in a small square smoking and talking on the little patch of grass at the top of the cliff opposite the houses. Now nearly all of their houses have been sold to distant town dwellers who take up residence for a few weeks in the summer. Only one man, a retired fisherman, remains with a wife and two daughters.

Medical Services. The quaint mid-eighteenth century house with its many small, low-ceilinged rooms, now known as Primrose Hill, has always been known as 'The Doctor's House'. Adjoining and built onto it were living quarters for a bachelor groom, a stable and a coach house. The short steep incline which leads down and onto the village-Hoprig road, is still, in spite of there having been no doctor there for 60 years, known as the 'Doctor's Brae'. The earliest known name was a Dr Hooper who was in practice in the early 1840s. More than likely he was followed by the Drs Black, who followed father and son till nearly the end of the century. The doctors in those days were under the direct jurisdiction of the laird, and the last Dr Black was dismissed over a supposed injustice to a local patient. A fairly rapid succession of doctors followed. These doctors did all their own dispensing, but the practice must have been a poor one for in 1923 the last doctor moved his residence to Dunbar, but came back each afternoon to hold a surgery in a room in the village square. Gradually more Dunbar doctors found patients in Cockburnspath Parish, and now some families even choose a doctor from Duns. The system apparently works well. Very occasionally patients are sent to Peel Hospital, Galashiels, but most serious emergencies and surgical cases are sent to Roodlands Hospital at Haddington. Less urgent cases, and cases of terminal illness, go to Belhaven Cottage Hospital, Dunbar. The medical care is entirely satisfactory, and the ambulance service most efficient.

Woods. There have been great changes in the woods of the parish during the last few years. Penmanshiel Wood, cut down during the First World War and replanted in 1924, has been cut down again and again replanted. Firs are the basis of this replanting for the soil is not acid enough for the growing of first-class larch. This big wood runs to 300 acres in extent and adds greatly to the beauty of the countryside. Many old and mature trees have been cut down in the Towner Glen during the past year. Another landmark that is missed is the small fir wood at the top of Ecclaw Hill. It has been cut down and immediately replanted and the young Scots firs are thriving. A good many acres have been planted in new places as shelter-belts on the upland farms, a total of about 450 acres in the last 10 years. Following the alterations to the A1 road at the tunnel, two or three small copses of hardwoods have been planted on top of the newly disturbed ground.

Animal and Bird Life. There has been little change in the fauna of the neighbourhood. Roe deer still inhabit their favourite places: occasionally a doe appears with twin fawns, and they seem to be much tamer than they used to be. Badgers are very scarce, but will probably return, for Ewieside is never long without them. Adders in reduced numbers still live in Penmanshiel Wood and are not uncommon on Whiteburn and other hill farms. Rabbits are beginning to recover from two attacks of myxomatosis, with the result that hares are again plentiful only on high ground. Stoats and weasels are in good numbers again. Foxes are flourishing, and the Berwickshire Hounds have several meets per season at Ecclaw, Whiteburn and the Star, and rarely fail to find. Red squirrels are to be seen in Dunglass and Pease Dens, but fortunately no grey squirrels have ever been reported. Very occasionally a blue hare is seen on Ewieside, but this is most often the result of a severe winter.

There has been no great change in the local bird life in recent years. Goldfinches have increased; the bullfinch, too, seems to have settled here, though scarce. Carrion crows have doubled their numbers, chiefly because of the lack of keepering on many large estates. Because so much more grain is now sown, the woodpigeons, whose numbers are governed entirely by the amount of food available, are in great abundance, and do infinite damage in newly sown cornfields and to young turnip plants. Apparently little owls have deserted us, but stonechats and tree sparrows are here. Very few wheatears are with us this year but siskins, yellowhammers and tits are as usual. Dunlins, crossbills and snow buntings come in their seasons and corncrakes (landrails) are back after a long absence. A raven and a pair of hen harriers have been sighted. Peregrine falcons still come but are now a rarity. Incidentally, it is interesting to note that the place-name 'Siccar Point' has nothing to do with 'making sure': it is actually derived from 'saycar', the fishermen's name for the peregrine falcon. They used to nest there in bygone times. The fulmars are now established all the way round the coast, always reaching a little further south, though they worked their way round from St Kilda about the time of the First World War. Redstarts and reed buntings we do not often see.

Flowers. There is an infinite variety of wild flowers but nothing peculiar only to this district. One flower, however, has become a menace in recent years: willowherb. It seems to have rooted itself on every unused square inch of ground and is now fighting a lusty battle with the bracken.

Climate. It used always to be a boast of the Cockburnspath people that they had almost the driest climate in Britain. The average rainfall was held to be about 23 inches per annum. Snowstorms, which may be a mere nuisance round the village, can lie deep enough to block all roads for as long as nine weeks in the hills. Really serious floods seem to come only once a century! In 1847 a great flood burst the banks of the Chapelhill Mill Pond, and caused great damage in the lower part of the village, while about two miles away the flood bore hundreds of tons of built-up soil from the North British Railway embankment where it crosses the Tower Glen. In 1948 the flood washed away all the railway bridges south of Grantshouse and closed the line for months. Little harm was done to Cockburnspath on this occasion, however. Gales cannot be said to be frequent but do cause damage every few years.

Agriculture. Farming, though still the biggest employer of labour in the parish, has suffered not only a vast but a sad change in the past 40 years. Older farmers may look back nostalgically to the old days and simpler ways of farming, but economic facts show unmistakably that there is no going back. Much has been lost through the abandoning of old fashioned crop rotations, and few farms are in anything like as good heart as they were when under these unbreakable rules. The artificial manure-spreader and the chemical control of woods have made possible economic advance, but the day may come when nature takes its as yet unseen revenge. No one can deny the already apparent effect on bird life, small animals, frogs and insects, and we wait to see if the end result may not affect man himself. Saving of time and labour are at the root of many of these changes. Farm hands now are reduced to one or two, though in busy times casual help may have to be found.

One great improvement, however, must be kept in mind — the elimination of much of the hard manual labour. Starting with potatoes, there is no longer a line of men and women planting them by dropping single potatoes into a drill. A tractor, a planting machine and two men on the back are all that is needed. There is no longer the lifting of heavy bags. Artificial manure is delivered on pallets and thereafter handled by a forklift. Turnips and swedes are sown as single seeds by a space sower. This has meant the end of the singling with a hoe, an endless, soul-destroying job. Come the harvest, instead of cutting, stooking, leading-in, stacking, thatching and threshing, the combine can deal with five acres an hour. Being in bulk, the grain goes mostly straight to the brewery with no more lifting of heavy bags. And so, given average weather, the previously long drawn-out harvest is soon at an end. Nevertheless, this time of combine-harvesting is one of acute anxiety for the farmer. The barley having to be left till it is thoroughly ripe, an hour of high wind can shake out hundreds of pounds' worth of the best grain, leaving only worthless straw. So precarious is it that, weather conditions permitting, the combine is often kept going all night.

Yet in the old days, despite long days, dawn to dusk without a farthing of overtime, the farm folk, both men and women, loved the harvest! In good times the harvest often brought the reward of a 'kirn', a dance held in the granary about the end of December. The farm hands spent many of their winter nights before this dance decorating the rafters with holly and ivy and paper streamers. One fiddler and his friend with a melodeon provided the music and the farmer laid in a barrel of beer for the men and cases of lemonade for the girls. The dance went on into the 'sma' oors'. Halfway through the proceedings the steward would stand up to announce that tomorrow would be a whole holiday. Prolonged cheers! Holidays were few and far between then. The only universally recognised one in Scotland was New Year's Day. Christmas Day, Good Friday and other sacred days were worked without question. Now, all farm people have 21 days' holiday with pay as a statutory rule.

In arable farming, there have been marked changes in cropping. Very few oats are grown and a little less wheat than formerly. The large barley acreage has in the last few years been split between spring and winter barley, the latter having the advantage of an earlier sowing and a fortnight or so's earlier ripening. It is not, however, of such high quality and does not malt well. Its great and increasing use is mostly for cattle fattening. The livestock side has altered too. The really up-to-date cattle courts now have a raised concrete platform between two courts with feeding troughs on either side. A tractor with turnip-cutting machine scoops up a hopperful of turnips, switches on the power, and the cut turnips are delivered on each side alternately as the tractor moves along the gangway. This is a great saving of time and energy.

Turning to the beef industry, cattle feeding is mostly for the low, in-bye places. The higher-up, stock-rearing farms keep to the breeding side. Some of the larger places have immense herds of cows. Quite often these are of mixed breeds but all must have big, substantial frames. Times have changed much in the breeds of crossing bull used. Between the wars the Aberdeen Angus was the only one to be thought of, but the Hereford with its greater weight and its ability to thrive on poorer pastures displaced the Aberdeen Angus bull to a great extent. Now the French Charolais is fighting for first place with the German Simmental; but the A.A. and the Hereford are still used in this parish and may continue to be.

Sheep stocks too have changed. The long-standing half-bred ewe has been largely replaced by the not only more prolific but cheaper grey-faced ewe. The Oxford ram is now rarely used for the low ground flocks, the Suffolk being the present favourite. This cross gives a leaner, more attractive lamb carcass. In the hill flocks of black-faced ewes, apart from the pure bred black-faced ram, necessary for the keeping up of the flock, the blue-faced Leicester has completely superseded the Border Leicester ram for the production of the mule lamb.

One animal not often seen on the farm nowadays is the pig. Economically they are out at the present time, and one large farm in the district which specialised in pork has had to change over completely to another way of farming.

It is cheering to realise how much land on the high farms has been reclaimed during the past 30 years: a total of 756 acres. Most of this land has been reclaimed from heather or blaeberry ground. According to the old Scots saying, 'Under whins, gold. Under bracken, silver. Under heather, copper.' Every acre will repay the trouble and cost. Some of this may be allowed to lie in grass in the years to come but will nevertheless be of greater grazing value than ever before.

Several farms have erected grain silos. Occasionally 50 feet in height, they are useful for storing feeding grain for long periods and have proved a great success.

A list of comparisons will express the agricultural changes in financial terms.

Wages	1950	1983
Shepherds	£11.5/-	£94.90

Stewards	£11.0/-	£91.90
Tractormen	£5.2/-	£84.60
	(5-1/2 day week)	(5-day week)

N.B. Nearly all farmers actually pay £30-£40 higher than these minimum rates at the present time.

Comparison of Values:

	1951	*1983*
	per ton	*per ton*
Barley	£15-£20	£90-£100
Wheat	£20-£25	£120-£130
Oats	£26-£33	£80-£90
Potatoes	£10	£50-£60
Cows	£70-£80	£600-£700
Calves	£35	£300-£350
Tractors	£550	£8000
Combines	£500	£30,000
Ewes	£6-£7	£50
Lambs	£4-£5	£40-£50
Hill Ewes	30/—40/-	£25
Hill Lambs	50/—60/-	£18
Rent per acre	£3-£4	£27-£30
Land per Acre	£25-£30	£300-£400

Agricultural Returns:

	1951	*1983*
Cattle	854	2655
Sheep	16,235	17,172
Horses	31	30
Pigs	6	6
Poultry	2765	322
Labour	128	35
Casual	51	10
Barley	1239	724 (Winter)
Barley		2539 (Spring)
Wheat	134	320
Oats	907	41
Potatoes	282	126
Turnips	568	333
Rape	115	53
Hay	364	565
Silage		466
Kale & Other Crops		1
Peas	128	14
Oil Seed Rape		14

1983

THE PARISH OF COLDINGHAM

by The Rev. J. B. Davie M.A. and the
Rev. W. Howard Purdie M.A.

THE PHYSICAL BASIS

Coldingham is a village and a coast parish of north-east Berwickshire. By road it is three miles from Eyemouth, four and a half miles from Ayton and three and a quarter from Reston Junction, this being 11 miles north-west of Berwick-upon-Tweed and 46 and a half east-south-east of Edinburgh.

The Parish of Coldingham is one of the largest parishes in Berwickshire, and it offers a great variety of scenery. Part of the parish lies alongside some of the most magnificent coastline in Scotland. The parish on the east is bounded by the coastline, beginning a little north of Eyemouth and extending for some 12 miles along the coast as far north as Fast Castle. The great cliffs are an imposing sight, rising in places to well over 500 feet above the sea, and are the favourite haunts of sea birds. The best known of the cliffs, though not the highest, is St Abb's Head, on the summit of which is situated a lighthouse and an Admiralty Signal Station.

A change in the parish boundary took place as from May 1891 by order of the Boundary Commissioners for Scotland. Coldingham had a detached part of 80 acres, at Highlaws, surrounded by the parish of Eyemouth. It was transferred to Eyemouth. The population involved was 16 persons.

There were also 1,417 acres of Oldhamstocks parish situated at the north-west end of Coldingham parish near Butterdean, which were annexed to Coldingham parish. The population involved in the transfer was 86 persons. The result of the alterations was to give a final population of 3,016 persons in place of the pre-change population of 2,946 persons. The present parish is bounded north and north-east by the North Sea, east by Eyemouth and Ayton, south-east by Ayton, south by Chirnside, south-west by Bunkle, west by Abbey St Bathans, and north-west by Cockburnspath.

There are five villages in the parish: Coldingham, St Abbs, Reston, Auchencrow, Grantshouse.

The editor wishes to acknowledge the assistance given by Mrs J. B. Davie in preparing the MS left by her late husband.

About a mile to the south-west of St Abb's Head lies Coldingham Loch, the only inland sheet of water of any significance in the parish. Though so near the sea, it is yet 300 feet above sea level, and it is remarkable in this respect that no stream flows either into it or out of it. The springs that feed it and the channels that drain it are underground. It has abundance of trout.

To the south-east of St Abb's Head lies the picturesque little village of St Abbs, situated right on the sea coast. It is of comparatively recent origin, having come into existence early in the 19th century, providing dwellings near the sea for the fisherfolk who had formerly lived at Coldingham. The village consists of over a hundred houses. An outer and an inner harbour were constructed, but they are difficult to approach in stormy weather. Near St Abbs is Coldingham Bay where there is a very pleasant sandy beach which is a favourite with holiday makers.

The road from St Abbs runs south-east to Coldingham, an old historic village nestling very prettily in the valley. No matter from what direction one approaches Coldingham, the picture before one's view is very pleasant indeed as the village with its red tiled roofs and its ancient Priory on a slight elevation in the midst comes into view.

If one takes the road north from Coldingham, after a steady climb for three miles, one comes upon a great stretch of moorland, through which the road makes its way for almost another three miles. This moorland at one time provided common grazing ground for the inhabitants of the parish. It was afterwards divided into a number of small farms which still exist. The greater part of the moor still remains in its natural state, and is used for grazing sheep and raising game. There are also some small quantities of peat moss. Its highest point is Drone Hill where the Air Ministry has a radar station which played an important part in the last war.

We have now reached the extreme northern boundaries of the parish. To the north-west the main Edinburgh to Berwick road enters the parish just above the little village of Grantshouse on the A1. There is a railway station here, and the bus junction from Duns, the county town. A little to the south-east of Grantshouse the road meets the Eye Water and runs alongside it for several miles. This is the only river of any size in the parish. It flows in a south-easterly direction to the village of Ayton before turning north-east to reach the sea at Eyemouth. Along the course of the Eye there took place some of the worst devastation during the disastrous Berwickshire floods of August 1948. After a 24 hours' downpour, which the already saturated earth could not absorb, the modest Eye rose to a raging torrent, and along its course flooded homes, ruined crops, and, within the confines of the parish alone, destroyed seven railway bridges as well as a number of road bridges. Railway traffic was disrupted. Energetic measures were at once taken to meet the situation, and in a matter of 10 weeks temporary bridges were erected and railway communications re-opened. Since then permanent bridges of longer span have been built, the course of the river has been widened and its banks strengthened as a precaution against further contingencies of a similar kind.

Following the main road from Grantshouse, we pass Renton, the name being all that remains of what was an ancient village. Then we come to Houndwood, which at one time was richly wooded, and was the hunting seat of the Priors of Coldingham Priory. Three miles further on is the village of Reston. It is a lively little village, and has an auction mart for the sale of stock and agricultural implements. It was at one time a railway junction for Duns and St Boswells. This branch line has recently been closed; but being on the main Edinburgh to Berwick line it is still an important railway station for the parish. It only remains to mention the little hamlet of Auchencrow, two miles south-west of Reston. It is supposed to have derived its name from an Anglo-Saxon or Dane who occupied the land and called it after himself — Aldengrave, which gradually became Auchencrow.

There are no hills of any height in the parish, the highest being about 860 feet. But the country is by no means flat; it consists of a series of undulating valleys which are for the most part closely cultivated. Hedges and copses fringe the fields. There are small patches of wooded land here and there, and one timber plantation of about 250 acres.

The rainfall in the district is normal. Spring is characterised by keen, biting north-east winds. In summer and autumn there are frequent gales. There is also frequent fog from the sea especially in May, though in June of 1955 the fog horn at St Abb's Head sounded a record number of hours for that month.

HISTORY OF THE LOCAL COMMUNITY

The story of Coldingham goes back to ancient times. It is mentioned in Bede's 'Ecclesiastical History'. Though the village existed long before the Priory was built, it was the latter which gave to Coldingham its prosperity and importance. In 640 A.D. Ebba, the daughter of the King of Bernicia, fled from her father's house to escape an undesirable marriage. She set off by sea and a storm drove her ashore at a point near St Abb's Head, which was named after her. In gratitude to God for her escape from the storm she founded a convent, and she herself became its first Abbess. St Cuthbert on more than one occasion visited the nunnery. At St Abb's Head can still be seen a few ruins which mark the place where the convent once stood.

There seems to have been a church in Coldingham as early as 830 A.D., built through the beneficence of a Northumbrian King. In 1098 A.D. Edgar, King of Scots, founded the Priory of Coldingham. This he did in gratitude to God for a victory which had regained him his father's throne. Evidently, before the battle, St Cuthbert appeared to him in a vision and directed him to take his consecrated banner from the

Plate 14. The bridge over the River Tweed at Coldstream.

Plate 15. A view of Coldstream in the 1950s.

Convent at Durham and to carry it at spear point in the van of his advancing forces. If he did so, he would win the battle. Edgar did as he was directed, won the battle, and then built the Priory and dedicated its altar to the perpetual memory of St Cuthbert. He gave the Priory over to the Benedictine Monks of Durham, and richly endowed it with lands, not only in the parish of Coldingham itself, but in places as far distant as Swinton and Paxton. There are still preserved in the archives of Durham Cathedral over 1,000 charters and documents of various kinds pertaining to Coldingham, which are a mine of information about conditions in Church and State in the Scotland of the early centuries. The Priory became extremely wealthy and one of the most influential houses in Scotland. The Prior sat as a baron in the Scottish Parliament and exercised feudal jurisdiction over a wide district. He was at one time served by a retinue of over 70 functionaries, a number scarcely surpassed by the greatest noble of the land. Around the Priory there grew up a considerable town with an extensive wool trade, which by the middle of the 14th century is said to have surpassed all other towns in the sheriffdom of Berwick in the number of its inhabitants and the accommodation it provided for travellers. Edward I of England established a weekly market and an annual fair in the town. The market place and cross are still to be seen, a reminder of former prosperity. The Prior, like most of the Anglo-Norman barons of the Merse, found it expedient to swear fealty to King Edward.

Because of its situation close to the English border, Coldingham was inevitably exposed to the hazards that beset the frontier communities in those troublous times. All through the Middle Ages both the town and the Priory suffered frequently in the incessant frays of border warfare. On a number of occasions they were occupied by the English, and the Priory suffered damage by fire at the hands of both the English and the Scots. Edgar's original building of the Priory was destroyed by King John of England in 1216. This was replaced by a new and greater building of cathedral proportions and splendour. The Priors, however, were in a most unenviable position, for, with the swaying fortunes of border warfare, they found themselves forced to swear loyalty now to an English King, now to a Scottish King. The Priory also was in a most awkward position — situated in Scotland, and yet under the jurisdiction of England. In the 15th century the Priors took steps to safeguard themselves and the Priory by entering into an agreement with the powerful border clan of Home whereby the latter were to act as bailiffs of the Priory and its lands and receive a share in its revenues, in return for their protection. One Scottish King ignored this agreement to his sorrow. In 1485, James III, finding himself without funds for the endowment of the Chapel Royal which he had built at Stirling, proposed that Coldingham Priory should be suppressed, and its revenues appropriated to the support of the new royal shrine. Though sanctioned both by the Pope and the Scottish Parliament, the King's proposal met with violent opposition on the part of the Homes and other powerful nobles, which led to the rebellion which ended in the Battle of Sauchieburn, where James was slain in 1488. In 1509, the Priory's long connection with Durham was severed and it was attached to the Abbey of Dunfermline. As the confused times of the Reformation drew near, the fortunes of the Priory waned, and it came under the control of lay commendators, for the most part favourites of the King, and these lay commendators did not scruple to use the Priory's revenues for their own enrichment. In the end, all its lands, like those of other religious houses, passed into secular hands. The nave and the transepts of this 13th century church were destroyed by the Earl of Hertford in a great border raid in the 16th century. Then in 1648 on his way to Dunbar, Cromwell, finding the Priory fortified, set his guns on an adjoining hill and destroyed the whole building, with the exception of the north and east walls of the choir, which still remain standing, and form part of the present parish church. The first parish church was built in 1660, by building south and west walls to the original north and east walls of the choir.

In 1854 the churchyard was excavated and the original foundations of the Priory were exposed. Some interesting relics were also discovered. A new porch and vestry were added to the church and improvements were made to the interior furnishings. The Priory has thus had a long and interesting history, and we can say that, with the exception of 12 years after it was destroyed in 1648, it has remained a place of worship for over 850 years.

The parish is full of places of historical interest. Near St Abb's Head, and north of it, are to be found early British fortifications. One of them is a three-walled camp, with the sea 430 feet below. North-west of Auchencrow, there is a chain of camps. An old Roman road led through the parish. Near Auchencrow is Billie Castle, which like all Border castles had an eventful history during the Border feuds. Three miles north-west of St Abb's Head on a rock overlooking the sea there stands Fast Castle, 'firm and sure on the rock will aye endure'. It is mentioned in 'The Bride of Lammermoor'. The summit of the rock on which the Castle stands is triangular in shape and isolated from the mainland by a distance of 24 feet. There is little remaining of the Castle. It was struck by lightning in 1871. Due to its unique position, the Castle took a prominent part in Border warfare. It has also the distinction that Margaret Tudor, sister of Henry VIII and future Queen of James IV, found hospitality within its walls on her way north to her marriage.

Before leaving places of such historical interest, it might be well to note the architectural features of the Priory. The Priory Church was built in the form of a cross. We know from excavations the position of the nave, aisles, transepts and choir, together with the Chapter House, Dormitory, Refectorium, one or two small rooms and cloister garth.

The north and east walls of the choir are now all that remains, of any significance, of the 13th century Church. They reveal a style of architecture which is partly Norman and partly First Pointed. The height of the walls is divided into two parts — a wall arcade in the lower, with a series of pointed arches; and a window arcade in the upper, with a central passage formed in the thickness of the walls. The arches have moulded shafts and very finely carved capitals ornamented with various kinds of foliage. The exterior of the building corresponds to the interior. The lower part of the walls has a series of Norman arches, and the upper part lancet-shaped Gothic windows with columns at the sides. The archway to the south aisle still remains as restored in 1854. But many of the remains of the Priory were taken down by the villagers who used the stone to build their houses; and in some of the oldest houses in the village the ecclesiastical stone can still be detected. In 1855 two bodies were discovered in a vault, with two-foot foundations remaining, near the west end of the building. The graves were built of stone, laid about six inches thick, and partly cut out for the head and shoulders. These were the tombs of two Priors of Coldingham who held office in the 13th century. Two large slabs, protected by iron gratings, preserve the authentic date and record.

A number of changes have to be recorded in the Church history of the parish.

After the Disruption of 1843, a few Free churches were built in the parish, at Coldingham, Reston, Grantshouse and St Abbs. The Church in Coldingham — St Andrew's — was built in 1793 and rebuilt in 1870. Dr McDougall gifted a fine Hall equipped with a good library in memory of the Rev. A. B. Robertson, minister of the church from 1856 to 1899. Later he installed and endowed a pipe organ in the church in memory of his wife. The Church at St Abbs was gifted by Andrew Usher of Northfield, and given to the fishermen of St Abbs. Mr Usher also built the St Abbs harbour. Up to the Union of the Church of Scotland with the United Free Church of Scotland in 1929, there were at least six ministers working in the parish. There are now four ministers at work in the parish. In these conditions it has been found necessary to unite congregations in the parish, and unions have been effected in Coldingham and Grantshouse and Houndwood. In Coldingham, the ancient Priory is now the sole place of worship, and a scheme was envisaged to improve its furnishings to make it a place of worship more in keeping with its long history. In 1955 most of that scheme was completed, by turning the seating across the church, and facing the congregation towards the 13th century east and north walls. This was made possible by forming a slightly raised chancel platform which would accommodate a Communion Table, Pulpit, Baptismal Font and Lectern. The new furnishings were dedicated on Easter Sunday, by the Rev. Ronald Selby Wright, Canongate Church, Edinburgh.

The only Church in the parish is the Church of Scotland, and those parishioners belonging to other denominations, who are relatively few, travel to Eyemouth to worship in their respective churches there. A hundred years ago there were six churches in the parish, all well attended, and many of the people travelled long distances to go to Church, and not a few went on foot. All that has changed. There are now only four churches in the parish and these are sparsely attended. Only a small percentage of the people in the parish are regular attenders and take an active part in Church life. At the same time, most would claim to have a Church connection, and ask for the Church's services at a baptism, wedding, or funeral, but do not feel any obligation to give practical support to the Church. This is understandable, especially with regard to the financial support of the Church, when it is remembered that it is not so very long ago since the Church was almost entirely supported financially by the wealthy, and very little was required of the parishioners, but now, with the more equitable distribution of wealth, the Church is depending for its financial support upon a class of people which has not been educated to give. In the new era of the Welfare State, parishioners will have to learn the rightful place of the Church in their midst, and their obligation to it.

The present manse at Coldingham was built in 1801. There was, of course, a manse before that date, but on a different site. In 1694 — the date of the earliest parish records — extensive repairs seemed to be made to the manse and offices. The present manse was enlarged in 1828. It was further enlarged during the ministry of the Rev. Henry Maclaurin Lamont, B.D. (1898-1942) who added two rooms and a front porch. The manse has 14 rooms, including bathroom and small dressing room, but apart from being too large for modern needs, it is well equipped with modern conveniences. It is pleasantly situated, bounded to the south by lawns and trees and to the north and east by the glebe — a field of four and a half acres. The sea is about a mile distant and makes a pleasant view from the top windows. There is an old-time walled garden with flowers, fruits and vegetables. The stone of which the walls are built has obviously been part of the Priory. Just beyond the garden is the Priory itself.

POPULATION

In 1801 the population of the parish of Coldingham was 2,391. By 1861 the population had reached the highest total ever recorded, 3,241, an increase of 850. Thereafter the population gradually dwindled until in 1951 it reached the very low figure of 2,302, the lowest so far recorded. The figures since 1861 are as follows: 1871, 3,093; 1881, 3,173; 1891, 2,946; 1901, 2,813; 1911, 2,749; 1921, 2,830; 1931, 2,398; 1951, 2,302 (M. 1,098, F. 1,204). It will be noticed that the biggest drop in the population took place between 1921 and 1931. In these ten years the population decreased by 432. In the 20 years between 1931 and 1951 the population decreased by another 96, making a total decrease of 528 in 30 years.

The history of the parish of Coldingham during the last hundred years reflects the wide changes which have taken place throughout the countryside in that time. No longer is Coldingham the centre of a thriving industry as it was when Edward I of England established a market there in 1305. The writer of the second Statistical Account indicates that then the market and the annual fair had almost dwindled to nothing. Now it has ceased to exist. There is no industry apart from agriculture. In agriculture far-reaching changes have taken place. The parish is fully up to date in its agricultural methods. Most of the ploughing of the land, the sowing of the seed, the gathering in of the harvest is done by machinery. Only a very limited number of horses are in use. The new machinery has offset to a large extent what would have been a very serious situation for agriculture — the continual drift from the land which has taken place within the last hundred years, and which has been even more marked in recent times.

This tendency of the population to drift from the country into the towns is a serious problem in Berwickshire. The same forces are at work here as elsewhere — better amenities in the town, and lack of modern amenities in the country. Although farm cottages are rapidly becoming modernised and equipped with hot and cold water and electric light, they have not yet reached the standard obtaining in the towns. And further, most of these cottages are removed a considerable distance from the towns, and thus from the centre of entertainment, which is offered in such variety nowadays. The unrest among farm workers took place after the First World War and was intensified after the Second World War. Agriculture could not offer the same prospects as industries in the towns. The parish of Coldingham, therefore, in common with other country parishes, has suffered this continual flow of its population to bigger centres of industry. In the village of Coldingham itself, the complexion of the population has greatly changed. It is now a village largely consisting of older people. The village population is somewhere in the region of 350-400. Of that number about 25 are between the ages of 15 and 20. And most of these young people will have to leave the village to find jobs. They go mostly to places in Scotland and England. Very few have emigrated. With regard to the older people who remain in Coldingham, there are very few left who are called 'natives', who have been born and bred and lived all their lives in the parish. Most of the old people are 'incomers'. Coldingham with its delightful situation, its nearness to the sea, and its proximity to Edinburgh, has also become very popular with those who are looking for a congenial spot in which to spend their years of retirement.

In view of these facts the future of the parish is not very bright. The only hope is that agriculture may be able to offer more attractive prospects to the young people. At the moment the farm workers, in addition to the local people, consist of those who have come into the parish from Northern England, from Ireland, and the neighbouring counties of Scotland. There are also one or two Germans who settled in the parish after the war.

WAR MEMORIAL

There is a War Memorial in Coldingham which contains 39 names for the 1914-18 war, and eight names for the 1939-45 war. The War Memorial is for the ecclesiastical parish of Coldingham only. For the former Quoad Sacra parish of Houndwood which included Grantshouse, Houndwood and Reston, there is a War Memorial in Houndwood churchyard which contains 29 names for the 1914-18 war, and four names for the 1939-45 war. The War Memorial in St Abbs takes the form of a plaque in the village church. It contains 65 names for the 1914-18 war, and seven names for the 1939-45 war. In addition to the War Memorials there are memorial plaques in most of the churches.

PUBLIC AND SOCIAL SERVICES

During the past hundred years one of the most significant changes has been the growth of public services, such as water supply, sanitation, electricity and transport. In addition statutory authorities and voluntary bodies have greatly developed health services, youth services, education and help for the aged. The parish has greatly benefited from these new developments.

The first change which revolutionised rural life was the advent of the motor bus. Formerly, to travel any distance, one had to go by horse and waggonette from Coldingham to Reston Station, a distance of about four miles. Now there is a regular bus service by which Coldingham is linked up with other towns and villages. There is a good service three times a day north to Edinburgh or south to Berwick and Newcastle. There is also a good local service. Only the remote parts of the parish are not served by bus. The bus service is not so good for those in the parish who wish to travel inland, say to Duns, the county town. But certainly the bus has changed the whole aspect of country life, bringing the people into contact with the towns, the best shops, and the most up to date forms of entertainment.

A new water scheme has been planned for the county in which the parish will benefit. It will be a year or so before this scheme will be in full operation. When it is in operation it will be a great boon to those places in the parish which have been inadequately supplied. At present Coldingham and St Abbs are well served. The water contains a large percentage of lime, is good for drinking, but very hard. Reston, Grantshouse and other places in the parish have their own supply. Most farms have their own private water supply, usually from nearby wells. In a widespread rural community it takes a much longer time to provide modern facilities than in the town, because the obstacles to be faced are much greater.

As it is with the supply of water, so it is with the supply of electricity. Many parts of the parish are not supplied with electricity, or have only been supplied recently. Coldingham and St Abbs were provided with electricity just previous to the Second World War, and Reston has had electricity within the last few years. Grantshouse has still to be supplied. Farms which are a distance from the main grid, and that includes the majority of farms in the parish, make their own electric power — with a few exceptions. In some cases the farm cottages are also lit from the system which supplies the farm house and farm. But there is still a long way to go before every cottage in the parish is supplied with the amenities which electricity provides.

Calor gas is very popular. It is sometimes used for lighting, but mostly for cooking purposes. It is quick and efficient, and is a great boon in remote places.

With regard to sewerage, the smaller villages lying inland are worse off. They depend upon septic tanks. There is, however, an efficient system of sewage disposal in Coldingham and St Abbs. It is also expected that with the new water supply there will come a better system of sewerage for the major portion of the parish. Refuse is collected throughout the parish once a week.

The County Council is responsible for the upkeep of roads in the parish. These roads have been greatly improved within the last hundred years; the main roads are in very good repair, but still, in parts, very winding, and thus unsuited for fast traffic. Minor roads are in good condition, with one or two exceptions. Streets are clean, but narrow. In Coldingham they are of the old-world type, conforming to the pattern they have had for many hundreds of years. At the time of writing the streets in Coldingham, St Abbs and Reston only are lit by electricity.

Education has advanced in this parish as it has elsewhere. The last hundred years have seen schools built or enlarged in all the villages of the parish. A good education is now the birthright of every child of the parish. At first, these schools were placed under the authority of the local school board, but more recently the authority has been centralised in the county education committee.

Each village is provided with a primary school. The largest school is in Coldingham. This is a four-teacher school and has 98 pupils. Coldingham draws some of its pupils from as far distant as Old Cambus, six to seven miles away, just outside the bounds of the parish. The smallest school is in Auchencrow which is a one-teacher school with 15 pupils. The other schools are two-teacher schools, Reston with 58 pupils and St Abbs with 26 pupils. Renton school is now closed. A new school with modern equipment has been built at Grantshouse. It was opened in

February 1955. At Coldingham a headmaster is in charge; at the others the head teachers are women. The small one-teacher school at Cairnbank which served the moors, was closed in April 1921, probably because of the decline in population. Pupils in that area are accommodated at Coldingham school. Before the passing of the Education (Scotland) Act (1945) most of the primary schools kept small numbers of non-qualifying pupils up to the age of 14. With the raising of the school leaving age to 15, a process of centralisation was carried out at the secondary stage of education, and all pupils who have completed the primary stage of education proceed to Eyemouth Junior Secondary School. For the sake of convenience, Auchencrow pupils who have finished their primary course go to Berwickshire High School, Duns. A small number of pupils do continue their education. A few of these proceed to the universities. None of the schools in the parish have any endowments of their own. The family life of the children is not disturbed whether they are attending junior or secondary schools. All schools are linked up by the bus service provided by the Education Committee. This concentration of the higher classes in central schools is probably inevitable in a sparsely populated county like Berwickshire, and no doubt it has its advantages; but the life of rural parishes like Coldingham has lost something though the resultant lowering in the status of the parish schools and the loosening of the local loyalties of the younger generation. As elsewhere throughout the County, children are supplied free of charge with books and stationery, and excellent dinners are served at all the schools at a low cost. 'Further Education' is provided at all schools through evening classes, which are well supported, the classes most in demand being those on drama and crafts like dressmaking, leatherwork and basket-work.

The Berwickshire County Library supplies the needs of the reading public of the parish. Supplies of books are sent to villages or schools at regular intervals from the central library at Duns. These books are mostly light reading, but books of the more serious kind and books for study can be supplied to those who desire them. The Library is well supported in the villages, but it is more difficult for those in outlying parts of the parish to make use of the scheme. That does not however entail much hardship for the farm workers who, as a general rule, are not inclined to spend much of their leisure in reading.

There is one resident doctor in the parish; he resides at Coldingham. There is no hospital in the parish. The nearest clinic is at Eyemouth. Those who require surgical treatment are usually sent to Edinburgh Infirmary, 48 miles distant. The distance is a disadvantage in cases of emergency, but apart from that, in Edinburgh Infirmary, parishioners receive the best medical skill in the country. The National Health Service has proved a great benefit to everyone in the parish.

There are also several voluntary social services run in the parish. The youth is largely catered for by the Churches. Most of the Churches have Youth Clubs or Fellowships where young people can get together for games, discussions, study and handwork. These clubs or fellowships are a comparatively recent venture of the Churches in an attempt to gather and keep the young people within the fold of the Church. While these Youth Clubs are usually well supported by young people, it can hardly be claimed that the Church has succeeded in its main purpose, though it is still true to say that the Church is the centre of village life.

As Eyemouth is quite near, some of the youth in Coldingham, St Abbs and Reston take part in amateur operatic or dramatic productions organised in that town.

The Women's Rural Institute flourishes in the parish. There are branches in Coldingham, Reston, Grantshouse and Auchencrow. The membership varies from 70 in the larger branches to 15 in the smaller. The branches meet monthly and provide a programme which is both instructive and entertaining.

With the introduction of the 44-hour week, everyone enjoys much greater leisure, and many have made use of that leisure to take up hobbies of various kinds, such as cage birds or carrier pigeons; or they may be interested in drama or singing, and there is always gardening. Most houses in the parish have a good-sized garden attached, and most of these are very well kept. It is interesting to note that in the winter months the Education Authority runs classes for those who are interested in drama, sewing, dancing, international affairs, and so on. These classes have not been largely attended, but have proved very helpful to those who have attended them.

HOUSING

There is a shortage of houses in the parish, though of course the problem is not as acute as in the towns. Farm workers have their own cottages which are attached to the farms where they work, and these cottages have been, or are in the course of being, modernised. The county council has also built houses for agricultural workers, each consisting of a living room and two bedrooms. Four of these have been built in Reston and eight in Coldingham. In addition to these the county council's housing programme for the parish since the First World War has consisted of 38 houses built in Reston, 12 in St Abbs with six in process of construction, six in Grantshouse, with 12 in process of construction, and 28 in Coldingham. These houses generally consist of a living room, two or three bedrooms, kitchenette and bathroom. All have gardens. The older houses are of various types, from the small cottage to the large villa. Most of them have been modernised with up to date conveniences. On the whole, there is not much overcrowding in the parish. In fact, since a large proportion of the population consists of retired people, many of the households consist of only one or two occupants. A large percentage of the houses, especially in Coldingham, are owner-occupied. The community life is vigorous but suffers from the lack of young people. The number of children in the parish has greatly decreased; it is in the new housing schemes that the greatest numbers are to be found. In one new housing scheme, in Coldingham, consisting of 20 houses, there are some 30 children. The average number of persons per house in the new housing schemes is four. Young married couples have to wait a considerable time before a new house is available for them. In the meantime, they must either live with relations or rent a furnished house or rooms, or buy a house.

Each village in the parish has a shop or shops. These consist of grocery shops, baker's shops, and one butcher's shop. The services of the Post Office are available, and there are two deliveries of letters and parcels daily. The Commercial Bank of Scotland and the Royal Bank of Scotland have branches in the parish which are open one day each week. There are garages and motor engineers in Coldingham, Reston and Grantshouse. Blacksmiths' shops are still to be seen, but no horses. Blacksmiths now earn their livelihood by repairing, or making parts for machines. In Coldingham there is a market garden, and a nursery which specialises in rock plants and Alpine plants. There is a small tree plantation a few miles west of Coldingham. In addition to the shops, the parish is well served by vans from various merchants both from within and from without the bounds of the parish. These vans carry a large variety of goods and are specially welcome in remote parts of the parish.

AGRICULTURE

There are four types of soil in the parish. Land near the sea consists of light clay and gravel; land in the Reston-Coldingham area is good loam; in Coldingham Moor there is moorland with considerable areas of bog and peat moss; and land with a north-west exposure in heavy clay. The acreage under tillage is 8,845 acres; that under grass 10,871 acres; and that under rough grazings, 3,295 acres. There are 71 farms in the parish averaging 277.7 acres each, and 73 per cent of these are owner-occupied. Where the farms are tenanted, the average rent per acre is 21/-. The farms are taken under lease as a general rule for 14 years. There are also some 30 small holdings under 25 acres.

The latest and most up to date machinery is to be found on most of the farms. Farming by machinery has made all the difference to agricultural production, and also to the conditions and working hours of the farm labourers. It was at one time the general rule for those working on the farm to be hard at it from early morning to late at night. All that has changed. Now it is possible by means of machinery to do the same work in a much shorter time. Like all other workers, farm workers have their 40-hour week. At busy seasons they do work longer, but all such extra time is counted as overtime, and obtains a higher rate of pay. Wages have greatly improved, as well as conditions of employment. But still, there is an acute shortage of labour on the farms. The coming of machinery has to some extent offset what would have been a very serious situation.

At one time St Abbs was a flourishing fishing village. There are now few wage earners in the village, the population consisting, as one fisherman put it, 'of widows and spinsters who depend upon the popularity of St Abbs as a holiday resort for their living'. The fishing industry has fallen upon bad days, due to many causes, and not least to the present high cost of fishing gear. Previous to 1914 St Abbs had 21 large fishing boats and 12 yawls. Now there is only one large boat, and five yawls, and there are insufficient men to man even these. Most of the fishermen are over 60 years of age, there is no one to take their place and it would seem that with them the fishing industry is likely to pass from St Abbs. The young men are not attracted to the fishing, for it requires long hours — sometimes 12 or more hours a day — and the life is hard. The financial returns are not attractive, for a young man can get a job in another industry, work fewer hours and get higher pay, without the hard conditions of sea life. Some have taken up a more lucrative form of fishing such as whaling, which occupies them during the winter months, and in the summer they find other work. Probably also keen foreign competition has contributed to the present conditions in St Abbs.

THE WAY OF LIFE

In the foregoing sections we have seen that great changes have occurred in the life of the parish which have made for a much higher standard of living and an altogether much easier life for the farm labourer, and the workers generally. They have a much broader outlook on life than their forbears had. Not only has modern transport made it possible for them to travel regularly outside the bounds of the parish to see how the rest of the world is living, but most of them have lived through two world wars, and as members of the armed forces have travelled far and wide. They do not accept ideas or customs simply because they have been handed down through the generations. They have learned to think for themselves and to decide for themselves the right kind of conditions under which to live and work.

The children have greatly benefited. Their parents want them to be brought up in healthy surroundings, and to have the best of education. Every child gets a good education up to the age of 15. The parents of today expect these things for their families. Family life in the parish has not suffered as the town life has from the many attractions which draw young people away from their own firesides and from the family fellowship. It is true that families no longer make their own entertainment as they once did, and they find it only in a limited way in the villages. Most of their entertainment must be found in the nearby towns, and because of the distance and expense involved, their visits to these towns cannot be too frequent. Family life on the whole is happy and contented.

The attitude to work has changed. At one time there was nothing but work. Many found in their work a considerable pleasure and developed great skill. Now, work only occupies one-third of the day, and is generally regarded only as a means of earning one's bread and butter and obtaining a fair share of the amenities of life. Because work has become largely mechanised, it tends to become monotonous, dull, and uninteresting. The consequence is that people look forward, more than ever, to their leisure time, put greater emphasis upon it and guard it jealously. They like to get some thrills into their leisure time to compensate for the dullness of their work. Besides the 'pictures' they are interested in different kinds of sport, and especially if any gambling is associated with these sports. The Football Pools have become very popular, giving life its necessary thrill; 6d or 1/- may win a substantial cheque. The cost of living, however, being high, it is a common thing for wives and mothers also to do part-time work and that not only among the farm labourers and other workers, but also in many cases in the middle classes.

The people of this parish are quiet and law-abiding. They also work quietly and without rush. In the same way, any changes that take place do so slowly and in leisurely fashion. Sorrow, tragedy and death are accepted calmly as the inevitable portion of us all. One of the great changes which has taken place during the years has been the people's attitude to the Church. What that change has amounted to is rather difficult to say. Outwardly it would appear that Church services are no longer attended as they once were. But it is very doubtful whether the people of today are any less religious than the people of 100 years ago. It has to be admitted that the people of former times who went to church did so for many reasons which were certainly not religious. The people today have no religious reasons, or at least not sufficiently strong religious reasons for going to Church, and so they do not go. In that respect they may be more frank and honest than their forebears. But this attitude of the people to religion and to the Church makes one thing very clear, that, spiritually, people have developed very little in these hundred years. Spiritual development has lagged far behind material progress and that is the cause of the unrest that lies deep in the heart of man.

Apart from spiritual rebirth, which would be the greatest blessing that could fall upon this parish and upon the world of our time, the future of the parish of Coldingham lies with the future of agriculture. Our country depends more than ever upon the produce of the land. At the moment young people are drifting away from the land. We must attract them back; we must provide them with all modern facilities; we must help them to discover the advantages and joys of life in the country which are unrivalled by anything the town or city can offer.

1955

COLDINGHAM

by T. D. Thomson

By 1985 there had been considerable changes in this ancient parish. First, on the ecclesiastical front only one resident minister of the Church of Scotland remained; Grantshouse congregation had been united with Reston linked with Houndwood, and that had later been linked with Ayton; St Abbs had been linked with Coldingham, and they are due to be linked with Eyemouth by 1992, ending a succession of resident pastors that will have lasted nearly 900 years.

While on this topic it may be remarked that recent archaeological researches have indicated that the remains at Nunnery Point are unlikely to be pre-mediaeval, that there may have been a monastic settlement, if not a Roman station of some kind, at Kirk Hall, and that something considerably older than the Priory may underlie the ruins of Edgar's Walls at Coldingham. Unfortunately it has not yet been possible to carry any of these investigations to completion. Properly funded, Coldingham could be an archaeologist's paradise.

In the countryside numerous farms had been laid together, as had their fields, with effect on the hedgerows and the fauna and flora that lived in them. There had been considerable afforestation on Coldingham Moor where also further portions had been brought under cultivation. Much of the arable land has been devoted to the monoculture of barley. The future of Coldingham Common, on the Moor, has been the subject of some discussion; meantime, the area immediately round the Long Moss is being placed in the hands of the Nature Conservancy Council and declared a Site of Special Scientific Interest. St Abb's Head and its immediate hinterland now belong to the National Trust for Scotland and are managed jointly by that and the Scottish Wildlife Trust as a nature reserve which attracts many thousands of visitors each year, and the waters round the Head have been declared, by the fishing and conservancy interests jointly, as the nation's first voluntary marine reserve.

Coldingham continues to attract its visitors, especially in the summer months, and they are served by two large caravan camps and a small one, as well as by the large Youth Hostel at the Sands (which brings something of a cosmopolitan flavour to the area). There are also chalet developments at Westloch and Press Castle. Apart from the transients and the holiday-makers a good deal of accommodation has been required by people employed in the construction of the Torness power station, which has also provided jobs for a number of local inhabitants; most of these, unfortunately, will go when the station is eventually commissioned.

There has been a considerable reduction in the farm population and many of the farm houses and cottages no longer house farmers and farm workers. Some are the homes of those who work elsewhere and others house retired folk or have become holiday cottages — these last are also to be found in Coldingham, where there are a dozen or so, and in particular in St Abbs, where three-quarters of one street is empty in the winter; this may be good for the rates, but not for the community. However, community feeling in St Abbs has been sufficiently strong to defeat a recent proposal to close its one-teacher school.

Tourism therefore flourishes, as does agriculture, while fishing has experienced something of a revival, and the two main villages have expanded somewhat in the past thirty-five years, particularly Coldingham, where there have been three main building developments since the war and a fourth, private one is under way at the time of writing. Reston, on the other hand, has suffered badly from the closing of the railway station — there is now not a single railway station in Berwickshire; throughout the parish there is a feeling of an aging population with, however, the hope that before the next Statistical Account is prepared demographic imbalances may have been ironed out and the rural areas of the country restored to full health.

1985

THE PARISH OF COLDSTREAM

by the Rev. A. E. Swinton of Swinton, M.A.

BOUNDARIES AND EXTENT

According to the second *Statistical Account* the original name of the parish of Coldstream was Lennel from the village which stood on the north bank of the Tweed. This village was destroyed by the English in their predatory incursions; and 'in 1716 a new parish church was built at Coldstream, which was then becoming the most populous district of the parish'.

'The parish extends seven and a half miles in length, and somewhat more than four in breadth; it is of an irregular rectangular shape, and has the parish of Ladykirk for its boundary on the east; while Tweed separates it from England on the south.'

The parish of Coldstream covers an area of 19 square miles divided between the landward, which has a population of 1839, and the burgh of which the population is 1294. The parish is well wooded and there are some beautiful trees, especially in the policies of Hirsel, Lees and Lennel. Dundok wood at the Hirsel has some fine Scots firs and contains one of the best collections of azaleas and rhododendrons in the country. They are situated on one of the few patches of peat in the Merse and therefore flourish there. The trees on this patch of soil were blown down in a great gale about a century ago. The Earl of Home seeing that the peat would not give sufficient hold to the roots of tall trees, conceived the idea of planting rhododendrons. The Scots firs mentioned above, being rooted in firmer soil, withstood the gale. At Lees there is a splendid Spanish Chestnut and at Lennel some very fine Larches.

The Valuation Roll shows a gross value of £22,845 made up of £11,920 for the landward and £10,925 for the burgh. Owing to the derating of agricultural land the rateable value of the landward is only £3,706, that of the burgh being £10,564.

ESTATES

The Hirsel, which is the seat of Earl of Home, K.T., besides the mansion house and policies includes the farms of Hatchednize, Darnchester, Castle Law, Fireburn Mill, and Haigsfield, besides other land outwith the parish.

Lennel, the seat of Mrs Sitwell, includes, in addition to the mansion house and policies, the farms of Coldstream Mains, Lennelhill, Oxenrig and Todhilrig.

Milne Garden, the seat of Captain J. D. D. Hotham, consists, besides the mansion house and policies, of the farms of East and West Mains.

Lees estate was broken up in 1932 after the death of Sir George Marjoribanks. The mansion house, policies and fishings of Lees are owned by Captain L. S. and Major J. M. Briggs. The nuns of La Sagesse, Newcastle are tenants of Lees House which they use as a holiday home for themselves and the children of their school.

The mansion house of Hawkslaw is owned by Major Askew of Ladykirk and is let.

THE BURGH

The domestic and street architecture of Coldstream is of modest aspect but of conspicuous artistic merit and is mainly of good 19th century type.

There is a memorial column, 70 feet high, to Charles Marjoribanks, M.P., who was returned to parliament at the time of the Reform Bill of 1832. It is surmounted by an effigy in carved stone, and a small granite obelisk to another member of the same family. A fountain carved in freestone with four dolphins which are assembled as supporters of a large circular basin (cut from one stone), is situated in the Market Place.

In the vicinity of Coldstream there is a beautiful octagonal garden temple at Lees, of Regency design, and a large obelisk of splendid proportion in blocks of cut freestone, in the Hirsel policies.

Hirsel House, of regular frontage in three storeys, an extensive mansion built at various times during the 19th century, is situated beside the Dail Knowe, site of the former and much earlier manor house. The south-east end dates from the beginning of the 17th century.

Lees House, a 19th century construction adjoining remains of an older mansion, has a frontage which is a masterpiece of architectural style. The stabling, built before the present house, has a tower of 'Strawberry Hill Gothic' character.

At Lennel the 18th century mansion has been altered and extended; it has pleasant architectural character. The garden terraces are extensive; they are built upon the sloping bank of the ground descending to the river and are enriched by architectural features, carving and statuary.

The parish church (1908) has a columnar interior in the manner of Sir Christopher Wren and a tower of Scots aspect belonging to the former building (1716) adapted to the later construction. There are

Plate 16. The west end of Coldstream after a snowstorm, 1950s.

Plate 17. Coldstream in the 1950s.

three other churches, two of which have conspicuous towers; one tower with buttressed angles has noticeable attractiveness. The Town Hall has a frontage decorated with Palladian pilasters supporting a pediment with entablature. The interior timber-work roof is of good architectural character. There are two bank buildings; one is expressive of Victorian model and aim.

Cottage homes (remains of former days) are interspersed here and there; even in the main thoroughfare they exist — formerly thatched, now tiled or slated.

Stone cobbling of first rate craftsmanship once extended throughout the town pathways, the gutters and the courts. Despite layers of cement upon these cobbles, they reappear occasionally after frost.

High Street is now the principal thoroughfare. It is about a quarter of a mile long; at each end there are small terrace houses and separate dwellings, some of which are of late 18th century type; others are of Regency design with iron railings of pleasant pattern, and some are of later period. The influence of 18th century Bath and of 'New Town' Edinburgh, slight but discernible, marks the character and the aspect of this street. The roof levels are harmonious and suited to the width of the street; the shops, with dwellings above, are designed in two storeys with basements and attics; fenestration and ornamentation are in the best taste and little alteration which is incongruous (at this time, 1950) has taken place in the original facades.

The ancient traffic route southward led to the ford at the bend of the river adjoining the lower, and older, part of the town. Here there are examples of earlier types of Scots dwelling houses, but the prevailing pattern in two streets, which are parallel with High Street (on the higher level), is the Regency type of small dwelling in hammer dressed or in cut stone, but the modern habit of cement facing (instead of renewal of decayed lime-jointing) has greatly damaged the pleasant aspect of many well built stone houses in Coldstream.

The use of cement in place of lime mortar, in repair of freestone work, induces gradual decay when the usual atmosphere in the district is humid.

There are two hotels and two inns. General Monck's two lodgings, one in the Market Place, the other at what is now Number 62 High Street, seem to have disappeared or left only slight traces of their remains. A tablet on a building situated on the north-east portion of the Market Place indicates the vicinity of what was probably the site of a very ancient inn and also General Monck's first lodging during the period of his 23-day visit to Coldstream along with his men of Fenwick's and Hazel's regiments. (They had already spent ten years with him in Scotland.)

The Abbey church and all buildings attached (possibly 19 or 20) have entirely disappeared (two carved capitals were recently unearthed). This church may have been situated in or near to the large open square or Market Place which is surrounded by dwellings and some shops. The Abbey church, burnt in 1545 by the Earl of Hertford, was repaired; it existed after repair for 76 years and was finally destroyed by its owner, Sir John Hamilton of Trabrown, in 1621 after 456 years of usage as a place of worship and of service to the common cause. Charles Rogers edited for the Grampian Club *The Chartulary of the Cistercian Priory of Coldstream* (1879).

Several town lanes, stone-walled on either side, typical of inhabited windy places, still exist.

Smeaton's Bridge (1763-66), a work of importance and of architectural merit, carries the roadway across the Tweed connecting Berwickshire with Northumberland. Another stone bridge, across the Leet, of one semi-circular span of good design, gives entry to Coldstream at the western end of the town where the local flour mill, now disused and in disrepair, is situated. A portion of this building, remodelled, is now the local Fire Station.

The Hirsel, the ruins of Lennel Church, and various defensive constructions are described in the *Report on the County of Berwick* by the Royal Commission on the Ancient Monuments of Scotland (1915), pp. 54-58.

The burgh is governed by a Town Council consisting of a Provost, two Bailies and six Town Councillors elected for the three Wards. The Provost was provided with a chain and robe of office about 1923. The Town Hall was built in 1862 as a Mechanics Institute on a site gifted by Thomas Fair. It consisted of the present Town Hall, library and billiard room. Its main purpose then was to provide evening classes for working men. Owing to financial difficulties the buildings were taken over by the town. The billiard room is used as a Working Men's Club. The library is run as a subscription library and also gets books from the County Library. Fiction, travel, and biographies are most frequently in demand. Newspapers are available in the reading room. A wing to provide dressing rooms for the stage was added in 1897. A room inside the main door was made into the Town Council Chamber about 1938. Cinema films are shown in the Town Hall four times a week.

AGRICULTURE

The agricultural statistics for the parish are:

Tillage	3,564 acres
Rotation Grass	1,828
Permanent Grass	1,757
Rough Grazings	56

Agriculture is the occupation of the inhabitants of the landward part of the parish. The soil is very fertile and all kinds of arable and stock farming are carried on. At Coldstream Mains Mr James McGregor has a dairy farm with a celebrated herd of Red Poll cows. There are 19 farms in the parish, of which seven are farmed by their owners. The average rent per acre is from 23s. to 33s. Tractors have superseded horses for farm work; and combine harvesters which reap and thresh the corn are being widely used. A recent development in haymaking is to rake the hay off the ground into a baler, the bales being stacked in cocks for drying.

The status of agricultural workers has greatly improved since the last *Account* and their cottages have been brought up to date.

OTHER INDUSTRIES

As already stated agriculture is the occupation of the inhabitants of the landward part of the parish. Agriculture has produced the largest industrial concern in the burgh—John Rutherford and Sons, Engineers, which began in 1899 as a millwright's business carried on by father and son alone. Some years later machinery was installed to deal with more elaborate work. The development of oil engines increased the demand for engineering repairs. The coming of the tractor, followed by all kinds of agricultural machinery and electrical plant, including milking machines, resulted in rapid expansion and now about 150 men and women are employed. The Lennel knitwear factory was started during the Second World War, in what used to be the Scout Hall and Golf Club house, as a finishing factory for goods from Hawick firms. It is now making complete articles with its own stamp as well as doing finishing work. It employs about 45 people. Forsyth's Bakery in High Street was taken over by Thomas Forsyth in 1932 and fully mechanised. It employs about 50 people and does a retail trade all round the neighbourhood, besides wholesale business further afield and catering. In the years 1937-39 its bread and Scotch currant loaf won medals in Glasgow and London. There are two smaller bakeries. There are two large grocer's shops and several smaller shops. R. Carmichael and Sons was opened in 1832. Meikle and MacDougal dates from 1834 but was taken over by Brough's of Newcastle in 1949. There are two chemist's shops; the Tweedside Pharmacy was established in 1863. There is a branch of the Tweedside Independent Cooperative Store. There are branches of the Bank of Scotland and the British Linen Bank.

HOUSING

Since the First World War the Town Council has erected 135 houses. Seventy-eight were erected between the Wars and 57 after the Second World War including 25 prefabricated houses. The houses are surrounded by gardens which are well kept and have greatly improved the appearance of the town.

WATER

Water is supplied from a reservoir to which it is pumped from a well at Lees. Water power from the Tweed is used for this, or if it is insufficient, electricity.

TRANSPORT

Prior to the advent of the motor bus, passengers to Coldstream travelled by railway to Cornhill station where a bus from the town met the trains. As most of the passengers to that station were destined for Coldstream, it was re-named Coldstream about 1922. Coldstream is a junction between the double line from Berwick to St Boswells and the single line from Coldstream to Alnwick via Wooler. The latter line has long been closed for passenger traffic. Coldstream is now served by a number of buses. They run to Kelso and Berwick with connections at both places and to Edinburgh (three or two and a half hours) and Newcastle. The all night Edinburgh-London buses pass through Coldstream and take up passengers for the South there. The roads in the parish, like all others in the county, are very good. The road to Cornhill crosses the Tweed by the handsome stone bridge built by Smeaton in 1766.

Plaques with a line showing the height reached by the water in the flood of 13th August 1948 have been placed in the Market Square and above the Nuns Walk. The Tweed rose a little above the 1831 mark and the Leet, dammed back by the swollen Tweed, flooded some houses in Leet and Duke Streets and entered Market Square to a depth sufficient to float canoes.

EDUCATION

There is one school at Coldstream; the school at Hirsel Law was closed in 1933. The school has infant, primary, junior and secondary departments. It is a central school for secondary education serving Coldstream, Ladykirk, Swinton, Eccles and Leitholm. The staff numbers five men and ten women, and there are 290 pupils who mostly go in for agriculture and allied trades. Parents are both cooperative and interested especially in their children's young years.

THE CHURCHES

The old parish church for Coldstream district was at Lennel. Only a scanty ruin survives, but the churchyard, which has been extended more than once, is used for burials. In its place a church was built in Coldstream in 1716 of which only the tower now remains. The tower contains a clock which is the property of the town. The rest of the building, renovated in 1798, was taken down in 1904, and the present fine structure completed in 1908. The church possesses an ancient handbell inscribed, 'This is Lendon Handbel'. It has a set of pewter Communion vessels dated 1739, comprising two flagons, four cups and five platters. In present use is a solid silver set dated 1890 consisting of two flagons, four cups and four platters. In the church are old colours of the Coldstream Guards which were solemnly deposited there in 1921. When the parish church was transferred to Coldstream a manse was built in the Duns Road. It was replaced by the present manse in 1830 and fell into ruins which were taken down to make room for a housing site in 1927.

St Cuthbert's Church is a fine building with a very attractive tower and some good stained glass windows. It was built in 1907 at the cost of Mrs Black of Lanton. It was originally known as the West Church and housed a former United Presbyterian congregation. In 1950 a union was effected with the Rodger Memorial Church, formerly a Free Church, and the name was changed to St Cuthbert's. The future use of the Rodger Memorial Church has not been settled at the moment of writing, but it will probably be made into a hall.

Hirsel private chapel (Episcopal) was opened in the 1880s. In 1897 this iron chapel was replaced by the present beautiful stone building. It was re-erected on a site beside the Lennel road as a mission of Christ Church, Duns, with the dedication of St Mary and All Souls. St Mary was the dedication of the ancient Lennel Church. All Souls was added in memory of those who fell at Flodden, many of whom were buried in the precincts of the Convent at Coldstream.

The iron church was replaced in 1914 by a stone church of simple design ending in an apse. The interior is very beautiful and its timber roof much admired; all its furnishings are of fine quality. When the building debt had been cleared off the church was consecrated by the Bishop of Edinburgh on St Columba's Day 1933. The charge is now an Independent Mission. In 1919 the Hirsel Chapel was closed; the Earl of Home joined the congregation and became joint patron with the Bishop.

There are about 50 Roman Catholics in the neighbourhood. Mass is said in the Drill Hall twice a month except when the nuns of La Sagesse are at Lees, when Roman Catholics attend Mass in their chapel on Sundays. The Order of La Sagesse was founded in 1703 at St Laurent-sur-Sevre, Vendes, France.

The parish church has 808 members, St Cuthbert's 550 and the Episcopal Church 73 communicants. There are three Sunday schools. The parish church has 95 scholars with an attendance of 72; St Cuthbert's 55, attendance 40 and St Mary and All Souls 18, attendance 10.

CLUBS AND SOCIETIES

The membership of the various clubs and societies is as follows: Boys' Brigade, 36; Life Boys, 24; Girl Guides, 20; Youth Club, 30; Women's

Rural Institute (W.R.I.), 100; Cricket Club, 40; Football Club, 100; Tennis Club, 40; Bowling Club, 65; Golf Club, 100; Literary Society, 75. It is worth remarking on the vitality of the Literary Society which continued to hold its meetings all through the war, while similar societies in other places ceased to exist. The lectures are not confined to literary subjects; there are debates and musical evenings. The W.R.I. has a very successful dramatic section. Other activities include branches of the British Legion and Royal Air Force Association, a Burns Club, a Darts League, and a Homing Pigeon Club. There is a Masonic Hall in which two Lodges meet — a Craft Lodge, St John and Royal Arch Lodge, Hirsel 466, and the Women's Voluntary Services Branch has been re-formed.

There is good fishing for salmon and trout in the Tweed. The salmon fishing commands high rents. In 1950 Coldstream began holding a Civic Week.

CHARACTER OF THE PEOPLE

Nearly everyone is loosely attached to a church and, but for the faithful few, attendances are poor, except in the case of Roman Catholics, apart from Festivals and Communions. United Services in the parish church on the Day of Remembrance attract large congregations. Some people never enter a church at any other time. The Midnight Eucharist at the Episcopal Church on Christmas Eve is attended by large congregations including many Presbyterians. The people are law-abiding and on the whole sober. Football pools coupons go into many houses, but I have seen no evidence of excessive gambling.

BOTANY

Mrs Swinton, Recorder of The Wild Flower Society for Berwickshire, reports that the following interesting plants have been found in the parish: Goodyera repens, Galium boreale, Rumex maritimus, Impatiens glandulifera, Rubus caesius, Lathrea squamaria, Lectuca muralis, Lactuca sceriola, Epipactis latifolia, Aspidium aculatum.

ANIMAL LIFE

The writer is indebted to Major the Hon. Henry Douglas Home for the following information. The variety of its topographical features gives the parish a richness of bird life unequalled in most other districts of a similar area. The long southern frontage of Tweed, the lesser valley of the Leet, the large areas of mixed woodlands and the lake sanctuary (27 acres) at the Hirsel, all provide interesting species apart from the normal bird life of an arable and pasture countryside. During the last 30 years about 140 different species have been seen in the area. Of these 89 species have definitely nested; more species nest in the Hirsel grounds than in any equal area in Britain. The first pair of turtle doves to nest in Scotland was recorded in 1946 and the great increase of Pied Flycatchers along the old timbered banks of Leet has been most remarkable. The Lake at the Hirsel offers a wonderful sanctuary for wild fowl of all species, and rare visitors like the Great Northern Diver, Bittern and Smew have been seen from time to time. Amongst the smaller birds Hawfinches, Marsh Tits and Warblers of all sorts have increased noticeably in recent years. Two species, Kingfishers and Dippers, have decreased alarmingly in the last 15 years. Landrails have also decreased, as in Scotland generally.

Red Squirrels which were very scarce for 15 years are now becoming numerous. There has been a great increase in Roe Deer during the last ten years, as many as 17 being seen on one day in the Hirsel woods. A doe with five and a half inch horns was shot at Hirsel. Foxes are very numerous. Most of the big woods at Hirsel have Badger 'Setts'. The biggest is a huge mound of great antiquity on a steep bank of Leet in Kimcham Dene. Otters are numerous in Tweed and Leet valley. All the smaller mammals are common. Each winter some stoats with 'Arctic' coats are trapped. Bats are common and moles very numerous.

1951

COLDSTREAM

by Rev. Iain D. Penman

The present population of the town of Coldstream is 1731.

The size of the Hirsel Estate was reduced in 1951 on the death of the 13th Earl of Home by the sale of Darnchester and Castlelaw Farms to pay death duties. The present Lord Home entered a disclaimer to become Prime Minister for a time in 1963-64. He also served two periods as Secretary at the Foreign and Commonwealth Office, 1960-63 and 1970-74.

The estate continues to engage in commercial farming and forestry, but in recent years has employed an agricultural management company and the Forestry Commission to run operations on the estate.

Retained under the personal control and direction of Miss Caroline Douglas Home are the grounds and policies of the Hirsel House. These are open all year round to the public, who come in considerable numbers to see the bird population of the lake, to walk, and to view the excellent museum which is accommodated in the buildings of the Homestead. Included in these displays are exhibits from excavations carried on over a number of years which have uncovered a chapel and associated graveyard, complete with stone coffins dating from the ninth century or earlier.

More recently, encouragement has been given to the creation of a craft community. This includes a silversmith, lapidarist, leatherworker, woodturner, potter and weavers.

The mansion house at the Lees has now been demolished, while the mansion house at Lennel has become a nursing home for the elderly.

In the interests of safety Duns Road was blocked off at its junction with the High Street and a new road, Guards Road, created, cutting through what was once the glebe of the parish Church manse. The manse has since become Trafalgar House, a local authority residential home for the elderly. It now has a Day Centre attached to it.

Other noticeable physical changes include the new bridge over the Lees at the west end of the town. The fountain that once graced the Market Square has now been removed to the museum. It was removed to accommodate the visit to the town of the Coldstream Guards when they received the Freedom of the Burgh in 1968. A freestone monument to their Tercentenary in 1960 now stands in Henderson Park. This park has a magnificent view of the River Tweed and Cheviot Hills. It was created out of the former tennis court of Dr Henderson's house and is named in honour of this doctor whose family gave such long service as general practitioners to the town and surrounding district.

Since 1950 the remaining two Church of Scotland congregations have united. They now use the original Parish Church as their place of worship, and the former St Cuthbert's Church as halls. St Mary's and All Souls continues as a congregation of the Scottish Episcopal Church served by a non-stipendiary priest. There is a Roman Catholic congregation.

Since the reorganisation of local government Coldstream has ceased to have a Provost or Town Council, but has a district councillor who sits on Berwickshire District Council. The Community Council is active in local affairs and in the interests of the town.

Trends in agriculture away from stock to arable farming are particularly pronounced in the parish. The growing of soft fruit is common, as is the intensive growing of vegetables such as cauliflowers, brussels sprouts and broccoli. A conservative estimate of the decrease of labour on farms in the area is about 40 per cent.

Servicing the needs of the agricultural community continues to provide employment to a large number of Coldstream's inhabitants, although many travel further afield for work to places such as Berwick-upon-Tweed.

The engineering firm of John Rutherford and Sons Ltd. has continued to diversify into manufacturing of grain handling and other farm equipment, and farm building. Including its garage concerns in Coldstream and Cornhill, it had 130 employees in 1985. There are other agricultural services in the town too.

Already well known for its Scotch Bun under the trade name of 'Forsythia', T. Forsyth and Co. was a large-scale bakery situated in premises between the High Street and Duke Street. A considerable employer before 1954, the firm then began to produce oven-ready pastry. This business grew enormously and 'Jusrol' pastry is now a household name. Unfortunately, planning permission was refused to develop a factory in Coldstream, and a factory was built at Berwick-upon-Tweed. It has continued to employ a number of Coldstream people in its large work force.

Since 1985, when the Primary School transferred to a modernised building, the original school building has been developed as workshops.

Tourism has grown steadily in the past few years and Coldstream has a Tourist Information Office which was opened by Her Majesty Queen Elizabeth II.

In the field of housing, there has been a large expansion of public housing over the period. Public housing was built in the 1960s at Cheviot Terrace, Duke Street and Parkside. In the 1970s Hillview and Priory Hill were constructed. In addition there was the provision of sheltered housing, with some public housing, at Gowanlea. A well-planned and attractive complex, it has proved a real asset in maintaining the increasing number of elderly people in their own homes.

Private housing development has taken place at Lennel Mount, Woodlands Park and Lees Mill Drive. There has also been construction of flats by housing associations at Market Square and in Nursery Lane.

People now prefer to live in public or private housing in the town rather than in tied accommodation on farms. There is less pressure for farm staffs to live on farms with a decrease in stock and the increase in personal means of transport. Coldstream is also a popular place for retirement.

Absent from the 1951 Account is any mention of the Cottage Hospital which celebrated its centenary in 1989. This hospital has performed a singular service to the population of the area. The hospital, for many years, was the place where most children in the area were born. The Maternity Unit closed in 1988 when the Borders General Hospital opened. In 1976 a modern Health Centre was opened alongside the hospital as the base for a multi-disciplinary medical team, headed by three General Practitioners.

In 1951 Coldstream boasted a Junior Secondary School with 287 pupils. In 1955 a new Secondary Department was constructed. It was opened in 1957 and continued until 1968. Thereafter only the primary school remained; the roll in 1968 was 208. In 1985 the building was totally refurbished. The roll was then 153, with 40 in the Nursery and the trend upwards. The Hall and Community room are now available to a large number of outside organisations when not required for educational purposes.

Coldstream continues to support an unusually large and varied range of voluntary activities and support for charitable purposes.

1990

THE PARISH OF DUNS

by R. G. Johnston, O.B.E., J.P.,
formerly County Clerk of Berwickshire

NAME AND ORIGIN

The Parish, apparently at its formation, adopted the name of its only Town — Duns — which derives its designation from its situation on Duns Law, originally on its north-west and west slopes, now on its south slopes. The Celtic word descriptive of a hill or fort is Dun. The pure French for a sandhill — and the Law is composed largely of gravel and sand — is Dune. If the origin of the Town be of the Norman period the second alternative is not unlikely (c.f. Dunes, Dunekirk — Dunkirk). A Norman presence, at any rate, would seem to be indisputable as pillars bearing traces of undoubted Norman workmanship were found embedded in the masonry of the Parish Church taken down in 1790, to be rebuilt in 1791, a little to the north of its immediate predecessor's site.

BOUNDARIES

No change has taken place in the Parish Boundaries since the date of the last Statistical Account (1834). These are: on north-east and east by Bunkle and Preston Parish; on the south-east by Edrom Parish; on the south and west by Langton Parish; on the north-west by Longformacus Parish and on the north by Abbey St Bathans Parish.

The extreme length of the parish is about six miles from south-east to north-west; its mean breadth about three and a half miles, and its extent 11,404 acres of which 275 acres are within the Town boundaries. Its configuration is so irregular that a more definite description than the foregoing is not practicable, beyond the statement that towards its northern and southern extremities its breadth is between three and four miles, and in the middle somewhat less than five miles.

POPULATION

In 1789 the Parish Population was 3,324, of which 1,000 were outwith the Town, created a Burgh of Barony by James IV by Charter in favour of the then Superior of the Town, George Home of Ayton and his son John, dated 23rd February 1490.

The Population of the parish (P) since 1801 including the Burgh, and the Burgh (B) since 1851 included in the parish figures and also separately shown are as follows: 1801, P.3613; 1811, P.3082; 1821, P.3773; 1831, P.3469; 1841, P.3162; 1851, P.3407, B.2567; 1861, P.3505, B.2556; 1871, P.3602, B.2618; 1881, P.3353, B.2437; 1891, P.3137, B.2198; 1901, P.3199, B.2206; 1911, P.3042, B.2069; 1921, P.2818, B.1868; 1931, P.2677, B.1768; 1951, P.2877, B.2028.

Of the 1931 population of the parish 1248 were males and 1429 females, and of the 1951 parish figures, 1320 were males and 1557 females.

The inhabited houses in 1951 were 863, of which 629 were within the Burgh.

It may be noted as indicating the incidence and fatal nature of smallpox in earlier times that in 1733, 130 children died of that disease, in the parish, within the space of three months.

PHYSICAL CHANGES

Landward. Probably the greatest change, since the last Statistical Account (1834), with the greatest resulting convenience to the parishioners, was the construction, following on the passing of the Berwickshire Railway Act 1862, of a railway single track line from the East Coast Main Line at Reston via the parishes of Chirnside and Edrom, and the southern boundary of this parish to a terminus immediately adjacent to the Duns-Coldstream Highway (road A6112) and about half a mile south of the Town's Market Square. The line was later extended via Marchmont, Greenlaw, Gordon and Earlston to St Boswells.

As a result of the Border floods in August 1948, when six and a half inches of rain fell in Duns Parish, in particular, in 24 hours, bridges carrying railway lines between Duns and Marchmont, Grantshouse and Reston collapsed, and a lake of large dimensions was formed immediately adjacent to the main line between Reston and Ayton; services on the whole branch line ceased. Passenger and goods service were resumed between Reston and Duns in May 1950, but passenger service between these points was discontinued definitely on 8th September 1951, on the stated ground that this department of the service was being run at a loss.

Another great boon was the substitution, commencing shortly after the termination of the First World War, of bitumen-binding for water-binding of the highways.

Bridgend Farm, the house and other buildings of which and a portion of its land are within the Burgh, ceased to be a separate holding some 20 years ago, the land being allocated to Rulesmains and Peelrig Farms, and to Duns Town Council for housing purposes. The farm house and other buildings have ceased to be used for purely agricultural purposes.

The mineral spring known as Duns Spa Well, discovered in 1747 and situated between Nisbet Rhodes and the adjoining stream, was misdiverted during intended improvement of site operations in 1840 and trace of it lost. The structure then erected to disperse its waters has disappeared during the present century, probably for building purposes of some nature.

A new burial ground to serve the whole parish, was laid out by the Parochial Board (succeeded in time by the Parish Council and County Council) on the Preston-Dunbar Road, immediately outwith the Burgh Boundaries, in 1858. Since extended north-eastwards, it is now administered by a Joint Committee composed of representatives of the County Council and the Town Council. The County Council have recently erected 16 houses under the Housing Acts at Bridgend, Duns and two for road workmen a short distance west of Clockmill.

The tile works which functioned for about a century on the high ground rising from the south side of the 'Bogs', south of Rulesmains Farm, ceased operations about the middle of the last century. Traces of the foundations of the buildings relating to the works are still evident.

BURGH

Public Park. The area between the part of the Duns-Coldstream Road (A6112) known in modern times as the Station Road, and the eastmost of the Earl's Meadows, extending to some 12 acres, forming part of the extensive bog bounding and protecting the Town in byegone days on the east and south, was purchased and presented to the Town by the late Mr Smith of Whitchester in 1891 and thereafter fenced on the Station Road side with massive railings and gateway, and laid off, by the late Sir James Miller of Manderston.

Tollhouse. This building, erected in 1846 at the junction of Bridgend and Station Roads, for the purpose of collecting Tolls or dues for the upkeep of the highways from passing vehicles, was taken down in the penultimate decade of last century.

The Barn-End. This bottle-nosed building comprising dwelling-house and shop (licensed grocer), and forming the western extremity of the line of buildings situated between North and South Streets, which before these buildings were erected formed a single highway (the High (HIE) Street), and the two adjoining buildings on the north-east, were bought by the County Council and demolished as a road improvement.

The 'Barn' was in all probability used by the Town Administration as a store for the meal which was purchased by them in the 17th and 18th centuries, as sustenance for the poor. The greater part of the sites are laid out by the Town Council, as an ornamental garden plot, by arrangement with the County Council.

225 houses have been erected under the Housing Acts by Duns Town Council at Bridgend, Brierybaulk, Earlsmeadow, Easter Street and Tannage Brae.

New Road. A New Road bearing this name was constructed at the south end of Newtown Street, connecting the latter with Langtongate, about the middle of last century.

Churches. The Burgher, sometimes known as the Burgher Meetin, alias the West Kirk, situated at the head or west end of Gourlays Wynd (formerly known as Riding School Wynd) was closed in 1895 and now forms two dwelling-houses; and the Anti-Burgher, latterly known as the East Kirk, has been converted into a cinema.

The Church erected in the Station Road at the time of the Disruption in 1843, known as 'The Boston' in memory of Thomas Boston, the celebrated Scottish Divine born in Duns, has (1953) been closed for public worship, its congregation uniting with that of the Parish Church. The Relief, otherwise known as the South Church, is still active. A Scottish Episcopal Church was erected in Teindhillgreen in 1854. A Roman Catholic Church was erected in Bridgend in 1882.

SCHOOLS

A primary school for the parish was erected in the Langtongate of Duns in 1881 at a cost of £5,760. Pupils of suitable age from the margins of adjoining parishes are now also accommodated therein: the pupils number 357 and teachers 11. A secondary school, which now receives pupils from the county generally and is now known as Berwickshire High School, was erected in Newtown Street, in the last decade of the last century and enlarged in the first decade of the present century. The pupils attending number 522 and teachers 29. A new school building of that standard is planned to be erected adjoining the west end of the Burgh in the 'Sawmill Park', immediately to the south-west of the south approach to Duns Castle. There is also a one-teacher primary school at Millburn with 10 pupils.

OBJECTS OF INTEREST

Edin's Hall (Broch). This type of building, which is only found in Scotland, is the workmanship of some of the early visitants from other countries, perhaps Scandinavians or Saxons.

'In general form the construction of this hill fort is oval, lying with its main axis nearly north and south, measuring some 500 feet by 380 feet overall and some 360 feet by 280 feet in the interior.' (Ancient Monuments Report).

It is situated on the northern slope of Cockburn Law, distant from the Whiteadder about 200 yards westwards.

LANDWARD

Duns Castle. The Lands of Duns with their Tower or Castle were granted by Robert Bruce to his nephew Randolph, Earl of Moray, who rebuilt that structure in 1320. Part of that erection is incorporated with the present castle.

Duns Law (714 feet above sea level). In 1639 and 1640 Covenanting Armies under General Leslie, afterwards the first Earl of Leven, were encamped on the Law; a block of old red sandstone on which, according to tradition, the Army's Standard was hoisted in 1639, still exists in its original position, it is believed. There are also distinct traces of entrenchments.

As already mentioned it was on the north-west and west slopes of the Law that the town originally stood and in that position it was burnt and pillaged by English troops in 1544, 1545 and 1558. These slopes are known as the Bruntons (corruption of burnt town).

BURGH

The house in which Thomas Boston was born — 17th March 1676 — is situated at 11 and 13 Newtown Street.

Cockburn's Town House. This building in a well preserved state, forming 43 and 45 Market Square, was the Town House of Cockburn of Langton who was for a long period prior to 1698 Superior of the Burgh.

Tolbooth Cells. These are under the Town Hall. The Commissioners of Supply for the County consented to the erection of the Town Hall in 1816-17 on condition that the Feuars who were paying for its erection provided cellars as a 'Tolbooth for malifactors'.

Mercat Cross. The Cross erected by Robert Hay of Drummelzier and Duns in 1792, a short distance west of the site of the Town Hall, was taken down in 1816. It was re-erected in 1897 (Queen Victoria's diamond Jubilee) in the Public Park.

INDUSTRIES

Agriculture is still the staple industry of the parish. Excluding those which are only partly in the parish, and land in grass let on a seasonal basis, it has 27 farms, 23 with rentals ranging from £125 to £428, and three with rentals from £25 10s. to £82, all varying in rental according generally to type and size. Seven are owner-occupied.

The acreages etc. of these farms are furnished in an appendix hereto.

There are no government-owned small holdings in the parish.

Farm produce has, meantime, minimum prices guaranteed by the government and subsidies or grants are given by the government for various types of farm stock and purposes connected with a farm.

The remuneration of the farm workers is fixed by the Scottish Agricultural Wages Board acting under statutory powers. Male whole-time workers, of 20 years or over, employed by the week or for longer period, are paid a minimum weekly wage of £5.16s. and women of 21 years or over employed on like duration, a minimum weekly wage of £4 8s. (1953).

The week is five and a half days, with hours varying according to season, from 42 to 48 (1953).

The internal combustion engine has revolutionised the operative methods of cultivation. Practically all of the implements are drawn by tractor. In the last few years the combine-harvester which thrashes and bags the grain and bales the straw has made its appearance. This mechanisation of farm work has greatly reduced the number of regularly employed farm workers. Casual workers, largely composed of displaced men from the continent, and Irishmen, are considerably employed. It remains to be seen whether this re-arrangement of cultivation operations benefits, or otherwise, the cleanliness and fertility of the soil.

Most of the farm cottages have been fully modernised, including the installation of electricity where the 'Grid' is available.

The yearly hiring market which was held for at least a century on the first Tuesday in March, when yearly contracts were entered into for a year from the following Whitsunday between farmers and farm workers, ceased about the beginning of the First World War.

The weekly corn-market, for the purposes of which the Corn Exchange (now a garage) was erected in Duns in 1865, ceased about the third last decade in the last century, Berwick's Saturday market being substituted.

Blanket manufacture is carried out on a large scale at Cumledge.

A branch of a Hawick Knitwear Company operates in the Burgh and is presently housed in the Town Hall.

Cammo Foundry at Clockmill carries on an extensive trade in the supply and repair of agricultural implements.

There are two quarries being operated in the parish, both for road making or repair purposes at Borthwick — on Duns Castle Estate and near Cockburn Farm, in Abbey St Bathans Estate, the former tenanted by the County Council and the latter privately.

Gas is supplied to the Burgh from the works of the Scottish Gas Company adjoining Duns Railway Station.

There are motor-engineering works and contractors for various types of work, all on a moderate scale, in the burgh.

There is only one master tailor and no maker, only repairers of boots and shoes, in the town.

The town has a full quota of vendors of merchandise for everyday requirements.

LANDOWNERS

The principal owners are Colonel G. H. Hay of Duns Castle and Manderston Estates Company.

Plate 18. A view of Duns from Bridgend, 1950s.

Plate 19. Cockburn Law from the Duns–Grantshouse road, with the farm of Hoardweel in the foreground.

SOCIAL LIFE

Till the present century was underway the only holiday generally was New Year's Day in the Landward Parish. The Burgh also held holiday at that time, occasionally extended to several days, but the last Wednesday in June was also a holiday in the Burgh. Now a fortnight's holiday with pay is general throughout the country.

The motor car has enabled social life to be extended both for visiting and for recreations such as football, cricket, badminton and golf — of late years carpet bowling and country dancing have been revived.

The Burgh instituted in 1949 a Town Festival Week commencing on the first Sunday in July, the leading personages being a Reiver and his Lass, each with two supporters elected by the suffrages of the town's people; and a Wynsome Mayde, a pupil of Duns Primary School, chosen by her fellow pupils. The appointments subsist for one year.

During the week the Duns Common is visited by the Reiver, his Lass and supporters and followers usually numbering 60-70, and a sod cut and brought to the town.

The Mayde is crowned as Queen during the Week with full ceremonial in the Public Park, unless weather forbids.

Buses (Scottish Motor Transport) give a moderate service to Edinburgh and various parts of the Borders.

Organisations on local lines include: Duns History Society; Duns Rural Institute; Duns Church Woman's Guild; Duns Toc H.; Duns Church Youth Clubs; Dramatic Societies; Women's Voluntary Service; Boy Scouts and Cubs; Girl Guides and Brownies; Air Training Corps; Army Cadet Force; British Legion; Freemasons; Curling Club; Ornithological Society; Beekeepers Association; Horticultural Society; The Working Men's Institute erected and organised by public subscription in 1877.

LITERATURE — BIBLIOGRAPHY

A Public Library, established in 1768, has existed in some form since then. Public Library functions, in Scotland at any rate, are now the responsibility of Education Authorities. The County Central Library, established as such in 1920, is in Duns. At present it has a stock of 31,000 books, housed in a new building erected in 1939 at 49 Newtown Street.

Included in the stock are the following books relative to the parish:

1. Baron-Baillie Court of Duns Minute Book 1732-1793.
2. Duns Heritor's Sederunt Book 1725-1785. (Heritors' Records from 1872 are preserved in H.M. General Register House, Edinburgh.)
3. Duns Guilds: Cordiners; Hammermen; Skinners and Glovers; Taylors and Weavers' Records — 1673.

4. Duns and its environs (Duns Dings A') — R. G. Johnston.
5. Hays of Duns Castle — F. S. Hay.

There is a definite movement toward developing the County Library not only for lending books but also for reference and information purposes, and as a repository for local historical documents.

HABITS OF THE PEOPLE

The most conspicuous, and not the least impressive, change throughout the nation generally, and to which this parish is no exception, is in the decline in Church attendance. It is abundantly clear that the House of God has no longer an attraction for a large proportion of the population of the nation. The root causes do not readily come to the surface.

A regrettable general change, and one which is evident in this parish also, is the steadily diminishing good-neighbourliness, possibly due in a measure to the gradual provision of state aid in its various aspects. Can it be that the cessation to a large extent of the old and widespread Scottish custom of the conveyance of New Year's Greetings to one's neighbours and intimates by 'First Footing' is wrapped up in this change?

A further conspicuous alteration of habits has been the apparent urge of people generally to move frequently around by some form of conveyance or other, without any really specific purpose other than the seeking of change, in a larger measure as an expression of indefinable discontent.

Walking as a pastime has practically become a lost art, except for a very limited few and most of these on few occasions.

HISTORICAL INCIDENTS

There is a tradition which illustrates the scarcity of wheat in Berwickshire in early days — e.g. during the reign of King Alexander I (1107-1124), and its existence in Duns. It is said that Alexander, who had no relish for the unleavened bread of his subjects, during a peregrination through the Merse was assailed by the qualms of hunger, which he had no means of satisfying to his taste, till the Royal Party reached the Town of Duns. A loaf of white bread being procured there, the hungry monarch's appetite was at length appeased with its appropriate aliment.

Duns Park — The ground south and west of the Castle was the assembly place of the Scottish Army in 1318, before the assault on Berwick under Randolph and Lord James Douglas. The King (Robert Bruce) was probably present at Duns, although not at the actual assault, as a charter under the Great Seal, in favour of Alexander, the Seneschal, undated, narrated that the lands conveyed therein, viz. Kynbrigham (Kimmerghame), were resigned into the King's hands, in presence of his magnates at the Park of Duns.

Barbour, in his poem, tells how Bruce laid his plans for the assault:

'At ewyn thow sall enbuschit be
In Dwns Park; bot be priue,
And I sall ger the erle Thomas,
And the lord alsua of Douglas
Athir with a sowme of men,
Be thar to do as thow sall ken.
The marchell (Keith) but mar delay
Tuk leve, and held furth on his way;
And held his spek priue and still,
Quhill the day that wes set him till,
Than of the best of Lothiane
He hym till his tryst has tayne,
For schyrreff tharoff than wes he.
To Duns park, with his menye,
He come at evyn priuely.
And syne with a gud cumpany
Sone eftyr come the erle Thomas
That was met with the Lord Dowglas
A rycht fayr cumpany thai war
Quhen thai war met to giddyr that.'

1315, circa June 24: Rauf le fiz William and Simon, warde to the King, inform him that the news from Cumberland and Northumberland is that Sir Robert de Bruys is in the Park of Duns, etc.

In 1316 the Earl of Moray (Randolph) granted 'at the Park of Duns,' in the King's presence, a charter to the Monks of Newbottle (Newbattle) of an annuity of 2 merks payable from the lands of Kingside (near Priestlaw).

In 1333 another Scottish army assembled in Duns Park, under Sir Archibald Douglas, preparatory to a movement for the relief of Berwick, then besieged by the English. The army marched from Duns on the morning of 20th July to the attack, which took place at Halidon Hill, where the main body of the English army was assembled. The result was disastrous to the Scottish army. In that morning Berwick was a Scottish possession. In the afternoon it was an English possession, and has so remained since.

In 1377 Duns Park was the scene of the following: it would seem that in August 1376 one of the yeomen of the Earl of Dunbar had gone for some reason or another to Roxburgh (St James's) Fair, and was there killed by some Englishmen. The following year the Earl and his brother with their followers suddenly appeared at the Fair, 'killed many Englishmen and set fire to the toun'. The Earl of Northumberland, notwithstanding the truce then existing between England and Scotland, entered the Merse and, after despoiling the lands of Lord Dunbar, encamped 'at Dunes-woode'.

Seemingly Percy's men met with little opposition in their march through the Merse, and when they reached Duns they relaxed their vigilance. The Merse men and hill men, who had been watching from neighbouring heights, saw that the Englishmen were off their guard, and in particular that the arrangements for securing the cavalry horses during the night were carelessly near to the camping ground of the men.

The English forces were routed by a strategem, described by Redpath in his 'Border History' as follows: 'His (Lord Percy's) further progress was stopped by a contrivance of the shepherds and peasants in the neighbourhood, who bethought themselves of employing in the defence of their country, a very simple sort of machine which they commonly made use of to frighten away from their corn the deer and wild cattle which then abounded in the hills of Lammermuir. These were a kind of rattle, made of dried skins distended round ribs of wood that were bended into a semi-circular form and fixed at the end of long poles. The bags being furnished with a few hard pebbles and vigorously shaken by a rapid motion given to the poles, made a hideous noise; and an unusual number of them being employed on the tops of the adjacent hills, the horses of the English took fright and, breaking away from their keepers, ran wildly up and down the neighbouring field, where they became a prey to the people of the country. The army also awakened with the strange noise, and finding themselves deprived not only of their war horses, but of many of their beasts of burden, retired on foot towards the Tweed in precipitation and disorder, having left their baggage behind them.'

It is not definitely recorded that any actual fighting took place in Duns Park, but the local men could hardly be expected to miss such an opportunity; moreover, before the Englishmen could escape they had the morass — close to the foot of the park — to cross. Tradition, however — passing from father to son down to the end of the last century — has it that a bloody battle was fought at what is now the west end of the town, when the little burn which flows from just south of the primary school to its junction with Langton Burn 'ran with bluid "for three days", hence the name Bluidy Burn,' which it retains to this day. It is not improbable that the town's motto 'Duns dings a',' may take its origin from the incident.

In June 1497 a skirmish took place at Duns, in which a marauding party of Englishmen seems to have been defeated by the Homes.

In the accounts of the Lord High Treasurer, it is recorded that on 8th June, 'the maister of Home's man and Stevin Nesbitt, Lang Patrich Home's man,' each received 42 shillings for bringing tidings to the King of the Battle of Duns, the reward being an indication, in its amount, of the issue of the affair being in favour of the Scots.

Chevalier de Beauté. During the infancy of James V and the regency of the Duke of Albany, the Earl of Home, who held the post of warden of the Eastern Marches and who apparently did not see eye to eye with Albany, was decoyed along with his brother William to attend a Parliament in Edinburgh, where they were seized, beheaded, their goods confiscated and their heads affixed to public places.

In the place of the Earl, Albany appointed as warden a French knight named De La Bastie, who for his handsome person was called 'Beauté', with Dunbar Castle for his residence.

This merciless treatment of the Homes naturally gave bitter offence to the Home family, and in particular to the Homes of Wedderburn, who all were nearly related to the slain. David Hume, the head of the Wedderburn clan, burning with desire for revenge, sought eagerly for an opportunity to obtain it. With his brother-in-law, William Cockburn, Wedderburn laid siege to Langton Castle in pursuit of a claim of Cockburn's. De la Bastie, who was holding a Court at Kelso, summoned Wedderburn to meet him the following day on the road between Kelso and Duns, which the latter agreed to do on condition that he should be allowed full liberty of returning when he thought proper. They met about two miles from Kelso, and for some time conversed amicably enough, until they reached 'the heath to the north of Fogo' somewhere near what is now the site of Gavinton, when a fierce altercation took place.

The Warden, realising that there was trouble brewing, took flight on his horse — a very swift one — which had belonged to the slain Earl, but 'being overburdened with trapping of great weight and unaccustomed to "French furniture", he was unable to proceed at full speed'. The Warden reached the ford called 'Cornifurd' (now Pouterlynie) half way between Langton and Duns, before Wedderburn's followers, who were besieging Langton Castle and had heard the tumult, could arrive to prevent his passage. He then continued his course through the middle of Duns (i.e., Langton Gate — Market Square — Easter Street) to the Stoney Moor, with Wedderburn and his followers in full pursuit, while one Dickson (or as others call him, Trotter), one of Wedderburn's pages, who had been left at home (probably with a good idea of what was likely to happen), hearing the tumult of the chase leapt on one of his master's horses, galloped from Wedderburn Castle across country, and overtook the Warden at the Stoney Moor. He kept attacking the Warden, who was no doubt endeavouring to cross the Whiteadder at the Broomhouse Ford on his flight to his residence at Dunbar, and in consequence of that distraction got off the firm into soft ground, where his horse fell. The Warden, starting to his feet, defended himself strenuously until John of Manderston and Patrick Home, David's brothers, came up and slew him. His head was cut off, publicly exposed on Duns Mercat Cross for some time, and thereafter exposed at Wedderburn Castle. The body was buried where the slaughter took place on 20th September 1517.

The hair of De la Bastie was preserved in a 'kist' at Wedderburn

Castle until 1810, when it was thrown into the fire by Miss Jean Home.

Tradition has it De la Bastie had been warned by an old seer, sometime prior to the event:

If eer ye cross the Cornie Syke
The Corbies will get yir banes to pyke.

An interesting account, in manuscript, of the life of Seigneur de la Bastie, called by his countrymen of France the 'White Knight', came into the hands of the writer a number of years ago and can be seen in the County Library, Duns.

In 1556 a meeting of Commissioners of both kingdoms was held in the town with the alleged purpose of settling disputes, but apparently the meeting was fruitless as two years later the English burned the town.

On 14th November 1566 Mary Queen of Scots passed through the town on her way from Langton, where she had spent the night, to Wedderburn, with a great retinue.

1613. John Weemes, A.M., Minister. In his time there lived near to the town of Duns a poor woman, generally believed to be possessed by an evil spirit. The Earl (afterwards Duke) of Lauderdale, when a prisoner in Windsor Castle in 1659, sent an account of her to Mr Richard Baxter who has published it in his 'Certainty of the World of Spirits'. The Earl, then a boy at school, used to hear conversations about the possessed woman between his father and the Minister of Duns, who was fully convinced of the fact of the possession. This clergyman and some other clergymen proposed to the Privy Council a fast for her benefit; but it was not allowed by the bishops. 'I will not,' said the Earl, 'trouble you with many circumstances; one only I shall tell you, which I think will evince a real possession. The report being spread in the country, a knight of the name of Forbes, who lived in the North of Scotland, being come to Edinburgh, meeting there with a minister of the north, and both of them desirous to see the woman, the northern minister invited the knight to my father's house (which was within ten or twelve miles of the woman) whether they came, and next morning went to see the woman. They found her a poor ignorant creature and seeing nothing extraordinary, the minister says in Latin to the knight: 'Nondum audivimus spiritum loquentum!' Presently a voice comes out of the woman's mouth: 'Audis loquentem, audis loquentem'. This put the minister into some amazement (which I think made him not mind his own Latin); he took off his hat and said: 'Misereatur Deus peccatoris'. The voice presently out of the woman's mouth said: 'Dic peccatricis, dic peccatricis'; whereupon both of them came out of the house fully satisfied, took horse immediately and returned to my father's house at Thirlestane Castle, in Lauderdale, where they related this passage. This I do exactly remember. Many more particulars might be got in that part of the country; but this Latin criticism, in a most illiterate ignorant woman, where there was no pretence to dispossessing, is enough, I think.' — Chambers' Dom. Annals. Vol. ii., pp. 43-4.

The story is 'verified' by a reference to the Privy Council Record, under 13th July 1630, containing an order for bringing before them Margaret Lumsdaine, 'the possessed woman in Duns,' together with her brother and father-in-law, that order might be taken concerning them 'as the importance and nature of such a great cause requires'.

Cromwell's Occupation — In 1650, after the Battle of Dunbar, Cromwell placed a garrison in Duns. The duration of stay does not seem to be recorded.

In 1715 — Thursday, 20th October — General Mackintosh halted in the town at the head of 1,500 Highlanders and proclaimed at the Mercat Cross the 'Old Pretender' as James III of England and VIII of Scotland.

In 1826 the town played a considerable part in an episode, which had its starting point at Edrom Churchyard, although its inspiration and incentive were created in Edinburgh. About the third decade of last century there was in Edinburgh a celebrated anatomist, Dr Knox, who apparently had difficulty in finding for his anatomy classrooms a sufficient number of corpses, and thus a keen, or what today would be called a 'black' market arose therefrom. Men, mostly from Edinburgh, but obviously in league with local gravediggers, made visits to various country churchyards, removed to Edinburgh corpses which had been a little time previously interred, and disposed of them for dissection purposes; Edrom in that year had a visit. Mr Howden, farmer of Whitelaw, and Mr Mark Cossar, a Duns inn-keeper, were returning in a gig from Gifford Fair, in the late autumn, and in the early morning, having no doubt had 'the last one for the road' at Longformacus, where there was then an Inn. As they were arriving at the top of the Hardens Hill, they met a conveyance, with three passengers in the front seat. Something in the attitude of the centre figure attracted their attention as the vehicles met, and suspicion, encouraged possibly by 'bauld John Barleycorn,' prompted them to turn their horse and follow the trio in their conveyance. The driver of the latter at once laid whip to his horse. The Berwickshire men being more determined than ever, did likewise and soon overhauled their quarry. Seeing that they were outpaced, two of the occupants sprang out and fled across the moors, the remaining occupant of the now halted and obviously undirected vehicle, being sagging, helpless and inert. Howden and Cossar investigated the position and found they had a dead man on their hands. They brought the trap with the corpse in it to Duns. It was in due course identified as that of a man named Peter McGall, buried a day or two earlier at Edrom, where the Beadle-cum-Gravedigger had been for some time suspected of being in league with the 'resurrectionists'.

Indignation in the town was intense, more particularly as there had been, shortly before this occurrence, an obvious attempt at a 'resurrection' in the Duns Churchyard. The horse was claimed by a Kelso innkeeper, who was able to prove that he had hired it out in the ordinary course of business. The gig was put into the coach house now forming the subjects belonging to, and used as a store by the Town Council, adjoining No. 6 Murray Street, in the yard forming the back entrance to Murray Place, etc. The gig remained there till the following March, when a rumour spread that it had been claimed by, and would be handed over to, the owner. The town rose in anger. The coach house door was smashed by a sturdy blacksmith, the gig hauled out, pulled round the town and brought to the Market Place. The Riot Act was read by the Sheriff, who had been hastily summoned from his house, but the crowd paid no attention, broke the gig to pieces, and speedily burned them.

The coffin in which McGall had been buried was found under a culvert, practically always dry, about a mile from Edrom, on the Duns road via Buxley in this parish. Beneath the culvert were found, and remained at any rate till the beginning of the present century, iron hooks, on which it is believed previously resurrected subjects had been duly hung to await removal. The bridge is still known as 'McGall's Brig'.

A lady then living in Allanton by name of Mary Manuel had the experience — probably unique — of dressing McGall before interment and of re-dressing him before re-interment. A grandson of his, who lived in Duns, died recently there.

NATURAL HISTORY

The principal sanctuary for wild-life in the parish is to be found in the extensive policies and surrounding woodlands of Duns Castle which in particular shelter a heronry.

Among the rare non-aquatic birds, noted in the parish, most of which were observed and doubtless all of which are to be found in the Duns Castle domain, may be included: The crossbill, fly catchers (pied and spotted), dove (stock), goldfinch, hawfinch, jay, landrail, thrush (missell), tit (marsh), raven, redpoll (lesser), siskin, woodpecker (great spotted and green).

Notes. 1. The goldfinch was so numerous when Duns Castle was being rebuilt in 1821, that some men about Duns made their living by catching them between harvest and spring with bird lime and selling them as cage-birds (Muirhead). It was not recorded in the parish for at least two decades prior to the mid-nineties of last century, when it was found nesting at Duns Castle Gardens.

2. The great spotted woodpecker was first noted in the County in the 1793 Statistical Account (vol. VIII p. 74) for Ladykirk Parish. It was noted first in this parish in the summer of 1894 nesting in the Castle woods, where it has nested regularly since. A male-bird was seen on two occasions in the writer's garden, and also in other gardens, all adjoining Duns Public Park, in 1951.

The green variety has been noted in the Castle woods, for several summers past (1953).

3. The corn-crake, which up to the early part of the present century was regularly and widely heard, in spring and summer, has apparently abandoned its visits to this parish, in common with a great part of the South of Scotland.

Duns Castle lake has regularly breeding and evident there, the mute swan, mallard duck, coot and water-hen. Among its occasional visitants noted, may be included teal and tufted duck, widgeon, shoveller, pochard, pintail, golden eye, gadwall, whooper swan, grebe, Canada goose.

Skeins of geese (pink-foot) are frequently seen and heard (one being overhead at the moment of writing) moving regularly in the autumn and winter between their feeding grounds and Hule moss, a considerable extent of water on the Greenlaw Moor.

Roe deer appeared from an unknown quarter in Duns Castle Woods, some 30 years ago, and have extended to the uplands of this and adjoining parishes in numbers requiring periodic reduction by organised shoots.

Red squirrel, once seen frequently, are rare.

The grey squirrel, fortunately, in view of its particular destructiveness, has not found its way to the parish, nor, so far as recorded, the County.

Badgers are in evidence.

1953

Agricultural Statistics as at 4th June 1953 (supplied by the Department of Agriculture for Scotland)

Crops (acres)	
Wheat	136
Barley	890
Oats	797
Potatoes	160
Turnips and Swedes	471
Sugar Beet	36
Rape	92
Other Crops	172
Ryegrass and Other Rotation Grasses and Clover for Mowing	478
Ryegrass and Other Rotation Grasses and Clover not for Mowing	1264
Total Arable Acreage	4,496

Permanent Grass for Mowing (Hay)	61
Permanent Grass not for Mowing	1828
Total Acreage, Crops and Grass	6385
Rough Grazings (not included above)	2848

Livestock (numbers)

Horses	81
Cows in milk and cows and heifers in-calf — Dairy	143
Other Dairy Cattle	56
Cows in milk and cows and heifers in-calf — Beef	408
Other Beef Cattle	861
Sheep and Lambs	12,909
Pigs	1274
Poultry	4968

Labour (numbers)

Regular Workers	102
Casual Workers	23

Classification of Holdings

Acreage (Crops and Grass)	*No.*
1+ to 5	9
5+ to 15	13
15+ to 30	5
30+ to 50	4
50+ to 75	1
75+ to 100	3
100+ to 150	5
150+ to 300	12
Over 300	5
Total	57
No. rented	46

REFERENCES

In addition to the references given above, various aspects of the history of the town and parish are dealt with in the relevant volumes of the Berwickshire Naturalists Club and the Proceedings of the Society of Antiquaries of Scotland. The Royal Commission on Ancient and Historical Monuments and Constructions of Scotland (Sixth Report, 1915) pp. 60-69 provides a list and description of ancient monuments and constructions in the parish. The manuscripts of Robert Mordaunt Hay of Duns Castle were reported on by the Historical Manuscripts Commission in 1909 (Report on Manuscripts in Various Collections, vol. V, pp. 1-71).

The old parochial registers in the custody of the Registrar General, New Register House, Edinburgh, include baptisms from 1615 and marriages and deaths from 1797 and 1798 respectively. Church records in the General Assembly's Library consist of Kirk Session Minutes of the Duns East U.F. Church, 1882-1923, United Presbyterian Church Synodical Record, 1878-1900 and Free Church Records of the Presbytery of Duns and Chirnside, 1843-1900. Agricultural returns relating to acreage, livestock and produce, 1866-1911, are preserved in H.M. General Register House, Edinburgh.

1953

THE PARISH OF DUNS

by Rev. Hugh McKay

CHURCHES

A prominent citizen of Duns, now deceased, once lamented that 'there used to be five Presbyterian churches in Duns and now there's only one'. This is no reproach to the Kirk; that there were once congregations of the Parish, Free, Burgher, Anti-Burgher and Relief persuasions sprang solely from the Scots' predilection for identifying differences and erecting them into principles. Never was there any pastoral justification for the existence of five Reformed congregations in a community of 3000 people, burgh and landward.

The ending of this fragmentation was achieved in 1976, with the long-foreseen re-union of the charges of Duns Old and Boston and Duns South as Duns Parish Church. The Old Kirk (extensively renovated in the early 1970s) became the sole place of worship and the former South Church building was sold. It now (1985) houses an Antique dealer's business.

The former Boston Church in Station Road — erected originally and against the wishes of the Kirk Session, as a 'Chapel of Ease' for the parish Church, but astutely retained in possession by its promoters who, in 1843, took it with them on adhering to the cause of the Disruption — became for a time after 1953 a public hall, and later a textile factory. It was demolished in 1985 to make way for sheltered housing.

The Parish Church was gutted by fire in 1879, amongst the losses being that of the organ — the first to be installed in a Church of Scotland building with consent of the General Assembly. It was about the same period, in 1864, that the present Manse was built, some 50 yards east of that mentioned in the 1834 Account. The Glebe was compulsorily acquired in the 1970s by the Town Council for housing.

A section of the churchyard bordering Currie Street was removed in widening the latter as part of a new road connecting Bridgend with Newtown Street to bypass the town centre.

Christ Church (Scottish Episcopal) in Tiendhillgreen and Our Lady Immaculate and St Margaret (Roman Catholic) in Bridgend continue as full incumbencies. The Faith Mission maintain a hall in South Street.

PUBLIC BUILDINGS

The demolition in 1966 of the Town Hall was an occasion of much controversy, the stour of which has not wholly subsided nearly 20 years later. Other buildings which have disappeared in recent years include the Public Library of 1874, removed c. 1968 to make way for new Police Station premises; the Corn Exchange, now the Swan Garage; the Auction Mart, now Aitchison's Bridgend Garage; Eggler's Castle behind the north side of Market Square; and Balmoral Buildings, taken down to open the east end of Newtown Street for the bypass.

On the positive side can be placed the building of the new Berwickshire High School and the extensions to Duns Primary School (the latter, however, not unconnected with reductions in the establishment of village schools in the landward area), and the erection of a new hospital for general and for geriatric patients at the Knoll with day-care facilities and a doctors' surgery.

TRANSPORT

Private transport by car is no luxury in the area, the closure of the railway after the flood of 1948 not being seriously compensated for by other public facilities.

INDUSTRY

A number of modest light industries are located at the 'Industrial Estate' to the south of the town, between the former railway station (now an agricultural machinery depot) and Cheeklaw Farm. Food-processing and building components are amongst the enterprises, as is chicken breeding. A major industrial loss has been that of Cumledge blanket mill, closed in the 1970s.

EDUCATION

New school buildings have been mentioned above and to them should be added the conversion of the old High School into the Borders Agricultural College (formerly Berwickshire Agricultural and Technical Centre).

SUMMER FESTIVAL

In 1949, Duns Summer Festival ('Reiver's Week') was instituted, incorporating the existing celebration of Crowning the Wynsome Mayde o' Dunse. It has established itself as one of the recognised 'riding festivals' of the Borders, supporting and supported by Principals from most of the Region and beyond. Selkirk is a possible exception, the Soutars having never quite forgiven the Men o' the Merse for what they consider the undisciplined way the latter behaved at Flodden in 1513. In 1985 the 'Week' was experimentally reduced to five days, but in the previous year it coincided with the visit to Berwickshire of Her Majesty the Queen, and the Principals and followers had the privilege of riding past Her Majesty and HRH the Duke of Edinburgh in front of Berwickshire High School, where she had been entertained to lunch by the Borders Regional Council.

VOLUNTARY ORGANISATIONS

To those previously listed (not all of which, however, survive) are to be added such bodies as The Rotary Club of Duns, Duns and District Round Table, the Parish Church Young Woman's Group, Christ Church Ladies' Fellowship, Berwickshire Civic Society and branches of several charity fund-raising organisations. Coffee mornings, sales of work, sponsored walks, swims, rambles and so on, claim the support of the public steadily throughout the year, and are as steadily supported. Duns is a low-income area; it is not low on generosity towards deserving causes.

LOCAL GOVERNMENT

From 1661-1696 and again from 1903-1975, Duns was the County Town of Berwickshire. In the last-named year the Local Government (Scotland) Act completely restructured the system and Duns became part of Berwickshire District within the Borders Region. Duns was retained as the District Council centre, but the Regional Administration fled to Newtown St Boswells. It would be accurate to say that the change, ten years on, is still not universally regarded as the crowning gift of parliamentary democracy. In fact Duns was one of the first areas to set up a Community Council under the Act, but the impression was gained swiftly by most of those involved that the framers of the legislation had devised the name without seriously allocating a function within the new structure. It remains to be seen whether the system will continue in its entirety, for there is now talk of eliminating one of the tiers from the scheme in Scotland as a whole.

CHURCH ATTENDANCE

This has undoubtedly given cause for concern — but it always has. Even 120 years ago, the Parish Kirk Session was considering 'how to induce young people to come to Church'; their answer was to instal an organ! The Roll of Communicants in the Parish Church currently stands at 771 and has been slightly increasing since 1982.

NAME

The derivation is clearly Celtic, from Dun = hill fort. The suggestion made by an earlier writer of a 'pure French' origin is of the slenderest pretensions. The name was spelled *Duns* originally (so far as one can find regularity in any spellings, whether of names or other words) but from the 1720s the form *Dunse* is found. The old spelling was formally re-adopted at a public meeting in 1882. (A charming little book called *Glimpses of the past in Lammermuir* was published in the last century. It deals mainly with Longformacus, but in one or two passages refers to what is clearly Duns under the pseudonym of 'Drinkwell'. Whether this alludes to the numerous occurrences of the element 'well' in local place-names — Wellfield, Wellnage, Cruive Well, Ladywell — or to the habits of the townsfolk, the present writer is unclear.)

EDIN'S HA' BROCH

Modern scholarship is tending to date lowland brochs to the Roman rather than the Saxon period. The element 'Hall' in old place-names should be treated with caution. Not infrequently it is an Ordnance Survey misinterpretation of 'ha" = 'haugh' = flat ground by a river.

JOHN DUNS SCOTUS

The renowned mediaeval Franciscan theologian has been claimed as a native by several places, but in 1966 the Franciscan Order signified its acceptance of the tradition that he was born in Duns, of a younger branch of the family of Duns of Grueldykes, in 1265. Following an International Congress at Oxford to mark the 700th anniversary of Scotus's birth, the Order erected two monuments in Duns, a cairn at the Castle's Pavilion Lodge on the site of the cottage long pointed-out as his birthplace, and a statue of somewhat daunting aspect in the public park. On both of these Scotus is entitled 'The Subtle Doctor', the usual English mis-translation of 'Doctor Subtilis'. The Latin word *subtilis* means 'accurate' or 'down to earth', and certainly not 'subtle' in the faintly-derogatory modern sense. John Duns Scotus (whose followers the rival school of the Dominican St Thomas Aquinas dubbed 'dunces') maintained — against the Thomists — the doctrine of the Immaculate Conception of the Blessed Virgin Mary. This explains the dedication of the present Roman Catholic Church in Duns, its pre-Reformation predecessor being named after the Holy Trinity.

1986

THE PARISH OF EARLSTON

by Dr. John M. Burns and Rev. David W. Torrance

Earlston, formerly known from early times as Ercildoune, lies in very attractive Border country. The village itself is located in the Leader valley — Leaderdale or Lauderdale. The boundaries of the civil parish have remained unaltered over many years. It is bounded on the north by Legerwood, on the north, east and south by Gordon, Smailholm, Nenthorn and Mertoun and on the west by Melrose. Traditionally, as in so many other parts of Scotland, the boundaries of the ecclesiastical parish have coincided with the boundaries of the civil parish. On the west side, the boundary followed the river Leader, in this area the boundary of Berwickshire. In 1963, however, the boundaries of the ecclesiastical parish, but not the civil, were altered so that the parish crossed to the west side of the Leader and was made to extend from the Kedzlie Burn in the north to the Packman's Burn in the south so as to include within the ecclesiastical parish the farms of Clackmae, Craigsford Mains, Craigsford and Sorrowlessfield Mains. To the north there was also an adjustment to the parish so as to include the whole of Chapel-on-Leader and Chapel Mains.

TRAFFIC AND TRANSPORT

The village is well located in relation to the central Borders, lying on the main north-side route of the A68, the Edinburgh to Newcastle road and at the western end of one of the principal links through Berwickshire. By road it is 33 miles from Edinburgh, seven miles from Lauder, five and a half miles from Melrose, and six from St Boswells, six miles from Gordon and seventeen miles from Duns. Following the floods in August 1948 when so many Border bridges were washed away, Border rail services were curtailed. The last train to Earlston station was a 'special' in 1962. Thereafter the railway and station were closed and the only means of transport since then has been by road. There has been, in recent years, considerable improvement and realignment of the A68 through the village itself and from the village to the south end of the parish, with the construction of a new bridge over the Leader. More

recently improvements and a realignment of the road, with considerable cutting away of rock, have been carried out to the north of the village. However much these improvements have been made in the interests of road safety, inevitably they have necessitated the felling of many valuable trees, some of many years' standing. The removal of these trees, coupled with those lost as a result of Dutch Elm disease and those felled as a result of a recent wind storm, has affected and marred the beauty of this stretch of road, particularly to the north of the village. Despite that, however, the two mile stretch of road past Chapel and Carolside, continues to be one of the most attractive stretches of road in the Borders, particularly in spring and autumn.

The area to the west of the A68 has been considered for the construction of a possible Earlston by-pass road. The Regional Council in December 1978 produced a feasibility study, suggesting four possible lines extending westward across the haughland. No decision for the by-pass has yet been made by the Scottish Development Department and the Regional Council at present considers that there is insufficient reason to press for the construction of a by-pass, which is regarded at present as a matter of low priority. In the opinion of the Earlston Community Council, the by-pass, if constructed, would further mar the beauty of this area, and possibly remove or affect public amenity.

POPULATION AND HOUSING

The village has shown progressive growth over the last two decades. In 1971, the population was 1415 and in 1981, it was 1610 which is an increase of 195 people or 14 per cent. There are 816 homes in the civil parish of Earlston. There are approximately 696 homes in the village itself. Of this number, 262 homes belong to the Local Authority. 128 of the Local Authority homes have been modernised since 1983 or are in process of modernisation. The present programme of modernisation is hoped to be completed in 1988.

In the local plans for the area which have been produced by the Department of Planning and Development of the Borders Regional Council, in terms of the Local Government (Scotland) Act 1973, three preferred housing sites have been identified. These are at Thistle Cottage which has planning permission for eight dwellings and is at present being advertised for sale, at Rhymer's Avenue and in the Glebe adjacent to the Health Centre, which have the capacity for about eight and 35 dwellings respectively. It is suggested that these would be adequate to meet demand up to 1991 and that land at Haughhead Road would be suitable for housing development in the longer term. It is recommended that land at the first three sites be allocated for private housing. Such projected development would further increase the population, although the proprietor of the land at the third site (the Church of Scotland) has not indicated at present any desire to sell or convert the land from agricultural use.

INDUSTRY AND EMPLOYMENT

Earlston is fortunate among Border villages for the number of businesses and industries located within the parish. It has continued for several years to be a substantial employment base, drawing workers from surrounding areas. According to the Scottish Border Business Directory, excluding shops, there are 30 businesses and industries in Earlston parish. Most of these are small. Twenty-four employ between one and ten people: two employ between 11 and 50 people: one employs between 51 and 100 people and three employ over 101 people. Consequent upon this and because the Border Region has not suffered as severely as the rest of the country from the present economic recession, unemployment in this parish has remained well below the present national average for Scotland. Of those unemployed, the present average for Scotland is 15.6 per cent. In the Border Region as a whole it is 9.6 per cent. For the Galashiels Employment Office Area it is 7.9 per cent. This compares with 2.1 per cent in 1975. The number of unemployed in Earlston, which is included within the Galashiels Employment Office Area, is probably lower than the number in Galashiels itself and is probably around 5 or 6 per cent. The exact figure for Earlston is not recorded. Sadly, however, one of the largest employers, Kings and Co. Ltd., have intimated that by the end of this month (February 1986) 24 people will be made redundant. These include two staff, 15 fitters and seven drivers. Their redundancies result from a decision by the company to close their East End workshop. The main reasons for the closure were outlined as Government restrictions on road spending, increased competition, and a decrease in demand for materials in the area. The company will continue to employ 34 people at Earlston, 23 at Craighouse Quarry and 14 at Dunion Quarry near Jedburgh. Servicing of the vehicles based in Earlston will now be done in Edinburgh. Happily the other main employers of labour in the parish, Rodger (Builders) Ltd., A. and R. Brownlie Ltd., and Hamish Morrison Ltd., are all at present maintaining their full work-force.

There are three principal industrial areas in Earlston — at Rhymers Mill, Station Road and the East End. At Rhymers Mill, there is a considerable area of under-utilised space which could accommodate some form of development. Station Yard is the main industrial site. The Regional Council wants to continue to encourage existing firms to develop and expand in existing industrial areas through the more intensive use of existing sites and through the redevelopment and modernisation of existing buildings. In the light of the present unemployment situation, there is an urgent need for the creation of new jobs and establishment of suitable new industries and enterprises with good growth prospects.

FARMING AND AGRICULTURE

Farming continues to be a most important industry and employer of labour. There have been in recent years, as throughout the rest of the country, considerable changes, both in the manner of farming and in the number of people employed on farms. Agricultural statistics from Earlston Parish during 1985, are as follows:— The total area of land registered under the 21 agricultural farms or holdings in the parish is 3470 hectares. Approximately half this land is tenanted (ten holdings); the remainder is owner occupied or under a 'family type' tenancy, where the owner has an interest in the farming of the land.

Excluding the farmers, a total of 76 people are employed on these farms. Forty-two are full-time, the remainder are part-time or seasonal.

The total area cultivated is 1540 hectares. The following crops are grown —

Wheat	224 ha
Barley	1016 ha
Oats	32 ha
Combining peas	30 ha
Oilseed rape	50 ha
Potatoes seed	33 ha
Potatoes maincrop	18 ha
Turnips/Swedes	117 ha
Kale/Cabbage	7 ha
Forage rape	10 ha
Strawberries	2 ha
Raspberries	1 ha

The total area of land under pasture is 1420 hectares; approximately 760 acres is less than five years old.

Silage/Hay	570 ha
Grazing	850 ha

The area of rough grazing is 415 hectares. Farm woodland extends to 60 hectares. The stock carried in 1985 is as follows —

Dairy cows	70 (mainly Friesian)
Beef cows	500 (mainly Hereford, Friesian or Blue-greys)
Replacement Heifers	100
Bulls	13
Calves under one year old	450
Breeding Ewes	5250
Breeding replacements	2000
Rams	200
Sows and Gilts	30

Laying Hens	7500
Other Poultry	26500

In recent years agriculture has come under considerable financial pressure. In response to over-production and surpluses, prices have begun to fall and margins have been squeezed. Recently farmers have diversified into alternative crops such as Oilseed Rape, which are not in surplus. This trend is likely to increase in the future. There has also been a general increase in cropping at the expense of livestock as farmers have tried to maintain profits.

Cereal yields on good land in the parish have risen to around 7 tonnes per hectare for wheat, 6 tonnes for winter barley and 5 tonnes for spring barley.

MEDICAL SERVICES

Although there have been doctors in Earlston since at least 1700 and there has been a pharmacy since 1868, these remained the only medical facilities until the 1940s, when the 'Clinic Hut' was built on the East Green to house Child Welfare and Chest Clinics and a Physiotherapy service. With the opening of a Health Centre in Kidgate in 1984, all the village medical services were integrated under one roof — a primary care health team comprising two General Practitioners (plus a third in training), a District Nurse, a Health Visitor, a Physiotherapist and a Chiropodist, as well as visiting staff who include a Speech Therapist, an Audiologist, an Occupational Therapist, a Social Worker and the Community Psychiatric team from Dingleton Hospital.

As the doctors moved out of their old premises in Summerfield, their place was taken by three dentists from a Galashiels dental practice who provide a dental service on three days per week in addition to the previously existing school dental service. The village still has its pharmacy which provides 'medicines by van' for Gordon and Greenlaw. Another medical service which has had secondary benefits for isolated corners of the parish is the 'Border Courier' bus service, which combines the collection of laboratory specimens from all the Border Cottage Hospitals and Health Centres with a public transport service to villages such as Redpath and Legerwood which would otherwise have no bus service.

Earlston still has an ambulance based in the community, a reminder of the ambulance run by the Earlston and District Ambulance Association in the days before a national ambulance service was established.

SERVICES FOR THE ELDERLY

Like all Border communities, Earlston has a high proportion of elderly citizens. 14.1 per cent of the Scottish population are over 65, and the

Earlston figure of 16.2 per cent is near the Border average of 18.2 per cent. For over 75s the figures are 5.8 per cent (Scotland) 7.9 per cent (Borders) and 7.6 per cent (Earlston) (1984 figures). Unfortunately, the geographical development of Earlston's housing has meant that few of the 'pensioner's cottages' are on level ground, and the proposed development of old people's flats at Thornfield by Eildon Housing Association is a welcome addition to the sheltered housing complex of 20 flats in the square, known as Hanover Close. Although there are no Day Centres or hospital facilities for the elderly within the village, there are 14 home helps, and a Lunch Club and 'Meals on Wheels' provide essential services for many of the elderly.

LAW AND ORDER

The Church, the village school, the village doctor, the village post office, the village chemist and the village policeman all contribute to the identity (and the survival) of any rural community. Although Earlston has managed to retain most of these institutions, there has been a gradual withdrawal of police services in the 1980s. The two police houses were vacated in 1980 and 1982 and later sold, and although the police station still remains as an office for occasional use, it is not manned, and mobile police patrols are sent from Melrose and Lauder. Although the village does not have high crime rates, vandalism, 'glue-sniffing' and the abuse of heroin and other hard drugs have not left the village untouched, and the doubling of national alcohol consumption since the War has been reflected in Earlston's drinking trends and consequent social and medical problems.

EDUCATION

Education facilities have grown rapidly in the last 20 years. The village always had its own primary school, but before 1967 secondary pupils had to travel to Berwickshire High School at Duns. From 1967, when the school was renamed Earlston High School, pupils began to spend first some, and then all of their secondary education at Earlston and the catchment area of the school gradually expanded to include pupils from the primary schools at Earlston, Channelkirk, Lauder, Melrose, Newtown St Boswells, St Boswells, Gordon and Westruther. Although there has been a fall in numbers attending the primary school in the last 20 years (220 to 183), the High School roll has risen from 111 to 561, making a total of 744 pupils and 60 teachers in the village.

A major extension to the High School buildings (including a lounge for community use) was completed in 1982, and in 1983 the primary school separated from the High School under a new headmaster.

SPORTS CLUBS AND FACILITIES

Earlston has always maintained an active interest in sport. Some 100 year old clubs continue to flourish (the Rugby Club, the Bowling Club and the Curling Club have all celebrated centenaries in recent years) and other newer clubs have joined them — a Badminton Club, and an Angling and Sea Fishing Association, a Homing Pigeon Club, a recently revived Tennis Club and Earlston Rhymers Football Club. Although the village lost its Golf Course during the War, and the Cricket Club did not survive the loss of their pitch at Carolside, golfers, curlers and indoor bowlers continue to travel to enjoy their sports nearby and the village has a bowling green, a rugby pitch and a football pitch — in each case the clubs have recently bought over the pitches and built or renovated clubhouses. The High School sports facilities include a Sports Hall opened in 1972, a Trim Track opened in 1978 and tennis courts opened in 1984, all of which are used by the community as well as the school.

Although many of the Earlston sports clubs can boast of recent successes, mention should be made of Black Hill Harriers, who were found in 1978 and started to compete in track athletics in 1982. In the subsequent three years they have won the Edinburgh and District League twice and been runners up once. Earlston Rugby Club who stayed aloof from the national leagues for several years, joined in 1982 and were Division Seven Champions the next year. Unfortunately their Autumn Sevens Tournament (traditionally the first of the season) has been deserted by some of the First Division clubs and has had to be moved to a Spring Sunday.

EARLSTON CIVIC WEEK

Most Border towns and villages have a Common Riding or similar Summer Festival, but until 1973 Earlston had no event. In that year, Earlston Civic Week was started, with the aim of providing 'a week of entertainment for the whole village'. The week's proceedings include family sports, dances, talent competitions, fancy dress parades, and a final firework display. Although Civic Week has neither the historic ceremonies nor the mounted ride-outs which add colour to many of the other Border festivals, it manages to involve a higher percentage of the village's population than many of these.

SHOPPING FACILITIES

Shopping facilities ebb and flow as shops open and close, but in the mid-eighties Earlston supports a butcher's shop, two newsagents, three grocers and a greengrocer, a pharmacy, a hardware shop and an agricultural merchant, a Post Office, and electrical shops and a draper's shop. Other commercial establishments include three public houses, a bookmaker, two ladies' hairdressers, and a bank, and an architect and a solicitor have recently opened branches in the village. The trends of the eighties — fast food and video technology — are represented by a video library and a baked potato 'carry-out', but there has also been a recent appearance of the traditional 'fish and chip' shop. Among older shops (and older technologies) which have disappeared are a watchmaker's shop, a mens' barber shop and the cinema which functioned in the (now demolished) Corn Exchange.

Tourists are catered for by two of the public houses which have bedrooms, five bed and breakfast establishments and a small café which looks after passing trade on the A68 well enough to have gained honourable mention from Egon Ronay's inspectors.

LOCAL GOVERNMENT

Until local government reorganisation in 1975, Earlston was in the County of Berwickshire, but thereafter it became part of 'the District of Ettrick and Lauderdale' and sends a District Councillor to Galashiels. It is also part of Borders Region and together with St Boswells and Bowden, sends a Regional Councillor to Newtown St Boswells. Although both councillors stand as Independents, national political parties have branches in the village. In parliamentary terms, our Member of Parliament is no longer the representative for 'Berwickshire and East Lothian', but for 'Tweeddale, Ettrick and Lauderdale'.

Earlston has a Community Council which takes an active and concerned interest in the welfare of the community. The Community Council has a full complement of members.

ENVIRONMENT

Whereas the whole parish is attractive, parts of the parish are areas of special beauty, namely the Leader valley, particularly the areas of Chapel and Carolside and of Cowdenknowes and, to the east and south, the area of Mellerstain. A good part of the parish is hilly, although the only high elevation is the Black Hill (1031 feet), on top of which can be distinguished the three concentric rings of an early British fort, and from which a magnificent view can be obtained of the surrounding Border country. The Community Council has suggested that due consideration should be given to the possibility of designating part of the parish as a Conservation Area. The Regional Council proposes to undertake consultation with the Community Council and the residents of the area concerned in order that this possibility may be more fully considered.

BUILDINGS OF ARCHITECTURAL OR HISTORIC INTEREST

The parish has a number of buildings of national interest, listed under the standard categories A, B or C. Three of these are listed under the category A. These are:

Cowdenknowes: In the 16th century, as the initials carved on the lintel of the former principal entrance would indicate, the mansion belonged to Sir James Home and his wife Katherine Home. At that time it consisted of three distinct parts, a tower, the mansion dated 1574 and a small tower now in ruins. All were originally connected by curtain walls and enclosed a courtyard now occupied as open gardens. A modern wing now connects the tower with the mansion. It is the home of the present proprietor Miss Jean D. Burns.

Mellerstain House: This is the home of Lord John Binning, heir of the Earl of Haddington, and of Lady Binning. The house is a unique example of the work of the Adam family. The two wings were built by Adam in 1725 and the main block by his famous son Robert about 40 years later. The interior decoration and ceilings by Robert Adam are very fine.

Mellerstain stables and cottage block: These have attractive ranges.

There are seven buildings listed under the Category B. These are:

Rhymer's Tower: It is said that in the 13th century it was the residence of Sir Thomas the Rhymer (or Rimor or Rimour). What remains today is an ivy-clad ruin of a small keep.

The Old Bridge: It is a hump back bridge, spanning the Leader Water. It has two arches with a centre cutwater and was built possibly in the 18th century.

Carolside: A late 18th century mansion, it has three storeys and a basement. There are three sash windows, a facade with centre projecting porch and a flight of steps, a low parapet and moulded cornice. One-storey flanking wings have bowed ends.

Norman Cottage, Mellerstain: It stands in Mellerstain policies, in the park.

East Lodge, Mellerstain: This is a one-storey building. The pediment has a circular window.

Mausoleum, Mellerstain: The pediment is supported by Corinthian pilasters. There is a centre doorway in rusticated surround. There are three parapet urns and a flanking balustrade. It is dated 1736 and carries an inscription.

Kirklands: This is a two-storey 18th century mansion. It is harled with rusticated stone dressings. It has a sash window facade, a centre columned porch and hipped slate roof with sprocketed eaves. There are various additions and offices to the rear. It stands in walled policies.

There are three buildings listed under category C. These are:

Earlston Church and Graveyard: Of special note are a Cross slabstone, the Rhymer's stone and the Burgerhuys bell dated 1609. There are interesting monuments in the church yard.

Rhymer's Mill: It has a date stone and was rebuilt by C. and M. Whale in 1842.

Whiteside Tower: Little now remains but the vaulted basement.

The former New Bridge over the Leader Water was listed under category C. It had three arches carrying the main road across the Leader. A few years ago it was replaced by a modern single span bridge.

Earlston Parish Church: Earlston Church is a branch of the National Church and is the only Protestant church in the parish. Members of other denominations who come to reside in the parish tend to associate themselves with the Parish Church, rather than travel elsewhere to worship.

Earlston was given by Walter de Lindsay to the monks of Kelso in the early part of the 12th century. In 1171 it was given by the monks of Kelso to the Priory of Coldingham, in exchange for Gordon. On the 20th March 1242, it was dedicated by Bishop de Bernham and brought into conformity with the Church of Rome. The present church was built in 1892 to replace an earlier church built in 1736. The present building is probably the fourth or possibly the fifth building on the site. In the middle and latter part of the 18th century, two secession churches were established. These united in 1887 and took the name of St John's. In the Act of Union in 1929, St John's became a congregation of the Church of Scotland and in 1946 united with the Established Church. The united Church, which became known as Earlston Parish Church, agreed to worship in the Established Church building. The name Ercildoune previously used for the parish Church was dropped.

In 1904, a small hall was built adjoining St John's for the use of that congregation. Thereafter and for many years, the West Free Church building was used as a hall by the Established Church. It was sold over 30 years ago and became used first as a garage and now as a shop and store for agricultural supplies. After the union in 1946, St John's Church was converted into a large hall, although lacking kitchen facilities and running water, so that the united congregation had the use of two halls, a larger and a smaller. In 1985, the large hall was sold and demolished. The small hall which had originally been given for sole and exclusive use as a church hall for all time to come, was retained and the congregation plans to enlarge and improve it.

The Church is financially self-supporting. In 1985, in addition to giving £1,428 to the Aged and Infirm Ministers' Fund, £100 to the Pension Fund, £132 to the Housing and Loan Fund and £108 in aid to the Maintenance of the Ministry Fund, it gave £1,814.08 to the Mission and Service Fund for mission at home and abroad. It gave £353.06 to Christian Aid and £152 to the National Bible Society for Scotland. Earlston Church remains as one of an increasingly fewer number of churches, which is not linked to another church within or outside of the parish. There is one morning and evening service each Sunday, with the exception of July and August when there is no evening service. In addition, the minister conducts worship on the afternoon of the first Sunday of the month in Redpath, in the community hall, and on the afternoon of the first Tuesday of the month in the Sheltered Housing in Hanover Close. Although the Church is not linked to any other, the minister acts as Chaplain in Dingleton Hospital which has approximately 350 beds. In addition to visitations, he conducts worship in the hospital each morning, together with mid-week services.

In 1985, the Communion Roll was	751 persons
The number admitted by profession of faith was	9
The number admitted by restoration was	4
The number admitted by certificate was	5
The number removed by transference with certificate was	10
The number baptised was	12
The number of deaths in the parish was	27
(of whom 19 were church members)	

The various church organisations, Woman's Guild, Young Women's Group, Sunday School, Bible Class, Youth Fellowship, Brownies, Guides, Cubs and Scouts, although not as large as might be desired, manifest a healthy vigour. Recently a Beaver Colony of 22 Beavers has been created and also a Venture Scout Unit. Because of the present leadership of the latter, the Venture Scouts in addition to many outdoor activities, are able to take part in the Duke of Edinburgh Award Scheme.

Both the Toddlers Group and the Play Group are very active. They meet regularly in the Church Hall, but are not Church Organisations.

Quaker Meeting: There is one Quaker in the parish. Meetings are held in her house but those attending come from outside the parish.

Catholic Church: The Catholic Church, although not having a church building, has a small hall which is used for worship each Saturday evening, when Mass is celebrated. Earlston comes within the Catholic Parish of Melrose. There is no resident priest in Earlston. The parish priest resides in Galashiels. A survey was conducted recently and it would appear that those who were baptised in the Catholic Church or were brought up as Catholics number 70, although the number of practising Catholics is around 30. Happy relations exist between the two religious communities. Occasionally representatives of the two communities meet together, as on the World Day of Prayer, the annual midweek service in St Andrew's, Drygrange, during the week of Prayer for Christian Unity, or other special occasions. There is no history of distrust between the two communities in this parish.

(The writers of this article would like to express their gratitude to the Borders Region Planning Department for their provision of information. They would like to thank Mr James McLean, B.Sc., an Adviser with the East of Scotland College of Agriculture, for the provision of agricultural statistics and Miss Anne Hughson, M.A., for help received.)

1986

THE PARISH OF ECCLES

by the Rev. John L. Douglas, B.D.

The name Eccles is derived from the Greek and Latin 'Ecclesia' signifying an Assembly or Church. Eccles earned the name of the 'Church' parish because in pre-Reformation times there was situated within its bounds a nunnery and four churches; the nunnery and church at Eccles; churches at Leitholm, Birgham and Mersington. There is no trace of the last. Leitholm was on the Chapel Knowe, behind the present manse; Birgham has a few ruins in the north-east of the churchyard; Eccles nunnery was large and famous. It was founded in 1154 by Cospatrick Home, Earl of Dunbar. Like many other Border places, it was frequently ravaged by raid and open war.

In 1545 the Earl of Hertford completely demolished both convent and village. There are extant today two cells within the property of D. G. Greig, Esq., of Eccles; also the fish pond remains, and some of the underground conduits and walls. Excavation would probably bring many things to light. The present church has stones in its walls that have passed through fire. In 1567 the land returned to descendants of the original donors.

GEOGRAPHY

According to the *Ordnance Gazetteer of Scotland* the boundaries of the parish are as follows: 'On the N by Fogo, E by Swinton and Coldstream, S by Northumberland and by Sprouston in Roxburghshire, SW by Ednam and Stichill in Roxburghshire, W by Hume and NW by Greenlaw. Its length, from ENE to WSW, varies between two and five-eighths and six and three-eighths miles; its utmost breadth is five and a half miles; and its area is 12,488 and three quarter acres of which 70 and three quarters are water.' Lambden is reputed to have been included in the parish but is now in Greenlaw. However, the Lambden inhabitants take part in the communal and church life at Eccles at the present time.

The parish lies mainly with a southern exposure in that rich agricultural valley called the Merse. The northern part has heavy clay soil and is slightly later in maturing its crops. When heavy snow falls there is a noticeable difference in the thaw between north and south. The main road leading by the Tweedside is hardly ever blocked. The soil around Birgham is light and sandy. The parish is pleasantly but not richly wooded and the two World Wars have not denuded the landscape to any noticeable extent. The River Tweed is the main river and for part of its course is the boundary between Scotland and England. Opposite Birgham at the Redden Burn three counties meet, Northumberland (parish of Carham), Roxburghshire (parish of Sprouston) and Berwickshire. Other small burns are the Leet, Liprick and Lambden. Fresh water pearls used to be gathered from the Leet.

There are three villages in the parish: Eccles towards the west end, Leitholm two miles eastward and Birgham two and a half miles to the south. Leitholm derived its name from the Leet; and Birgham had once been 'Brigham', but there is no trace of the brig which gave it its name. It is possible that the churchyard road which leads down to a ford may have once led to a bridge. Birgham was noted a century and a half ago for its Bicker Makers (wooden porridge bowls). The name 'Crichton Cottage' perpetuates the name of the makers. What was once a fourth village, Hassington, has fallen into decay and there are now only a few houses.

ESTATES

Eccles parish has an unusually large number of mansion houses. It is a convenient centre for fox hunting. When the writer came to live here 26 years ago there were large and enthusiastic meets of the hounds. The territories of the Duke of Buccleuch and the Berwickshire Hunts meet at the Greenlaw-Coldstream main road. However, fox hunting is rapidly dying out over the county, due to high taxation. The grandeur of the great landowners has departed and only skeleton staffs strive to keep house, gardens and grounds. Double hedges, to give cover for the foxes, were once a special feature of this area. Mr William Foreman, a hedger in Eccles, was known afar for his trim and tidy hedges. He was a master of that art. He died three years ago.

This countryside is also a good preserve for game, splendid fishing being also available. It is distant from industrial undertakings and is of great natural beauty with rich fertile soil and a genial climate. Its southern vista toward the Cheviots makes a beautiful outlook, while to the north the ground rises gradually toward the Lammermoors.

Eccles House is in the hands of the third of the present line of owners, Denis G. Greig, Esq. The village of Eccles is his property, as well as Eccles Mains, Loanknowe and Harlaw. Mr Greig has served his country in both World Wars. The previous owner, Sir John Paterson, is reputed to have built Eccles Stables out of money which he won at cards off the Duke of Roxburghe. A most unusual feature is the clock in the Stable Tower, which marks the time with one hand only. It is said to be unique in Scotland and that there is only one similar in England. Another inhabitant of Eccles worthy of mention is the Sub-Postmaster, Mr David Pitt. His father developed a type of leek which under the present David Pitt has gained world renown, the variety known as 'Pitt's Lyon Improved Leeks'. Bedlington dogs, bred by Mr Pitt, have also been champions at Cruft's Show, London, and at other exhibitions.

Stainrigg, an old house, with coats of arms embellishing its front, has just been purchased by R. W. D. Boswell, Esq. The late laird, Miss Lucy Ramsay, died a few months ago. Stainrigg Mains and Eccles Bankhead comprise the estate. The farmer of Bankhead, Mr Adam S. Hamilton, has just retired at the age of 84 after spending 60 years on this farm. When over 70 years of age, he discovered that he possessed the gifts of a water diviner and the present writer has had ample proof of his ability with the hazel twig.

Anton's Hill takes its name from a well dedicated to St Anthony upon its policies. It was at one time a place of pilgrimage for healing. The Hunter family long occupied this home. A daughter married to Lieutenant Colonel A. G. Bates, D.S.O., one of the heads of the famous Cunard White Star Shipping Line, is the present owner. The farm of Orange Lane is on this estate. The name has intrigued many people. One explanation is that John 'Orwin' was farmer there in 1774. There is a quaint sundial on the gable of the farmhouse.

Kames, at one time called Bessborough, was renamed after the famous Lord Kames. Benjamin Franklin was once entertained under its roof. The present family is that of Menzies, the head of the publishing firm of that name. Colonel Menzies commanded the Glasgow Highlanders (H.L.I.) in the First World War.

Bughtrigg in the last 20 years has had two eminent owners — men of the sea. Admiral of the Fleet, Sir William May gave notable service in the First World War. Then followed Admiral Sir Bertrand Ramsay.

Purves Hall was the home of Captain Bowlby, R.N. Sir John Hume Campbell of Marchmont had owned this land and much more; but by bad management and carelessness it all passed out of his hands.

Belchester is the home of Colonel Wilson. His wife is one of the Hunters of Anton's Hill.

Springhill, situated on Tweedside, is the residence of Lord Dunglass, M.P. for North Lanarkshire. He is the heir to the Earldom of Home. His father, the Earl, and he are respected and beloved by their tenantry. Birgham and Homebank (with Haigsfield) are their property.

Many of the farm houses are very considerable, and are occupied by owner-farmers. Mersington and Springwells are examples.

Several of the estates have been broken up within recent years, and Bartlehill, Kennetsideheads and Eccles Newtown are also now in that category.

FOLKLORE

An old rhyme about the Lambden Burn says:

'Its twists and turns, its hooks and crooks
Fill the bowie, And fill the Kirn.'

Here is a Border couplet, which must be a few centuries old:

'Bughtrig and Belchester
Hatchedknowes and the Peel
If ye canna get a wife
In ane o' thae places
Ye'll ne'er dae weel.'

In Leitholm there used to live Tibbie the Witch. She was greatly feared and she could buy cheese at her own price and get milk for nothing. A village woman at last plucked up courage to tell Tibbie that she could no longer spare milk. The woman's cow milked blood.

Here is a rhyme which is passed down by mouth from generation to generation in the parish. Let me explain that, just across the parish border from Whitrig, into a thicket on Hatchednize ground, and near the main road, there is a shallow grave dug which is kept open by the roadmen. Tradition says that a maid had a tryst with a man at that spot, and she, arriving early, climbed a tree and waited. She appeared later at the 'Kirn', held at Hatchednize that night; she recited these verses and more. One of the young men went out, and was never seen again.

'One Moonlight Night as I sat high
I looked for one, but two passed by.
The leaves did shake, my heart did quake,
To see the hole the rogues did make.'

Did they intend to murder her, or simply to frighten her? We shall never know.

CUSTOMS

Creeling is still practised at the local weddings and is considered lucky. Properly done, a creel with a rope on it should be placed on the bridegroom's shoulders and the basket gradually filled with stones, until he pays ransom. His bride meanwhile attempts to release her husband. Now, it usually consists of a rope held across their way, and the bridegroom quickly pays something in the region of 10s. to get clear passage.

'Barrin' oot Day' is still held sometimes at the local school. The pupils bar the schoolmaster out.

SAYINGS

The Borders have many sayings of their own. The use of the expression 'hard up' to explain anyone, or anything in poor condition is in every day use. It has no connection with the colloquial expression in other parts, where 'hard up' means in financial straits. The word 'shabby' is also used in much the same way; for example, ill persons are shabby. It does not mean 'down at the heel'.

PLACE NAMES

Several names are falling into desuetude. Banghousewalls appears in the parish stipend location. Then names such as Molesmill, Ayton Hall and Cloverhall are still used, but the buildings have disappeared or almost so.

MONUMENTS

The most notable monument is a cross, opposite Crosshall farm cottages. A few years ago the Berwickshire Naturalists' Club placed a strong metal rail round for its better preservation. The old name of this farm was Deadriggs, which signifies that a battle was fought there. A local tradition says that it marks where a Governor of Hume Castle fell, and there are weird stories that his head was severed from his body two miles away and that it was here that his body fell from his horse. The Liprick was said to have run with blood for 24 hours. The most likely explanation is that it is a monument to one of the Percys of Northumberland who was killed here in engagement with the rival family of Douglas. The designs are now hardly recognisable but from the *Statistical Account* of 1831 we learn that the east side had the figure of a naked man, and a greyhound, the greyhound being the Percy crest.

Leitholm Peel is now an ivy-grown ruin. It was the stronghold of the family of Dicksouns who were once a great power in the parish.

There is an old well in the park in front of Stainrigg. There is a tale that one of the Kings Charles took refuge within it.

The Loupin Stane outside Eccles Church is still in good preservation. It is reminiscent of the days when the farmer's wife mounted the horse behind her husband. The antiquities of Eccles are described and illustrated in the *Report on the County of Berwick* of the Royal Commission on the Ancient Monuments . . . of Scotland (1915).

A historic place in Birgham is worthy of mention and it has no monument. It is the Treaty Field where in 1290 arrangements were made for the marriage of Prince Edward to Margaret of Scotland. This field is in the corner field where the Eccles Road meets the Birgham-Coldstream main road, to the south of the new Orlit houses. Because of its historic association, it was not used as a building site.

MODERN MEMORIALS

A fine grey Celtic cross stands at the west end of Leitholm. It is the War Memorial for the First World War and was the first to be erected in Scotland for those who fell in that War. A block of stone has been set in front of the cross on which are the names of those who gave their lives in the Second World War.

In Eccles church a beautiful and valuable stained glass window commemorates the fallen of the two Wars. The window was designed and made by Mr Douglas McLundie of the Abbey Studio, Edinburgh.

RECENT OUTSTANDING EVENTS

Aerodrome. During the First World War there was a landing field for aircraft at Eccles Tofts. In the Second World War a large aerodrome was begun on much the same site but extended eastward, and was named Charterhall. An Anti-Aircraft Unit was stationed at Purves Hall. The Home Guard took their due part in local defence and an outlook post was set up at Bartlehill. A number of bombs were dropped on the parish, especially Springwells, but there was no loss of life.

The spring of 1947 is remembered for the very severe snow which lasted for nearly three months. For three days Eccles was cut off, mail was brought in on horseback, and caterpillar and wheeled tractors had the greatest difficulty in going out for supplies of bread. The roads leading north and south were filled level with the hedges. It was nearly a week until the milk could be removed from the dairies.

The flood of August 1948. Very heavy rain began to fall in the evening and poured extremely heavily until, without warning, it was evident that a serious flood had developed. None of the burns or culverts could contain the volume of water and many bridges were swept away. All kinds of animals, including horses, were swept away and much property. The water in the Fishpond Park at Eccles was about 10 feet deep. The pressure of water finally swept away the south half of the churchyard wall, six feet high and it lay scattered over and blocking the roadway. The wall has been rebuilt only to about half its original height. It was the worst flood within living memory.

POPULATION

Over the last 26 years there has been a slow but steady decline in population. Soon after the writer came to live here in 1924, farmers began to put off horses and increase the acreage under pasture. It was an economic move to counter the depression. Farms such as Eccles Tofts and Eccles Newtown had eight to ten pair of horses; these were reduced to a matter of four, a man less for each pair of horses. Men thus left out of employment sought work elsewhere, and very, very few of these persons have returned to the land. The coming of war in 1939 meant a tremendous ploughing up of pasture, but that has been mainly achieved by mechanisation. The employment of Italian and German prisoners of war helped the situation, and now a number of European displaced persons ('D.P.s' for short) have helped to fill the gaps. Some of these men are doing a really good job but they vary greatly in usefulness.

Plate 21. The Eyemouth fishing fleet in the early years of the century.

The population of this parish is preponderantly Border Scottish, composed almost entirely of persons born in either Berwickshire or Roxburghshire. Many families move round a focal point such as Kelso or Duns which they refer affectionately to as 'oor district'.

In recent years very few have emigrated. A few young men went to Canada soon after the close of the First World War and they have made good in the country of their adoption.

In the parish a few Irishmen are to be found, but they are mostly seasonal workers. There are a few Englishmen, who are in gentlemen's service. Northumbrians are hardly accounted strangers, but there is not so much coming and going as one might expect. The terms for removing are different, and so is the dialect.

The only foreigners are the displaced persons from Yugoslavia, Poland, Lithuania and other parts of Europe.

There is a small admixture of Gipsy blood to the rural stock. This is accounted for by Yetholm Gipsies who have settled on the land. There are no Jews in this part. During the height of Hitler's persecution of the Jews, it was necessary for the parish minister to issue a certificate to a lady born at East Printonan and residing in Germany, to the effect 'that there was no Jewish blood in her veins'.

There is a likelihood that the decline will be stayed and that the population figure will become fairly static, or even increase, due to the improvement in agriculture and the provision of better houses.

At the moment there are more young persons, indicating more work and money, on the farm places, than in the villages. Leitholm in particular, tends to be peopled mostly by old and retired persons.

Here are the census figures since 1801: 1801, 1682; 1841, 1946; 1851, 1892; 1901, 1433; 1911, 1449; 1921, 1245; 1931, 1132; 1951, 1023. At the moment among the youthful marriageable persons, the males will out-number the females about two to one. This is most unusual.

PUBLIC AND SOCIAL SERVICES

Water. There is no general public water supply. The Berwickshire Scheme, which is bringing water from a reservoir fed by the Watch Burn at Longformacus, is in process of construction, and pipe laying throughout the Middle District is making rapid progress. It is due to reach this parish within a very few years and will be a great boon to the whole community.

Eccles Estate is meantime served by a private supply installed (perhaps about 1920) by the late James L. Greig, Esq. An engine pumps water from the disused quarry to two concrete tanks on Eccles Hill, a distance of one mile. Birgham has a private supply belonging to the Earl of Home. Leitholm is badly served with water, there being only wells, of which there are 22. Most estates and farms have now some private supply tanks; at the moment water boring is in process at Eccles Newtown.

Electricity. This useful commodity is gradually being introduced throughout the parish and the work is behind schedule. Leitholm is the only village so far provided with street lighting and it was installed a year ago. More than half the farms (they have a priority) have the national grid supply. A number of the larger houses generate their own electricity for lighting purposes.

There is no coal gas supply in the area. Paraffin stoves and lamps meet the needs of a good proportion of the people, and great progress has been made in kerosene equipment. A recent product, Rural or Calor Gas (Butane Gas) has become very popular. It is delivered in metal containers by motor van to households.

Scavenging. Until recently there was little provision for the removal of refuse. Unsightly dumps in the vicinity of the villages of Leitholm and Birgham were common. Now a twice-weekly motor refuse van collects refuse, and carries it off to Swinton Quarry.

Drainage. There is no general system of sewage. Septic tanks are constructed where necessary.

Roads. Great progress has been made in the surfacing of the parish roads. A quarter of a century ago the roads were rough and dusty, now they are mostly tar-macadamed and smooth.

The same progress is visible in means of transport. There being no railway line through the parish, it was isolated and inconvenient. A bus service with a solid rubber-tyred bus, had commenced between Kelso and Berwick. Now there are three passenger routes through the parish, via Eccles, via Birgham and via Hassington. Birgham is on the main Edinburgh-Coldstream-Newcastle route. Eccles connects with Kelso, Berwick, Duns and Greenlaw. The Scottish Motor Traction Company operates most of these routes and this company (along with others) has been recently nationalised. Every evening buses pass Orange Lane on their way from Edinburgh to London (time 13 hours). The return fair is £2 10/-.

Communications. There are three post offices, one in each village. Most parts of the parish are served by two deliveries and two collections of mails. Most of this is done by postal van now, but the postman mounted on his bicycle is still seen in Birgham. Different parts of the parish are served by different postal towns. Eccles is under Kelso, but for some years was under Greenlaw; Leitholm and Birgham receive their mail from Coldstream.

Telephones. A great increase in the number of subscribers has taken place within the last ten years. There are public telephone boxes in the three villages and a Royal Automobile Box at Orange Lane. There are automatic exchanges at Leitholm and Birgham. The use of telegrams is on the decrease.

Education. There are three schools in the villages. Eccles and Leitholm are staffed by a Headmaster and assistant, Birgham has a Schoolmistress. Eccles has 41 pupils, Leitholm 37 and Birgham 15. Some 10 pupils attend primary schools outside the parish. The schools have been kept up to date with central heating (except Birgham) and electricity in all three. The fabrics are administered by Coldstream and District Education Sub-Area Committee. For all other matters the County Council Education Committee control the schools. Children over three miles distant from school are conveyed free and the same holds for children under eight years who are more than two miles away. When the school leaving age was raised from 14 to 15 years after the recent war, children over 12 years were removed from Eccles and Leitholm and sent to either Coldstream Junior Secondary School or to Duns High School according to their ability. At present they are 10 in number. Within the last four months a system of hot meals conveyed from Coldstream to the three schools has been introduced. Medical and dental services are available for all children by means of travelling clinics.

Local Government. Eccles is one of the few county parishes divided into two wards, returning two members to both the County Council and the District Council. In recent years the County Council has gathered more and more power into itself. The latest development is an attempt to overcome over-centralisation. The Parish Council was abolished some years ago, but now a Parish Committee of about five members has been appointed in a consultative and advisory capacity. The County Councillor, Maxwell Walker, Esq., Springwells and the writer, who is District Councillor, are *ex-officio* members. The churchyards are administered centrally by a travelling squad of men with modern grass-cutting machines. The church, manse and churchyard came under the care of the Heritors, but on the abolition of Heritors in 1925 the Council was entrusted with the churchyards. Birgham churchyard is cared for by a local man. Leitholm cemetery is a private company managing its own affairs.

Health Services. There is no doctor resident within the bounds. Doctors from Kelso, Coldstream, Greenlaw and Duns serve the community. Residents requiring hospital treatment are conveyed to Kelso, Coldstream or Duns Cottage Hospitals. The more serious cases go to Edinburgh Royal Infirmary and other Edinburgh hospitals which have recently been set up. Peel Hospital, near Clovenfords, was erected as an Emergency War Hospital, and it plays a large part in the art of healing in the South-East Border. A good fleet of ambulances helps in the transport of the sick and ailing. Gordon Hospital now deals with long chronic cases. At Leitholm, a Queen's Nurse is situated, and she attends the sick in their own homes and carries out the duties of a midwife. She is provided with a house and car. All health services were recently taken out of voluntary organisations into the hands of the State.

CHURCHES

The parish is served with two churches — Eccles and Leitholm. Since the Union of Churches in 1929, they are both Church of Scotland. There are very few residents of any other denomination. The old Parish Church was built in 1774. It superseded a fine Gothic building in the shape of a Cross, simply because the latter was too small. When the present incumbent was ordained, the present building was too large, seating fully 1000 persons, with box pews and a heavy gallery three quarters round the building. In 1929 an ambitious scheme of internal reconstruction was embarked on, and today it is one of the most modern, comfortable and beautiful churches in the district (roll 324). The old pew backs form the wall panelling. The Death Bell is exhibited on a window. The moulder, by mistake, has done the lettering in reverse. Corrected, it reads: 'For the parish of Ekkles 1715'. The Church Bell is dated 1659 and has inscribed upon it, 'Fear God Ye People of Eccles'. Early in its history the present Eccles Church figured in Court of Session decisions: (1) 'That a Belfry but not a steeple must be provided by the heritors, though a steeple once attached, forms part of it'. (2) 'A family pew is first assigned to the Minister, then the heritors in order of the amount of their valued rents, choose family sittings — 17 Dec. 1776'. A panel was installed in 1930 with the names of the ministers since 1567. Here are two incidents connected with those names, reflecting the times in which they lived. John Cook, who was inducted in 1663, was deprived by the Privy Council for not praying for Their Majesties William and Mary, and refusing to read the Proclamation of Estates. Matthew Dysart, inducted in 1731, seems to have been a man of strong character. His election was disputed, and the militia were called out to restore order. Henceforward he preached with a pistol on either side of the pulpit. He is reputed to have died much respected.

In Eccles vestry there is a photograph of Rachel Pitt, who lived to be 103 years. When she was 96 years old she robed the writer. She is buried in Gordon churchyard. On her tombstone there is recorded the death of a full sister, 120 years earlier. This sister died young, 17 years before Rachel was born! This case must be almost unique. Church services are conducted fortnightly in Birgham Hall; and at Eccles Tofts monthly, by the parish minister. Sunday schools are held at Eccles (68) and Birgham. Woman's Guild (36), Youth Fellowship and other organisations are all in a flourishing condition. A small hall was made internally within the church building, at the reconstruction. Electricity has just been installed.

At Leitholm there is a church seating about 200 (roll 210, Sunday school 30). It was first an Original Secession Congregation, then United Presbyterian, then United Free and is today part of our National Reunited Church. It is a plain building about 110 years old, with a loyal congregation, serving the needs of the east end of the parish. The

Union of 1929 has benefited this congregation both in numbers and in financial assistance from the endowments of other parishes. The Rev. Michell Dabb has just become the minister.

In Birgham there is a Scottish Episcopal Mission with its own premises. It is under the charge of the Rev. Alan Swinton, M.A. of St Mary's, Coldstream.

YOUTH ORGANISATIONS

Boy Scouts have operated in the parish since 1925 and have their headquarters at Eccles. The troop normally numbers about 18 boys. The troop has a good record, having won the County Flag on three occasions. Five boys and their Scoutmaster were present at the International Scout Jamboree held at Arrowe Park, Birkenhead in 1929. Baden Powell, the Scout Founder, was Camp leader.

Girl Guides have their meetings in Leitholm and there is also a Brownie Pack. There was a Guide Troop in Eccles for some years, but it is now in abeyance. The Leitholm troop serves the whole parish.

SOCIAL ACTIVITIES

A Dramatic Club in Eccles has achieved noteable success under the direction of the present schoolmaster, Mr John Stark, MA. Badminton and Table Tennis are also enjoyed.

Eccles, Leitholm and Birgham all possess really good village halls. Eccles Hall was the Free Church. It closed for worship and the congregation was dissolved in 1922, all its members joining the parish church. For several years it was disused, then in 1940 Mrs M. E. Greig, the widow of the late laird, had extensive alterations and additions made to the building, and she passed it over as her personal gift to the community. It is an excellent hall. There are Trustees and a local Committee of Management of which the minister and schoolmaster are *ex-officio* members.

Leitholm Hall, a brick building of suitable size, was built by public subscription about 1910. It is administered by a local committee. Concerts, whist drives and dances are popular events in all three halls.

Birgham Hall was also built by public subscription in 1909. It is constructed of brick. The Earl of Home is Trustee, and there is a village committee.

Evening classes are held in the local schools under the head of 'Further Education'. Recently these classes have become less strictly educational. Popular classes recently held are country dancing, leather work and dressmaking.

Football is the most popular outdoor sport and is indulged in by a large number of the youths. Eccles Young Men's Guild team did well prior to the Second World War. Today Birgham has a very strong team and has won the Kelso and District Cup for 1950. Leitholm too has a good team in the field.

Quoiting has lost place and favour in recent years, but Leitholm still has a keen and active club.

Women's Rural Institutes are functioning in the three villages, Leitholm and Birgham branches for about 20 years. The Eccles branch was commenced three years ago. These Institutes are social, recreational, and educative and are linked by the Scottish Federation.

Playing field. A movement has been set afoot to acquire ground adjacent to Eccles Hall as a playing field. The schoolmaster leads this project and there is no doubt that it is a commendable one and worthy of success.

Political parties are not specially active. The Farm Servants' Union is allied to the Labour Party. The present Member of Parliament is Mr J. J. Robertson and he is a Labour Member. The Conservatives and the Liberals have each their own committees.

HOUSING

The housing shortage is not so acute here, but there is a clear necessity for more and better houses. Wherever people are able-bodied there is work for them on the farms; the needs of the aged, who wish to retire, raise difficult problems. A farm worker has a deduction of 3s. to 6s. per week from his wages according to the condition of his house. The new Orlit houses in the parish will have a rent of 17s. 6d. to £1 per week, so that the farm worker in a 'tied' cottage has a great advantage, which probably he does not always realise. In most cases good gardens are provided, and in many cases the tenants take pride in their gardens. However, some are becoming negligent. The change from yearly to monthly engagements is partly the cause of this, as a man is never sure that he will reap what he sows. The monthly engagement has not come up to expectations, especially for the worker. Some think a change to three or six months engagements at specified dates would be welcomed. At the moment 18 permanent prefabricated houses of the Orlit type are being erected in the parish. Eight are in course of construction at Eccles. Six are well advanced at Birgham, and four are to be built at Leitholm. Here is a general census of houses — Total number in parish, 324, made up thus: Mansion houses, 8; large and commodious, 50; cottages, 248; new orlits, 18; Eccles area, 126; Leitholm area (1 Inn), 136 houses; Birgham area (1 Inn), 62 houses. More than half of the cottages have been modernised, with bathrooms, electricity and general improvements installed. In a few years it is fairly certain that all cottages will be reconditioned. Farmers with poor cottages have difficulty today in securing workers and keeping them in their service. Eccles village is the property of the Laird; the village was rebuilt about 1905 and has a tidy and attractive appearance. However, due to changing times, the need of running water and modern sanitation inside all the houses is felt. Leitholm has a number of owners, but most of the houses are owned and/or occupied by retired persons. Birgham has also a number of private owners, but the Earl of Home is the largest landowner. Overcrowding does not exist to any extent. Better houses, e.g. with upstairs windows built out, and smaller families have altered this. The farm cottages in this part are above the standards in many other Scottish counties. Building Societies have made little difference to housing here.

AGRICULTURE, INDUSTRY AND COMMERCE

The agricultural statistics, supplied by the Department of Agriculture for Scotland, are as follows:

Tillage	6125 acres
Rotation Grass	2978 acres
Permanent Grass	2006 acres
Rough Grazings	29 acres

Of the 38 farms, 34 are full-time. 77 per cent are general cropping farms, but there are also some which combine stock-rearing and feeding, and some stock-rearing only.

A review of agriculture over the last 25 years reveals that the First World War brought a boom, but by 1928 the main activity of the parish was entering a serious depression. The farmers countered this by lowering wages and turning arable land into pasture. A married man's wage fell to about 30s. per week, with a free house and a few perquisites. The Second World War called for a great plough-up of pasture, and owing to large Government subsidies agriculture in 1950 is booming. Wages are now about £5 for a tractor driver, £6 for a shepherd, and women workers, when available, earn 74s. per week. Casual workers, or those on special work or piece work may earn much more. Dairying is a new departure in this parish and is carried on with considerable success. Eccles Tofts, Eccles Mains and Mersington (the last using the most modern equipment) are stocked with Ayrshire herds. Here is a list of the main crops raised in the parish, the more important being mentioned first: wheat, oats, barley, turnips, potatoes, sugar beet, rape silage (beans, peas, oats and tares), grass drying, cocksfoot grass seed, canary seed, soft fruits.

At present about one quarter of the farmland is in pasture; it carries about two lambs, three ewes per acre. The old system of fourth shift rotation is falling into disuse owing to the many artificial manure dressings now available.

Other occupations such as rabbit catching, timber cutting and engineering give employment to a fair number of the residents. Horses have almost disappeared from the land, and the pony and trap are a curiosity — very different was the case a quarter of a century ago. There are several general merchants in the parish and vans (motor) from

Kelso, Coldstream, Greenlaw and further afield bring bread, clothing, ironmongery and even jewellery to the house door. The Co-operative Society from Kelso have a good share of the local trade.

Several years ago five smithies were active in the parish; now, Hassington is the only one active, and it is combined with a motor engineering business.

Salmon fishing provides both a pastime and a business, the Tweed water being the property of the Earl of Home. Birgham Dub, comprising the Weil, the Cradles, the Dub Pool, the Corbie and the High Scar, is world famed. In the spring season of 1950, 485 salmon averaging 8 to 9 lbs. were landed. The heaviest was 27 lbs. In recent years the heaviest salmon landed, in the autumn season, was 44 lbs. Fishing gives employment to some of the Birgham men. There are joiner's shops at Birgham and Leitholm. Some men are engaged in the building trade, and there is a firm of slaters and builders in Birgham. Several of the girls travel to Kelso or the surrounding towns to work in offices or shops or Kelso Laundry. Very few of the girls are meantime entering domestic service.

THE WAY OF LIFE

The people have a loyalty and pride in their community, and they are good neighbours to each other. There is no sharp distinction between rich and poor, and there are not the great social extremes such as exist in some parts. The prestige and power of the great landowners have almost passed away, but there is good co-operation between employers and workers, and a personal contact in almost every case.

The people live well, and they eat a substantial diet and of greater variety than formerly. Except for a shortage of sugar the local population have hardly felt the food shortage and restrictions of the recent War. Many households rear a pig, some keep hens, but only a few now keep a cow. Even the farmhouses find it difficult to get milkmaids. The folk dress much better, and the whole status of the farm worker has been raised. Twenty-five years ago women workers on the land were sometimes referred to under the old name of 'Bondagers'. That was not a title of servitude but simply stated that they were bound for a year. The women wore large black straw hats with coloured bands and the hat was held on with a scarf. Men who are not bound are said 'to work to their own hand'.

People move about much more freely now; an evening trip to a theatre in Edinburgh is occasionally indulged in. Many persons in all walks of life have motor cars, some largely for business purposes, others simply for pleasure. Some have motor cycles; at the moment many of the farm workers are purchasing expensive racing cycles. There are fairly good bus services, and this method of travelling is cheap. Railway travelling from such places as Kelso is largely ignored. For generations the farmers have gathered on Fridays for the Market and their families usually accompany them; in the same way the farm servants have foregathered in Kelso Square on Saturday evening. The cinema, the fish and chip and the ice-cream shops are centres of attraction. The pubs have their share of trade, but the cinema has become a powerful rival. 'Picture' buses also run specially to Kelso on Wednesday and Thursday evenings. Sunday is quite well observed and attendances at the churches fairly good. However, there is much indifference towards the Christian faith, and the sense of attendance as a matter of conscience or duty has departed. Most of the people are pleased to claim church membership, and attendance at Communion can be an inspiring sight. A bus brings members from Birgham to the Communion.

There is little crime and most people are loyal law-abiding citizens, living peaceably. There is a noticeable increase in gambling, especially on horse racing and football pools, but there is little drunkenness. Until a few years ago a policeman was stationed at Leitholm, but now all police work is done by a police car operating from the Coldstream Station.

Most homes receive a daily paper and perhaps a weekly magazine. Almost every home possesses a wireless. A county scheme makes library books available for all at the nearest school.

Home life is a reality, and good parents maintain the highest traditions of Scottish family life. Only a very small number of mothers go out to work every day, but many mothers lend a hand at the busy seasons on the farm. Old age and widow's pensions, and family allowances have lightened the lot of those most in need. The people of Eccles are an industrious kindly folk, intelligent and contented. They look into the future with fresh hope and confidence, for when agriculture is good they all prosper.

1950–51

ECCLES

by David Thomson

ESTATES

The farms on Eccles Estate were sold in 1980 to Mr John Fullarton of Haddon and are run from Loanknowe. For some years previous to that, the land on Eccles Mains had been let annually as grass parks. Sadly, the farmhouse and buildings have been unoccupied for some time. They are now in an advanced state of disrepair and do much to spoil the otherwise tidy and well-kept image of the village. The houses in the village, formerly part of the Estate, are being sold off as they become vacant. Mr James Greig, son of the late owner, has retained the shooting on the estate and also a house at the stables which he uses as a shooting lodge.

Stainrigg has had several owners since the death of Mr R. W. D. Boswell in the late 1970s. The farms of Stainrigg Mains and Bankhead which originally comprised the estate are now farmed by Mr Robin Boswell as one unit from Bankhead. Mr Jeremy Bates now owns Anton's Hill, while his brother, Martin, owns neighbouring Belchester. Both families are connected with the arts, Mr Jeremy Bates being an accomplished organist, while Mrs Martin Bates paints under her maiden name, Sue Ryder, and was responsible for the much acclaimed portrait of the Princess of Wales in her wedding dress. The three farms on Anton's Hill Estate are let to tenants, although Grizelrig and Orange Lane are now run as one unit, the farmhouse and steading at Orange Lane having been sold.

Kames, at one time called Bessborough, was renamed after the famous Lord Kames. Benjamin Franklin was once entertained under its roof. The Menzies family have occupied the house for some years, the present owner being Mr John Menzies. All the farms on the estate have been taken 'in hand' as they became vacant, and the extensive new steading at East Mains attracted a great deal of interest when it was built in the early 1960s.

In recent times Bughtrig has had two eminent owners, both men of the sea. Admiral of the Fleet, Sir William May gave notable service in the First World War. There followed Admiral Sir Bertram Ramsay who was responsible for the naval operations for the invasion of North Africa in 1942 and for 'D' day in 1944, the Normandy bridgehead which led to the end of the War in Europe. Tragically, he was to die soon after in an air crash. He had married a Menzies from Kames and Bughtrig is now owned by their younger son, Brigadier Charles Ramsay O.B.E., who has acquired the farms of Langrig and Pittlesheugh.

Purves Hall is now run as a hotel, there being a boarding kennel for dogs in the stables. The land at Purves Hall was acquired by Mr Robert McDonald, tenant of the adjacent farm of Ecclestofts. At Purves Hall he formed the Woodside Stud where two or three thoroughbred stallions are kept. Here, New Brig finished his stud career, he being the sire of Mr McDonald's Scottish Grand national winner, Young Ash Leaf, who herself has bred some good winners.

Springwell, for long owned by the Home family, was sold in 1985 on the death of Lady Bridget Douglas Home.

FARMS

Few changes in farm occupancy have taken place in the last 30 years apart from those mentioned in connection with Eccles, Kames, Anton's Hill and Bughtrig. Stonefold changed hands several times before being acquired by the Cavers family from Crosshall, and Kennetsideheads is now owned by a member of the Mitchell family from neighbouring Legars. The occupancy of Hardacres has moved to Mr Jackie Fleming, a nephew of the former owner. In nearly all the other farms in the parish there are sons who will follow their fathers, a healthy state of affairs indeed.

As in the other areas, there has been a marked reduction in farm staffs within the parish. Whereas in 1950 wages were about £5 per week, most workers would now earn more than £100 per week. The need for farm cottages had decreased in a similar way, especially as some people prefer to live in the villages or towns and travel to their work. Several 'rows' of farm cottages have been knocked down or converted to other uses, although at Springwells four new cottages have been built to replace those demolished. The letting of cottages for holidays does not appear to be as prevalent in this parish as in other areas. Some farm cottages have been sold when little more than ruins and renovated by their new owners. Particularly good examples are at Stonefold and Bluehouses.

VILLAGES

Eccles. When Eccles congregation was linked with Greenlaw in 1976, Eccles Manse was sold to Mr Roger Dodd whose wife is the daughter of Mr Andrew Czynski, the last tenant of Loanknowe Farm.

A feature of the village is the industry which takes place at the east end. Messrs Forsyth, Commercial Motor Engineers, Messrs Waddell, Joiners and Messrs Oliver, Road Transport, all provide much needed employment as well as excellent services. Mr John and Mr Ian Forsyth have built houses to the south of the Orlits and Mr Norman Oliver has built a house to the east of the village hall.

Sixteen Orlit houses were built in the early 1950s and known as Kirkfield. These were refurbished in 1983–84, the occupants being housed in mobile homes while the work as being carried out. Some of these houses have been sold to the tenants.

Leitholm. While there has been considerable improvement and renovation of existing houses, no private housebuilding has taken place since the last report was written. However, two lots of council houses were built in the early 1950s known as Mansefield and Ramsay Crescent, and some of these houses have been sold to the tenants. An attractive playground has been formed on the site of the old smithy which greatly enhances the appearance of the village. To the north of it have been built bungalows specifically for the use of pensioners.

Birgham. The main feature in Birgham has been the construction of some extremely attractive houses. Built about 1970, these have a magnificent situation high above the Tweed, several being owned by retired people. There has been other private housebuilding in the village as well as the reconstruction of existing houses. All but two of the Orlits, built by the council in the 1950s and known as Treaty Park, have been sold to the tenants.

CHURCHES

Several changes have taken place in the parish in recent years. Services at Ecclestofts and in Birgham Hall ceased in the 1950s. In 1959, Leitholm being vacant, the congregations of Eccles and Leitholm were linked under the Rev. J. I. C. Finnie who had, in 1951, followed Rev. J. L. Douglas as minister of Eccles. In 1976 Eccles and Leitholm were transferred from the Presbytery of Jedburgh to the Presbytery of Duns. That same year, Mr Finnie retired and, after much discussion, the linking between Eccles and Leitholm was broken. Leitholm was then linked with the multiple charge of Swinton, Fogo, Whitsome and Ladykirk, under Rev. Alan Cartwright, the manse being at Swinton. Eccles was linked with Greenlaw under Rev. Frederick Levison, the incumbent there at that time. The manse at Greenlaw became the manse of the linked charge and, as reported elsewhere, Eccles manse was sold. Mr Levison retired in 1977 and in 1978 Rev Ian Paterson was inducted as minister of Greenlaw and Eccles. When he retired in 1985 yet another change took place, and the linking between Eccles and Greenlaw was broken. The minister of Gordon, Westruther and Legerwood retired in the interests of readjustment and Greenlaw was linked with these three congregations. Eccles was then linked with Coldstream under its minister, Rev Ian Penman. This seemed a wise move as, although Eccles and Birgham had been limited for many years, some Birgham inhabitants worshipped in Coldstream and some in Eccles. Now they all had the same minister.

As with most country parishes, church membership and attendance have fallen dramatically. While in Eccles in 1950 there were 350 on the roll and 200 attending communion, the roll now contains 150 names with 65 attending communion. However, there is no lack of vitality either in the Session or in the congregation. There is an active Sunday School, although most of the pupils are under 10 years of age, and every year at Christmas a nativity play is performed in the church. This has become a popular tradition and is extremely well attended. There is also an enthusiastic Guild with 16 members. While Eccles is fortunate to have a morning service every Sunday, at Leitholm this takes place only every fortnight, making the task of the minister and office-bearers that much more difficult. However, the congregation is in an extremely satisfactory state with a flourishing Woman's Guild having 21 members. There are 135 on the Leitholm Roll with about 50 attending communion.

SCHOOLS

In the early 1960s the school and schoolhouse at Eccles were demolished and new ones built on the same site. In 1980 Leitholm School was closed and the pupils transferred to Eccles, which is now a two-teacher school with about 30 pupils, nearly all being conveyed by school transport daily. Whereas previously the children went up to the village hall for meals, the new school has its own facilities. The school boasts its own computer and for swimming lessons the children are taken to Duns. At 11 years old everyone now goes on to the High School in Duns, Coldstream being entirely a Primary School since 1968. Birgham School was closed in 1953 and the children now attend Coldstream.

AGRICULTURE

Since the 1950 report, the changes in agriculture have been considerable. Previously, there was a large flock of half-bred ewes on most farms, with a shepherd in charge. Now, apart from Bartlehill which has one of the leading flocks of pedigree Suffolk sheep in Britain, there are only a few small flocks of breeding ewes and no shepherds in the parish. To compensate for this, far more land is under the plough, and instead of the age-old practice of rotational farming, continuous corn growing has taken over on some farms, apparently with no detrimental effect on the land and certainly not on yields. The acreage of winter grain has risen dramatically with some farms sowing practically all their cereal acreage in the autumn. Apart from the much higher yields of grain obtainable, there is the added advantage of harvest commencing earlier and being spread over a longer period. The growing of winter barley on a large scale has only commenced in the last decade. Previously the crop was very susceptible to mildew and other diseases, but these can now be kept in check by spraying. The spraying of weedkillers, fungicides and pesticides is becoming ever more frequent and widespread, and while it causes considerable anxiety to conservationists, it is doubtful if it does much harm if used intelligently and responsibly. Peas, beans and, in particular, oil-seed rape are now being grown as break crops. To some extent these replace swedes and turnips which are practically non-existent. Fields of vegetables are now being grown on certain farms. Potatoes are probably the only crop for which the acreage has remained fairly constant, although they are mostly lifted by mechanical harvesters rather than by squads of school children.

Large and modernised dairies still exist at Ecclestofts and Mersington and these have been joined by equally efficient units at Hassington West Mains and Kennetsideheads. It is very unusual to find so many cows being milked in such a predominantly arable parish.

The house cow is a thing of the past, it is doubtful if a single pig is fed in the parish and even poultry are in very small numbers.

In spite of the large reduction in the labour force, the farms in the parish have, in general, a pleasing and well-kept appearance. A great many new buildings have been erected, some for feeding cattle but most for drying and storing of grain. Wherever possible, care has been taken to see that these blend into the countryside. Fortunately, unlike in some parishes, no high tower silos for grain or silage have been erected.

COMMERCE

Apart from those already mentioned in connection with Eccles village, there have been a surprising number of commercial developments within the parish.

On the site of the Cocked Hat Covert at Whitrig, a Transformer Station was built when the electricity line from Cockenzie was brought through in 1966. Shortly afterwards a depot was set up next to it by the agricultural spraying contractors, Chafers. This has now been taken over by Messrs Thomas Sheriff, agricultural engineers, who have several workshops in the Borders. Across the road is situated the sawmill of Mr Albert Ross. This is a real success story. Mr Ross, whose father was the tenant of Harlaw, started up in a very small way in the timber business when he returned from the war. Now he has one of the most modern plants in the country at his Woodside sawmill, employing several men. He has also built two very attractive bungalows on the site. In 1963 Mr Robert Boswell built the well-known filling station on his own land at Orange Lane. It has since been purchased by Mr James Blacklock who owns the garage in Leitholm. Another garage is that of Mr Dominic Buckley at Hassington. Mr Buckley, a very successful Rally driver himself, has considerable expertise in preparing rally cars and so, apart from serving the local community, his business covers a very much wider area. In 1980 a drier and grain store was built on Charterhall aerodrome by Border Grains. The plant has a storage capacity of ten and a half thousand tons. A further 10,000 tons can be stored in the two hangars which are leased from Major Trotter of Charterhall. At the former steading at Orange Lane David Hall has set up in business as a builder and there are still firms of joiners in Leitholm and Birgham.

SHOPS AND PUBLIC HOUSES

There has been a marked reduction in the number of shops, especially in Leitholm where there remains only a general store and a post office. In Eccles, a small shed behind one of the Orlits acts as a post office, selling a few items as well and a similar shed in Birgham does the same job, but here there are no post office services. The Fisherman's Arms in Birgham and the Plough at Leitholm are the only public houses in the parish although Purves Hall Hotel now provides bar and restaurant services.

PUBLIC SERVICES

Water. The Watch reservoir has given Berwickshire a fine water supply and nearly all the farms and houses in the parish are connected to it.

Electricity is almost certainly in all homes and there is street lighting in the villages, some would say to an excess, particularly in Eccles. Three lines of pylons now cross the parish. The highest line, put up in the mid 1960s and coming from Cockenzie, passes east of Eccles village, and the third line from Torness which is under construction in 1986 passes east of Leitholm. Much discussion took place before the routes for all these lines were finalised, with considerable opposition from some quarters, and while they are certainly a blot on the landscape, they are nevertheless essential to the demands of modern living.

Gas. A main pipeline for North Sea gas was laid through the parish in 1970 with a valve station at Hassington W. Mains. From this, a branch line supplies certain houses in Leitholm.

Roads. While the main roads are well maintained, the same cannot be said of some of the minor roads in the parish. Apart from surfaces breaking up, roadside edges and drains seldom receive attention and many farmers have taken upon themselves to do this work. Roadmen do not now appear to attend to roads in their own locality but are conveyed in squads throughout the Region, after working long distances from home.

Refuse. In order to minimise the incidence of rubbish dumps, there is a weekly collection of refuse throughout the district.

Sewage. Sewage works have been constructed in all the three villages.

Transport. There are regular if infrequent bus services to the nearby towns, and when these are not available, the routes are covered by Post Buses. The public are also welcome to make use of school transport.

THE HOME

While much has been done to modernise many of the houses in the parish, there have also been great improvements made in furnishing and in interior decorating. Fitted carpets, central heating and electrical appliances such as cookers, washing machines, refrigerators and freezers are to be found in a great many houses. Colour TV sets are to be found in nearly every house while telephones are still increasing. Except for the elderly most families own a car, and many make use of it to do their shopping at supermarkets in local towns. This has made travelling vans uneconomic, and although bread and milk are still delivered regularly, other vans are seldom seen. There is however a travelling library run by the Region which visits the parish regularly.

SOCIAL ACTIVITIES

Because people can watch television or use their own cars to reach nearby towns, social activities within the villages have been sadly curtailed. This is especially so in Birgham where all the leisure activities would appear to take place in Coldstream. There is, however, a small youth club for 7-12 year olds. Each village boasts a flourishing W.R.I., there being 18 members in Birgham, 28 in Eccles and 30 in Leitholm. Badminton takes place in Eccles Hall weekly and occasional dances are organised — everything being run by the Hall Committee. In Leitholm the Quoiting Club is still in existence and the village hall appears to be in constant use. It is used regularly for badminton and carpet bowling. There is an Evergreen Club for senior citizens started in 1970 by Mr Cooper and a playgroup every Monday which is visited by Gus the Bus. This is a playschool double decker bus run by the Regional Council which visits rural areas.

HEALTH SERVICES

There are now health centres in all the local towns, and, as far as possible, patients visit the doctors there rather than the doctors having to travel to people's homes. The doctors are ably supported by district nurses and health visitors. Until recently maternity cases were catered for in the local hospitals, but when it became impossible to get sufficient midwives, it was necessary for the expectant mothers to go to Edinburgh. However, they normally return to a local cottage hospital when their babies are about 48 hours old. Other patients requiring treatment go either to Peel or to one of the Edinburgh hospitals.

POPULATION

There continues to be a marked drop in population. For Eccles and Birgham there are 300 in the Electoral Roll and for Leitholm, 310. The approximate numbers living in the actual villages are Birgham 130, Leitholm 120 and Eccles 60.

1986

Plate 22. The old railway line at Eyemouth.

Plate 23. Grantshouse in the 1950s.

THE PARISH OF EDROM

by Helen Brunton and Margaret Harrower

PHYSICAL

The parish covers 14 square miles approximately of level land drained mainly by rivers Blackadder and Whiteadder which flow through the parish from west to east, the Whiteadder forming the northern boundary, and join at Allanton.

Parishes bordering Edrom are: north, Bonkyl (Buncle, old spelling); north-east, Chirnside; east, Hutton; west, Duns; and south, Whitsome and Swinton.

The present population is approximately 361, a big decline in 100 years. In 1881 population was 1514 and even 50 years ago in 1931 the number was 1015.

There are only three villages in the parish, Allanton, population 90; Edrom, population 25 and Sinclair's Hill, population 13.

The parish is mostly agricultural land with approximately 20 farms, all very intensively farmed. Edrom, being part of the Merse, is very fertile: wheat, barley, potatoes and root crops are all grown. In recent years many farms have grown oil-seed rape and protein peas. Stock on the farms is mainly cattle, both breeding and feeding, and here again changes have taken place in breeds from the Aberdeen Angus, Shorthorns and Herefords of the past, to Charolais, Simmental and others which grow more quickly with leaner meat. Sheep, in lesser numbers, are also reared. There is one substantial dairy farm with milk going to the Milk Marketing Board by road tanker.

In recent years mechanisation has increased rapidly with the result that fewer permanent agricultural workers are needed on each farm. One no longer sees large squads of men and women in the fields, hoeing, haymaking, binding and stooking sheaves or gathering potatoes. Now, at busy seasons, extra casual workers are employed and some farms use contractors who bring their own machines and employees. Little hay is made now, the change being to silage which is stored for winter feed in pits or in huge silos which tower on many farms and certainly do not contribute to the beauty of the landscape.

Most farms have their own grain driers to deal with the increased acreage of grain, but near Edrom village there is a large grain drying and storage complex owned by a group of grain merchants to which grain is brought by road from a wide area. This does not offer high employment as it is mostly mechanically operated. Work horses have disappeared from the landscape since the 1930s. There are riding horses and ponies kept at some farms. Changes in wages have been tremendous. For the agricultural worker the last 60 years have seen a ploughman's wage of 22/- per week in 1925 soar to a present tractorman's wage of £100 per week. In each case there are 'perks' to add to these figures, usually a free cottage, sometimes produce like milk or potatoes. Tradesmen's wages and charges have increased in similar ratio.

The landscape has changed greatly in the last 50 years with many hardwood mature trees being felled - particularly on the large estates which were sold up. Hedges, too, have often been torn out to enlarge fields in order to facilitate work with large machines. Recently however, there has been more replanting, but mostly softwoods, such as Sitka spruce, which grow and mature quickly. These new woods do not offer as much shelter, nesting and food to birds and small animals as do mixed woods of oak, plane, beech etc.

Before the 1914 war, the several mansion houses and estates in the parish employed many workers both indoors and outdoors, with other tradesmen in the villages supplying goods and services also. Through taxation and other factors some of these estates have been broken up, the farms usually being sold to the tenants, and in several cases the mansion houses have been demolished. Broomhouse, Blackadder, Allanbank, Kelloe, all have been demolished over the years. Kimmerghame is still occupied by the Swinton family as it has been since 1760 and part of Nisbet House still stands and is occupied. Edrom House has had a complete change of use, as it now houses part of the International Cello school where students from various countries live and study music.

The three villages in Edrom parish have changed little in appearance except for modernisation and good roads, with telephone wires and T.V. aerials above the roofs. A few new private houses have been built in each and four council-owned houses in Allanton and four in Sinclair's Hill. A number of cottages and houses are only used as holiday and weekend homes and this is true of many farm cottages no longer needed for workers. This tends to alter the structure of the villages, as the holiday owners are not truly part of the community.

Many small trades and shops which used to serve the area have now disappeared, leaving only a Post Office and shop in Allanton. No shop remains in Edrom since the Post Office closed in 1969. Travelling shops still serve villages and farms but with more people owning cars, much shopping is now done in Duns, Berwick and further afield. As in many rural areas bus services are infrequent and not always convenient as to timing to intending passengers, although recently there has been a slight improvement.

With no large employer or industry in the parish, a large proportion of people not connected with agriculture work elsewhere — in Duns, Berwick, Coldstream, Kelso and Eyemouth, most travelling by car daily.

EDUCATION

There were originally three public schools in the parish, Allanton, Edrom and Sinclair's Hill, each with a good number of pupils from village and surrounding farms. Allanton and Sinclair's Hill closed in the 1930s and the pupils were transferred to larger schools in Chirnside and Duns. Edrom school continued for some time with one teacher instead of two, then with a falling number of children on the roll, pupils were transferred in 1965 to Chirnside, travelling by school bus. For some years the building was used as a school for disabled and spastic children. It is now used as a village hall.

CHURCHES

For many years there were two churches serving the parish, Allanton Church and Edrom Church — the latter being the Parish Church built in 1732. The last minister of Allanton was there for over 60 years and on his death the congregation joined with Edrom congregation. The church building and manse were sold and are now occupied by a transport and farming concern. Edrom Church was later linked with Bonkyl and Chirnside under one minister, both smaller congregations still holding services in their own churches and managing their own finances. Edrom Manse was sold, the minister of the linked churches living in Chirnside Manse. The Sunday schools are small these days — a far cry from the past when a large contingent of scholars marched from Whitsome, Edrom and Allanton to Blackadder House to hold their summer picnic there. Races were run, a piper played and tea was provided by the Houston Boswall family.

The weather in this area is not usually subject to extreme changes but two events are worthy of note. In 1881 the lowest temperature in the British Isles was recorded at Blackadder Gardens — 22^{0}F below zero — 54^0 frost. On 12th August 1948 the Border countryside experienced a tremendous deluge in 24 hours. The rivers Blackadder and Whiteadder flooded many acres in the parish and swept away stocks and crops, but fortunately no human lives were lost.

COMMUNICATIONS

Previous to the 1948 floods, the area was served by rail, there being regular trains between Reston, Chirnside, Edrom and Duns. This branch line connected with the main rail network to Edinburgh and south to England. In other parts of Berwickshire several bridges were washed away in the flood and as a result the Edrom branch line was closed. Edrom station buildings eventually became a private dwelling. Motor transport, both public and private, has taken over from horse transport and the steam train.

As in the rest of Britain the telephone has revolutionised communications, both in the home and business, but is especially beneficial in rural areas.

SOCIAL SERVICES

Great changes have come to the parish with the advent of electricity in 1951, and the supply of main water from the newly constructed Watch Reservoir in 1953.

Road surfaces and drainage improvements have been carried out through the years by the Regional Council and many farm roads have also been improved. There is a much welcomed County Library van which reaches most parts of the parish to bring books to housebound people unable to reach the library at Duns.

The Women's Royal Voluntary Service also delivers meals to invalids and housebound people several times weekly, the meals being cooked in the Chirnside school kitchens.

MEDICAL SERVICES

The parish has no resident doctor or nurse, but is served from the practice in Chirnside and from the Knoll Hospital and Health Centre in Duns. Community nurses, taking over from the former district nurses, now cover the area from Duns. Radio communication in their cars has helped doctors and nurses to reach patients anywhere in the parish with no delay.

POLICE

As with the medical services, the parish is served by police from outwith the area, travelling by car and van with radio contact. Fortunately there is little crime in the parish and that of a minor nature.

ACTIVITIES AND LEISURE

Leisure pursuits in rural areas have been greatly affected first by the arrival of radio in the home and even more by television, and some activities have disappeared altogether. Quoiting used to be played in the villages and tennis in Allanton. However carpet bowling and indoor bowls are still very popular in Allanton and Edrom in the winter.

In the whole parish there is only one public house, the 'Red Lion' in Allanton. The Women's Rural Institute flourishes in both villages and there is a joint Senior Citizens' Club and church guild.

Sadly there are no youth activities in the parish; for these the youngsters have to go to Chirnside or Duns. Fishing is still a popular pastime although catches are small nowadays.

Edrom parish lies in countryside of great beauty and many visitors return year after year to holiday in cottages and hotels in the area and surrounding parishes. We who live here are content and happy in our small but peaceful and beautiful parish.

ALLANTON

(including the Manse and Allanbank Mill)

Allanton is the biggest village in Edrom parish. The main street runs uphill from the confluence of the Whiteadder and the Blackadder and at first sight looks much as it did at the beginning of this 20th century. But as one reaches the top of Allanton hill the differences appear. The thick growth of trees at the entrance to Blackadder Drive was cut down about 1916. The wide side walks, once roughly paved with cobblestones and known as 'causies', are now covered with tarmacadam. The pretty little grass field opposite the gates has also lost its trees and is now the site of four bungalows and two workshops. The gates into Blackadder House were removed when the house was sold in 1925 and are now at the entrance to a public park at Morpeth, Northumberland.

It is interesting to compare the number of houses, population and occupations in 1914 and 1986.

OCCUPATIONS

1914	*1986*
Blacksmiths	Social worker
Slater & Plasterers	Joiners
Grocers: 2 shops, 1 licensed	Farmer
Tailors: 3 businesses	Lecturer (on staff at Moray House)
Cobbler	Architect
Estate workers	Agricultural engineers
Papermill employees	Clerkesses
Builders: 2 businesses	Farm workers
Bakery	Home-helps
School headmaster	Worker at Torness power station
Dressmakers: 2	Sempstress
Sweet Shop	Factory workers
Artist	Potato pickers
Red Lion Hotel	Baptist minister
Maids	Postmistress

Woodman	School janitor
Farmworkers	Teacher
Gardeners	Design engineer at Dexters
Manse: Rev C. Blades	Secretary
Sawmiller	Red Lion Hotel
Farmer	Contractor
	Shop assistant
	Farm and contractor

In 1914 only four persons worked for employers outside the village (except for those working on Blackadder Estate). There were no unemployed. Six persons were retired.

In 1986 23 persons work for employers in Duns, Berwick, Eyemouth, Chirnside and on farms.

One person is unemployed. 22 persons are retired or widowed.

In 1914 there were 42 houses in the village, 144 inhabitants, 51 being children.

In 1986 there are 52 houses; 101 inhabitants, 16 being children.

In 1914 there were seven shops; nine businesses employing people from both within and without the village.

In 1986 there are no businesses employing workers. There is one shop/post office. There are four council owned-houses, eight bungalows have been built. Five houses are now holiday homes, two houses have been demolished, two are for sale, two houses have been sold but are still unoccupied.

The village school was closed in 1932, and is now as the village hall. Children attend school at Chirnside until aged 12 then go to Berwickshire High School in Duns, travelling by bus.

Allanton Church was closed in the 1950s. The congregation was united with Edrom and later with Bonkyl and later still with Chirnside.

Innovations. Water supply from the Watch Reservoir in 1953. All houses now have bathrooms. Roads were tarmacadamed. Telephones and electricity (1951) were introduced. The first letter box was installed in 1916, and the Post Office in the 1920s. Street lamps appeared in 1953. Bus service commenced in 1920s. First car appeared in village in 1914; now most families own a car. Bridges were built over Whiteadder and Blackadder in 1841 and 1851.

1986

THE PARISH AND BURGH OF EYEMOUTH

by Rev. D. M. Walker

The Parish boundaries, which have changed little since the reports of 1792 and 1835, are as follows: from Callercove Point the line runs through Hallydown Farm, excluding the farm buildings, to the Ale Water river. Continuing down the Ale Water to the River Eye the line runs down the Eye to the Tollbridge and thereafter follows the new line of the Burgh.

From the Killiedraught Bay the boundary of the Parish runs in a southerly direction until it reaches the Eyemouth-Coldingham Road (A1107) at approximately 70 yards above the 'four roads crossing'. The line continues south-east to Netherbyres Old Lodge across the Ayton-Eyemouth Road (B6355) to the middle of the River Eye. Continuing down the centre of the Eye River to the Toll Bridge it runs along the north side of the Eyemouth-Burnmouth road (A1107) to the garden boundary of the Gunsgreen Hill Farm Cottages. The line breaks off north-east and runs parallel with the River Eye to a point 2300 feet distant. Then turning south-east it runs 2500 feet and finally turning east it meets the sea a little above Scout Point.

The variation of the Burgh boundary took place only recently, in 1946, and has an important bearing on the growth of the town. It made possible the development of a housing scheme stretching from the Burnmouth Road along the south bank of the Eye towards the sea. This is an important development, taking quite a section of the town across the River Eye and is regarded by the County Planning consultant as bad development, but the Town Council feels that it centres the town to the Harbour, a feature which is desirable in the fishing community. These opinions hinge on the future development of the Burgh and this will be more fully discussed under the heading of Industries and Commerce.

HISTORY OF THE LOCAL COMMUNITY

The industrial revolution and the mechanisation of many hand processes have brought changes to the Parish and Burgh. Eyemouth has, however, not experienced industrialisation to the same extent as many other parts of the country; nevertheless the products of the industrial age have been accepted and used readily. For example, methods of fishing and the types of vessels used have undergone many changes. Sails were replaced by engines towards the close of the 19th century.

The storm of 1881 (October) which resulted in the death of 129 fishermen, would not have created such a tragedy at the present day for the sailing vessels of that day were uncontrollable in the face of such a storm. The steam drifter, using the drift net in the catching of herring, was the type of large vessel mainly in use in the 1930s. Smaller vessels were fitted with paraffin burning engines and used fishing lines, each line containing 1000 hooks. Grim stories are still told by the old folk of how limpets were used as bait. As young boys and girls they would walk to the Cove, a distance of ten miles, to gather limpets. The use of mussels instead of limpets to bait the lines involved the fishermen's wives in four hours of hard work, every evening or early morning, shelling 1000 mussels and baiting the line. Even in the 1930s there were still a few line boats with their paraffin burning engines. During the past 10 years the seine net boat has ousted the small line craft and the large drifter. The seine netter using a diesel engine can quickly be turned from white-fish-catching to herring-catching and is a much more economical vessel than the drifter. Echometers, wireless receiving, transmitting, as well as direction finding apparatus have all brought changes. Electricity is greatly used on board the vessels.

A similar story can be told of agriculture. Farmers such as David Gray of Northburn and John Raw of Linthill were among the foremost to make use of agricultural machinery. The tendency has been for the small farms to become concentrated into larger holdings and today agriculture in the parish of Eyemouth and Berwickshire as a whole, has become a highly mechanised process involving the use of mechanical sowers and combine harvesters.

The Parish and Burgh have also responded to the facilities offered by modern transport. A Branch railway from Burnmouth to Eyemouth connects the town with the London and North Eastern Railway, now British Railways. This link was responsible for developing the fishing as an industry, enabling wider markets to be reached. The buses offer also a good passenger transport service, particularly to Berwick and Edinburgh, and the town is fast becoming a popular holiday resort.

As in all parts of Scotland the industrial age has brought with it a considerable secularising of the life of the community, strict sabbath observance having been greatly relaxed.

The farms of the parish are as follows:

Farms	*Owner*	*Occupier*	*Acreage*	*Tillage*	*Pasture*
Northburn*	Mr R. Wood	Mr R. Wood	67	40	27
Anedale*	Mr J. Craig	Mr R. Wood	167	160	8
Highlaws	Major Sandison	Mr Craig	169	161	8
The Mill Farm*	Sir Chr. Innes	Capt. John Webb	82.5	59.5	23
Hallydown	Mr Purdie	Mr Purdie			
Linthill	Mr Fleming	Mr Fleming	322	212	94 (16 woodland)
Old Linthill House and Market Garden	Milne Home Estate	Mr W. Moffat			

Farms marked * were originally part of the Milne Home estate to which many owner-occupied houses in Eyemouth still pay feu duty. Highlaws Farm was the home farm of Highlaws House, at present occupied by Major Sandison.

Linthill farm has only come into the possession of Mr Fleming during the present year and was occupied by Mr John Rae who rented it from Mrs Home Robertson, it being part of the Milne Home Estate.

Northburn farm was purchased by Mr Wood in 1945 and was previously occupied by Mr D. Gray.

Local folklore, customs and traditions. There is little to mention of folklore of a historical nature, but a report such as this should mention features of a distinctly local flavour such as dialect, superstitions and customs. The dialect of the people is very broad, some of the vowels being much lengthened, particularly the vowel 'a' which is lengthened to the sound of 'aw'. Many broad Scots words are in everyday use and phrases of the sea and navigation are woven into everyday speech. Superstitions closely associated with the fishing still exist but do not hold such a command over the views of those who hold them. It is, for example, regarded as unlucky to meet a minister while going down to the boat; certain words are taboo such as pig, salmon, rabbit.

A ceremony instituted in 1939, and revived in 1945, at the close of the Second World War, may continue as a custom of the Burgh in years to come: namely the Crowning of an Eyemouth Herring Queen, the Queen being the Eyemouth Fisherman's daughter with the highest marks out of the first two terms' examinations in the third year of the High School. On the appointed day the Queen is sailed from St Abbs on one of the Eyemouth boats and is met by a large escort of the vessels of the port. The crowning ceremony was for the first time performed by Lady Burness of Netherbyres, and thereafter the retiring Queen has placed the crown on her successor's head. The site chosen for the ceremony has always been the flat piece of ground between Gunsgreen House and the Lifeboat Station.

Historical Buildings and Monuments. The buildings mentioned in the previous reports are still standing but Gunsgreen House, owned by Mr Sanderson of Gunsgreen Farm and rented as a Boarding House, is in a very weathered condition, the roof in particular being much in need of repair. Old Linthill House, though showing the marks of passing years, is still a remarkably find old building.

A monument in the form of a broken mast erected, after 1881, at the entrance to the new cemetery will ever remind Eyemouth of one of the most disastrous days in her history and of the hazards of the fisherman's life in the days of the sailing boats. On 14th October 1881, a violent storm arose while the fleet of fishing boats was at sea and 129 men were lost. The old cemetery in High Street is now regarded as a place of interest by visitors to the town. The ground of the cemetery is much higher than street level and tradition has it that a fresh layer of soil was placed on the cemetery after an outbreak of plague. The gravestones disturbed by this work were collected and built to form a small square or watch house at one corner of the cemetery.

There are no ecclesiastical records earlier than the Disruption or the middle of the 19th century. A Kirk Session Minute Book beginning in the 1840s reveals that Lamberton Toll on the Scottish border was as favourite a place for eloping couples as Gretna Green in the west. The minute book contains quite a few cases of couples who on their return to Eyemouth have been compeared by the Kirk Session and rebuked for their irregular marriage.

There are various endowments for religious purposes, all now collected by the General Treasurer of the Church of Scotland on behalf of the Auld Kirk. About 1870 the Rev. Stephen Bell of the Auld Kirk claimed that tithes should be paid upon fish landed. To this proposal the fishing community strongly objected. The minister took the matter to law and won his case, whereupon the fishermen must have decided to free themselves of the responsibility by offering a settlement by an investment which to this day realises £60 per annum. Feelings ran very high during the dispute and an effigy of the minister was burned on the Manse lamp-post. At other times, however, Mr Bell's ministry was received with more appreciation and records show that he died during the year of the fishing disaster in 1881 having spent himself nobly on behalf of his parish. A further sum of £43 is received as interest from the sale of the Glebe in 1934 to the Eyemouth Town Council for housing development.

POPULATION

The population figures of the Parish and Burgh of Eyemouth are as follows: 1801, 899; 1831, 1181; 1851, 1488; 1881, 2935 (maximum); 1901, 2487 (change of boundary during intercensal period); 1911, 2561; 1921, 2573; 1931, 2321; 1935 (as disclosed by overcrowding survey) 2256 with say 30 floating, 2286.

It is a well known fact that during the past 20 years agricultural areas such as Berwickshire have suffered from a continual drift of the rural population towards the towns. This has been due to various causes such as more congenial employment, a greater variety of opportunity and better housing conditions. Considering that agricultural workers in the years 1930 to 1938 were receiving 26/- to 30/- per week, the drift was inevitable. It is estimated that in the years between the 1914-18 and 1939-45 wars an approximate total of 22,000 left the Berwickshire area. In certain respects Eyemouth experiences the same trend. The census figures remain fairly static, but young people leave to find more congenial and well paid work in the city. Fishing returns during the decade 1929-39 were extremely meagre, when the industry reached its lowest ebb. Apart from the two industries, agriculture and fishing, there were few opportunities for the progressive boy or girl and the result has been not only a static population figure, but more worrying still, the failure of the fishing industry to attract young men who will continue the basic industry of the port. When the fishing industry boomed during the war years, 1939-45, the young men were all in the forces and by the time they returned, the attractiveness of the fisherman's calling had again lost any strong financial appeal. Eyemouth, as a parish and burgh, like the whole of Berwickshire requires to be developed by establishing various industries, otherwise the population will not provide that cross-section of people so necessary for a full community life.

For the most part the population is composed of people born in the parish, but municipal, ecclesiastical, professional and key positions tend to be held by people who have come into the town. No immigration to the town of people from other parts of Scotland, England or Ireland could be traced in the history of the last five or six generations. The rural population of the parish tends to move around every few years but better economic conditions have considerably eased this problem and the radius of migration was never very large.

PUBLIC AND SOCIAL SERVICES

The Water Supply. Prior to 1878 pipes were run from Highlaws Spring and Mattly Wood Spring on the Burnmouth Road. In 1878 water was conveyed by five inch pipes from springs along the Ale River. In 1885 an additional supply was sought from St Ebba's Well in Ayton Castle and Bell's spring, the water being brought by four inch pipe and connected to the Ale Water supply at Balabraes Bridge. In 1905 the Linthill Haugh Supply was tapped and brought to the town by six inch pipes running side by side with the old five inch pipes.

There is no surface reservoir of the normal type, but Linthill Haugh contains a large gravel bed which is filled by seepage from the Ale to form an underground water supply of considerable extent. A shaft has been sunk into this gravel bed and the main pipe, six inch in diameter, leaves this shaft about 15 feet below the surface. The supply amounts to 120,000 gallons per day which just meets the needs of the Burgh. During the years 1935 to 1950 the supply dwindled considerably to around 70,000 gallons per day and much inconvenience was caused by economy of supply. In 1950 the trouble was diagnosed as due to corroded pipes and, after scraping of the pipes, the supply originally promised by the system has become available. Only the 1905 six inch pipe was scraped. The water reaches the town via the tank west of Victoria Road and with housing development above the level of this tank the water is pumped to a high level tank at Airedale. It is the intention of the Town Council to augment the supply to a high level tank by the county water scheme at present being developed, thus eliminating the cost of pumping. The houses at Bridgend and Gunsgreen were supplied with water from a spring south of Eyemouth outflowing to the sea about half way to Hawkness point. This supply has become so unreliable during the past few years that all the properties dependent upon it have transferred to the town supply, now conducted across the Gunsgreen housing site.

Electricity. Electricity reached the town in 1935-36 and was supplied by the Scottish Southern Electricity Supply Co., Galashiels. The supply is now the responsibility of the S.E. Scotland Electricity Board. Eyemouth has not had a transformer capable of meeting the town's needs during the past few years and the problem is not being overlooked, since the S.E. Scotland Electricity Board are intending to place two transformers at upper Houndlaw and Gunsgreen housing site to augment the output of the original one at a point west of Victoria Road. The supply is the standard one of 250 volts A.C. reduced from the grid system of high tension current. The costs for domestic purposes are, flat rate 4.1/2d per unit, contract rate 5/- per room per quarter and 3 farthings per unit.

Gas. The local gas supply now under the control of the S.E. of Scotland Gas Board is steadily improving. The plant has been modernised and a new gasometer of more generous capacity has recently been built.

Sewerage and Sewage disposal. The present system is a most unsatisfactory one from a health point of view since the main sewage pipe discharges into the harbour entrance without use of a septic tank or filter. Only the cleansing power of the tides makes it possible to tolerate such a system. The new housing area at Gunsgreen discharges sewage direct to the sea, well south of the town and it has often been planned to tunnel the fort and discharge the sewage from the main town direct to the sea at a point north of the town. There is no indication of any grants being available for the purpose and the finances of the Council would prohibit such a scheme as a local charge.

Roads, Streets. 1. Certain streets within the Burgh have now been classified as main roads under the care of the County Council, namely Church Street, High Street, Harbour Road, Chapel Street, Albert Road, Coldingham Road, Victoria Road and Northburn. The Town Council is responsible for the other streets but the work is done by the County and charged to the Burgh in the county requisition. Much improvement has been made to the streets, the old cobbles having been covered with tarmac and in Chapel Street a very dangerous bottleneck has been removed.

2. Cleansing is the responsibility of the Town Council. An efficient service for removal of waste is provided and much of the town refuse is dumped over the North Point of the Port.

3. Street lighting is good. The main streets are lit by electricity controlled by a time switch. A few streets are still lit by gas but the system is recognised as antiquated. The Harbour lights are of the sodium arc type and are the responsibility of the Harbour Trust.

Education. Schooling is provided in Eyemouth for children from the primary classes through to the third year High School and thereafter pupils intending to take the Higher Leaving Certificate travel by school-bus to Duns.

The school buildings are unfortunately not centred in one block. The original primary building was built in Albert Road in 1876. The secondary school buildings were built at various stages in 1923, 1936 and 1950 in Coldingham Road. The school now serves a wide area for secondary education, children being conveyed by bus from Burnmouth, Ayton, Auchencrow, Reston, Renton, Cockburnspath, Coldingham and St Abbs. A meals canteen serving 600 meals per day to the children was built in 1945.

In 1936 the Scott Bursary of £100 was founded by ex-Provost William Scott, the interest of which is awarded to the writer of the prize-winning essay in the third year of the Eyemouth High School. The essay is set and corrected by the Auld Kirk minister.

In 1938 the school acquired a large stretch of playing field which has been extensively developed by the Eyemouth Youth Panel as a camping site and playing field, and the local football club has co-operated with the Youth Panel to lay off an excellent football pitch with a grandstand. In 1944 the Youth Panel converted three rooms in the Albert Road school into a Youth Hall.

The number of children in 1950 on the roll of the school in the following age groups were:

Infants	5- 7	107
Primary	7-12	127
Secondary	12-15	235

The Eyemouth people are making full use of the facilities provided in Further Education classes, the following subjects being attended in the winter session: handicrafts, drama, music and dancing, pipe band music and folk dancing. There is an annual amateur operatic production.

Health Services. Eyemouth was fortunate in having laid a good foundation for the National Health Service to develop. There was, for example, an active committee of the Queen's Institute of District Nursing and with the dawning of the National Health Service in 1948 the capital of the Committee was devoted to the equipping of an up-to-date clinic situated in the High School playing field. There was also an ambulance committee constituted with three members of the town council, three representatives of the Nursing Association and three representatives of the Red Cross. The ambulance gifted in 1935 by Sir Christopher Furness in memory of his mother was controlled by this local Committee. With the National Health Service in operation the ambulance committee still functions and now controls two vehicles serving the area of Eastern Berwickshire. Originally the Eyemouth Ambulance was maintained by the annual collection of a householder's membership fee. Now the

Committee receives payments on a mileage basis from the St Andrew's and Red Cross Scottish Ambulance Services.

VOLUNTARY SOCIAL SERVICES

Youth Organisations. There is a Troop of Boy Scouts, a Company of Girl Guides and the various churches have clubs for young people. Under the auspices of the Auld Kirk a children's film show is given weekly during the winter months. There is ample accommodation for youth activity. The various halls available are: St John's Church Hall, the Auld Kirk Hall, the Congregational Church Hall, the Episcopal hut and the Youth Hall under the management of the Youth Panel.

There are numerous women's organisations. Four of the churches have Woman's Guilds. There is an active branch of the W.R.I.

Much of the music, drama and art in the form of handicrafts is centred in the further education classes provided by the Education Committee of the County Council. A voluntary effort which has set a high standard of musical appreciation is found in the work of the Eyemouth Choral Society, under the conductorship of Mrs David Fairbairn, L.R.A.M. Mrs Fairbairn established her choir in 1939 and during the war years much good work was done in east Berwickshire by the choir in the gathering of funds for various war charities. Since 1945 the choir revived the name of the Eyemouth Choral Society and concentrates upon the rendering of Handel's *Messiah* every Christmas and the presenting of a first class concert in the spring of each year, when some work demanding the devoted collaboration of music lovers is mastered.

There are no Friendly Societies[1] interested in the insurance and benefits of members and even membership of the large Trade Unions is apt to be haphazard. Only during the past few years have fish workers, for example, become members of the Transport and General Workers Union, and those of the community engaged in agriculture have become members of the Farm Servants' Union, but the individual enterprise of the fishing industry has dissociated the community from the mass membership of Trade Unions which is a feature associated with the large industrial areas.

A Fishermen's Mutual Association was in existence before 1945, but was re-established in that year as The Fishermen's Mutual Association, Eyemouth Ltd. This association now acts for half the boats and also acts as one of the major buyers in the port for the inland market. It also auctions and markets the catch of crabs and lobster from the boats in the neighbouring village of Burnmouth . Since the end of the war in 1945 the number of fish hawkers has greatly increased. Vans leave Eyemouth every day to supply many parts of south-east Scotland. Larger

[1] Mr Carnegie who was in charge of Parish relief until the National Health Act of 1948 is of the opinion that the Friendly Society disappeared with the National Health Act of 1911.

buyers send fish on lorries or by train to Shields, Newhaven, Glasgow and London. During the past three years an interesting development has been established by the firm of John Burgon and Sons. Lobster tanks have been built in one of the yards near to the harbour entrance and lobsters brought from many other ports are kept alive for the market by a continuous circulation of sea-water through the tanks. Lobsters are sent periodically to Southampton for use on the Queen Mary and the Queen Elizabeth.

CHURCHES

There are a surprising number of denominations in Eyemouth considering that the total population is just over 2,000. They are as follows: two Church of Scotland charges, the Auld Kirk and St John's; a Methodist Church, a Congregational Church, a charge of the Scottish Episcopal Church and a Roman Catholic Chapel. Going back 120 years the only Church was the Auld Kirk, and the other denominations have established their churches during the past century. St John's was a United Free Church before 1928 and was created by a Union of the Free Church and the United Presbyterian Church. The building of the U.P. Church has become the local cinema. There have been periods of religious revival in the community but the proportion now of church members tends to follow the nationwide trend of approximately a third of the population. There is a small group known locally as 'the pilgrims', accepting in the main the doctrinal point of view of the Plymouth Brethren. There is also a Masonic Lodge and hall.

POLITICAL PARTIES

Eyemouth is not politically conscious, a fact which goes hand in hand with the lack of industrialisation and the scant Trade Union activity. On the occasions of a General Election there is an uprising of political fever which lasts only a few weeks and quickly dies down again. There is a small branch of the Labour Party which has been in existence since 1945 and during the past 50 years there have been similar occasional attempts at the stimulation of political interest. Town Council Elections have not been contested on a Party basis as in the industrial areas.

MISCELLANEOUS

The British Legion has an active branch which has established a well equipped recreation hut on the Fort Road near Northburn Farm. The Hut was opened by the Earl of Haddington in 1950. The war years 1939-45 stimulated a branch of the Red Cross and until 1948 there was the local Committee of the Queen's Institute of District Nursing. The

Red Cross and the District Nursing Committees combine their representatives on the Committee of the Eyemouth Ambulance Association mentioned before under Health.

HOUSING

The following statistics in round figures can be given under the heading of Housing.

Total number of houses in Burgh 650, in Parish 50

Rooms	*Older Types*	*Council Houses*	*Total*
2	38	12	50
3	126	174	300
4	110	90	200
5	98	2	100
over 5	50	—	50

Owner-occupied houses 332. Rented houses 368. The number of gardens is approximately 400. Total rateable value of town £14,800. 3/- in £1 is spent locally which gives a proportion of three quarters to county expenditure and a quarter locally. Number of persons per room approximately one. Overcrowding is limited. The real problem is that houses of the older type have become unfit for habitation or do not conform to health standards in that there is a lack of conveniences.

There is a wide difference of standard between the old terraced type of house and that set by the new council houses. A few of the older blocks, such as Chapel Terrace and Renton Terrace, have been condemned, but people have still to live in them owing to the acute housing shortage. The terraced houses built by their owners in the last 20 years of the 19th century, such as Home Street and Houndlaw Park, are good houses and have easily been brought up to modern housing standards. The houses built by the Town Council are of the flatted or semi-detached cottage type. The planning consultant of the County Council has expressed concern at the spread of the town to the Town Council Housing at Gunsgreen across the River Eye. There is a risk of the town being divided into two sections. The Town Council sees no cause for anticipating such a sense of division since the bond of the family relationship in Eyemouth is much stronger than the sense of community. Interest in civic affairs is apt to be stimulated more by the personal need of the moment (almost always a housing one) than by the wider motives rooted in a sense of community.

AGRICULTURE, INDUSTRY AND COMMERCE

All the farms have become highly mechanised, and dairy-farming, carried on by Northburn farm and the Eyemouth Mill farm, requires a

Plate 24. The old A1 road at Grantshouse, 1950s.

very high standard of efficiency to satisfy the Health Department of the Berwickshire County Council.

The main industry associated with Eyemouth has been the fishing but there are conflicting opinions as to the future of this industry since it has been subject to booms and slumps. The inter-war years, the 1930s for example, saw the fishing industry at an extremely low ebb when the fishermen earned the ridiculously low wage of 15/- to 30/- per week. The world war of 1939-45 created a boom, but since 1946 the catches have tended to fall. A reason for alarm could be found in the fact that boats are all owned by men over 40 (many of them well over 40) and young people are not entering the industry because of its fluctuating returns. Nor are the girls of the town interested in the working of the fish, but are turning to more congenial work. The female labour engaged in the working of the fish is not drawn from the younger section of the community. Methods of fishing have changed. The sailing boats have gone. The herring drifter has come to be regarded as uneconomic, and smaller crafts — 45 to 85 feet with diesel engines — operate seine nets of the trawl type. The 85 foot vessel, also diesel driven, can be turned during the seasonal fishings from white fish to herring. The seine net method of fishing is recognised as exhaustive upon the supply of fish and most destructive of young fish of an unmarketable quality. It is difficult to forecast the future of the industry. The Harbour Trust is pressing the Scottish Home Department for a grant towards a new harbour with an entrance formed through the rocks south east of the Bay. Such an improved deeper harbour would have considerable effect upon the trade and life of the community. But one industry which has brought fluctuating returns during the past 30 years is not sufficient for Eyemouth, just as agriculture, the basic industry of the County, is not sufficient for Berwickshire. Until Eyemouth and Berwickshire can show in a cross section of its population that they are involved in a variety of industries, the drift of the population from the small burghs, as from rural areas, will go on.

A new post-war development has been the establishment of two branch factories in St John's Church Hall and the Auld Kirk Hall. St John's Hall houses a branch of E. Gardiner & Sons' Tweed Factory, Selkirk, employing 30 girls in picking and darning, and the Auld Kirk Hall houses a branch of Turner, Rutherford & Co.'s Hosiery Factory, Hawick, employing about 30 girls on individual sewing machines. It is known that Messrs Gardiner & Sons have procured a factory site on the piece of land between the playing field and the cemetery but building costs seem to prohibit the establishment of a permanent factory. It is the hope of all those interested in the welfare of the town that these industries, new to Eyemouth, and producing export goods, will remain for many years and ultimately be housed in their own factories.

The town has possibilities as a holiday resort and the recent coast erosion bill will provide the money for a sea wall which, with the north side of High Street cleaned of dwellings, should form an attractive sea front. The Town Council is now negotiating with the Scottish Home Department for the erection of a portion of the sea wall from St Ebba's Place to the gas works where the problem of erosion is most acute. The cost of this portion is estimated at £30,000 and the cost of the whole sea front at around £90,000. A sea wall was built in 1901 by public subscription but the pounding of the storms of only two winters saw the whole thing in ruins.

The town is well supplied with shops which include a branch of Tweedmouth Cooperative Society Ltd., which is now responsible for a considerable proportion of the milk distribution in the burgh. There are also a fair number of private traders, e.g., grocers, butchers and bakers.

THE WAY OF LIFE

Eyemouth in the past has relied for its livelihood on the fishing and the fisherman's way of life has a great influence upon the life of the community. The individual spirit of enterprise and self reliance is cultivated in a daily routine which brings five or six men together aboard a small craft to wrest their living from the sea and share their fortunes, good or bad, from week to week.

Family ties are strong and children are well cared for. This age of transport communication and mass distribution of goods has not yet extinguished the broad dialect of the people, but on the other hand, the homes of the people reveal that they move with the times in modern appliances and in an easy acceptance of the benefits of buses, radio, electric sweepers, irons and washing machines.

The writer would be inclined to say that civic consciousness and civic pride have declined. For example: among the municipal houses, common ground at the street corners becomes intersected with paths which are the shortest distance from point to point. Municipal trees and shrubs have suffered abuse to the extent of extermination. Civic consciousness is lacking in a community where little interest is shown in municipal affairs except from a personal point of view. A further sign of the lack of civic pride, is this: the community enjoys football not by playing it but by watching the game being played. There are good tennis courts and a putting green which are municipally owned. There is a healthy golf club and a flourishing bowling club. There is a public library open, at present, on certain evenings of the week. It has only recently been approved by the County Council Education Committee to have the library and reading room open every day.

The affairs of the town are reported regularly, week by week, by the 'Berwickshire Advertiser' and the 'Berwickshire News', both published in Berwick-on-Tweed.

The town is remarkably free from crime, and cases of juvenile delinquency respond well to periods of probation.

People enjoy their leisure and industrially the interest is focussed upon the fishing. The season of summer visitors from June to August is becoming important to the community life and Eyemouth enters with its visitors into the joy of the holiday seasons.

Despite the lack of interest in muncipal and civic affairs, specific organisations, mentioned in this report, have their enthusiastic members and in general there is a kindliness and neighbourliness which is shown at its best to those in sickness, loneliness and distress.

1950s

PARISH OF EYEMOUTH

by Rev. David Lindsay, B.D.

TOPOGRAPHY

For practical purposes the area under consideration in this Account will be broadly that of the Eyemouth Local Plan (Borders Region 1981). The main topographical features are the River Eye Valley, the River Mouth (Harbour Entrance), the 80 foot high peninsular promontory known as the fort, the bay and beach, the cliffs to the south-east. This part of the coast is generally regarded as being of national significance for geological research and education.

A small area of low elevation (Gunsgreen Picnic Area) in the north-east gives way to sharply sloping ground rising to Gunsgreen farm (146 feet). On the north-west bank of the river the low elevation of the harbour area again gives way to rising ground that levels in the Barefoots and Deanhead housing areas before rising again to Hallydown hill (298 feet). The landscape is largely open and exposed. Established tree growth is generally restricted to the Eye and Ale river valleys and the woodlands around Netherbyres and Highlaw House.

HISTORICAL NOTES

At the time of the publication of the last Account, Eyemouth was a small port busy with general trade. The years that followed, however, saw a remarkable change in the activity in Eyemouth harbour. There was a transformation from general trade to an almost exclusive concentration on fishing. This was obviously a crucial factor in moulding the character of the present-day town.

Friday, 14th October 1881 was without a doubt the blackest day in the history of Eyemouth. Ignoring the warnings of the weather glass, of an impending storm, the Eyemouth fishing fleet put to sea. Of the 45 boats that sailed that day only 26 returned. One hundred and twenty-nine men, half of the male fishing population of Eyemouth, were lost on that terrible day. Seventy-three women were widowed and 263 children left fatherless at a single stroke. As the Rev. D. McIver records in his book, *An Old-Time Fishing Town: Eyemouth* —

'There was weeping on every side, there was nae a hame unbereft, Fathers and brothers and lovers — there was hardly a man of them left.'

Like every other community in the land Eyemouth suffered its share of losses in two World Wars. Sixty-three men fell in the First World War and 27 in the Second. The town was generally unscathed from enemy action. On one occasion however, in February 1942, a lone bomber made an attack on the harbour area. A fishing boat was completely destroyed and some buildings badly damaged. Fortunately there were no serious injuries to the populace. Eyemouth was of course part of the coastal defence network. The remains of gun mountings and other World War II structures can still be seen on the promontory known as the 'Fort'. (See also sections on Churches, Fishing.)

The notable buildings mentioned in the previous reports are still standing, (Old Linthill, Netherbyres, Highlaw House, Gunsgreen House). Gunsgreen House is the most prominent building in Eyemouth, designed by James Adam about 1753 and purchased by Patrick Home of Billie in 1764. In 1948 the house was stated as being in bad repair. At the time it was used as a boarding house. It is now owned by Berwickshire District Council and is the home of Eyemouth Golf and Sailing Clubs.

The 'Auld Kirk', the former Parish Church, was built in 1812 by Alexander Gillie, a Berwickshire architect. In 1954 the congregations of the Auld Kirk and St John's (the former Free Church) united. After worshipping alternately in both buildings the united congregation finally decided on the Free Church building on the corner of Victoria Road. The 'Auld Kirk' was purchased by Berwickshire District Council and sadly deteriorated through lack of use. In 1981 the Auld Kirk was restored and now houses the Eyemouth Museum and Tourist Information Centre.

The old Cemetery in the High Street is a rather unusual place, in that about 1849 it became full because of a cholera epidemic and had to be remade. The level was raised by about eight feet and a new cemetery was made on top of the old one. Immediately to the right of the entrance is an old watch house. This is a unique structure in that it is constructed from the old tombstones removed in the relayering. The Memorial in the centre of the cemetery depicts a broken mast and is to the memory of the fishermen lost in the Great Disaster of 1881.

The Fort is the local name ascribed to the peninsular promontory in the north-west of the parish. Recent archaeological digs have confirmed the existence and lay-out of the mid-sixteenth century fortifications. Great interest is aroused by indications of a much earlier settlement on the same site. Two cannons pointing seawards now take pride of place on the Fort Point. The cannons, 32 pounders, were probably cast about 1830. It is thought that they were positioned on the Fort in the 1850s during a French invasion scare. The gun carriages were restored by the pupils of Eyemouth High School in 1966.

POPULATION

The population figures are as follows: 1755, 792; 1801, 899; 1831, 1181; 1851, 1488; 1881, 2935; 1921, 2563; 1931, 2321; 1961, 2161; 1974, 2797; 1977, 3300. The population of the burgh grew steadily in the 19th century, reaching a peak in 1881 (the year of the Great Fishing Disaster). During the first part of the 20th century it declined to 2161 in 1961, since when it has again risen.

This recent increase has stemmed from a large influx of people into the town, particularly during the 1970s. This came about as a result of the previous (Eyemouth Town Council) and existing local authorities policies on attracting industry with the provision of housing.

Migration has played a considerable part in the increase of population in the last two decades, particulary since 1971. There is a high proportion of young women in Eyemouth when compared with the Borders region as a whole. There is a lower proportion of retired people when compared with the Region and Scotland as a whole. The immigration of young families has resulted in an increased birth rate against regional and national trends.

AGRICULTURE

Agricultural activity is of course limited and restricted to the fringes of this small but relatively built-up parish. The local farming scene was however no exception to the dramatic changes in methods following the end of the Second World War. Increased mechanisation resulted in fewer workers and the removal of horses from the land. The use of artificial fertilisers, herbicides and insecticides has also produced dramatic increases in yields.

With the exception of that land recently given over to housing developments, it is basically the same area, as outlined in the previous report, which is under cultivation. Up until the 1960s there was some dairying activity, particularly at the Northburn Farm. The farmhouse and buildings are now incorporated within the built-up area of the town while the land which was retained is utilised as a caravan park.

Market gardening takes place at Biglawburn and Gunsgreen Market Garden. The Acredale, Highlaws, Hallydown, Linthill and Mill farms are mainly arable. Barley is the main crop with a half again of wheat. A great number of potatoes and turnips are grown, and to a lesser extent other vegetables: beans, brussels sprouts and peas are produced, some for the local frozen food processing. Silage grass is cultivated as, to a limited extent, is oil-seed rape.

In the main, livestock tends to be fat-stock cattle, normally Charolais crossbred, with some Suffolk crossbreed sheep.

FISHING

Along with the mechanisation, the development and increased efficiency in agriculture, changes of an almost revolutionary nature have occurred in the fishing industry.

At the close of the 19th and the dawning of the 20th century the old 'Zulu' and 'Fifie' sailing yawls were replaced by the 'steam drifters'. The steam drifter was a large boat sometimes 80-90 feet in length. Paraffin engines for smaller vessels were introduced at the end of the first decade and subsequently replaced in the 1940s by the more efficient diesel engine. The largest of the present-day boats in Eyemouth now have engines capable of developing 570 H.P. Indeed the auxiliary engines of 114 H.P. are as powerful as the main engines of the boats of the 1940s.

Those boats most recently added to the fleet have tended to be large (60-80 feet), constructed from steel and built outwith Eyemouth. This compares with the smaller (50-60 feet) wooden vessels, built in the 1960s and early 70s, which make up most of the present-day fleet. The yard of the Eyemouth Boat Building Company Ltd. (formerly James Weatherhead) was opened in 1841. Eyemouth boats are traditionally constructed from timber. Along with a number of smaller local firms, the Eyemouth Boat Building Company provide an engine and boat repair service. The majority of Eyemouth boats are well equipped with modern handling gear. Fishing has not fallen behind in the electronic revolution. Navigational aids, sonar-echo meters, fish finding equipment and radio have vastly improved the lot of the present day fisherman.

The late 19th and the early part of the 20th century was probably the foremost period of 'small line' fishing from Eyemouth. A single line could contain as many as 1,000 hooks, each of which had to be baited by hand. The use of mussels in place of limpets to bait the lines gave the fishermen's families a great deal of hard work. Wives and children would spend hours gathering and shelling the mussels in addition to baiting the lines. From the month of March to early September most of the boats took to the herring fishing which was carried out with the aid of drift nets.

The era of the 'steam drifter' (1930s-40s) saw the introduction of the 'great line' fishing. Cod and halibut were caught on lines baited with herring. In the herring season hundreds of women were employed in the gutting, salting and packing of the herring into barrels. The quayside was normally crammed with lines of barrels, a great many being loaded directly for export on to foreign boats from the Baltic ports. The herring being a migratory fish, many of the Eyemouth boats would follow the shoals, travelling from the north-west, down the east coast as far as Yarmouth and Lowestoft. By land the 'fisher lassies' of Eyemouth would 'travel the herrin', working the fish in many a port.

The Second World War saw the requisitioning of a number of the large steam drifters. This and other factors led to a reduction in the length of the Eyemouth boats. The post-war years heralded the introduction of the seine net and the demise of line fishing. Along with the gradual increase in boat length in the late 1970s, there developed the concept and practice of 'pair trawling'. In this method, two boats work together to cover a larger area.

In a bid to conserve rapidly dwindling stocks, herring fishing was banned on the east coat in 1976. (Limited fishing for herring is to be introduced in July 1983). As herring fishing is seasonal in nature, the ban was disastrous. Most fishermen adapted well to concentrate on white fish. A small number of boats fish exclusively for prawn. Lobsters are caught locally and stored in ponds prior to transportation to London and directly to European markets.

Like the tide, over the years, the fortunes of the Eyemouth fishermen have ebbed and flowed. In the past, many a fisherman found it difficult to earn a living. Today, for some it is often similar but many others have reaped well from the harvest of the sea. The restrictions and quotas resulting from Britain's entry to the E.E.C. are not welcomed by the majority of Eyemouth fishermen, although they do benefit from boat building grants.

Mention should be made of the Eyemouth Fishermen's Mutual Association. Re-established in 1945, this cooperative with 100 boats and 600 members covers the greater part of the fleet. The Association provides marketing, transportation, chandling and insurance facilities. Cessation of normal supplies of ice necessitated the formation of a separate co-operative and the building of an ice-plant. This has proved very profitable and beneficial.

EYEMOUTH FISH LANDINGS 1981

Type	*Weight in metric tonnes*	*Cash Value*
Demercal	5938	£2,990,648
Shell Fish	308	209,815
Cod	2221	1,293,970
Haddock	2269	1,021,694
Whiting	963	378,053
Plaice	207	109,069
Lemon Sole	100	124,137
Dog Fish	84	23,159
Winkles (Hand Gathered)	75	17,560
Crabs	162	58,212
Lobsters	20	98,180
Norway Lobsters (Nephrops)	252	206,285

(Listed — Main Species Only)

THE HARBOUR

It is perhaps interesting to note that in 1794 only six fishing boats were working out of Eyemouth. The early nineteenth century however saw a dramatic increase in fishing, resulting in a fleet of around 50 operating in 1881.

In that year the fishermen of Eyemouth set up a fund for the purpose of extending the harbour. These improvements took place in 1887 when the harbour was deepened and extended to nine and a half acres. Further improvements were carried out at the end of the century, notably the finishing of the quay wall and the deepening of the entrance. The most recent alterations were completed in 1962, when the entrance was moved from the west to the north. It was hoped that the changes would lessen the degree of silting. This was successful up to a point but silting still occurs, depending upon the strength and direction of prevailing winds. At present, the maximum draught is 14 feet. The entrance is 60 feet maximum width.

THE LIFEBOAT

The first lifeboat stationed in Eyemouth was the 'James and Rachel Grindley' in 1876. This was of the pulling (oars) and sailing type. The first motor lifeboat came to Eyemouth in 1937. After the alterations to the harbour in 1962 the lifeboat was moored in the harbour and the shed no longer used. The present boat is the 'Eric Seal' of the 'Waveney' class with twin 260 HP engines and was commissioned in February 1974.

INDUSTRY AND EMPLOYMENT

At the present time Eyemouth has a rather specialised economy based on fishing, fish and food processing and tourism. At times concern is expressed over the lack of diversification in the industrial base. The former local Town Council did well to attract new industry and established a small industrial estate but concern is also expressed at the loss of Development Status. This action, with the consequent loss of grant aid, has resulted in the non-utilisation of some of the small factory units on the estate.

Almost half of the working population are directly or indirectly dependent on the fishing trade. A great part of the remainder are employed in the frozen food processing which has developed since 1967. In 1971, 75 per cent of the working population were employed in Eyemouth, five per cent in Berwickshire and 20 per cent elsewhere. Major employers outwith fishing interests would include E.L.B.A. (East Lothian and Borders Association of Growers), specialising in frozen vegetables, and C. W. Dexter of Chirnside, paper manufacturers.

In recent times the construction of the Torness Nuclear Power Station near Dunbar has created new employment opportunities. The Eyemouth Boat Building Company continues to be a steady employer although very much subject to the placement of new boat orders. In comparison with the Borders Region as a whole unemployment is relatively high, and there is a clear seasonal trend with a peak in winter.

Tourism has increased. The number of enquiries at the local Tourist Information Centre has risen from 6000 in 1967 to 14,000 in 1979. The six hotels within the town are small but there are a good number of bed and breakfast establishments. Day trippers perhaps form the greater part of the visitors to the town. Visitors who stay for longer periods tend to reside at the caravan site. In 1981, as part of the commemorations of the 'Great Fishing Disaster Centenary', a museum was established in the 'Auld Kirk' (the former Parish Church). The museum is of a local nature with an emphasis, though not an exclusive emphasis, on the town's fishing heritage.

The Eyemouth Tapestry commemorating and commissioned for the Centenary of the 'Disaster' is worthy of note. The Tourist Information Centre is now housed in the museum entrance. A 'town trail' was introduced in 1983 and in the same year Eyemouth became a major interest point on the 'East Coat Fishing Heritage Trail'.

HOUSING

In 1981 Eyemouth had 1340 habitable dwellings; 340 of these were built between 1971 and 1977. This increase in housing stock was associated with a 30 per cent increase in population, which represented the most rapid increase in any Border town at this time.

Since 1945, 84 per cent of the houses built in Eyemouth have been built for the local authority. In 1981, 64 per cent of Eyemouth's housing stock was within the public sector compared with 41 per cent in the Border Region and 54 per cent in Scotland. There are no plans substantially to increase local authority stock, the current emphasis being on the improvement of existing property.

Private sector dwellings are sited throughout the town with concentrations in the Barefoots Estate, the new Gilsland Estate and the old town. The latter is an area of mixed use, residential, commercial and industrial. The old town area presents an attractive but decaying townscape in need of enhancement and conservation. The Royal British Legion Housing Association Ltd. are presently constructing 'Swan Court', a sheltered housing unit in the old town area. This unit will complement 'Linkum Court', the local authority's existing sheltered housing unit situated at Deanhead.

TRAFFIC AND TRANSPORT

Eyemouth has a favourable location close to the A1 trunk road, 50 miles south of Edinburgh and 60 miles north of Newcastle upon Tyne.

The North British Railway constructed the east coast line in 1846 with a branch line and station in Eyemouth linked to the line in 1891. This branch line connected with the main line at Burnmouth and was used for the transportation of fish and passengers. The station and branch line closed in 1962. The nearest railway station is now at Berwick-upon-Tweed, nine miles to the south of Eyemouth.

Bus services between Edinburgh and Newcastle pass through Eyemouth four times daily (Monday to Saturday) in both directions. The 'Courier Service' provides a daily link with Galashiels, five days per week. While available, public transport is limited and journey times are long. There is much dependence on private cars.

With its narrow streets and mixed use Eyemouth has considerable traffic problems, particularly in the town centre and harbour area. The situation is aggravated in the summer months with much conflict between fish lorries, delivery vans, local traffic, visitors' cars and pedestrians. The Traffic Management Scheme (one-way system) introduced in 1976 has done much to alleviate the problem. Lack of car parking space remains a source of constant irritation.

PUBLIC SERVICES

Education. Educational provision is covered by a High School (six year secondary), Primary School and Nursery School. Eyemouth High School is fed from nine primaries within eastern Berwickshire. In the 1970s a growth in the school rolls corresponded with the increase of population within Eyemouth. In 1975 the High School roll stood at 467 compared with 534 in 1980 and 552 in 1983. Three temporary classroom porta-cabins were sited at the High School in the period of increasing numbers. The Eyemouth Primary School roll in 1983 was 360. In 1980 it was reported that there was no spare capacity within the school. Accommodation is functional, although great inconvenience is experienced through the lack of an Assembly/Gym Hall. The playing fields serving both schools are advantageous but do not comply with Scottish Education Department standard sizes.

A public library is situated in Market Square. This library is much appreciated and well used but the premises are far from adequate for the largest population in Berwickshire. The museum housed in the 'Auld Kirk' provides an additional educational facility.

Health. The opening of a new health centre in 1983 brought together the main health services of the town. In addition to the four General Practitioners, there is provision for District Nursing, Nursing Treatment, Community Health and Physiotherapy. The services of a dentist, chiropodist and optician are available elsewhere within the town. The nearest hospitals are at Berwick-upon-Tweed and Roodlands in Haddington. Specialised treatment, including most maternity work, is only available in Edinburgh or other large centres. The building of the Borders General Hospital near Melrose will be of little advantage with respect to travelling and transportation from Eastern Berwickshire.

The Coldingham Road Cemetery, opened in the late nineteenth century, is still in use and was recently extended. As the nearest Crematorium is in Edinburgh most funerals are by burial.

Police, Fire and other Emergency Services. A police station (manned part-time) and a 'retained' fire station are located in or close to Coldingham Road. A sergeant and six constables are housed within Eyemouth. An ambulance and driver are normally available in the town. Coastguard and lifeboat services are also based in Eyemouth. The present lifeboat 'Eric Seal', commissioned in February 1974, had by 1983 answered 33 calls with 10 lives saved.

PUBLIC UTILITIES

A gasometer sited within the town and connections to the national electricity grid ensure a constant and regular supply of gas and electricity.

The supply of water and disposal of sewage present problems. These problems were aggravated by the increase of fish and food processing and by the seasonal increase in population. In the summer months the daily population often doubles, making heavy demands on the inadequate facilities.

As with most of Eastern Berwickshire, Eyemouth water is supplied from the Watch Water reservoir. Apart from some augmentation from ground sources, at the present time there is little spare capacity to meet the increased demand.

Untreated sewage is discharged directly into the sea by two outfall pipes. The rocky coastline and sea currents around the outfalls, mix, disperse and dilute the effluent. Any further development within the town will however necessitate suitable settlement and treatment facilities.

RECREATION AND LEISURE

Indoor sports facilities include the District Council swimming pool (25 metres), with toddlers' pool and sauna facilities, a squash court, and public use of the High School games hall. The Royal British Legion premises are used for snooker and indoor bowls. The cinema is very popular and offers a variety of entertainment in addition to films.

Outdoor recreation is catered for with the school playing-fields, two football pitches and one hockey pitch at Gunsgreen, three tarmac tennis courts at Coldingham Road, a private bowling green and nine-hole golf course. The beach is one of three in Berwickshire and is very popular in the summer season. Sub-aqua diving with particular attention to the special marine conservation area is increasingly popular as is sea-angling. Eyemouth Sailing Club use the former lifeboat house for storage.

CHURCHES

As is quite common in fishing ports of its size, Eyemouth has a relatively large number of religious denominations.

The Parish Church, Church of Scotland, congregation can clearly trace its history back to at least 1690. It is evident however that in one form or another (Presbyterian or Episcopal) the Church of Scotland was in existence in Eyemouth in the earlier years of the Reformation. From the time of the Reformation there has occurred a notorious loss of Parish Records, Kirk Session minute books etc. There is a suspicion that at least some of these have fallen into the hands of well-intentioned but short-sighted amateur historians. Those records that have come to light are now in the keeping of the Registrar General's Office in Edinburgh. The following incident from Parish Church History is worth a mention. It concerns the Great Fishing Tithe Controversy. For a great number of years it was the custom that a fishing tithe was payable to the Superior for the upkeep of the parish Church School and for the benefit of the minister of the parish. It is recorded that in 1835 local boats were required to make a payment of £1.13s.4d. per annum. The proposal that the tithe should be extended to herring as well as white fish met with opposition. In the years leading up to 1855 there was growing hostility, culminating in the refusal to pay the tithe for that year. A period of civil unrest and disobedience followed. Violent demonstrations took place. Effigies, including that of the minister, were burnt. Police officers were assaulted. Arrests were made and several prison sentences imposed. It is perhaps interesting that a number of prominent landowners (notably of other denominations) took the rather unusual step of combining with the lower classes in what was in effect a workers' revolt. The dispute was eventually taken to arbitration with the result that the claim of the minister of the parish for all time was met by a payment of £1800. In the 1830s the influence of Methodism crossed over from England and the denomination established a foothold in Eyemouth. The present Methodist Chapel was built in 1905.

The E.U. (Evangelistic Union) Congregational Church of the Morrisonian tradition was established in 1861. The consecration of St Ebba's Episcopal Church took place in 1901. Roman Catholicism was re-established with the consecration of St Andrew's Church in 1961. The latest of many religious traditions to appear in Eyemouth is an 'American inspired' Free Baptist Sect.

WAY OF LIFE

Eyemouth continues to depend essentially upon fishing for its livelihood. Although the character of the town has dramatically changed over the last decade (1970-80), the fisherman's way of life continues to exert a considerable influence over the town. It is perhaps no great exaggeration to say that the community's pulse can be felt and measured by the prices and activity of the daily fish market.

While migration, improved communications and the advent of television and radio have exerted some influence, a very pronounced and identifiable local dialect continues to flourish. In addition to the rich parochial vocabulary many 'broad Scots' words are in daily use, with phrases of the sea and navigation also woven into everyday speech. It is perhaps unfortunate that for some there is a tendency to follow the distasteful trend of using obscene language rather than the more acceptable and more expressive local vocabulary.

As in many towns there is a kernel of common surnames e.g. Collin, Lough, Dougal, Dougall, Aitchison, Craig etc. To avoid confusion many nicknames have evolved and are still in common use. Many have sea-faring connotations. Some are compilations of the name of a boat with the skipper's Christian name. Occasionally a skipper is simply known by the name of his boat. Some of the nicknames or bye-names are handed down from generation to generation while others are of a more modern and temporary character. To add to the complexity of identification, many of the women folk retain the use of, or at least are referred to, by their maiden name.

Superstitions associated with fishing still exist but no longer exert any significant influence. The god 'Mammon' tends to command a larger following than any gods of superstition. At one time on meeting a 'Jonah' (a minister in clerical dress or sometimes a particular female credited with bringing bad luck), many a fisherman would turn back rather than put to sea. Some words, e.g. pig, salmon, rabbit, are still regarded as taboo. As with the language, fishing superstitions are often carried over into everyday life. One of the first motor cars to be seen in Eyemouth was observed making a manoeuvre in the Market Square. One old fisherman remarked to another 'My did you see that? He's gone agin the sun' — this being a navigational exercise that few fishermen would perform with a boat.

The annual crowning of the Eyemouth Herring Queen is a colourful pageant popular with locals and visitors. The ceremony was instituted in 1939 and revived as a 'Peace Picnic' in 1945. At present the Queen is always a third year pupil of Eyemouth High School and is elected by her contemporaries. On the appointed day, usually in July and traditionally on board one of the most successful boats of the year, the Herring Queen sails from St Abbs to Eyemouth. The Queen is then met and escorted by a flotilla of the flag-bedecked vessels of the port. The first Queen was crowned by Lady Furness of Netherbyres and thereafter the retiring Queen has placed the crown on her successor's head.

In 1981 the people of Eyemouth commemorated the Centenary of the 'Great Fishing Disaster'. On Sunday 11th October worshippers filled the Parish Church, with audio-equipment relaying the service to worshippers in the hall. Civic dignitaries and representatives of organisations joined the people of Eyemouth in a very moving service of remembrance. On Wednesday, 14th, exactly 100 years from the day of the Disaster, the lifeboat, with the Parish minister aboard, put to sea. The party having taken station seaward of the Hurkur Rock, a brief service was conducted and an anchor-shaped wreath of remembrance was committed to the sea.

One of the special events of the Commemoration was the opening of the Eyemouth Museum. The museum is housed in the 'Auld Kirk', the former Parish Church. Two exhibits are worthy of special mention; a carefully reconstructed interior of a late nineteenth century fisherman's cottage and the Disaster Tapestry. The latter is a beautiful canvas work-embroidery produced by a team of 20 Eyemouth ladies. Employing 500 colour variations, this beautiful work of art depicts the storm, its aftermath and symbolism of perseverance and hope for the future.

A long-established custom on Easter Sunday is the presentation to children of an orange in addition to the traditional egg. The origin of the custom is lost in antiquity but may have something to do with the health value of fresh fruit to seafarers. In former times Easter was an occasion for children to be rigged out in new clothes. After church it was also the practice for most of the townsfolk to enjoy a family picnic at 'Maggie Murphy's' (a field near Millbank on the road to Ayton).

One of the most remarkable characteristics of the Eyemouth people is the absence, to any great degree, of class consciousness. It is a tolerant society with first name referral commonplace, regardless of an individual's position or status within the community. The establishment of the industrial estate and the expansion of the house building programme of the 1970s has transformed the formerly close-knit society. A new influence results from migration from the north-east of England and to a lesser extent from the West of Scotland. The latter tend to be retired people who spent holidays in Eyemouth in the pre- and post-war periods. At times a minority may express some antipathy towards the incomers or 'interloupers'.

While many of the townsfolk enjoy healthy outdoor pursuits, there are others who prefer the less healthy atmosphere of licensed premises. At the present time, in addition to a licensed grocer, there are six hotels, three public houses and three clubs. Civic pride needs much encouragement. The modern curse of vandalism has not missed Eyemouth. Dog fouling is an obnoxious problem and excessive litter often abounds in the town. While the 'pernicious trade' of smuggling has long since ceased there is perhaps a continuing disrespect for the full letter of the law in a somewhat *laissez-faire* attitude to salmon poaching.

If these be somewhat negative attitudes they are more than matched by many positive attributes. In addition to a great number of special charity events held throughout the year, not a week passes without a coffee-morning in aid of some local, national or international cause. In times of trouble and despair, neighbourliness abounds, and that undeniable spirit of love, care and compassion remains a true and faithful characteristic of Eyemouth life.

1983

THE PARISH OF FOGO

by The Rev. John C. J. Hunter

The Parish of Fogo is situated in the middle of the County of Berwick. On the northern boundary the Parish of Langton touches it at a point, and then in a clockwise direction the surrounding parishes are Edrom, Swinton, Eccles, Greenlaw and Polwarth. The parish is included in the farming district of the Merse.

The area is stated at 5651 acres, of which about 17 or 18 are water. The surface is of a rolling character, being rather hilly both lengthwise and across. The parish presents a pleasant aspect, for it contains many moors and strips of woodlands or groups and lines of trees; the soil is mostly a light or medium loam and is obviously very fertile; and the division into fields is chiefly by hedges. The elevation varies from about 200 to 500 feet above sea level, most of the land being between 300 and 400 feet. There is one river, the Blackadder, which, flowing in a considerable depression, partly intersects the parish and partly forms its boundary with Edrom.

The only community centre is the hamlet of Fogo, comprising eight houses, the church and the school. It is four miles from Duns, five from Greenlaw, about 12 from Kelso and 16 from Berwick-upon-Tweed.

The meaning of the name Fogo is uncertain. The popular explanation is Bog Glow. Natural conditions in the valley of the Blackadder would suit, and some support might be found in the farm named Bogend.

There is not sufficient material for a history of the parish, but a few notes, chiefly about church matters, may be put on record.

It might be expected that the parish would suffer severely in the wars between England and Scotland and this is borne out by one ecclesiastic who in the reign of David II petitioned the Pope for a benefice in addition to Fogo because he could get nothing from Fogo on account of the wars.

Fogomoor seems to have had some local importance down to the 17th century as a place for assembling military forces. The church and parish were appropriated by Gift of Cospatrick Earl of Dunbar in 1159 to the Abbey of Kelso. The incumbent was accordingly a 'perpetual vicar'. An interesting record in the manuscripts of the Earl of Home tells how, in October 1555, the Abbey was warned to hasten to collect

Plate 85 The village of Gordon in the 1950s or 1960s

teinds of corn because the Earl and his tenants could not allow the crops 'to byde forthir hazird of wodder and kep forthir and mair skaith'.

The church was consecrated on 29th March 1243 by David de Bernham, Bishop of St Andrews. The dedication is unknown. The Bishop consecrated a chapel of St Nicholas in the parish on 2nd April 1242, but no information about it has been found beyond the mention in the Bishop's Pontifical.

A conventicle was held at Fogomoor in 1678, the preacher being the celebrated William Veitch, afterwards minister at Peebles and Dumfries.

The names of a few of the perpetual vicars are known. David, Vicar of Fogo, swore fealty to Edward I of England in 1242 during the War of Independence. Henry de Smalham held the vicarage along with a canonry first of Dunkeld and then of Glasgow, from about 1349 till 1354 when he became Archdeacon of Teviotdale. Since he is described as a Master of the English Nation of the University of Paris and a Scholar of Canon Law, he was plainly a non-resident. James of Tranent, Vicar of Fogo, witnessed a deed in 1475. In 1543, Adam Kinghorn witnessed a deed at the Monastery of Dunfermline, but since he is described as Vicar of Fogo and Chamberlain of the Monastery, he was probably non-resident.

Shortly after the Reformation Fogo was served by a Reader, under a Minister for Edrom, Duns, Longton, Fogo and Polwarth. There is a complete list of Ministers from 1540 to the present day. The Episcopal Minister in 1643, William Methven, was deprived for nonconformity, and the Minister at the time of the Disruption, John Baillie, 'went out'. The Patron was the Crown.

The repairs to the walls and roof of the church in 1755 noted in the Second Statistical Account must have been a practical rebuilding, as the church shows no substantial antique features. As far as is known the only structural alteration since the beginning of the 19th century is the erection of the Charterhall Gallery at the west end in 1853. The church was repaired in 1927 in terms of the Church of Scotland Property and Endowments Act, 1925, and at that time, the low building at the east end was adapted to make a vestry. This building is believed to have been the chancel of the pre-Reformation Church.

As it stands the church is a pleasing example of a typical country church. It is shaped like a T with a short leg. There are two laird's lofts with outside stairs, one at the west and the other at the east end. The open belfry on the west gable is graceful and well-proportioned. The windows are of very various shapes and sizes, but the large window facing south is admired for its design. The pews are rather straight backed and narrow, and there are a few box pews. The small pulpit, on the north or back wall, facing the leg of the T, has a conical canopy. The only modern feature is electric light.

There is a tradition that there were vaults under the church, and there is an indication of an arch in the back wall just above ground level. The manse was built in 1843 and has received some modernisation from time to time. The church possesses two hammered silver communion cups with long stems and narrow bowls. They were made by Patrick Borthwick, Edinburgh and were presented in 1662 by George Trotter of Charterhall. The church also possesses a small portable Baptismal Font, made of pewter, maker Robert Whyte. The bell is the product of the famous foundry of John Meikle and bears the inscription in Latin, John Meikle made me, Edinburgh 1694. The Communion Table was given by Colonel David Milne Home of Wedderburn, who resided at Caldra and was an elder of Fogo Church, shortly before he died on 19th November 1901, and the small pipe organ is the gift of his children in his memory.

The original school is believed to have been the now disused classroom and vestibule adjoining a cottage at the side of the road. In 1864 a large classroom was built on a contiguous site, and the old classroom was used for the infants. About 20 years ago a new classroom and cloakroom were added to the building of 1864. Central heating was introduced. The playground was fenced off from the road, and a playshed erected. The old classroom then became a store. Fogo is now one of the best small schools in the County. There used to be a headmaster and an assistant, but from 1945-1953 there was a schoolmistress only; in 1953 the staff was increased to a Headmistress and an Infant Mistress. The schoolhouse, having been enlarged and improved from time to time, is a good modern house.

The most remarkable feature in the ownership of land has been the way in which the estate of Charterhall has been extended in the parish since the last Account. It has descended in the family of Trotter of Mortonhall and Charterhall and has acquired at various times the farms of Fogo East End, and Eclestofts, of which a small portion is in the parish, and part of Caldra Farm, and it has enlarged its interests in Fogo common from one third to the whole. The other estates have been sold and divided. The present owner of Marchmont House holds only one farm in the parish, Clerkenville. Harcarse and Bogend with Cairnsmill are now separate properties. Caldra House and policies have been disjoined from the farm, and Caldra Farm, although still one farming unit, has been divided between two proprietors. There are thus six proprietors in the parish: Major H. R. Trotter, owning Charterhall Estate, Mr A. G. E. Calder, owning Bogend and Cairnsmill, Messrs Edward Webb & Sons (Stourbridge) Ltd., owning Harcarse, Sir Eric V. de la Rue, owning Caldra, Sir John H. F. McEwen, owning Clerkenville, and Lord Brocket, owning part of Caldra Farm.

The mansion houses in the parish are Charterhall and Caldra House. Both proprietors are resident.

The Roman Camp at Chesters is almost obliterated. Fogo Bridge was repaired in 1843 and being very much in use, is hardly an antiquity.

Part of a square keep is built into the farmhouse at Harcarse. In the church there are two heraldic panels. One, carved in stone, is the arms of George Trotter of Charterhall, dated 1671. The other is the painted arms of Sir Roger Hog, of Bogend and Harcarse, Lord Harcarse, a Senator of the College of Justice whose portrait hangs in the Parliament Hall, Edinburgh.

Among habitations which have gone to ruins and are likely to disappear are Kirsty Miller's near Fogomoor Crossroads, Pilmuir at Hunthall Roadend, Corbiehall between Caldra and Sisterpath, Oer Hall, near Sisterpath, and Rashie near Fogo Village. The name Rashie has been transferred to a new housing site at Fogo Village. The tile works near Harcarse have also disappeared.

A Roll of Honour preserved in the church records that 38 men from the parish served in the War of 1914-18. The War Memorial, a very well designed Lych Gate to the churchyard, incorporates a panel with the names of 10 men who fell. One name for the War of 1939-45 remains to be added.

During the War of 1939-45 there was a Royal Air Force Station at Charterhall. In the churchyard there is a War Graves plot where rest 16 airmen of the Canadian, Australian, and New Zealand Air Forces, as well as of the Royal Air Force and Fleet Air Arm. Three German airmen are also buried in the churchyard.

Parts of the Aerodrome were used after the war for a time as a European Volunteer Workers' Hostel, but most of the buildings are now in ruins. Certain government departments have stores in those remaining. Recently a motor racing track was formed from the runways, and the races attract large attendances during the season.

The floods of August 1948 did extensive damage to the banks of the Blackadder in the parish, and the road bridge near Sisterpath Mill and the footbridge at Fogo were swept away. The banks of the river have now been made good, and the bridges have been replaced.

The County Council have built four houses for agricultural workers at the west of Fogo Village; two, in one block, are of four apartments, and two, in another adjoining block, are of three apartments. This is the new Rashie.

One major change in general conditions is the abolition of the yearly engagement of farm workers from 28th May to 28th May and the discontinuance of the Hiring Fairs at Earlston, Duns, Kelso and Berwick. The results are evidently far reaching for this and all other agricultural parishes.

The older records of the parish are believed to have been accidentally burned a long time ago. The Kirk-session records begin in 1835. They contain lists of male heads of families, five of them with residences and occupations, drawn up between 1835 and 1841. Short extracts from earlier minutes are to be found in articles in old numbers of the 'Berwickshire News'. The Heritors' Records from 1801-1891, and the Parochial Board Records from 1841-1891 are in the Register House, Edinburgh. A rare book, 'Stray Leaves from a Border Garden,' by Mary Pamela Milne Home (Mrs Milne Home of Caldra), published in 1901, contains some interesting information about the parish and a few photographs of Fogo Village.

The figure given for the population at the census of 1951 should be modified for purposes of comparison. It includes the inmates of the E.V.W. Hostel at Charterhall, which was only a temporary establishment. The normal population in 1951 is accordingly estimated at 300.

The fall in population over the last century is not peculiar to this parish, and the explanation must be sought in the general causes of rural depopulation. Certain influences, however, seem specially strong in this parish. There are, and can be, very few kinds of employment in, or even near the parish. The fact that almost all the houses are tied to work on farms or estates, and that, apart from two mansionhouses, there is no purely residential property, has a restrictive effect. Because farm workers' families do not to the same extent as formerly desire to work on the land, and because women outdoor workers have almost disappeared from rural districts, the want of public transport discourages families, some of whose members require other work at a distance, from coming to the parish. It is difficult to estimate the effect of the almost complete mechanisation of farming in the parish. At first sight it would seem obviously to diminish population, but on the other hand there is a shortage of farm labour which is not met by mechanisation.

One age group, old people, is very small. Houses are available only for workers, and the few old people are living with relatives. The population is not truly resident, because change of job for the householder means change of home for the whole family. Even under modern terms of engagement, changes are fairly frequent. There are few natives of the parish in it, and the weight of circumstances is against natives being able to remain. Most farm servants belong to the county, and the nearer parts of neighbouring counties, particularly Roxburgh. There are a few from Northumberland. The staffs of the mansionhouses usually include some from the more distant parts of England.

Since the abolition of parish councils there has been no parochial public authority, or, since the disappearance of heritors' meetings under the Church of Scotland Property and Endowments Act, any body with only local responsibilities. Fogo is part of the Electoral Division of Fogo and Polwarth of the County of Berwick. It is included in the Middle District. The local representatives are one County Councillor and one District Councillor for the Division. The functions of the County Council far exceed those of the Middle District Council both in number and importance. The chief matters that fall to the District Council are the upkeep of a few rights of way, of two footbridges over the Blackadder, the oversight of a small village green and the care of the War Memorial.

The roads in the parish include one A road on the route from Duns to Coldstream and one B road on the route from Greenlaw to Berwick. The others are of lower classification. They are all with the exception of a few little-used side roads in excellent condition, and uphold the high reputation of the County Roads Department. The road system seems to serve local needs, though a cross road from about Fogo Village to near Fogorig, where there is at present only a farm service road, would probably be of great local convenience.

Rights of way are not much used and probably the list of them is not now known. Only two are in regular use, one from Fogo Village to Caldra Garden, the other from Fogo Manse to Hunthall roadend. One from Corbiehall to Oldhall is falling into disuse with the closing of Marchmont Station.

Public transport is very poor. The parish of Fogo joins heartily in the complaints about lack of transport in Berwickshire. Marchmont Station used to serve part of the parish, but since the floods of 1948 it has been closed and the rails lifted. The bus services are confined to Kelso to Duns on Thursdays and Saturdays, and Edinburgh to Berwick on Saturdays and Sundays. The times are not considered convenient. Most people who have to make a journey have either to get a lift from neighbours who have cars, or to hire a car from Duns or Greenlaw. It may be remarked in this connection that the farmers are very obliging with both their cars and telephones.

The farmhouses, with two exceptions, have telephones, and also the larger houses. A kiosk was erected in 1952 at Fogo village. Most telephones are connected to Leitholm exchange, but two go to Duns, and one each to Greenlaw and Swinton.

The post town for all the parish except one farm, which is under Greenlaw, is Duns. Most places have two deliveries each day. There are two letter boxes at Fogo and Fogomoor.

Until this year, when the County Water Scheme came to the parish, all water supplies were private. Most are likely to remain so for a considerable time. They require the pumping of water from wells by hose or mechanical means. The public main passes along the Berwick to Greenlaw road and several places near it have made a connection. There is also a branch main across the fields from Fogorig to Fogo Village, to which the four new agricultural houses and the school and schoolhouse have been connected. The water is much softer than that usually obtained from the wells.

There is a public supply of electricity in the parish provided by overhead mains by the South East of Scotland Electricity Board. It is fairly generally available. The mansionhouses, manse, church, school and schoolhouse and six of the farms (including the cottages) have electric light and power. Four of the farms and eight separate estate and farm workers' houses have no public supply, but among these one farmhouse and one farm worker's house have private lighting plants.

The obstacle to the extension of the public supply seems to be the cost of the connection.

Drainage is necessarily private for the various farms and houses. A drainage district has, however, been formed this year, for the village, chiefly to meet the needs of the new houses.

Primary education is provided at Fogo School and secondary education at Berwickshire High School, Duns. Twenty-five years ago the roll of Fogo School was about 60, when there was a headmaster and an assistant-mistress. The roll has been affected both by a fall in the number of children in the parish and by the centralisation of post-primary education. In 1945 the school was reduced to one teacher status, under a headmistress. The roll fluctuates considerably from around 25 to over 30, and this year an additional lady teacher has been appointed. School meals sent from the Greenlaw centre are available and almost all the children take them. Secondary pupils from the parish and district are transported by a special school bus which picks them up at assembling points on its journey through the parish by way of Charterhall, Fogorig and Bogend to Duns.

Doctors in Duns, Greenlaw and Coldstream have patients in the parish. The National Health Service takes patients, by ambulance if necessary, for attention in hospital or clinic, chiefly to Duns, Edinburgh or Peel.

The Parish of Fogo is a Registration District, and there is now a parliamentary polling place at Fogo for the parishioners who had formerly to vote at Greenlaw.

The churchyard is directly administered by the County Council. The maintenance and the gravedigging are done by a squad with headquarters in Duns who travel by motor van.

The parish church is the only one within the bounds. There are about 140 members. The kirk session has three elders. The church has a Sunday School with about 20 pupils staffed by two lady teachers and the minister. A church youth club with 31 members (25 young men and six young women) has been functioning for two years and is proving very successful.

There is a Unionist Association, which occasionally brings a speaker, usually to a function such as a whist drive and naturally it is most active at the time of an election.

The number of houses is 87. There are two mansionhouses, Charterhall and Caldra, 10 farmhouses, 53 farm cottages, 14 estate workers' houses, two blacksmith's houses, the manse, the schoolhouse and four new council houses, for agricultural workers. There are, in addition, three bothies.

The houses are distributed throughout the area and occur mostly in groups at the farms. Most houses are built of sandstone; some of them suffer from damp. One estate cottage was built between the wars, and two farm cottages and the four council houses were built since

1945. They are of brick roughcast. The larger houses, most of the estate workers' houses and a few of the farm cottages are detached. Farm cottages are usually in rows of from two to 10. The farmhouses are mostly commodious two-storey dwellings of from six to 10 rooms. The typical farm cottage is a two-storey house of either three or four rooms. The estate houses are various, including for example both the lodge and cottage styles.

During the last 25 years the standard in the farm and estate cottages has been greatly raised by reconstruction or additions, and by the introduction of modern equipment. At the beginning of the period few of them had water inside. Now all have water inside, but most have no hot water systems or bathrooms. Most have modern grates. The majority have electric light, some have both water and electric light and some have neither. These inequalities, which mean that houses in the parish range from good to excellent, will certainly disappear gradually as prices, supply of materials, and availability of services permit. There are no human problems connected with housing and there is no overcrowding in the parish. The mansionhouses and one farmhouse are owner occupied. The other farmhouses are occupied by either tenants or managers. By far the largest number of houses are tied to employment, the Manse and the Schoolhouse being restricted in their own way. It will be interesting to see how the new house for agricultural workers, which are not tied to particular farms, will fit into the structure of this parish.

All the houses have gardens, the smallest of which are adequate for the supply of vegetables for the household with space for flowers. The cottage gardens do not usually have fruit trees or bushes. Caldra House garden has a peach and tomato house. Most cottages have accommodation at the gardens, or behind, for pigs, and often there is space for keeping a few hens.

The occupations in the parish are chiefly connected with the land. One of the estates has a forestry staff of four, and two other properties have single foresters. There are three gamekeepers and one gardener in the parish. But most workers are engaged on farms in various capacities. Two separate master blacksmiths, one having an assistant, serve the needs of the community, but there has been no joiner for about 15 years. The mansionhouses and the larger farm houses have domestic staffs, and the other farm houses usually find help among the women or girls in their cottages.

There are 13 farm steadings in the parish, but only nine farming units. Two of them include a little land beyond the parish, and there are besides in the parish about 200 acres belonging to a farm just over the boundary. The sizes of the farms vary. Two are very large, about 1000 acres, two have 500 to 550 acres, two 300 to 400 acres, and three have about 200 acres. The acreage rent is about 28/- per acre.

One farm is managed by the resident owner, two have managers for the owners, and the remaining six are in the occupation of tenant farmers.

Very little of the farming land cannot be cultivated. The only land used as rough grazing consists of a few steep banks above the How burn on the northern boundary, and above the Blackadder, and a few 'haughs' beside the Blackadder which are not usually cultivated because they are liable to flooding.

The normal method is 'mixed' farming, with sheep as the essential stock, but during and since the war this has had to be modified by the cultivation of a greater proportion of the land for food production. The usual grain crops are oats, barley, and wheat with barley predominating. Turnips, mangolds, and kale are grown for feeding stock, and silage is also made for this purpose. Potatoes are grown extensively in spite of the difficulty of finding labour for planting and lifting. Sugar beet is also grown. In addition to the sheep, all the farms feed cattle. One farm has a large dairy of over 100 cows, and one has a pedigree Aberdeen Angus herd of cattle. All the farms have poultry, mostly on a commercial scale. Some of them breed and feed pigs to a considerable extent.

Agriculture therefore provides employment of various kinds. Two farms have stewards, and most of the others working stewards. They all have one or more shepherds. There is usually a cattleman who does other work during the summer. Where necessary there is a dairyman with men and women assistants. There may be one or more orramen, who are often skilled in special jobs such as stacking or making potato pits. One special feature of agriculture in the parish is the almost complete mechanisation. Cultivation depends on tractormen, who must be skilled not only in the driving and maintenance of the tractors but in the use of the various tractor implements, and in row crop work. Combine harvesters, which are now in common use, call for additional skill on the part of some of them. There are now few horsemen (ploughmen); indeed a minority of farms have work horses. Since the war women outdoor workers on a regular engagement, have practically disappeared. Casual labour for such work as turnip singling, hay making, harvesting, potato lifting and turnip shaving used to be supplied by Irishmen who lived for the time in bothies, but it is not now available to the same extent; only a few now come, and it appears they are not true casuals, but are rather workers on a seasonal arrangement. Casual labour is often provided by women from the cottages or by squads who are collected in Duns or Berwick, or round the countryside.

The woodlands in the parish amount to about 275 acres. Most of them are distributed on Charterhall Estate. Its largest wood is the Big Wood of 185 acres, others are the Easterwood of 36 and Printoran of 20 acres, and the total area is over 260 acres. The estate has a sawmill, and produces timber for estate and commercial purposes.

There are no shops in the parish. Food is mainly obtained from motor vans and to a lesser extent, clothing and footwear. Grocers, bakers and butchers from Duns, Gavinton, Greenlaw, Swinton, Chirnside, Coldstream and Kelso, make regular journeys in the parish, and meet the needs of the community adequately. Other commodities have to be procured from the towns.

Hours of work vary with the season. Saturday is half day, but at busy times such as harvest there is much overtime both on Saturdays and Sundays.

The community is loosely knit. Houses are scattered at intervals of about one and a half miles. Fogo village has not the size or the amenities to serve as a proper centre. It is therefore pleasant to record that there is considerable community spirit and that efforts for local purposes and good causes are well organised and well supported.

The social groups in the parish are fairly well defined as county society, farmers, estate workers and farm workers. Leadership on national or other important public occasions is expected from the laird of Charterhall.

The community is very respectable and orderly. Houses are comfortable and well managed. Children are loved and well cared for. There is much neighbourly kindness.

The standard of work is high and there is a real pride in the various agricultural, live stock and forestry skills required. The hours of work vary with the season and the length of daylight. Some households are awake by 5.30 a.m., most by 6 a.m. Some retire as early as 9 p.m. and most are in bed by 10 p.m. Bicycles are common possessions, and in the absence of adequate public transport, are much used. Many of the younger men have motor cycles. Motor cars are a necessity for farmers and others who have to travel on business. The use of leisure is as much an individual matter here as elsewhere, although no doubt it is influenced by local conditions. Much entertainment is necessarily of the stay-at-home kind. Games such as dominoes, cards and darts or hobbies such as fret work, occupy many of the evenings. Reading chiefly of fiction is to the taste of some. There is a branch of the County Library at the school. Most homes have a wireless set. Light music from both the Home Service and the Light Programme, variety, quiz programmes, discussions, weather forecasts, news bulletins, sports bulletins and sports commentaries seem to be the most popular items. Many listen to Radio Luxembourg.

Among amusements should probably be reckoned the filling up of football pool coupons which is widespread.

In the spring and summer much leisure time is spent in gardening, which affords great pleasure to some, although to others it is merely a necessity of country life.

There are several beekeepers in the parish. Most of them send their bees to the heather in the Lammermuirs. Many people follow the Berwickshire Foxhounds when they are in the district at a convenient time.

Local functions such as whist drives, concerts or dances are much appreciated. Sometimes parties are organised to go to entertainments in Duns or even Edinburgh. Dances are probably the most popular form of entertainment and young people travel considerable distances round the countryside to attend.

There is little organised sport. A Quoiting Club is at present in abeyance. At some farms there are teams which play summer football. The church youth club plays badminton. Agricultural shows are a universal interest. Duns and Kelso may both be counted local. It is a great event when the Royal Highland Show is in the Borders but many continue to travel to it when it is far away. Flower shows, bird shows, displays and competitions by organisations such as the W.R.I. attract many from the parish.

Many homes take a daily paper, a weekly paper, and a Sunday paper. The local weeklies, 'The Berwickshire News' the 'Berwickshire Advertiser' and also the 'Southern Reporter' have a wide circulation in the parish. They are the regular means of advertising situations on farms.

Most people go to Duns on Saturday for shopping, to attend football matches, or to see the films. Near neighbours visit each other in the evenings, but visiting more distant friends is most convenient on Saturdays and Sundays.

Most families in the parish are connected with the parish church. There are a few Episcopalians and a few Roman Catholics. Their churches are in Duns. Most people, whatever their church connection, have a kindly interest in the parish church and all welcome the minister in their homes.

Religion means more to the people than appears on the surface, for Borderers are not effusive. Attendance at church fluctuates a great deal, and is affected by weather and the amount of Sunday work. Few people attend every Sunday. Baptisms are usually at home, and are family and neighbourly occasions. The custom of large attendances at the celebration of the Sacrament of the Lord's Supper obtains in the parish. Many families take considerable trouble to enable their members to partake. In the judgment of the present writer the custom is evidence of true devotion. Marriages are more frequently in church than 15 years ago. The proportion has risen from 0 to about 50 per cent. Otherwise they are usually solemnised at the bride's home or in the manse. Funerals are a real mark of respect. Relatives and intimate friends are present at the service in the house and it is the custom for all who know a bereaved family, employers or employees, fellow workers or business associates, to follow the funeral from the house to form a reverent company for the service at the grave. Interment is not always at Fogo churchyard for the first death in a family may have occurred when they were at a farm elsewhere.

The future of this community is bound up with the state of agriculture. If agriculture continues to prosper, it is reasonable to expect that the standard of life will rise and that Fogo village will expand to become an adequate community centre for an important agricultural parish.

1952

PARISH OF FOGO

by Rev. Alan C. D. Cartwright

As with all parishes in Scotland there have been great changes in Fogo since the 1950s. Probably the biggest changes have been in the amenities available to every house of water, electricity and sewage. This has brought a great improvement in health and has done much to increase the life expectancy of people all over Scotland. Of course, in the country there has always been a fair proportion of people who lived to an old age because of the healthy air and abundant food. Thus in Berwickshire as a whole there are more people over 75 as compared to the rest of Great Britain (6.1 per cent compared to 5.4 per cent) and far more of pensionable age (22 per cent as against 17.7 per cent).

This however is not true of Fogo, as most of the people when they retire move into Duns or Coldstream, to the extent that only 6.5 per cent of the population of Fogo is of pensionable age. There are now also fewer children (18.1 per cent, compared to U.K. average of 22.3 per cent and Berwickshire of 21.9 per cent).

Fogo parish is not only different from the rest of Berwickshire in the proportion of older people and of children, it has also seen a greater level of depopulation. In 1755 there were 556 people in the parish (according to Webster's census) and this had increased to 604 by 1851. Yet by the 1981 census the population was down to 137 and by 1985 it has further reduced to 127. This drop in population is mainly due to increased mechanisation. In the late 1800s and early 1900s there were quite a few farms which had every cottage filled with workers and their families, but now there is, sadly, not one farm with all its cottages filled. Even those which have some cottages have not got the number of children of pre-war days.

Thus the numbers attending the school dropped dramatically, until in 1963 the school was closed. In the whole of Fogo parish there are now only six children of primary school age. When the school was closed various people got together and agreed to set up a playschool in the old school building. This has been very successful through the years and has many toddlers coming from Duns, Greenlaw, Gavinton and all the surrounding parishes. The young children obviously enjoy this small school atmosphere and it is rather sad that there is no small primary school for them afterwards. The children from Fogo go to Duns primary school as there is no school in Gavinton either; however some children have been taken by their parents to Swinton which has still got the homely small school atmosphere. The High School for the whole of the west part of Berwickshire is Berwickshire High School in Duns. The children from Fogo are transported by bus to both the primary school and the High School.

For quite a while some of the children went to the High School by train from Marchmont Station, but after the great flood of 12th August 1948, when part of the railway line was washed away (and various bridges throughout the Borders), the trains no longer ran between Duns and Greenlaw. The railway used to run along the northern boundary of the parish — the boundary with Polwarth — and this railway was well used by the people of Fogo. This common link between the parishes of Fogo and Polwarth created a bond which over the years has grown stronger, with the people from Polwarth (all 30 of them) voting in Fogo, and a common Community Council (shared with Gavinton). Strangely there has been very little linking of the two villages in the church, as over the years Polwarth was first of all united with Langton (Gavinton), with the minister staying at Gavinton, and then subsequently linked with the Kirk of the Lammermuir in 1983 with the minister staying at Cranshaws. Fogo, on the other hand, was linked with Swinton in 1967 and then united with it in 1976, and further linked with Leitholm in 1976 and with Ladykirk and Whitsome in 1978, with the minister staying at Swinton. So although Fogo and Polwarth have so much in common their ministers actually stay 17 miles apart.

Even though Fogo lost its resident minister in 1967 with the death of Rev. John C. J. Hunter (the writer of the 1951 Account), and despite its small population, there are still regular services once per month in its ancient kirk. There are extra services at Easter, Christmas, and Remembrance Day and the occasional evening service too. The little kirk with its two unusual 'laird's lofts' is an ancient one and has probably been on the present site since its foundation prior to 1159 (when it was granted to Kelso Abbey). Rev. John Hunter in his account says that the 1755 repair must have been in effect rebuilding and he may be correct. However the typical 'T' shape of Fogo suggests that it was a pre-Reformation kirk facing east, which probably fell into disrepair. After the Reformation, as the long Communion Table would take up a lot of room, there was need for further space and the short leg of the 'T' was probably added. The fact that two 'laird's lofts' (or galleries) — one at each end of the kirk — are both entered by outside stairs, is very rare, if not unique. Both of the lofts probably go back to the dates of their respective coats of arms. On the front of the east-end gallery is the coat of arms of Roger Hog, who lived at Harcarse, with the date 1677, whilst at the other end of the kirk is the coat of arms of George Trotter with the date 1671. Although the galleries have probably been altered over the years it is likely that they date back to the 1670s.

The two coats of arms relate to the Restoration of the Monarchy in 1660, and to the fact that many of the lairds decided to help the Church at that time in thanks for the Restoration. George Trotter, whose arms are above the west end of the kirk, also presented two silver Communion Cups to the kirk in 1662. These cups, still in regular use, are two of the oldest Communion Cups in Scotland; and the Trotter family, from Charterhall, still worship at Fogo, giving a double link with the people of over 300 years ago. The bell, which is rung before each service, also creates a link with those far-off days as it was made by John Meikle in Edinburgh in 1694.

The kirk is one of the few list 'A' historic churches in Scotland. This is because of the two 'laird's lofts' and also the 'box-pews'. These pews are little boxes with a table in the middle and pews going round the four sides so that a whole family could sit together. At Communion they would be sitting around their own private Communion Table, which is quite at variance with the idea of the Reformers, who wanted one 'Common' Table. The family box-pew was an innovation of the late 17th and early 18th centuries, so it may be that these box-pews go back to the 1755 repair of the kirk. Fogo is one of the few kirks which has retained its box-pews and for this reason is visited by quite a number of people who are interested in church history and church architecture.

It is hoped that in the near future the Historical Buildings Council will give a grant to Fogo Kirk in order that essential repairs to the roof and the woodwork can be carried out. Fogo Kirk is an historic building and it would be a loss of part of our heritage if it were allowed to deteriorate. Very little has been done to alter the kirk over the last 200 years except for the adaption of the low building at the east end as a vestry in 1925.

This building may have been the pre-Reformation chancel but, if this is so, it must have fallen into disrepair after the Reformation and subsequently been used as a burial crypt, for in it there is a stone with a skull and crossbones. An inscription beneath reads 'Memento Mori' ('Keep death in your thoughts'), below which there is a tree, (perhaps representing the 'Tree of Life').

There is another stone attached to the kirk — outside the south wall under the window of the leg of the 'T'. This strange stone depicts three people, two of whom have a banner across their chest saying, 'VIVE MEMO LETHE' ('Live being mindful of the river in the infernal regions'). Above the stone is an inscription only half of which can now be read; the second half reads 'WHO LOVED HIM WHO BOUGHT US DEAR'. This stone has been explained in various ways: the three figures may be Faith, Hope and Charity, or the engraving may depict the Fall of Man with Adam and Eve and the Devil in between.

Another interesting feature is the Lych Gate which is the Fogo War Memorial. Each Remembrance Sunday there is a short service in the kirk at 3.30 p.m., followed by the laying of the wreath at the War Memorial. The lych gate gives a pleasant shelter to those who are worshipping and remembering, and with the darkness just beginning to fall about 4 p.m., it is a poignant setting for the two minutes' silence.

John Oliver is buried at the back of the Kirk. As the gravestone states he was 'A wanderer throughout the Borderland'. This famous tramp — nicknamed 'Yorkie' (he came from Yorkshire) — died at Fogo East End in December 1933 and was buried in the parish kirkyard. Various people around the area, who remembered him with kindness, subscribed to a stone to commemorate him.

Fogo kirk and kirkyard is an idyllic spot and especially beautiful in the springtime, with hundreds of snowdrops growing around the gravestones, and later a profusion of daffodils along the Blackadder, opposite Fogo. Many people come from many miles just to admire the quiet beauty of Fogo.

Of course, Fogo is much quieter now than it was before, with the number of people living in the parish being less than half of what it was even a generation ago. This drop in the population has also meant that there is less need for mobile shops or public transport. In the 1950s and 60s there were quite a few delivery vans, perhaps two or three per day. Now in some places there are none at all and elsewhere there are only two or three per week. There are no buses going through the parish except for the school buses. This lack of public transport and of delivery vans means that there is even less chance of people moving into the parish unless they have work in it and also have a car.

When Rev. John Hunter wrote his account in 1951 very few people had cars or a telephone. Now most houses have at least one car and a telephone, and the proportion of both is much higher than in the towns or cities. By my estimate only two of the houses (out of a total of 49) in the parish do not have a car and probably only five or six do not have a telephone. A car and a telephone are practically essential for country life and no longer luxuries. The higher standard of living means also that all houses have electricity, hot water, and sewage. Most houses now have colour television and many also a video recorder.

The majority of the population live and work in the parish although there are a few who work in Duns or elsewhere. Most of them are involved in agriculture, either as farm workers or in one of the ancillary trades (agricultural or haulage contractors, blacksmiths etc.). Since 1951 there has only been one change in ownership of land, with Mr T. Baird now owning, and farming, Harcarse; but instead of many of the farms having tenants, all the farms on the Charterhall Estate are now run by the estate with a manager.

The most important change in the agriculture of the parish is the decrease in the amount of livestock, with many fewer sheep and cattle. This is a change which has affected the rest of Berwickshire even more, with few farms in the Merse having both sheep and cattle, and probably half of the farms having neither. Fogo has not suffered quite so much from the increased production of grain to the detriment of meat, but nevertheless there are far fewer animals now in Fogo and no dairy farms. Apart from those kept for private consumption there are no pigs or hens either.

However there are still a lot of wild animals: rabbits, hares, mice, rats, shrews, voles as well as stoats, weasels, foxes, badgers, mink, and roe deer. As there is still quite a bit of woodland throughout the parish (though most of it is coniferous) there is also shelter for many birds, including pheasants and partridges which attract people from all over during the shooting season.

The Berwickshire Hunt meets regularly in Fogo and has a large following. Before, many people rode with the hounds, but now there seem to be as many cars following as there are horses. Apart from the kirk and the playgroup, the Hunt is the only activity which takes place regularly in the parish — people go to Duns or further afield for their entertainment.

The community of Fogo is beginning to lose its identity because there is no school, no village hall, no clubs or societies. It is difficult to keep a community going when there are just over 100 people in it, but the regular monthly services in the ancient kirk keep some semblance of community feeling alive. There is normally an attendance of about 30, which can rise to over 50 on a Communion Sunday, ensuring that Fogo will continue as a parish for the forseeable future.

As Rev. John Hunter indicated in his account, religion means more to the people than appears on the surface, and the minister is always made very welcome at any house in the parish. Most marriages now take place in kirk, although it has recently been the case that Fogo girls have been married in Swinton kirk as it is bigger. However, there have been weddings at Fogo and quite a few baptisms too, when the little kirk has been quite full. (It holds about 150 with another 50 in the galleries.) There certainly has been an increase in funeral services in kirk, with about a third of the funerals now having a service in the kirk followed by immediate interment in the kirkyard. There also has been an increase in the number of cremations, with about a quarter of funerals going to one of the Edinburgh crematoria. The increase of both kirk services and crematorium services has also meant an increase in the number of women who now go to funerals. Even 20 years ago very few, if any, women would go to a funeral, but now it is commonplace; though some women remain in the kirk during interment.

The Berwickshire District Council keep the graveyard tidy and with the neat gravestones, the ancient kirk, and the lovely lych gate, Fogo is a picturesque place which is held dear by many a person (including this writer).

With the continuing depopulation there is not much hope that Fogo will thrive, but certainly it will be a haven of faith, peace, and tranquillity for many folk for a long time to come, and its beauty will continue to attract people far and near.

1986

Plate 26. The village of Hume.

Plate 27. The bridge over the River Tweed at Ladykirk.

THE PARISH OF FOULDEN[1]

by the Rev. Andrew Martin

THE PHYSICAL BASIS

The compact parish of Foulden, so far as its extent, boundaries and geographical features are concerned, remains much the same as stated in the second or *New Statistical Account* at the end of 1834, namely: 'It is 2 miles and 2 furlongs in length, and 2 miles and 1.1/2 furlongs in breadth, and is of a compact form. The northern conterminous parish is Ayton; the western, Chirnside; the southern, Hutton; and the eastern, Mordington. The southern extremity is traced by the river Whitadder'. The landscape has been denuded of many splendid trees, and by the cutting down of much beautiful woodlands, due in part to the two world-devastating wars and the consequent demand for timber. The extraordinary floods of 12th August 1948, when the Whiteadder changed its course, and devastated a considerable amount of good arable land (now in course of reclamation) made any changes there are, on the southern boundary. Climate and salubrity remain much the same as 100 years ago — comparatively mild and sheltered. While the parish is by no means immune from the diseases which modern civilisation has brought in its train, sickness and death are kept well in check. The parish has benefited very much from large scale preventive welfare work in this respect.

HISTORY

Under this section many changes and advances have taken place, probably many more than in many like rural parishes. In 1834, four-fifths of the land was the property of John Wilkie Esq, Foulden House. This estate was acquired by the Scottish Board of Agriculture in 1922 (after the First World War) for the primary purpose of providing small holdings for ex-servicemen. The farms were sub-divided into some 61 holdings, ranging from five to 80 acres. This change in land tenure changed almost everything in the life of the parish, and brought with it an influx of new people, a new community life, with new ideas and social life. It brought about a new way of living. It brought into existence small compact farms capable of maintaining a married couple with a small

[1] *See* also Mordington.

family without the employment of further labour. The tremendous advances of agricultural machinery, i.e. tractors, combined harvesters, etc., within reach of most, either by outright purchase or hire, have greatly facilitated hard work and made results possible that could not be attained by horse. This was particularly so in regard to the ploughing up of old grass lands required by the law during the Second World War.

Access to and from this parish has brought about tremendous changes; there is now a splendid bus service, running four to six times daily according to season, between Berwick-Duns-Galashiels. This has had a transforming impact upon the social life and habits of the inhabitants, with far-reaching consequences. The small village of Foulden was rebuilt (it is said on a Belgian model) by Sir James Wilkie and is picturesque with a beautiful southern outlook to the Cheviot hills. On the village green opposite is placed the First World War Memorial in the form of a Cross. In 1925 an adequate parish hall was erected by public effort. The school built in 1865 is commodious and in a very pleasing style of architecture in keeping with the village. The amenities of modern social life have thus been provided.

ANTIQUITIES

No fresh antiquities have been discovered during the past century. Foulden's antiquities consist of an ancient stone front (in the church) belonging to pre-Reformation times; a stone with a thistle carved upon it on the site of Foulden Bastel-House, and the George Ramsay Stone, 1592, in the churchyard. *See* the *Report on the County of Berwick* (1915) of the Royal Commission on Ancient Monuments . . . of Scotland, pp. 89-90.

The Tithe Barn is a long rectangular two-storeyed building of pleasant proportions. Though there is no record of its construction available, it is of early 18th century date. The cross stepped gables and the window details are characteristic of the period. Entrance is obtained by a flight of stone steps through a door at first floor level in the gable end. The ground floor is not vaulted, the first floor being supported by massive timbers. The chimney is not original, being a secondary feature. The building has been recently restored by H.M. Ministry of Works, and is under its care.

POPULATION

The population, in spite of the sub-division of the farms into holdings, has not greatly increased. The 1951 census revealed the population to be 294. This is partly explained by the fact that the holdings are not big enough to support large families, and partly by the continual drift of youth to the large towns and centres of industry. This drift shows little sign of being checked. It is one of the disappointing features of this small holding experiment, that it is not keeping, far less increasing, the population of the parish. In 1851, 100 years ago, the population (431) was almost double what it is today. Probably 50 per cent of the people were born in other parts of the Borders or of Scotland; a few owing to proximity, hail from England, none from other countries. The families who can go back three and four generations in this parish are not more than two or three, and these are craftsmen, viz: blacksmiths and joiners.

PUBLIC AND SOCIAL SERVICES

Here, as in other communities, there have been notable advances. The supply of water is short and irregular at present, but is likely to be rectified within two or three years by the big County scheme, actually begun.

Electricity was brought to the parish in 1949, and has been introduced into almost all the holdings however widely separated. It is proving a great boon, providing not only lighting but power for many kinds of agricultural machines, such as milking machines.

A modified scheme of scavenging was put into operation by the County Council in 1949. Sewage disposal is mostly by individual domestic septic tank.

EDUCATION

A two-teacher Junior School for children up to 11 years of age is maintained in the village. The pupils number 34. Transport for children living two or more miles away is provided. Mid-day meals are about to be provided: and dental and other medical treatment is given regularly. With the centralised county administration for education the old school board and the individual Parish Council have within the last century risen and passed away. The 'Further' education provisions have made evening classes in almost all subjects available, viz: drama, dancing, domestic science and others. They are not, however, taken advantage of to any extent.

Social activities are provided by such organisations as the Young Farmers' Club (membership 25, joint with Mordington), the Women's Rural Institute (50), the Church of Scotland Woman's Guild (joint 50).

Sports are well represented by football, badminton, carpet bowls and tennis, all of which have their clubs. Most of the working inhabitants have a weekly half holiday, and a week's annual holiday with pay, that is, those other than small holders. The very neat and commodious parish and village hall which was erected in 1951 has greatly facilitated all the above movements and activities.

HOUSING

Owing to the Government-sponsored small holdings scheme the housing in this parish is good. The houses were all built within the last quarter of a century and are compact and neat, if on the small side. They consist of living-room, two or three bedrooms, kitchenette and sanitary conveniences, including hot water, and about one-half have bathrooms. There is little overcrowding. Standards of living have risen both with regard to furnishings and food, and also pleasure.

AGRICULTURE, INDUSTRY

Agriculture is the staple work of this parish. The arable side has been greatly increased owing to the ploughing out demands and the maintenance of good prices. The great addition to the usual crops has, of course, been sugar beet which is extensively cultivated. Several holders specialise in early potatoes, and some in dairying, and there is one very large piggery.

Industry is represented by one motor haulage firm, one builder, with blacksmith and joiner. There are still two or three independently owned large farms, notably West Foulden (Mr Edward Scott) and Foulden Hill owned and farmed by George Hogarth, J.P. Foulden House with its beautiful grounds is now the property of Mr Robert Miller, a pioneer in the 'one day' chicken industry. The old family of Wilkie, connected with Foulden for centuries, has now no connection with the parish.

CHURCH AND RELIGION

Great changes in church life and administration have taken place locally as well as nationally. Before the Union of the Scottish Churches in 1929, the Presbytery of Chirnside had in 1927 formed into a joint charge, the parish churches of Foulden and Mordington. This readjustment of two congregations has on the whole been successful. The Union of the two great Presbyterian Churches of Scotland, terminated the system and responsibilities of the Heritors and placed new and heavy responsibilities in regard to the upkeep of all church properties on the local congregations. In many ways this has proved good. It has created a new interest in church fabric and many improvements have been made. The congregation is now within the bounds and jurisdiction of the new Presbytery of Duns.

WAY OF LIFE

The way of life of this rural parish has been greatly widened and enriched, the outlook likewise. Religion is still an influence in its life. The joint roll of the churches is 204. Attendance at public worship (joint average 60) leaves very much to be desired, and apathy towards the Church and its mission is still too prevalent. Religion must come to be a more potent factor. Family life must be deepened if it is to keep its place as the basis of our society. A better attitude to work and a better use of leisure must be attained if the great advances and enrichments of the last half century are to be conserved.

1951

PARISH OF FOULDEN

by Rev. W. G. Dunnett, M.B.E.

HISTORY OF THE LOCAL COMMUNITY

Possibly the biggest change that has happened since the last account is that the holdings as made up in 1922 are no longer 'small compact farms capable of maintaining a married couple with a small family'. It has been necessary for many holdings to be linked together to make more economic units.

Public transport in the form of buses can no longer be described as an excellent service; though buses still run through the parish between Berwick, Duns and Galashiels, but with no great frequency. However as most families now run a car, this lack of public transport is not as serious as one would expect.

Recently many of the houses in Foulden Village have changed hands. The Old School and Schoolhouse have been converted into dwellings, retaining their old outward appearance.

POPULATION

The population, like that of all similar places in this part of Berwickshire, has fallen steadily over the years. In 1982 the population of Foulden Parish was 201, while in this year of 1984 it is down to under the 200 mark. The reasons for this continuing fall are the same as before.

PUBLIC AND SOCIAL SERVICES

There is little change to report other than that there is now a sewage works for the area.

EDUCATION

A new school was built some years ago just east of the Nunlands road end. This adjoins the playing fields and is a very nice modern and open primary school. The number of pupils has been declining and it is now only just over the twenty mark, thereby retaining its status as a two-teacher school. There is a possibility that in the near future the school at Hutton will be closed and the children from there transported to Foulden. This may save Foulden School, since through the lack of young children in the parish the numbers are due to fall drastically in the next few years.

It is however a very lively and active school, taking a keen interest in the community in general. The head teacher, Mrs Robertson, draws the best out of the pupils and, while maintaining strict discipline, creates a happy atmosphere in which the children develop their own initiatives in a most excellent manner.

On leaving the primary school the pupils continue their education at Eyemouth.

HOUSING

There has been a considerable development in the way of housing, other than that associated with the holdings, in the last 50 years. An estate of council houses has been established at Kerrigan Way close to the new school. There are at present plans for the building of a number of private houses (nine perhaps or even as many as 24) adjoining this estate. In the grounds of the old mansion house there now stand six large modern houses set in the old grounds which still retain the old trees and grass.

Many of the holding houses have been modernised to include central heating and additional rooms.

AGRICULTURE AND INDUSTRY

Farming is still the main industry in this parish. The number of holdings has been considerably reduced as has happened in similar places, and the independent farms have increased in size.

There is now only one dairy farm run, by Mr McGregor, in the parish, where the main crops grown are barley, potatoes and turnips for winter feed. Sugar beet is no longer grown, but a new crop that is spreading in Berwickshire is oil-seed rape.

Industry is represented by one builder, one road contractor, one tomato and deep-litter chicken grower and a motor haulage firm.

CHURCH AND RELIGION

The union of the two parishes of Foulden and Mordington is working well. The bulk of the support for the church now comes from Foulden where services are held on alternate Sundays. The United Congregation is now linked with that of Hutton, Fishwick and Paxton with the minister (Rev. W. G. Dunnett, M.B.E.) living in Hutton. This linkage has turned out very well as there is considerable 'cross the Whiteadder' movement and relationships, and the road joining the two parishes makes this possible through the bridge over the river.

Membership of the church is fairly steady but ageing. As so many of the young people have to leave the district to find work there is a great lack of young leaders to take the place of the now ageing Session. In the Kirk Session there are two lady elders of whom one is Session Clerk.

WAY OF LIFE

There is within this community a good way of life, with people able to go about freely and without fear — a state of affairs not always to be found in other parts of the country. With the advent of television there is perhaps less of a social life, but nevertheless the S.W.R.I., the Woman's Guild, the Bowling and the Youth Clubs are well supported. Regular dances are held in the village hall and also whist drives. Religion is still an influence within the community, though attendance at public worship could, as in the past, be much better.

1984

THE PARISH OF GORDON

by The Rev. James Robson, B.D.

PHYSICAL BASIS

An agricultural parish in the western district of the Merse, Gordon is bounded on the west and north by the parishes of Legerwood and Westruther, on the east by Greenlaw and on the south by Hume and part of Earlston. It is roughly diamond-shaped and covers an area of 21 square miles. The River Eden forms the north-west boundary, the Blackadder runs along two miles of the north-east and the Hareford Burn on the south-west. The village of Gordon (formerly West Gordon) lies in the centre of the parish where the Greenlaw-Earlston and the Edinburgh-Kelso roads cross at right angles. East Gordon was once a village community but is now only a farm steading. The parish stands over 500 feet above sea level but none of the high ground is entitled to be dignified with the title of hills except the Knock Hill (891 feet). The atmosphere is clear and healthy owing to the general high situation.

HISTORY OF THE LOCAL COMMUNITY

Certain Norman nobles who helped Malcolm Canmore to recover his throne received from him gifts of lands in return and in 1057 Adam de Gordun took possession of his new estates, building his castle on a wooded eminence (beside the present railway station) still known as the Castle Park. These nobles were loyal both to King and Church. Richard, the grandson of Adam de Gordun, in 1171, when the Church of Gordon was transferred from the Abbey of Coldingham to the Abbey of Kelso, along with other donations, bestowed on the 'Church of St Michael in my town of Gordun in free and perpetual and unincumbered gift all the land from the cemetery to the louping stone of the priest . . . Alexander, and so toward the ditch which Walter a former priest had made, etc. etc.', which land, to exactly the same extent, constitutes the present glebe.

At the end of the 13th century, the Gordon family, probably because they also possessed lands in England, paid homage to the English King. Later on they gave their allegiance to William Wallace and King Robert the Bruce. Rewards followed in the granting of the barony of

Strathbogie, and some place-names have probably been transferred from the south to their new territory, e.g. 'Huntly' may well have come from Huntl(e)y Wood in this parish. By 1400 onwards, their interests lay almost entirely in the North. From the marriage (in 1408) of Elizabeth Gordon to Alexander Seton, who assumed the name of Gordon, come the families now represented by the Duke of Gordon, the Marquis of Huntly and the Marquis of Aberdeen. A branch of the family which remained in Gordon must have returned to the paternal name of Seton for over the door of Greenknowe Tower (built 1581 to replace the destroyed Castle) is a stone bearing the initials and coat of arms of the Seton family. This building, whose walls are in a good state of preservation, is now an ancient monument: in covenanting times it afforded shelter to Walter Pringle, the 'Laird of Greenknowe', to whom the estate passed by purchase in the 17th century. The estate must have been greatly impoverished by the fines which that zealous Presbyterian had to pay, yet it remained in the possession of his family until the 19th century when it passed, also by purchase, to the Fairholms, one of whom made himself famous by joining the expedition of Sir John Franklin and perishing along with that explorer. The property again changed hands, coming into the possession of Mr A. D. Forbes Gordon, but in the last few months the remaining farms have been sold to their present occupiers, so that only a minute portion of the parish is now owned by those bearing the name of the original founder.

Rutherfurd's *Southern Counties Register* (publ. Kelso, May 1866) states that the area of the parish is according to the Ordnance Survey nearly 9,739 acres, of which 105 are occupied by roads, nearly 26 are under water and the remainder (about one-fourth) of non-agricultural land consists of unreclaimed moor. These figures show little variation from those given at the present time by the Department of Agriculture, though a certain amount of drainage (about 200 acres) has been carried out, where practicable, on bog land in the southern part of the parish. 7000 acres are ploughable — 2300 are in crop with the rest in temporary pasture. The average rent per acre is 17/9. Stock carried on farms would amount to approximately 5,000 breeding ewes, 300 breeding beef cows and 120 milk cows on the three dairy farms. With the break-up of the large estates in this area (subsequent to the First World War), the 11 farms, which vary from 500-1100 acres, are all owner-occupied. There is at present only one tenant farmer in the district and his is one of six smallholdings.

The appearance of the parish has been materially altered since many trees were cut down during the 1914-18 war and the countryside is left bare with the fields divided by dry-stone dykes. The district contains a great deal of whinstone, and one method of clearing the fields in the past was to erect these dykes, often three feet thick. Where these have been broken down, however, it is often difficult to carry out even temporary repairs as dykeing is a lost art. Fifty years ago, there were half a dozen dykers in Gordon — now there are none, although efforts are being made in surrounding districts to attract such workers. In the Second Statistical Report, mention was made of the feus sold by Greenknowe estate to residents in the village who cultivated them in their spare time. All of these have passed into other hands; in most cases absorbed into the larger farms. It is a commentary on how work has become specialised: many of the villages possessed a field or two in connection with their businesses, e.g. the butcher required one on which to graze beasts for the period between purchase at the mart and disposal in his private slaughterhouse (now also a thing of the past); one or two in the village kept cows and purveyed the milk to the rest of the inhabitants who came to collect it, but this is now the province of two dairy farms who both deliver by pony and cart — though even here mechanisation may soon be supplanting the animal. Vans are being used increasingly, hence the fields are no longer required for horses or ponies as of old, so their owners dispose of them. One or two of those fields remaining in private hands are let on a year to year basis. The villagers have always possessed the right to cut peats in Gordon moss, though none now avail themselves of this privilege so highly prized in the 1830s; 'birks', however, are regularly gathered by many of the villagers, who, incidentally, are growing perturbed about the moss being treated as a dumping ground for all sorts of rubbish.

Some customs are still carried out in Gordon, but these are common to many Border parishes, e.g. blackening the feet of the bridegroom in the week preceding the wedding and 'creeling' the pair after they have left the church. As in other places in the Borders, the local inhabitants possess a nickname: in this case — 'Gordon Gowks'. The reason for this is lost in the obscurity of the distant past, but Robson's *Churches and Churchyards of Berwickshire* (1896) notes that when the heating apparatus was introduced into the church several years previously the workmen came upon a pit in which 76 skulls were huddled together along with a number of thigh bones. 'It was remarked (he states) that the skulls were extraordinarily thick and the thigh bones were acknowledged to be longer than those of the past or present generation!' Whatever truth may lie in that explanation, the old rhyme outlining the extent of the parish is still quoted:

'Rumbleton, Rumbletonlaw,
Middlethird and Bellitaw,
Hexpath of the yellow hare,
Gordon Gowks for evermair.'

The older inhabitants can tell of place-names that are gradually dropping out of use like the 'Beggar-raw' (Edenside road) on which an old worthy, Lockie by name, was building a dyke when passers-by informed him that he was working on the Sabbath. 'Pity-me', he exclaimed, and for a long time that spot went under that name. A field on

Upper Huntlywood was much used in covenanting times and has come down in history as 'the Pulpit'. The Bannock-knowe or Greenknowe farm lay on the old drove road from Kelso to Lauder, and when the monks crossed Greenknowe Moss over a causeway made of windle straws, they halted there for their midday meal.

POPULATION

The population of the parish has fallen by 46 per cent within the last century. In 1851, it stood at 983, the maximum ever recorded. Fifty years later in 1901, it was 791 and had dropped to 711 in 1911. At the 1921 census, it was 719, composed of 342 males and 377 females, showing a further drop in 1931 with 702. In 1951 it was 672.

These figures would seem to show that the reasons for the decline in population lie in the undoubted facts that families are smaller, and far fewer people are now employed on the farms owing to the mechanisation of labour. In the olden days one farm itself is said to have had a population of 90. It had 12 cottages and in one of these there were 15 children. While this was a unique instance, 20-25 children to a farm was quite common. With the increasing use of the tractor for all kinds of farm work there are not above 20 horses working on the land in the parish, whereas 30 years ago there would be 42 pair. This reduction in the number of horses kept means that there is a corresponding reduction in the number of women employed. The farm population nowadays is roughly three-quarters of the men employed when horses were used, and no women. About 10 to 15 per cent of the agricultural community over the age of 40 have been born in the parish or in neighbouring parishes, and about 40-50 per cent of the village population over the age of 40 are natives. Most of those who are not natives have come from other parts of Berwickshire, or from either East Lothian or Northumberland.

The average age of parishioners has always been high in Gordon. At the 1921 census there were 16 males and 12 females over 75 years of age; and two years ago this month a minister officiated at three funerals in the one day when the combined ages of the deceased amounted to 272. In the churchyard there is a very interesting tombstone commemorating Rachel Pitt who died aged 104 in 1932, exactly 122 years after her elder sister who died in infancy in 1810. Quite a number of retired people have made their home in Gordon and this has helped to arrest temporarily the decline in population.

PUBLIC AND SOCIAL SERVICES

Most of the public and social services are administered by the County Council to which Gordon returns one member. There is also a representative on the West District Council. The parish has an excellent sanitary system and a good gravitation water supply. Piped water has been available since 1895; electric light since about 1925. Practically all the houses in the village (96 in number) have hot and cold water, electric light and baths. The roads in this part of the county are well maintained by the appropriate section of the County Council. Ashes and rubbish are collected by lorry twice per week, a special scavenging rate being levied on the county for this purpose. The domestic water rate is payable by occupiers only. The telephone exchange was altered to automatic working in 1944. Three postmen working from Gordon cover a considerable area in the parishes of Westruther and Earlston as well as their own.

Gordon Hospital was the fever hospital for Berwickshire before the war but since then has not been fully occupied. One ward at present holds 14 elderly ladies and there is the possibility of another ward being opened this year. The hospital is under the Border Hospitals Board of Management. The assistant to the Greenlaw doctor resides in the village, and the Greenlaw district nurse also looks after Gordon.

Gordon school is a three-teacher one, of whom at present two are graduates. There are 72 pupils between the ages of 5 and 12 in attendance. The school has recently been redecorated; a new central heating system installed and a new classroom, staffroom and cloakroom facilities added. The pupils have every encouragement to progress in their education since full use is made of the many excellent broadcasts for schools and a projector is available for the showing of films — a great difference from the days when education was limited to the three 'R's'. The health of the pupils is ensured not only by the regular medical and dental inspections but also by the opportunities given for playing games. School dinners of two courses are served on each school day, giving all those who partake a balanced diet and obviating the necessity of carrying a 'piece' which prevailed in the past. Free milk is also available to all who wish it. The County Library allocation of books is also lodged in the school: it is well used by the children, but the adult population has little time or inclination for serious reading.

At the age of 12 all pupils are transferred to the main secondary school in the county town of Duns, being transported there by a special bus. Centralised education does not commend itself to the community here, and it is generally felt that many pupils would derive more benefit from completing their education at the local school, where their abilities and their family background would be better understood. Very few of the 25 pupils who travel to Duns intend to complete the secondary education open to them although the County Education Committee offer inducements in the shape of bursaries for University and technical courses whenever a pupil shows promise and the home circumstances warrant such a grant. Most of them leave once they attain the statutory age of 15, and take whatever opening presents itself, regardless of whether it is a blind-alley occupation or not.

Adult education is carried out under the auspices of the Education Committee who grant the use of the school classrooms and provide teachers and materials where the numbers warrant such a class being held. Handicraft classes are usually very popular, especially with the women folk, many of whom display exhibits at local and national shows. A country dancing class has also attracted many women, but few men. The latter prefer to attend the Carpet Bowling Club which meets twice a week during the winter and plays in various district leagues. A new hut has been bought by this club and will be erected in the course of the year. A football team drawn from the parishes of Gordon and Westruther plays in the Berwickshire League.

Gordon has been very fortunate in possessing a park in which are situated the bowling green and tarmac tennis court, and also an excellent hall in which many activities are carried on during the winter months. There is a Badminton Club with a membership of 30. There too the W.R.I. with a membership of 130 meets, and whist drives which take place every other week are well supported by the community. The W.R.I., besides holding a Burns Supper, sponsors an annual Flower Show at the end of August and there is keen competition and interest shown in this event. Among other hobbies and interests worth noting is the breeding of budgerigars. Four local breeders who are members of various societies compete in both district and national shows: half the first prizes in local shows are won by these four breeders, one of whom has also won six cups during the past season.

HOUSING

Here again the situation has been vastly improved in recent years. The days of the 'but-and-ben' and the thatched cottage are gone. The main street in the village does not present an appearance of uniformity — many of the smaller cottages were demolished to make room for garages and shops or to allow of extension to existing houses. Less than 10 per cent of the houses are three-roomed and so overcrowding is negligible. Twenty-four houses have been built by the local authority. Eight of these (upper and lower flats) in two blocks were built just before the War and 12 Crudens were built in 1946. All of these possess gardens which are very well kept. Eight houses are scheduled to be rebuilt and about three-quarters of the houses in the village are owner-occupied. The new local authority house-rents are high in comparison with the older houses in the village but, though people grumble at the rents, they prefer these new houses with their increased space and excellent situation. Applications for vacant local authority houses are dealt with by the West District Council on a 'points' system and can be allocated to persons living in other parts of the county. This feature of the system does not commend itself to the local population, and makes many young couples feel frustrated. There are sufficient farm cottages available. Usually only one man in each of these works on the farm, with the rest of the family finding work in other occupations. Most farmers are taking advantage of grants to modernise their cottages, and, where this has been done, the occupiers do their best to carry out improvements in redecoration and furnishing, taking a real pride in making their houses as bright and cheerful as possible. Many of these cottages are rent-free and the workers receive perquisites in addition to wages which are fixed by negotiation. The farmworker's life has changed immensely, with an assured minimum wage, much shorter hours with weekends practically free, and far better housing conditions. Few are without a wireless set and many make a weekly excursion to the cinema.

TRANSPORT

The Berwickshire branch of the former L.N.E.R. railway was put out of action in 1948 by floods which washed away a number of bridges. One of these has never been replaced and the line is now closed except for the passage of one goods train daily. During the severe storm of March 1947 roads round about were blocked for a week and the railway was only open as far as Gordon. Bread and other commodities could thus reach the station and parties came from the various farms as best they could to collect what they needed. Five hours to cover two miles was not an unusual occurrence then. With the change from passenger working, the local people often wonder how they would fare in the event of 'another 1947'! Since the closing of the railway for passenger working, the bus services have been augmented but these still leave much to be desired. Two workers' buses ply between Duns and Galashiels each day and there are three others which run between Berwick and Galashiels. The transport authorities consider these sufficient for the number of passengers carried, but local feeling is that the service could be vastly improved by one or two additional buses running at more convenient times. Two buses run on Friday and Saturday nights to the nearest cinema in Kelso and are well patronised. Many people, disgusted at the inadequacy of the bus services, have bought cars, especially when they require them essentially for their work. There is no industry in Gordon apart from a whinstone quarry which employs four men and a clerkess. Apart from girl assistants in the various shops, the others have to find work elsewhere in Earlston or Kelso. Many of the girls work in the tweed mill at Earlston, but this mill has sometimes been working on 'short time' lately, which results in less pay and an incentive to find a steady job elsewhere, even if it means leaving the county. Not many young men have emigrated abroad since there are contractors in the building and timber trades nearby who require a constant labour pool. This often involves living away from home for a period, but it is unavoidable when local work is not available.

There are only two trades of a century ago still carried on by members of the same families. The three tailors have disappeared since 'ready-mades' flooded the market. The other businesses, though now well-established, are of more recent creation. Gordon has three joiners, one blacksmith, two drapers, two bootmakers, two garages, one butcher and three grocers' shops, all of which carry on successful trading in the surrounding district. Two haulage contractors are kept busy, especially on market days. A policeman is stationed in the village but as this is a law-abiding community generally, with little drunkenness and no serious crime, his work is mainly concerned with technical offences.

There are two churches in Gordon. The parish church of St Michael was consecrated by Bishop David de Bernham in 1242. Nothing of the original church remains — it was rebuilt in 1763 and restored in 1897, two beautiful stained glass windows, each of three lights, being added later. There are 320 members and eight elders. There is a Woman's Guild of 30 who perform wonders at their annual sale of work. Two youth organisations have recently been attached to the church — a company of the Boys' Brigade and a team of 10 Lifeboys. A Girl Guide company is also shortly to be formed in the district. The United Free Church (built in 1843) has a membership of 39 and is served by a student pastor. Relations between the two churches are excellent.

WAY OF LIFE

The passing of the years also sees the passing of the 'old worthies' — men and women with a wealth of character written upon their faces and a downright attitude to life. Their descendants possess a far wider knowledge of the world and its ways acquired in many cases by service abroad in two wars. The dissemination of news by wireless and an appreciation of politics and current affairs through newspaper articles has also made people conversant with events occurring outwith their immediate neighbourhood. Yet with all this increase in knowledge of world affairs some things have been lost — not only knowledge of crafts but certain fundamental truths about life, including a sense of its purpose. A distinct cleavage has arisen between the spiritual and the temporal. Most people nowadays think in terms of this world only, and this attitude is reflected in their way of life. Work is coming to be regarded more as a means of gaining money to acquire material possessions or to participate in pleasures which appeal to them. The ubiquitous football coupon with its fatal attraction of 'easy money' contributes to this and people are no longer moved as in former days to make comparable, real sacrifices for their children's education ('it's state subsidised!') or for their religion: they feel themselves oppressed by the cost of living and by the cost of 'essential' pleasures.

With the rise of this materialistic view of life there has been a corresponding spiritual decline. For many people, to lead a decent respectable life based on Christian virtues is held to be quite sufficient. They would miss the Kirk were it to be removed but they do not wish to be troubled unless something drives them to it. Congregations nowadays include few men between the ages of 20 and 50 except on Communion Sundays. Women are more open to the need for a life based on religion and usually see to it that their children attend Sunday School. At baptisms and marriages people do realise more of the spiritual perceptions and the need for deepening their religious life but the effect generally wears off after a short time. Funerals are very well attended but here too there is a widely-held creed that the grave means the end of all life, and that it is simply a case of paying one's last respects to the deceased. Custom dies hard and the village is still 'bidden' to attend a funeral. Whether or not church attendance in the last century was largely based on custom and tradition, it was a good custom, ensuring that people were reminded of certain eternal truths without the practice of which life cannot be a success.

Parental control over the family is another thing which has vastly changed. Nowadays many children 'rule the roost' and good manners have often disappeared. The modern disintegration of family life has meant the disappearance of the old traditions — the family pew filled every Sunday to overflowing, and family worship which brought religion into the home throughout the week. The latter is now a quaint relic of the past in all except a very few homes. Sunday is nowadays regarded either as a day of rest or at least of freedom to enjoy oneself according to personal inclination. The younger generation are not so keen to provide amusement for others; there was a very successful concert party in this parish but the older members of it were wishing that more young people would come into it for training. Perhaps this passive attitude to amusement is due to the effect of broadcasting and the cinema.

As elsewhere people hereabouts grumble that government rules and regulations hamper the independent spirit, but there is no lack of enterprise in this community. Farmers and others are anxious to keep up with modern methods and, provided they will pay, are more than willing to use them and invest in new equipment. Whether further mechanisation will affect population is a debatable point but there is no likelihood of any substantial increase if adequate transport to larger centres of industry is not forthcoming. The outlook for the future depends on many things — material as well as spiritual — but without the recovery of the latter the community life will certainly be the poorer.

1952

Plate 28. The gateway of Ladykirk House.

THE PARISH OF GORDON

by The Rev. A. MacLeod

POPULATION

Since the date of the last Statistical Account, the parish population has further declined and now stands at 430. A number of retired persons from other districts have taken up residence here, but families are smaller these days and an increase in population seems unlikely.

TRANSPORT

The railway station has been closed for a number of years and the former site is now occupied by a timber yard. Bus services to and from local towns are infrequent, but the great majority of parishioners have cars, and indeed without them life would be very circumscribed.

EMPLOYMENT

As the tractor has replaced the horse, and agricultural machinery is in evidence everywhere, opportunities for employment on the farms have correspondingly declined. In Gordon Village there is now one joinery business, two garages, two contractors (one haulage, the other public works) and one engineering workshop. All of these employ a limited number. The timber yard also employs a few, but the coal agency and the quarry have both ceased to operate. Many have to travel to the nearer Border towns for daily work and the prospects for young people wishing to obtain employment in the parish are not encouraging.

EDUCATION

A new primary school was built in Gordon in 1974. It is a three-teacher school with 58 pupils and apart from commodious and well-appointed classrooms it has an excellent hall and canteen. The old school is used in the main as a store. Post-primary children travel to the secondary schools in Earlston and Duns. The Parent-Teacher Association is active both educationally and socially.

CHURCHES

The parish church of St Michael's has 168 members, seven members of Kirk Session and 11 on Congregational Board. In 1971 the parishes of Gordon, Legerwood and Westruther became a 'linked' charge under one minister, residing in St Michael's Manse, Gordon. This arrangement continues. Church attendance has declined here, as elsewhere in Scotland, but there are many loyal members and the children's organisation, called 'The Monday Group', is popular and well attended. The combined Woman's Guild (Gordon, Legerwood and Westruther) meets regularly during the winter months and has a good representative membership. The United Free Church in Gordon has 40 members and a resident minister who occupies the U.F. Manse.

HOUSING

The main factor to be reported since the previous account is the construction of the Glebe Park local authority housing scheme in 1970. This consists of 36 houses and a number of garages. A number of the older local authority houses have recently been modernised and much improved by the installation of centrally heated radiators.

PUBLIC AND SOCIAL SERVICES

There is no longer a resident doctor in the parish, nor a nurse, nor a policeman. Gordon Hospital was sold to private ownership some years ago and hospital services for parishioners are available at hospitals in Kelso, Coldstream, Duns, Galashiels, Melrose and Peel. Parishioners are registered with the doctors in Greenlaw and Earlston. The District Nurse visits regularly.

There are now only two grocer's shops in the village — one sells milk and newspapers; the other is a combined shop and Post Office. There is additionally a combined drapery/boot and shoe shop. The parish is represented on the Community Council and on the District and Regional Councils. There is one Justice of the Peace and one Registrar.

RECREATION

Television is vastly popular but there are additional forms of recreation. There are many enthusiastic gardeners and the annual 'Flower Show' testifies to their skill and zeal. The Bowling Club and the Angling Club attract goodly numbers. The mobile library visits every fortnight. 'The Gay Gordons', a club for O.A.P.s, meets in the village hall as does the Badminton Club for youngsters. Girl Guides use the school hall for weekly meetings. Adult Education classes have been discontinued as have meetings of the W.R.I.

Gordon Moss is no longer a dumping ground but is now a Conservation Area.

CONCLUSION

Changes recorded above which have occurred over the period of the last 30 years (approx.) could no doubt be paralleled in similar communities in the Borders. The steady decline in population and the current recession have had inevitable effects. This is a peaceful and friendly parish with roots deep in the past, and yet, with a lively and concerned outlook on the wider world, it retains the flexibility to adapt to meet the altering circumstances imposed by an ever changing society.

1983

THE PARISH OF GREENLAW

by Rev. Robert D. Higham

Greenlaw parish, as an ecclesiastical division, is part of the linked parish of Gordon St Michael's, with Greenlaw, Legerwood and Westruther. Greenlaw ceased to be a single parish in 1978 when it was linked with Eccles. Then in 1985 Eccles was transferred into a linkage with Coldstream, and Greenlaw was linked into the already existing linkage of Gordon St Michael's, Legerwood and Westruther. The linked parish is part of Duns Presbytery of the Church of Scotland which in turn is part of the Synod of the Borders. Greenlaw parish is in Berwickshire District of the Borders Region. It is 36 miles from Edinburgh, 10 miles from Coldstream, eight miles from Kelso, seven miles from Duns and 11 miles from Earlston. The parish area is 12,200 acres. At its longest it measures eight miles (13 km) on a north-north-west to south-south-east axis and at its widest it measures four and a half miles (seven km) on a west to east axis. The parish lies on the lower south-facing slopes of the Lammermuir Hills as they descend into the Tweed Basin, known in its lower course as the Merse. The highest point in the parish is Dirrington Little Law (1191 feet) at the northern extremity and the lowest lying land is at the southern extremity at Lambden Burn, which is just below 300 feet above sea level.

Greenlaw parish marches with Longformacus to the north, Polwarth and Fogo to the east, Eccles to the south and Stichill, Gordon and Westruther to the west. The descending altitude of the land from north to south is usefully recorded at the farms. Bedshiel stands at 740 feet, Halliburton at 643 feet, Greenlawdean at 550 feet. Greenlaw itself is at 475 feet and lies mainly on the eastern bank of the River Blackadder. Rising out of this valley to the south, Elwartlaw is at 525 feet, Old Greenlaw House at 650 feet, Crumrig at 500 feet, Easter and Wester Howlaws at 450 feet, Cowrig at 400 feet and Lambden at 300 feet.

The main surface drainage is the Blackadder Water which flows into the parish at Hurdlaw on the western boundary with Westruther at the confluence with one of its tributary streams, Evelaw Burn. The main feeder stream is the Fangrest Burn which is formed by the confluence of the Millknowe Burn and Bogpark Burn as they drain the south side of Dirrington Little Law. The Blackadder flows into Fogo parish, east of Lintmill Bridge. To the south two small streams, Thirlington Burn and Lambden Burn, the latter forming the whole southern boundary of the parish, flow into the Leet Water. All water drains down toward the Tweed. The northern part is moorland while the southern part is fertile.

Geologically the north of the parish is mainly upper old red sandstone. Dirrington Little Law is intrusive igneous felsite (felstone mica-trap). South of Greenlaw there are basalt lavas of carboniferous age and then in the very south, at Rowchester and Lambden the rock is Scottish calciferous sandstone also of carboniferous age. Sandstone has been quarried in several places in past centuries. The most important quarries were in the steep sides of the Blackadder valley above Greenlaw. The most notable was Corbieheugh Quarry. Sandstone for Leaderfoot Viaduct and other bridges on the Berwickshire Railway was quarried in the Blackadder valley. The soil maps reveals that Dirrington Little Law is well-drained peaty podsol; Weetfoot Bog and Dogden Moss are basin peat; around Bedshiel are poorly drained peaty gleys. The depth of peat in Dogden Moss is 10 feet in certain parts. The last time that peat was cut for fuel in any quantity was during the Second World War.

The Kaims, a gravelly ridge stretching from Polwarth Moss to become the northern boundary of Dogden Moss, in appearance looks like a prehistoric man-made earthwork. Kaim is a word of Celtic origin meaning encirclement. The ridge may have been regarded as a protective bank raised to defend an ancient settlement, but it is probably the former southern embankment of a glacial lake. It is 50 feet broad at base and varies from 30 to 40 feet in height and with several breaks, one being for the passage of the Fangrest Burn. The Kaims runs for two miles in a semi-circular configuration. It comprises brown forest soils derived from fluvio-glacial sands which are well-drained.

Bedshiel itself lies on brown forest soils derived from upper old red sandstone and marls, as do the following farms — Halliburton, Greenlawdean, Whiteside, Catmoss (no longer a farm), Easter Howlaws, Angelrow and Lambden.

Hule Moss comprises well-drained peaty podsols and poorly drained peaty gleys. The bottom of the Blackadder Valley near Greenlaw is alluvium as is the Rumbleton Burn to the west of the village. But in Greenlaw itself and flanking the valley there are brown forest soils derived from fluvio-glacial sands. Old Greenlaw, Elwartlaw and Crumrig have brown forest soils derived from lower carboniferous basalt lavas and upper old red sandstone. East of Castlemill and Angelrow are soil complexes derived from lower carboniferous sediments, basic lavas, upper old red sandstone and Silurian greywackes.

HISTORY

The purpose of Heriot's Dyke or Harrits Dyke is unknown. It is thought to have extended from Boon in Legerwood or from Harefaulds, an ancient British village, on Blythe farm, in Lauder parish, eastwards to Berwick. One of the few places where this ditch and dyke are still discernible is on Greenlaw Moor to the south of Hule Moss and stretching to the Fangrest Burn.

At the confluence of the Blackadder Water and the Fangrest Burn, known as the 'meeting of the waters', is Blackcastle Rings, about half a mile from where the vestiges of Heriot's Dyke meets the Burn. This ancient fortified camp stands 100 feet above the confluence on the east side. Another entrenched dyke, Black Dikes, begins to the north of the camp and reappears on the other side of the Blackadder valley, following the rim of the declivity and turning away south to Crawlee Plantation. Last century it was evidently traceable through Rumbleton and Rumbletonlaw farms in Gordon parish.

Several ancient burial barrows existed in the north-west of the parish, below Dirrington Little Law, until early last century, but they were demolished and the stone used for building dykes.

Examples of an early cultivation system, crooked rigs, occur in the parish. Crumrig farm gets its name from this system of ploughing land to conform with the curves in a stream in order to maximise use of the land.

The town of Greenlaw was originally sited near the present Old Greenlaw House, on an eminence or law. The name stems from the nature of the place, a green hill. New Greenlaw began to expand in the valley, on its present site, in the second half of the 16th century. By 1598 it was more populous than Old Greenlaw and parliament ratified a charter of burgh of barony in 1600. Property names extant today, which appeared in this charter, were Broomhill, Greenlawdean, Eastfield, Whiteside and Clay Dub. Greenlaw Castle was also mentioned in the charter. It may have been more of a mansion house than a fortified dwelling. The only evidence of the former existence of such a building is Castlemill farm, which must have derived its name from Greenlaw Castle.

Greenlaw became county town in 1696. Thereafter the most significant building projects went ahead. The present church had been rebuilt on its medieval foundations in 1675. But in 1712 the church was lengthened, a court house was completed and separating the two was a tolbooth or prison, also completed in 1712. The style of the prison had the appearance of a church tower, although out of proportion to the size of the church and without access from within the church. It is 60 feet high to the corbelled parapet. Above this rises an 18 foot steeple. The structure is unique and has earned Greenlaw church, Category A status as an historic building.

With church, tolbooth and courthouse standing together a rhyme became popular in the area —

'Here stands the Gospel and the Law,
Wi' Hell's Hole atween the twa'.

An inset in a map of Berwickshire produced for Hugh Hume, Earl of Marchmont, in 1771 depicts Greenlaw with the church, tolbooth and county house as the small town's most prominent features. On the green in front of these buildings, where the town hall has since been erected, are a well, the Mercat Cross and the Trone (official means of weighing goods). The arched part of the tower at ground level is said to have been the condemned cell, otherwise called the thieves' hole. In one of the cells in the tower are preserved some old graffiti inscribed by gardeners from Marchmont who had been incarcerated for ducking an old woman they had suspected to be a witch.

A new gaol was built in 1824. Then in 1831 the county hall was completed and the court house demolished. The new county hall was built in Grecian style. It accommodated the court, the sheriff and had rooms for all county meetings. Above the vestibule was a domed, fire-proof room in which the county records were stored.

The county hall was built at the expense of Sir W. P. H. Campbell, Bart. of Marchmont and presented to the county.

Greenlaw Church thereafter inherited the former prison as a tower, although proof of ownership was not settled until 1968 when the general trustees of the Church of Scotland verified that it became church property in 1925 under the Church of Scotland (Property and Endowments) Act.

Greenlaw's status as county town began to be eroded in 1853 when an Act of Parliament authorised that sheriff and commissary courts could be held in Duns. Trials by jury continued to be held in Greenlaw; but more police provision in the form of cells and offices was built in Duns. Eventually, a Bill making Duns the County Town was introduced to parliament in 1900. It was passed, after much delay, on 30th June 1903.

The history of Greenlaw Church is very much part of the history of the area. References to the area by the Venerable Bede in his account of missionary activity radiating into Northumbria from Lindisfarne, lead to the belief that a church was established at Old Greenlaw in about 700 AD. The first church on the present site was probably built and endowed by Cospatrick, second Earl of Dunbar, early in the 12th century. It was a mother church having dependent chapels at Lambden and Halliburton. The first known priest was Nigel in about 1159. Bishop David de Bernham of St Andrews (the Merse was in that diocese) dedicated the church in 1242. The patron saint may have been St Helen; a fair was formerly held on that saint's day, 3rd May, every year. In the 1860s fairs for the sale of cows were still held twice yearly in May and October. They had only local importance and ceased long ago. The first Presbyterian minister, David Home, took office in 1606, the parish having been served by 'readers' since the Reformation in 1560. The 'readers' were former Roman Catholic priests. David Home built a wooden bridge over the Blackadder at the head of Wester Row.

After rebuilding in 1675 and lengthening in 1712, east and west galleries were added in 1721. After 1784 the north loft was added. In 1855 the church was completed on a T plan by the addition of the north aisle. In 1883 most of the church was reseated, the outer stair to the east gallery was demolished and an inner stair erected. The pipe organ was installed before the end of the century.

While the tower was a prison there was a small window at the west end of the church for prisoners to observe the services. The tower houses the church bell and the town clock. The bell was provided under the will of Thomas Broomfield, Greenlawdean, who died in 1667. It was made in 1696 and refounded in 1726 and is inscribed with his name. Broomfield left funds to build a new bridge over the Blackadder at the west end of the town.

The town clock is maintained by the District Council.

Since the last Statistical Account in 1834, when there were two other churches in Greenlaw, there have been considerable changes. The 'Easter Meeting' was a congregation, which was part of the General Associated Synod, originally the Antiburgher Associate Division of the Secession Church. It had been founded in 1780, but a church building was not erected until 1855. It eventually became the Congregational Church and continued until the late 1930s. The building has been used for a garage business, as a store and is now used by a person running a vintage vehicle business.

The 'Damside Meeting' was a congregation of the Original Secession Church. It began in 1807 and joined the Church of Scotland in 1839. After the Disruption of the Church of Scotland in 1843, a Free Church congregation was formed, known as the Fairbairn Church after their first minister. The Free Church School was also established. The premises were the Fairbairn Hall which is the Church of Scotland's current church hall. A Free Church manse was built and this has become the present manse, the former 'Auld Kirk' manse having been sold after the Fairbairn Church united with the parish church in 1952. The Free Church had joined with the United Presbyterian Church to form the United Free Church in 1900, and then in 1929 the United Free Church rejoined the Church of Scotland and two Church of Scotland congregations flourished in Greenlaw until their union in 1952. The Fairbairn Church building remained empty until its demolition in 1979, except for providing storage space for a local second-hand furniture and antique dealer. The parish church building suffered damage to its foundations as a result of bombs being dropped on Greenlaw during the Second World War. Several houses in front of the church were destroyed or damaged and some billeted servicemen were killed. The shock of the blast disturbed the tower foundations and a crack developed in the tower. After some inadequate repair work in the late 1960s a major renovation project was launched in the 1980s. The first phase, the repair of the external fabric of the tower, was completed in

1986 and the second phase, repointing the church, renewing windows and roof drainage, was completed in 1989. The work qualified for grants from the historic buildings and monuments council of the Scottish Development Department. The roll of Greenlaw Church contained 247 members in 1988 of whom 100 communicated during the year. Members are divided into 14 districts, each with an elder. In addition there are five members of the Congregational Board.

The church has a Sunday School with ten children on its roll. There is a branch of the Church of Scotland Woman's Guild with 28 members, meeting once a month. A bible study and prayer group meets every week, attracting eight people regularly.

POPULATION

Since the time of the Second Statistical Account in 1834, when population peaked at over 1400 (1831, 1442), there has been an irregular decline: 1841, 1355; 1851, 1378; 1861, 1370; 1871, 1381; 1881, 1245; 1891, 1110; 1901, 1015; 1911, 941; 1921, 909; 1931, 889; 1951, 831; 1961, 777; 1971, 793; 1981, 770; 1988, 700. Of the present population of approximately 700, 597 are registered electors, 70 are children under age 12 and 33 are over 12 and under 18. Those of pensionable age amount to 170.

INDUSTRY AND EMPLOYMENT

The Bleachfield cottage is a continuing reminder of an important industry of the past. Linen webs were bleached in the open air near the Waulk Mill dam. Greenlaw Waulk Mill thickened, scoured and dyed cloth.

The Lintmill Bridge is another reminder of the handloom weaving industry, a cottage industry occupying many families in the 18th and early 19th centuries. Lint was grown in the parish. The Lintmill made the fibres ready for weaving. Machinery eventually killed the handloom craft industry. It lasted until the late 1850s in Greenlaw. Grinding mills functioned at Halliburton, Lambden, Slegden, Greenlaw Castle and in Greenlaw. The mill stream, which can still be traced from the Blackadder below Greenlawdean and running along the back of the caravan park, may have served both the Waulk Mill and the grinding mill at Greenlaw. The farmhouse and steadings at Greenlaw Mill are the site of one former mill, kiln and mill house.

Import of foreign grain and decline of the practice of providing farm workers with corn meal and porage oats as part of their wages reduced the need for local grinding mills.

Greenlaw was also famous for cabinet making, coopering and horn spoon-making. The latter two died out in the late 19th century.

The textile industry lives on in Greenlaw. James Renwick & Co., part of the Jaeger Knitwear Group, have a small factory in Greenlaw, employing 60 women, 20 of whom live in Greenlaw. The average weekly wage is £100.

Henry Steel & Sons Ltd. is a major building contractor employing 45 people. Apart from office staff, the bulk of the employees are tradesmen engaged in all trades relating to building construction, maintenance and repair. A. & R. Gold Ltd. is a grain merchanting company. They employ 14, seven of whom live in Greenlaw. The average weekly wage with overtime is £260. Most employees are lorry drivers.

In the old station yard is a vehicle spare parts and scrap business and a Massey Ferguson agricultural machinery agency.

Farming used to be a major provider of employment. But since the advance of mechanisation, employment had declined. Apart from the farming families, only 15 people living in farm cottages were employed in farming. A farm worker's basic wage is £150-£160 per week.

With improvement in the roads, increasing numbers of people work outside the parish. Some work in small factories in Duns, mainly fish processing. Some ladies are involved in nursing and domestic work at hospitals and homes for the elderly. They travel to the Borders General Hospital at Melrose, opened in July 1988, and to the Sue Ryder Home at Marchmont which took its first patients in November 1989. The Sue Ryder Foundation, which cares for patients with various physical disabilities and terminal diseases, took over Marchmont House, which lies in neighbouring Polwarth parish, in 1985. The comprehensive refurbishment will be complete in 1990.

Hamish Morison Ltd., one of the country's largest poultry businesses, has a breeder farm in Greenlaw, breeding hens to produce broilers. This is one of many such farms in Berwickshire. At Greenlaw seven workers are employed, each earning on average £145 per week.

Several representatives for companies are based in Greenlaw because of its convenient location for travel to the South-East of Scotland and North-East England.

There are several small businesses, including two second-hand furniture businesses, one of which specialises in antiques and has developed a good export business. This company now occupies the town hall, using it as a store and sales room.

The petrol station is part of a large company not based in Greenlaw, but it employs several ladies in petrol sales. The adjacent vehicle service and repair garage is run by a local motor engineer, who employs a local assistant.

There is a joinery business, an upholsterer who is also a cabinet maker, two painting and decorating businesses, a café with grocery shop, hairdresser, post office with general store, another grocer with video hire facility, two public houses which provide meals and bed and breakfast accommodation, a butcher, two electrician businesses, a caravan park and two bed and breakfast establishments.

When Greenlaw had a higher population and transport to larger towns was not so readily available, there were more retail businesses in the town. Going back 25 years there were two tailors, two drapers, a bootmaker, two bakers, a butcher, three grocers' shops, one petrol station, two vehicle repair garages with petrol sales, a cycle shop, a wallpaper and paint shop, a sweet shop, a post office and a hairdresser.

A few people live in Greenlaw who run businesses elsewhere, proprietors of a public relations business in Edinburgh, an interior design business in Kelso and shops in Galashiels and Kelso fall within this category. Since improvements in the main road to Edinburgh over Soutra Hill, Greenlaw is now on the edge of Edinburgh commuter zone and a few travel daily to and fro to employment there.

The Regional Council employs ladies as school caretaker and kitchen staff. Several ambulance drivers live in Greenlaw. A few ladies serve as clerks in the District Council Offices (Duns) and the Regional Council Offices (Newtown St Boswells).

There are a few self-employed casual labourers. Quite a number of housewives work part-time as home helps for the elderly, earning £2.50 per hour, while others with young children can earn £50 to £100 per week on piecework at home painting ornaments for a firm in Lauder.

Greenlaw is home to a few men who work off-shore in the North Sea oil industry or work overseas for oil companies.

Farming still plays an important part in the local economy, even though so few are employed on farms and no markets are now held in Greenlaw. There are four small holdings of less than 50 acres on the edge of the village and another one in the south of the parish. Two men live in the village who are employed on larger farms in the parish. One man works as a representative for a manufacturer of agricultural chemicals.

Ministry of Agriculture Parish Census Summaries reveal the change in the pattern of agricultural employment.

Greenlaw Parish

	Hired	*Family*	*Causal*	*Totals*
1951	58	15	28	101
1961	74		10	84
1971	32	17	5	54
1981	25	17	3	45
1988	27	21	2	50

Significant Holdings

1870 55 of which 28 were under 5 acres and 15 were over 100 acres.
1881 56
1891 62 rented: 59 holdings/owned: 3 holdings

1901 48
1911 39 of which five were under five acres and four were over 300 acres rented: 37 holdings/owned: two holdings
1921 35
1931 40 rented: 24 holdings/owned: 16 holdings
1961 33 rented: 3175 acres/owned: 8225 acres
1971 22 rented: 2396 acres/owned: 11415 acres
1981 16 rented: 2012 acres/owned: 11792 acres
1988 20 rented: 2077 acres/owned: 11277 acres

Marchmont Estate was once the largest estate in Berwickshire. Stretching from the Tweed to the Lammermuirs and including land in Lauderdale, the estate owned much of the parish and belonged to the Earl of Marchmont and his successors, the Hume Campbells. Sir John Hume Campbell sold Marchmont House and part of the estate to the grandfather of the late Robin McEwen in 1912. The latter's widow, Lady Brigid McEwen, has now sold the estate. The house is now a Sue Ryder Foundation Home.

The acreage figures show increased private ownership by farmers. (Compare the 1911 figure with the 1931 figure.)

The large country houses in the parish are Old Greenlaw, owned by the Hon. Felicity Douglas Home; Rowchester House, owned by P. H. Maresi, an American businessman; and Lambden House, owned by David Thomson, farmer and deputy Lord Lieutenant of Berwickshire.

Farms Today

Angelrow	240 acres	
Elwartlaw	420 acres	
Crumrig	161 acres	(land rented out)
Cowrig	220 acres	(land rented out)
Lambden	400 acres	
Easter Howlaws	300 acres	
Greenriggs	100 acres	
Gordonbank	150 acres	(land rented out)
Old Greenlaw	310 acres	
Greenlaw Mill	121 acres	
Greenlawdean	870 acres	
Whiteside	300 acres	} Marchmont Estate (on market at time of writing)
Castlemill	320 acres	
Slegden	455 acres	
Woodheads	450 acres	
Halliburton	3000 acres	} (hill farms)
Hurdlaw	400 acres	
Bedshiel	3000 acres	

Some land has been bought by farmers in neighbouring parishes. Rumbletonrig and Queenscairn own land in Greenlaw parish. The former

Wester Howlaws farm has been divided between three owners, two of whom are not based in the parish. Non-farming interests also own land. An example is the refuse disposal company in Duns, which owns 80 acres at Catmoss where the local tip is located.

Analysis of Land Use and Livestock Holding

	Corn Crops (acres)					*Green Crops (acres)*		
	Wheat	*Barley*	*Oats*	*Beans*	*Peas*	*Potatoes*	*Turnips*	*Rape*
1870	42	673	970	13	40	78	967	—
1881	52	640	1006	22	26	65	860	—
1891	10	415	1139	22		45	785	23
1901	—	499	1055			40	762	8
1911	3	461	938			51	701	33
1921	26	425	961	8		46	631	36
1931	53	182	772	2		29	475	43
1951	20	617	908	6	—	103	346	107
1961	137	856	541			57	309	57
1971	355	1795	324			—	260	14
1981	177	2507	190			34	182	28
1988	1170	1442	107		75[1]	35	112	212[2]

(1) for combining
(2) oil seed rape, previously fodder rape.

N.B. Other small crops than recorded here appear in the census. Only significant acreages are recorded in this statistical digest.

	Grass (acres)			*Woodland*	*Livestock (head)*						
	Hay	*Meadow*	*Hill Grazing*		*Agric. Horses*	*Dairy Cattle*	*Beef Cattle*	*Sheep over 1yr.*	*Sheep under 1yr.*	*Pigs*	*Poultry*
1870	194	1713		—	126	155	389	3821	3409	192	
1881	547	1575		188	118	130	305	4615	3239	188	
1891	370	2182	3455	134	126	134	450	5408	4291	132	
1901	265	2928	3005		129	99	372	5557	4917	111	
1911	364	3002	3005		114	116	404	6056	5733	112	
1921	462	2976	5191		112	98	322	5451	5119	121	
1931	542	4164	4971		115	199	528	8283	8486	152	
1951	664	2553	5944		21	169	896	7033	6161	153	4513
1961	761	4719	5746	127	—	170	1307	7300	8709	760	1990
1971	628	2034	8168	126	—	133	954	6843	6704	1347	318
1981	402	1400	8617	110	—	—	877	7053	7158	1368	158
1988	450	1352	7947	155	—	—	709	6721	6913	2322	58

Housing

Greenlaw parish has 353 habitable dwellings. The distribution is as follows:

Greenlaw	*Inhabited*	*Holiday Home*	*Empty*	*Total*
Bank Street	6			6
Blackadder Crescent	19			19
Church Hill	32			32
Church Street	9		3 (for sale)	12
Coldstream Road	2			2
Duns Road	20			20
E. High Street	30		4 (for sale)	34
Edinburgh Road	10			10
Fairbairn Court	20			20
Halliburton Road	3			3
Marchmont Crescent	16		2	18
Marchmont Road	14	2		16
Mill Wynd	10			10
Queens Row	6			6
The Square	6			6
Todholes	7			7
W. High Street	20	2	2	24
Wester Row	36			36
Farmhouses and cottages				
Angelrow	1		2	3
Bedshiel	2		1	3
Castlemill	2			2
Cowrig	1	2		3
Crumrig	2		1	3
Easter Howlaws	2	1	2	5
Eastfield	1		2	3
Elwartlaw	5			5
Flourishwalls	1			1
Gordonbank	1	1		2
Greenlawdean	6			6
Halliburton	2		3	5
Hurdlaw	1			1
Lambden	6			6
Old Greenlaw	5			5
Rowchester	3		1	4
Roweston Cottage (Inkbottle Lodge)		1		1
Slegden	2		1	3
Toll House	1			1
Wester Howlaws	3		1	4
Woodheads			3	3
Whiteside			3	3

Most of the housing dates from the 18th and 19th centuries and early 20th century. Local authority housing was erected in Greenlaw, beginning before the Second World War with houses in Wester Row on the west bank of the Blackadder. This development was completed after the war. In the late 1940s Blackadder Crescent was built. Then in the mid 1950s came Marchmont Crescent. Pensioners' houses (8) were built at Church Hill in the late 1960s and then the whole Church Hill housing scheme was added in the mid 1970s.

Pensioners' houses (7) have also been built in Wester Row and in 1984 Her Majesty Queen Elizabeth opened Fairbairn Court, a complex of 19 flats for the elderly with warden accommodation and surveillance developed by the Bield Housing Association.

ROADS AND RAILWAYS

Greenlaw stands at an important interchange in the Eastern Borders road network. The main road is the A697 Edinburgh to Newcastle route. The A697 begins at Carfraemill where it branches off the A68 to bring traffic to or through Greenlaw to Coldstream, Wooler and Morpeth where it joins the A1. The A6105 Berwick to Earlston Road crosses the A697 at Greenlaw, both routes sharing the West High Street. Just south of Greenlaw the B6364 turns south off the A6105 towards Kelso. The B6456 crosses the northern part of the parish, linking Duns to the main Edinburgh road. The Regional Council maintain roads leading to all the farms in the parish. But no road is preserved for traffic from the north of the parish into the village, except from Halliburton. It is clear that there were well-used drove roads leading into Greenlaw from the directions of Bedshiel, Wedderlie in Westruther parish and Kettleshiel in Longformacus parish. These would be important when Greenlaw was the County Town but have long since disappeared through disuse. Halliburton Road was formerly the main road to Edinburgh. It is shown as such in the 1771 map already alluded to. The present road and the old road run parallel for about 2 km.

Two bridges are maintained over the Blackadder in Greenlaw capable of carrying the maximum permitted loads of heavy lorries. The A697 is a route preferred by many long distance hauliers as an alternative route south or north to the A1. Traffic density, however, has not reached the level that would permit the installation of a pedestrian crossing with traffic lights in Greenlaw High Street, nor is it likely in the foreseeable future that a by-pass will be constructed.

Evidence of the former railway still exists. The embankment of the old line enters the parish from the west, running parallel with the Rumbleton Burn. The former platform is preserved at the Station House, now a normal dwelling house. The A6105 no longer passes over the former line on a bridge; but the bridge is still there. The raised embankment runs parallel with the Blackadder to where it used to cross the A697 on a level crossing before travelling east to cross the Blackadder by bridge en route to Marchmont Station. Disastrous floods in August 1948 destroyed this bridge. It was never rebuilt and passenger services were suspended.

The first sod in the construction of a railway linking Duns with the main line of the Old North British system at St Boswells was cut at Greenlaw on 14th October 1862. The Berwickshire Railway was officially opened as far as Earlston on 16th November 1863. The necessity to build the Leaderfoot Viaduct delayed completion until October 1865. There was a certain lack of vision in building the Berwickshire Railway because the North British Tweedmouth-Kelso-St Boswells line had already provided a rail route from the east coast since 1852, thereby obviating the need for another via Duns. The Berwickshire Railway remained independent until 1876 when it merged with the North British. The railway continued as a goods line after 1948, Greenlaw being the terminus, until 1965.

SERVICES

Fuel. There are no coal merchants in Greenlaw. Coal is delivered from Duns. There is no piped gas supply. Some householders use bottled gas. Electricity is also used for heating and cooking.

Water Supply. The first public water supply was piped from the Well Tree springs in 1829. In 1878 water was supplied from a small reservoir above Greenlawdean farm. Since 1952 Greenlaw has been connected to the Watch Water reservoir above Longformacus.

Street lighting was first installed during the winter of 1880-81.

Police were stationed in Greenlaw until 1979. The former police house is now a private dwelling in the East High Street. Greenlaw is now policed from the Duns Police Station of the Lothian and Borders Police.

Ambulance. The Greenlaw and District Ambulance was maintained by public subscription before the Second World War and until 1950. It was then run by the St Andrew's Scottish Ambulance Service until 1963 when the national organisation, The Scottish Ambulance Service, took over the responsibility. An ambulance is kept in Greenlaw.

Bus Service. Greenlaw is served by the Eastern Scottish Bus Company with services passing through the village connecting it with Duns and Berwick to the east, Earlston and Galashiels in the west and Kelso to the south. A small Border Courier bus service connects with the Borders General Hospital on weekdays. There is a school bus to the Berwickshire High School and a bus taking students to the Colleges of Further Education further afield.

Schools. Greenlaw Primary School, housed in new premises since 1969, has a roll of 72 children, about 20 of whom are brought in by bus

Plate 29. Mellerstain House.

from beyond the parish limits. The school's catchment area includes the former Hume parish area to the south; it extends as far as Rumbletonlaw in Gordon parish to the west and as far as Purves Hall in Eccles Parish to the east. Children in the north of the parish where no road connects farms directly to Greenlaw, go either to Westruther or Duns. There are four teachers, none of whom live in the parish. They travel in from Duns, Coldstream and Lempitlaw.

Decline in rural population is evident from the comparison to 1861 when the population was 1371, divided into 318 families with 100 children attending the Parochial School and 120 at the Free Church School. In those days each of the three churches had sabbath schools; the parish church had 70; the Free Church, 50; and the United Presbyterian Church 45. Thus 165 of the 220 children attending schools also attended sabbath schools. This compares to 10 out of 72 in the late 1980s.

Doctor. Greenlaw is now a 'single-handed' practice. In the 1970s two doctors served the village and surrounding district, attracting patients also from Hume, Gordon and Westruther. A medical centre was completed in 1988. The former School House was transformed for this purpose.

Bank. There is a branch of the Royal Bank of Scotland, open on weekdays.

Library. The Borders Region Library sends a mobile library van to Greenlaw every fortnight.

Inns. In 1834 there was one principal inn, the Castle Inn, one inferior inn and seven ale houses. Today the Castle Inn Hotel is still the principal inn. Matching the architectural style of the Town Hall opposite, it is a much older establishment. The old stabling still exists. The hotel has eight guest rooms, provides small conference facilities, a gymnasium, bars and dining rooms. Seven ladies are employed by the hotel. The Greenlaw Caravan Park offers sites for permanent and touring caravans and the tourist and holidaymaker can find bed and breakfast accommodation at two private houses as well as at the inns, the Cross Keys and the Blackadder Hotel, the latter formerly a temperance hotel. Other licensed premises in Greenlaw are the Social Club at the masonic Hall and the Bowling Club.

Town hall. After Duns became county town, the Town Hall was used for social functions. The Berwickshire Hunt Ball was held there until after the Second World War. During the War, Polish soldiers were stationed there.

In 1973 money was raised to turn the interior of the Hall into a swimming pool. It was opened by H.R.H. Princess Margaret. But when the Regional Council built a larger swimming pool at the Berwickshire High School, Duns, the Greenlaw pool declined in popularity and the hall lay derelict until it was let to an antique dealer, A. Brotherston, as a furniture store and sale room.

War Memorial Club. After the First World War, the premises of what had been the 'Good Templars' Club' were handed over to trustees to form a working men's club, providing darts, snooker and other pastimes. Called the War Memorial Club, it still continues but with a greater emphasis on providing recreation for youth.

Community Council. In order to monitor matters relating to the overall well-being of the community, the Council meets monthly, receiving reports from the District and Regional Councillors and occasionally inviting speakers.

CLUBS

Masonic Lodge. Lodge Blackadder 1350 of the Grand Lodge of Scotland was founded in 1926 as a daughter lodge of the Duns Masonic Lodge.

Youth Organisations. Brownies; Girl Guides (a few girls travel to the Guide Company in Gordon); Girl's Club; Friday Club, Youth Group (associated with the church).

Ladies' Organisations. Women's Rural Institute, Wives and Mothers Group, Church of Scotland Woman's Guild.

Sports Clubs. Fishing, Bowling, Football. Professional games, 'The Greenlaw Games,' were held until 1956. The Greenlaw Festival filled the gap which the cessation of the games created.

Greenlaw Festival. In 1960 a one-day celebration involving the crowning of the Greenlaw Maid, followed by sports and fancy dress competition was begun by the Girls' Club. Festival Week began in 1971 at the time when the now defunct Community Association was formed. The Festival continues to be held during the last week of June every year. It is run by the Greenlaw Festival Committee.

Charitable Bequests. The Marchmont Bounty of £50 per year was left by the late Sir W. H. Campbell in 1821 for the distribution of meal and coal to the poor of the parishes of Greenlaw and Hume from November to February. Responsibility for assessing worthy recipients and organising distribution is entrusted to the parish minister. The capital is now invested with the Church of Scotland General Trustees and the annual interest accumulates until there are sufficient funds to finance an equitable and worthwhile distribution.

1990

THE PARISH OF HUME

by Janet D. Blair

NAME AND ORIGIN

Hûm means 'at the heights' and indeed there is no other place in Berwickshire where you can look for miles in every direction until the distant hills break the view. In a document of 1159 it appears as Hûm (the dative plural of the OE Hoh). Gradually the û became like an O and so Hom evolved which changed to Home, but it was also written Hoom, Hoome, Holme, Houm, Houme, Hume and even Yem on an old tombstone. While Home remained the property of the Earls of Home, it retained the ancient spelling, but on 19th February 1766 the 3rd Earl of Marchmont bought it and changed its spelling to Hume.

DESCRIPTION OF SOIL AND SURFACE

As a result of volcanic action, there are five hills runnings from south-east to north-west. These are known as the Castle Hill, The Heughan (where the Scots hewed down the English and vice versa!) and the three Craigs. The last four hills are made of augitic trap. To the extreme west of the village at the Lurgie Craigs, the trap can be seen as hexagonal rods. The Castle Hill is basalt, with a 'crag and tail' formation due to the Ice Age. Between the hills are whinstone and basalt. There is a whinstone quarry which is not being worked at the moment. The old houses, the schoolhouse and the school were built of whinstone, with some red sandstone from the Catmoss Quarry close to the western boundary of this parish.

POSITION OF VILLAGE

Hume is located in Berwickshire at Lat. N55 40'5" and Long. W2 27'33"; or on an Ordnance Survey Map it is 36/704414 on the National Grid. The village lies between the Heughan and the Castle Hill. All buildings are on the north side of the road facing south. They used to stretch further west to Hume Orchard when there was a population of over 1000!

AGRICULTURE AND PRODUCE

Since the quarry closed, agriculture is the only source of employment in the parish. Otherwise people travel out to work in the neighbouring village of Greenlaw, or in Kelso or Duns. There are seven farms and several smallholdings. These were carved out of three large farms after the First World War to give employment to returning ex-servicemen, but with the improvement in farm machinery and the rise of farm contractors, the smallholdings are easier to work and the tendency of the Board of Agriculture is to make larger units as the sitting tenants move out, and sell off the smallholders' houses. All the farms grow barley and a little oats, hay and grass for silage. Two farms have large dairy herds, one Friesian and the other Ayrshires. The high land is not arable and supports sheep.

THE SCHOOL

No one knows when the first school was built, but there was a school 200 years ago, for John Spratswill's tombstone in the kirkyard states that he was the late schoolmaster and died in 1789. The beautiful Georgian schoolhouse was probably built by the Earl of Marchmont after he bought the village in 1766 and had the new houses built. John Spratswill may well have been the first occupant. The classroom was on the ground floor and the schoolmaster lived in the flat above which was approached by an outside stair. This building was sold in 1971 and demolished by the new owner. The new school building which stands today was attached to the Georgian house, which was converted into a private house for the schoolmaster. It was built just before the Education Act of 1870. The school has two rooms and had 78 pupils in 1873 and two teachers. By 1941 the roll had dropped to 24 pupils, and so it became a one-teacher school with a female teacher. The school was closed from 1947-48, when there was difficulty in getting a teacher because the schoolhouse had been sold to a teacher who had been there for 28 years. As a result of parental pressure a new teacher was found and the school re-opened. Six new council houses had been built in the village and one was allocated to the teacher. After 20 years, when the school hit the headlines by winning national competitions for projects, calligraphy and art, the roll dropped to 13, the teacher transferred to Leitholm and the school closed for good. It was sold along with the old schoolhouse in 1971 and has since been converted into a dwelling house.

THE CHURCH

The church, built in 1147 at the instigation of a monk from Kelso Abbey called Orm, was dedicated to St Nicholas. It was destroyed by

Cromwell's Ironsides in 1653. Now only the foundations can be seen in the churchyard, and the Verter Well (for baptising converts) in a nearby field at Homebyres. A christening bowl found there is in the Scottish National Museum, as is the Celtic-type church bell and an iconographic ring found in the castle. No attempt was made to rebuild a church, so the parish joined with Stichill, and when the new school was built permission was obtained to use it for a monthly service.

THE CASTLE

The castle stands on its base 742 feet above sea-level. Some people denounce it as a 'folly' because it was partly rebuilt on the old foundation in 1774 by the only son of the last Earl of Marchmont, who sat in the House of Lords as Lord Berwick as well as being Lord Polwarth. He died before his father in 1781. In 1931 the Berwickshire Naturalists' Club placed an indicator in the castle to mark the centenary of the founding of the club. It is a circular pillar of Creetown marble with a bronze plate on the top which indicates all the landmarks in England as well as Scotland and their distance from the castle.

The castle has played its part in Border history, being fought over and besieged several times. The former Statistical Accounts relate the story of Cromwell's Army and the garrison of Home under Sir Thomas Cockburn, who was related to the Homes. There were other visitors too.

James II and his Queen visited it at the time of the Siege of Roxburgh in 1460. It is said that the queen watched the engagement from a hill south of Home and that when the news of the death of her husband reached her, it brought on her labour pains and she was conveyed in a litter to Home Castle where her baby was born. The hill became known as Queenscairn.

James IV visited Home Castle in 1496 as Alexander, third Lord Home, was one of his friends. His queen, Margaret Tudor (sister of Henry VIII) was at Home when the Battle of Flodden took place in 1513, and again tradition has it that the queen watched on Queenscairn Hill for signals from the battlefield. Indeed a clear signal on a clear day could be seen as nothing impedes the view. Legend also says that the king's body was conveyed back to Home Castle by the Earl of Home and hidden in the well in the castle, and that if the well were drained his famous iron belt could be recovered. But the well was drained and no belt or bones were found. (The English had taken his body to the Abbey of Sheen in Surrey.)

Most interesting is Mary, Queen of Scots' visit in 1566. She was on her way back from Jedburgh and after her stop in Kelso on 10th November she decided to see Berwick. Sir John Foster, Warden of the English Border, was speaking to her when his horse reared up and attacked the queen's horse and his front hoofs hurt the queen's thigh so badly that she had to stay two days at Home Castle before she could return to Edinburgh.

On 7th January 1952 H.R.H. Princess Margaret attended a Meet in the Castle Field. She was a guest at Marchmont at the time.

Two Hume Stories

In 1516 the Earl of Home and his brother, William, were beheaded in Edinburgh and their heads were put on the Tolbooth Prison for four years for all to see. A French knight, Antoine D'Arcy, Seigneur de La Bastie, was made Warden of the Eastern Marches and given Home Castle. He was also made Governor of the Lothians and given Dunbar Castle, another Home property. De La Bastie captured Lady Home, imprisoned her in Dunbar Castle and fed her on bread and water. Lord Home's cousin, Sir David Home of Wedderburn, and his brothers wanted revenge. In the end they pursued and killed de La Bastie on his way to Dunbar, cut off his head and placed it on Home Castle where it stayed for two years till it fell off. This story is told in an old ballad.

The second story concerns the beacon at Hume which was one of a chain of beacons stretching from the ford at Coldstream to Midlothian and so to Edinburgh. In the time of Napoleon the sergeant on duty at Hume saw a fire at Coldstream and, mistaking it for a beacon, lit the Hume beacon. The men of the Hume Volunteers marched to Kelso and were the first volunteers to arrive, but it was all a false alarm and Napoleon never came after all!

In writing the above account I have left out material already used in the first two Statistical Accounts which concern Hume, and added material which I discovered in my own researches. Since the school closed, the children attend Greenlaw Primary School and the Berwickshire High School, being conveyed there by bus. The Post Office has been closed, and having to go into Kelso for their pensions is a great inconvenience to the older villagers. But it is not all doom and gloom — the village street lighting was installed in 1982!

1989

THE PARISH OF HUTTON

by The Rev. David S. Leslie

There have been no changes in the parish boundaries since the last Statistical Account of 1834 was compiled. The parish comprises the two small parishes of Fishwick and Hutton, joined together in 1614 to form the present civil parish of Hutton, Berwickshire.

The area of the parish is 5645.5 acres. The parish is roughly triangular in shape with the apex touching the roadway from the Tweed to the Whiteadder known to residents as the 'Boond' Road. The river Whiteadder forms the north-eastern boundary of the parish, the Tweed, the south-eastern boundary, while the parishes of Edrom, Whitsome and Ladykirk form the western boundary. The parish stands on the borderline between England and Scotland. The plain of the Merse extends from the Lammermoors to Whiteadder point, and Hutton Parish forms the most easterly section of it. The parish does not rise to any great height above sea level. The highest point in the parish is Gordon Law, a slight eminence on Sunwick farm. The surface of the parish is not uniformly flat; it is slightly undulating with no great variation of heights and hollows. The tidal-water from the sea at Berwick is traceable as far up the Tweed as Norham Castle, an indication that the surface of the parish is not much above sea level.

Most of the land is arable and the soil is of good grain-producing quality. In the Paxton area, and near the river banks, the soil is generally a rich loam, while in the centre of the parish, stretching well into the Merse, there is a belt two to three miles wide of stiff clay, which in some seasons presents the farmers with a difficulty in cultivating, if the season should be a wet one, but when seasons are favourable, produces magnificent crops of cereal and roots. The steep banks of the Tweed and Whiteadder which in places are inaccessible for cultivating are either planted with trees or put under grass for grazing.

During the war years from 1914-18 and 1939-45 much of the hardwood in the woods and plantations round Paxton House, Spital House and Tweedhill House was cut down and little has been done as yet to refurnish the denuded woodlands with growing timber. The general outline of the parish is one of great beauty. The banks of the Tweed and Whiteadder are specially attractive in the spring, summer and autumn seasons. The colouring of the rocks, water and woodlands all blend to form a beautiful landscape.

ROADWAYS

The parish is well furnished with roadways. Within recent years the County Council has spent a great deal of money on the upkeep of roads and great improvements have been made in resurfacing the roads with bitumenised stone metal which has enabled the roads to stand up well to the wear and tear of modern heavy motor traffic.

The principal roadways from west to east of the parish converging at Paxton Tollhouse are —

(1) Broomdykes — Harrogate — Paxton Loaning.
(2) Pistol Plantation — Sunwick — Spital Mains.
(3) Swinton — Fishwick — Paxton South Mains.

The main roads from north to south of the parish, converging on the Tweed Suspension Bridge Road are —

(1) Bluestone Ford — Sunwick Moor Road.
(2) Hutton — Hutton Mains — Broadmeadows Farm.
(3) Hutton Mill Bridge — Paxton North Mains — Paxton House Lodges.
(4) The 'Boond' Road running from Whiteadder Ford to Tweed Ford at Finchey and forming part of the borderline between England and Scotland is only a service road and is not kept up by Berwickshire County Council.

The 'Boond' Road touches upon an area of eight square miles, which, according to a natural division of territory, should be in Scotland with Berwick-upon-Tweed assuming its position as the principal town of the county which bears its name. As a result of centuries of warfare, the town of Berwick and the territory known as Berwick Bounds, after changing sides 13 times, finally passed from Scottish ownership in 1482 to become part of Northumberland and thus under English law. Lately, Sir Frank Mears suggested that for business reasons the town and bounds of Berwick should be included in Berwickshire.

During the August flood of 1948 two footbridges connecting Hutton and Chirnside Parishes at Bluestone Ford and Edrington Mill were swept away. Another, at Edrington Mill, connecting Hutton and Mordington Parishes was also destroyed. The footbridges at Bluestone Ford and Edrington have now been replaced. During the flood, when the waters of the Whiteadder and Tweed rose so rapidly and to an abnormal height, great damage was done to arable land bordering on the rivers and crops were washed away. In some places the course of the river Whiteadder was greatly altered. These alterations have been repaired and the river has now resumed its usual course. As a result of the flooding, Hutton Castle Mill, Hutton Mill and Clarabad Mill suffered considerable damage. The proprietors of Hutton Castle Mill and Hutton Mill have considered that it is not economically profitable to put the mills into working condition and both are now derelict. The proprietor of Clarabad Mill no longer uses water power to drive the machinery and has installed diesel oil engines for this purpose.

Two bridges for light traffic over the Tweed and Whiteadder have greatly facilitated road communication between Northumberland and Berwickshire. The Union Suspension Bridge over the Tweed at Tweedhill, built in 1820, was the first Suspension Bridge to be erected in this country. Only vehicles of two-ton weight or less are allowed to pass over the bridge.

Hutton Mill Bridge was erected in 1837 and is of great service for vehicles travelling from Hutton towards Foulden and Eyemouth. In the 18th century, before the present macadamised roads were constructed, there was an old loaning, bordering between Winfield and Sunwick farms, which is still called the Millers Loan. It is said by old residents that at one time the corn from Ladykirk Parish was thirled to Hutton Mill and the road for transit was made by way of Millers Loan, Sunwick Loaning, Hutton Bell, Paxton's Croft. The business of the small country mills is now passing to larger milling establishments in large towns which are better equipped with modern milling machinery and labour saving devices for drying grain and handling meal products. In the three mills of the parish, in 1900, 12 workers were employed. In 1952, three men are so employed.

TRANSPORT

Public motor transport for the district is suitable, but an additional early morning bus to convey workers from Whitsome, Hutton and Paxton to Berwick-upon-Tweed could with profit be introduced. School buses convey pupils over 12 years of age to Chirnside Junior Secondary School and to Duns High School. Extra buses for public service are usually supplied at holiday periods and for special sporting events.

FARMING

Farming is the principal industry in the parish. There are 31 farm holdings varying in acreage from 600 to 30 acres in extent. The area under tillage is 2674 acres, 2104 acres under grass, 919 acres barley, 452 oats, 97 beans, 240 wheat, and a considerable acreage is given to cultivation of root crops, potatoes, turnips, mangold, sugar beet. The livestock comprises 32 horses, 36 dairy cattle, 794 beef cattle, 4516 sheep (including lambs), 374 pigs, 4323 poultry.

The style of agriculture has altered considerably since the last Statistical Account was published. It has emerged from a system the most crude and barbarous to a system the most intelligent and enterprising to be found anywhere. During the second half of the 19th century no remarkable change in farming progress falls to be recorded. There are no special changes in the variety of crops cultivated, yet there have been advances and important ones. The application of thorough drainage has enormously augmented the acreage subjected to good husbandry. Lands regarded formerly as unproductive have been raised to the highest grade among grain and meat-producing soils. The introduction of artificial manures has greatly extended the available arable acreage, increased the yield and also made the cultivation of turnips possible on what was regarded as unsuitable soil and has, perhaps, nearly doubled the number of sheep sent to the butcher market. The progress in agriculture during the past 50 years may well be attributed to the help farmers have received from the researches of careful and intelligent scientists into the methods and doings of nature. Agriculture has grown during these years from an art into a science. Much information has been found of the greatest value to profitable farming, in publications describing the Chemistry of Agriculture and Plant Physiology, and through the researches and field experiments at various agricultural experimental stations throughout the country. Through the help of these researches in this country and on the continent farming is now being carried on according to truly rational and scientific principles. A general respect and deference is now paid by farmers to agricultural science and the desire is shown to make full use of its assistance. The discovery and use of selective weed killers is helpful to increased production. As regards the different crops of the farm, farmers have learned their different powers of assimilating these under the differing circumstances of soil and climate. As to farmyard manure, its intelligent preparation, conservation and application is now pretty thoroughly understood. Great advance has been made in draining, stock feeding and grass cultivation. A century ago great emphasis was placed upon livestock for the maintenance of soil fertility. One might almost say that it was only through livestock that the cropping capacity of the soil could be maintained. During the past century livestock on the farm has changed greatly in bulk, breed and quality. Improved breeds of cattle have spread throughout the country and better sheep and horses have been bred. Within recent years intense interest has been paid to the development of farm animals and high prices have been paid for outstanding prize standard specimens.

Another contrast relates to the use of mechanical power on the farm. A century ago the possibilities of steam power were eagerly considered. After centuries during which the strength of men and animals and the power of wind and water had been the means of performing work, farmers looked ahead to the time when the power of steam could be utilised for performing exacting duties of farm routine. On several of the larger farms in the parish steam engines were installed to do the work of threshing grain. There was great interest taken in the profitable steam engine which could be taken from farm to farm along with a mill for threshing corn. The engines were regarded as too heavy for solving the problem of applying steam power to the cultivation of the soil and for that reason were discarded. It was weight which defeated the inventor of that age and brought developments in power cultivation almost to a standstill until the internal combustion engine with its high power and light weight made possible the present day mobile farm tractor.

A century ago threshing was just becoming mechanised but most threshers were simply machines which did little more than knock out the grain. Screening, winnowing and straw-delivering devices had still to be applied. The flail on smaller holdings was still often used, and on the harvest field the scythe and hook were the main utensils for cutting the grain. In 1851 the possibility of mechanising the cutting of corn was shown in the county. Demonstrations were attended by interested farmers and caused the same sort of sensation as did similar demonstrations of combine harvesters during the war years. The new types of mechanised machinery on the farm, such as combine harvesters, ploughs, cultivators, beet harvesters, manure distributors, and spraying machines, have greatly added to the interest in farming as well as conducing to increased production.

Though the farm worker could not realise it, he too has benefited, as much as anyone, from this rapid mechanisation. The employer looks upon the machine as a means of reducing costs, a time saver and a means to increase profits. The introduction of new machinery has an ameliorating effect upon the lot of the farm worker by reducing drudgery and hours of work and raising the standard of living. Hard work, of course, must still be done on the farm, but, as far as possible, the machine is made to do it. The one great drawback for the farmer at the present time is the growing shortage of workers on the farm. The number of foreign employees on the farms is increasing. Principally, they are refugees from Poland or the Ukraine. At present (1952) there are seven families. It is to be regretted that boys of 15 years of age, brought up on the farm, on leaving school are seeking to become apprenticed in industrial jobs in preference to working on the farm. All over the country few youths are being trained as shepherds and in a few years' time its will be very difficult to procure this type of farm servant.

The status of farm workers has greatly advanced during the past 50 years. Improved farm cottages with modern amenities are gradually taking the place of cottages that half a century ago were considered adequate for the workers but are now considered obsolete. The average weekly wage for a farm servant is £6. Stewards, shepherds and cattlemen are paid on a higher scale. Overtime pay is given by farmers for seasonal work. Farm servants have now the Saturday half holiday and a fortnight's holiday with pay.

On several farms no cows are kept and milk is supplied to farm cottages and to the villagers in Paxton and Hutton from Tweedmouth Central Dairy.

The system of tenancy in connection with farm land was fairly general at the beginning of the present century. The pressure of increased taxation, during and subsequent to the first world war, led to several estates being broken up and separate farms being exposed for sale. There has been an increase in the number of owners of land and houses and especially of occupying owners of land. The break-up of large estates is accompanied by both advantages and disadvantages to the rural population and perhaps we are too near to the transition period to calculate the true result. Many long-time residents regret the changes that are so evident. The decline of rural trades and industries has been a feature of the last 50 years. The country blacksmith and joiner so valuable to the agricultural industry have either closed their shops or are finding it difficult to maintain themselves in business.

POPULATION

As in all rural parishes throughout the county there has been a steady decline in the number of people resident in the parish. The figures of the population of the parish since 1801 are as follows: 1801, 955; 1841, 1133; 1851, 1102; 1901, 750; 1911, 682; 1921, 655; 1931, 614; 1951, 556.

There are more women than men in the parish — 261 men, 295 women. The number of occupied houses is 161. Family houses consist of three to five rooms. There are a few two-room cottages. Houses in the villages are mostly owner-occupied. A few houses are rented, the average rental being £8 to £10. The health of the community is good and within the last ten years there have been no epidemics affecting children or adults. Under the County Welfare scheme, clinics are held monthly at Paxton and Hutton for mothers and young children. Doctors, dentists and eye specialists visit the schools periodically and attend to the physical health of the scholars. The average attendance of scholars at Hutton School numbers 36, at Paxton 34. Scholars over 12 years of age attend Chirnside Junior Secondary School or Duns High School. The teaching staff at Hutton and Paxton consists of two male teachers and two female teachers.

HUTTON VILLAGE

In olden days, Hutton, like many another village bordering the Tweed, would suffer a good deal from the constant raids and forays that were being continually staged and carried out, first on one side of the Tweed and then on the other. The uncertainty of the situation must have contributed considerably to the feeling of insecurity amongst the people and must have been one of the reasons for the undeveloped nature of the Merse plain during the feudal period.

When quieter days came and the people of the Borders were less disposed to quarrel with one another, the agricultural industry developed and became the settled interest of all classes. The air of prosperity began to spread gradually over southern Scotland and especially over

Berwickshire, and when this was seen by outsiders, and also the 'buirdly' build of the men of the Merse, it was then that the saying originated 'In the How-hole (Hutton) o' the Merse the men are a' bannock fed,' a confession of the fact that in the simple products of the soil are the necessary vitamins essential for the building-up of men of muscle.

HUTTON CHURCH

There is no mention made of a church at Hutton until the year 1243, although in all probability it existed prior to this; possibly in the time of King Edgar, as 'Huton' was one of the manors bestowed by that king to the monks of St Cuthbert, Durham. In that year the church was dedicated by David de Bernham, Bishop of St Andrews.

The contrast between the present-day buildings of church and manse and the buildings of long ago is very striking and one has no hesitation in saying the modern buildings are much more comfortable and suitable for the purposes for which they were intended.

The foundation stone of the present church was laid by Mr James Macbraire of Broadmeadows in 1834. The plummet and mallet used at the ceremony are preserved in the vestry of the church. The church was renovated in a handsome manner in 1937 through the generosity of a member of the congregation. The chancel and pulpit were gifted by the Milne Home family in memory of Colonel David Milne Home of Paxton, Wedderburn and Billie who died in 1918. An interesting collection of lead Communion tokens in use at one time in the church, dating from 1700, can be seen in the vestry. The Church Communion Plate is very chaste and beautiful. It consists of two large cups with the inscription 'In the Ministry of Adam Landels 1809', two large cups of the same design as the first two with the inscription 'In the Ministry of Robert Kirke 1870', two flagons of beautiful design and three pewter patens. There is one pewter baptismal basin. In 1908 an organ was introduced to assist in the praise part of the church service. Hutton Kirk Session consists of the minister and five elders. The roll of church members numbers 191. The church is heated during the winter months by a system of hot water pipes introduced in 1911. The bell in Hutton Church is a Flanders bell and bears the inscription 'Soli: Deo: Gloria: Johannes: Burgehuys: me: fecit 1666'. The inscription is printed in one circle on the upper part of the bell in beautifully clear and well preserved characters. The top part, above the inscription, is decorated with festoon work, the lower part, plain. Two very beautiful memorial windows have been put into the church by Mr Frank Gott, Mayor of Leeds, in memory of his grand-aunt, Mrs Macbraire of Broadmeadows.

Through the kindness of Lady Burrell, Hutton Castle, a beautiful hall was presented to the church in 1931 on the site of the old Butt's Cottage, granted by Mr Arthur Bell, Hutton Mains. The hall has been a great asset to the social life of the community and during the autumn and winter months ample facilities are provided for recreation and entertainments of a varied nature. The interior of the hall is bright and fresh looking. The pictures on the walls are quite a feature. They are framed photographic copies on a large scale of masterpieces and give the hall a well-furnished and dignified appearance.

There was a hospital at Hutton in early times. It was dedicated to the Apostle John. No traces of the building are now to be seen. It is believed to have stood near the present mansion of Spital House. In some records it is spoken of as Hutton Spital.

Hutton Manse is a commodious and beautifully built house erected in 1870. Electric lighting and regional water supply have been lately introduced.

FISHWICK CHURCH

Fishwick had, prior to the year 1614, a separate parochial existence. The church at Fishwick dates from an early period. It is now a ruin. It was used by the proprietor of Broadmeadows Estate as a family burial vault.

PAXTON VILLAGE

Paxton is a village in Hutton Parish. There are 51 inhabited houses in Paxton with eight new council houses in the process of erection. As at Hutton, none of the houses has water laid on. It has all to be pumped from wells, of which there are quite a number in the village. Paxton is beautifully situated, lying in a shallow hollow between the Whiteadder and Tweed. A new drainage system is being installed for the village and pipes to convey the regional water supply for the houses are being laid down. Electricity is already put into most of the houses and street lighting by electricity is now functioning. In a short time all modern amenities will be supplied to all the houses.

There is a church, a school, a post office, a telephone kiosk, an automatic telephone exchange and a village hall. This was erected two years ago. It is a very nice one and is suitable for the social and recreational needs of the community. It is well patronised for meetings of a varied nature.

There is one joiner — the only craftsman in the village. A few men are engaged in salmon fishing during the fishing season. Several men are engaged by contractors in the district and some on farms in the parish.

A beautiful church was built in Paxton village in 1907 under the auspices of the Mordington and Paxton U.F. congregation. The church was dedicated by the Rev. Alexander Whyte D.D., Free St George's, Edinburgh. The Rev. Patrick Geddes Hendry, Mordington U.F. Church, was instrumental in getting the church built and became its first minister. He died in 1929. Paxton and Hutton congregations became 'linked' in January 1950 and the Rev. David S. Leslie became minister of the two congregations.

An enthusiastic branch of the Women's Rural Institute was formed at Paxton nearly 40 years ago. The membership of the branch numbers 50.

Paxton, like Hutton, was a much larger village at one time than it is now. In the past it was, like all country places, practically self-contained and self-subsistent and the inhabitants depended very little on the larger communities for their livelihood.

The barony of Paxton was held by one of that name, who like many proprietors in the past held land both in England and Scotland. When quieter times came to the Borders, the Paxtons of that ilk, who at one time had considerable landed possessions, were left with only a few acres at Auchencrow. Sir Joseph Paxton who designed the Crystal Palace belonged to this family. Paxton village at one time had its own town lands and common on which the villagers had the right of grazing their cows. The town lands were let out in portions or crofts to the villagers for the cultivation of root and grain crops. From time immemorial a number of the villagers found employment at the salmon fishing on the Tweed and in days when the fish could be purchased locally Paxton was famous for its salmon 'sae fine'.

A local popular rhyme descriptive of the habits and customs of a day long past is as follows:

'Hutton for auld wives
Broadmeadows for swine
Paxton for drucken wives
And salmon sae fine.

Crossrig for lint and 'oo
Spital for kail
Sunwick for cakes and cheese
And lasses for sale.'

THE CARE OF THE POOR

Before 1845 the poor in the parish were in the care of the church. The State entirely relieved the church of the burden of poor relief in 1845. In the 1840s — 'the hungry forties' — there came a series of rainy summers resulting in the failure of the potato and grain crops. In 1843 came the Disruption, and the old Church, bereft of about half its ministers and members, could no longer bear the burden of relieving the poor. The Poor Law Act of 1845 provided for an elected body in each parish, called the Parochial Board, which was superseded by the Parish Council in 1894. An inspector of poor and a collector of rates were appointed in each parish. A central authority, called the Board of

Supervision, was set up. This title was altered in 1894 to the Local Government Board, later to be called, in 1919, the Scottish Board of Health. With present-day legislation, the incidence of poverty in the parishes throughout Scotland has been, to a great extent, eliminated.

The affairs of the parish, at one time considered and administered by the parish council, are now under the supervision of Berwickshire East District Council which is subordinate to the County Council of Berwickshire. The parish is represented by one member on the East District Council and by one member on the county council. There are two justices of the peace in the parish. There are two local representatives on the Chirnside Area Sub-Committee on Education, one representative to the County Education Committee. The Registrar's Office is at Hutton Schoolhouse.

WAR MEMORIALS

Two Celtic Crosses, one in Hutton village and one in Paxton village, were erected in memory of the soldiers who died in World War I. The names of those who died in World War II have been added.

COLLOQUIALISMS

There are several colloquialisms which are peculiar to the Berwickshire tongue. Some of the expressions are quaint and still in use in the daily conversation of those born on the Scottish side of the Tweed. These expressions are seldom seen in print and it is here that a grievance can be expressed at our modern method of school education. When a child goes to school he has to conform to a certain style of teaching. The method of acquiring knowledge has to be according to what is put before him on the printed page. He has to spell out the words and pronounce them in English. The words sound so different to what he is accustomed to hear in the home. When the pupil passes from the infant room to the upper classes and to the secondary school, he is, when he has reached school-leaving age, supposed to be able to speak, read and write good English, while in his schooldays he has never once been asked to converse in the vernacular or everyday language of the home or community in which he has been brought up.

In the parish vernacular I is ah, he is e, she is shi, we is wi or hiz yins, you is ee, they is thi or thae, my is mah, his is hez, ours is oors, your is yir, them is thaim. Some of the prefixes in use do not conform to the English standard — *a* for *be*, ablow, ahint, atween; *a* for *on*, ahaud (on fire); *mis* meaning unfavourably, misca, misdoot. Words in common use are feyre, Apreil hyred, tyred. *Buddy* is used as a suffix, abuddy, naebuddy, onybuddy; *ie* is often used as a diminutive or expressing affection: bairnie, lammie. The accentuation of many Berwickshire words varies from the English style: Advertēēse, Aprēil, Arithmētic, Commit-

tēē, diffīculty, interēsting, pōlice, mischēēvous. Some expressions in common use are: 'She has her ain adaes', 'Yin's aye wice ahinthand,' 'G-way' (surprise expression), 'A'm fair baizled,' 'A bangchap,' 'A'll come if A can wun', 'Gey nairra begaun' (mean), 'Ourecuisin' (cloudy), 'Nocket' (light refreshment), 'Oncome' (shower), 'Nickseat' (corner seat next fire), 'Pirry' (short tempered), 'Roadend' (joining of two roads), 'Rake' (a journey), 'Bring twae rake o' waitter frae the wall,' 'Rummal gumption' (common sense), 'jirble' (a drop of liquid), 'Gleed' (a glowing cinder), 'No sae baud' (well), 'goam' (to notice) — (used of person gravely ill) 'e never goamed me'.

EMINENT MEN

Colonel David Milne Home of Wedderburn, Billie and Paxton, M.P. for Berwick-upon-Tweed, President and Secretary for the Berwickshire Naturalists' Club. He was the writer of several interesting articles for the Club. He died in 1901.

George Muirhead LL.D. George Muirhead was born at Saltoun, Midlothian in 1845. He studied agriculture under Mr Hope at Fenton Barns. Later residing at Gifford Vale, he devoted himself to floriculture, shooting, fishing and taxidermy, in all of which he was proficient. In 1870 he was offered and accepted the post of factor on the estates of Paxton, Billie, Wedderburn and Milne Garden. He resided at Paxton Cottage for 19 years, taking over from time to time the management of several other properties in Berwickshire, and in addition, holding a government appointment as Inspector of Improvements in the Border Counties. In 1889 and 1895 he published two excellent volumes on 'The Birds of Berwickshire' which has become a standard work on ornithology. His poetic quotations, folklore and topographical plates greatly enhance the volumes. In his garden at Paxton he made an extensive collection of alpine and other flowering plants upon which no pains were spared to show them at their best. At Paxton he wrote several essays on the growing of cereals which were much appreciated by the Highland Agricultural Society who awarded him their gold medal. In 1889 he became commissioner to the Duke of Richmond and Gordon. In 1888 Mr Muirhead became a Fellow of the Royal Society, Edinburgh, Fellow of the Society of Antiquaries, Fellow of the Botanical Society of Edinburgh, and a member of the British Ornithologists' Union. He was an occasional contributor to the publications of these societies. In 1925 in recognition of his scientific attainments the University of Aberdeen conferred on him the honorary degree of LL.D. In 1897 he made an extended tour through Canada and the United States, visiting the government experimental farm and gardens. He died at Fochabers in 1928.

Sir William Burrell of Hutton Castle was a member of the shipping firm of Messrs Burrell and Son, Glasgow, which was founded by his grandfather. Sir William was born in 1861. His public spirit had been evinced in an active interest in civic affairs and in 1899 he became a member of Glasgow Town Council for the old Exchange Ward. He retired from the Town Council in 1906. Sir William has been a member of the Glasgow Royal Institute of Fine Arts since 1900. He purchased Hutton Castle from Lord Tweedmouth in 1918 and has made suitable additions and alterations to accommodate many of his art treasures. Sir William is widely recognised as a connoisseur.

In 1931 Queen Mary honoured Sir William and Lady Burrell with a visit to their beautiful home. Sir William received his knighthood in 1927. In 1944 Sir William and Lady Burrell presented to the City of Glasgow their entire collection of tapestries, pictures, porcelain, stained glass, silver and furniture. The collection is estimated to be worth £1,500,000. In addition to this magnificent gift, provision has been made for a special building to hold the collection. The building will be erected in the country near Glasgow. With this end in view further gifts amounting to £450,000 have been received by the Glasgow Corporation. The complete collection comprises 6,200 items, and since the gift was made additional items have been made to the collection. Sir William's collection of Gothic tapestries is the largest and most important in the world. No museum, no private collection either in Europe or America owns such a wealth of mediaeval masterpieces of this exquisite art. In the collection of pictures there are several masterpieces by some of the distinctive French and Dutch artists of the last century, marking a personal preference in tone, colour and subject, lending a character and distinction of its own. Objects of French 13th century painted glass, fine specimens of Chinese pottery and porcelain, Egyptian stone vases, Gothic limestone figures representing religious subjects are all included in this collection

In 1946 Sir William Burrell was awarded the St Mungo Prize. The prize is awarded every three years to the person who in the opinion of a selected body of representative citizens has done most during the preceding years for the good of the city by making it more beautiful, healthier or more honoured. Sir William was the third recipient of the prize. He was also made a Freeman of Glasgow at a private ceremony in the City Chambers in May 1944.

COUNTRY HOUSES

Hutton Castle, one of the most interesting of the old-time edifices that now remain in Berwickshire, is situated near the western boundary of the parish and is built on a steep bank overlooking the Whiteadder. The situation of the Castle seems to have been well chosen to serve the purpose for which it was originally intended and from an aesthetic point of view the situation is beautiful, looking across the flat green haugh to the silver strip of the Whiteadder flowing quietly under the shadow of overhanging trees. Towards the north-west of the Castle, about 100 paces or so, there is a ravine which has been partially filled up, and towards the south-west the dry ditch and mounds, which served to make the stronghold more secure, can no longer be traced. The broad-spreading lawns sweeping towards the south-west give the fortalice a picturesque and beautiful setting. Many of the old trees planted when the Castle was built have been preserved, and these, with their wide-spreading branches, add a charm to the place. The ancient Castle dates back to the year 1200 and figures frequently in history during the succeeding centuries when England and Scotland were frequently interlocked in warlike struggles.

When Sir William Burrell bought the Castle the whole of the interior was remodelled and a new kitchen wing was added. Additional rooms were built and the present building as it now stands is one of the most picturesque residences in the county. Externally the recent alterations in the building and surroundings have all been planned to bring out the full aesthetic value of the dwelling and its position, and in the changes made, the designer has been eminently successful. But, however much one may admire the beauty of the wide sweeping lawns, the castellated walls and the old trees — grim historians of many an ancient raid and foray — and scan the glowing shrubberies bright with the colours which summer suns win forth, one has only to be invited across the threshold to stand amazed at a house replete with treasures that are centuries old. One feels transported into another age. Long refectory tables grace the floor, rich-looking tapestries bedeck the walls while mailed figures stand sentinel. A subdued and softened daylight filters through the old stained glass and lights up the interior with irridescent hues. One generally thinks of securing a house and then searching for treasures to fill it, but in the case of Hutton Castle the treasures have been the fruits of a lifetime's collecting and the house has been remodelled to suit them.

On the south wall of the Castle there is a coat of arms with the initials A.H. and E.H. There are three birds (papingoes) and three stars in the first and fourth quarters respectively and a lion in the second and third quarters. The obliterated initials A.H. represent Alexander Home, the third spear of Wedderburn; E.H., Elizabeth Home, daughter of Patrick Home of Hutton Hall.

Broadmeadows House. At one time Hutton had its 'toon lands' and its common, on which the villagers had the right of grazing their cows. A portion of the 'toon lands' was divided up into sections or small fields suitable for the villagers to cultivate for the growing of root and grain crops. Eventually these sections of land passed into one tenancy and, possibly, into the possession of the more successful and progressive of the villagers. Most of the 'toon land' of Hutton came into the possession of one family, Ker of Broadmeadows. William Ker, the last of the Kers of Broadmeadows, died in 1801. In 1803, Broadmeadows passed into the possession of the Swintons of Kimmerghame and was held by them until 1825, when the estate was sold to Mr John Joseph Macbraire who at that time possessed Tweedhill and Fishwick. During his possession of Broadmeadows, Mr Swinton built a mansion house of substantial proportions in the Georgian style. When resident there Miss Swinton composed the air to the beautiful but rather sad song, 'Annie's Tryst'. When Mrs James Macbraire died in 1914, the Broadmeadows estate was broken up and sold. The estate comprised the farms of Hutton Mill, Hutton Mains, Broadmeadows Farm, Fishwick and West Fishwick. Each of the farms found different proprietors.[1] The mansion house of Broadmeadows and the home farm were sold to Mr J. Watts who demolished the greater part of it, remodelled the remainder and made the house more adaptable to modern requirements. The position of the mansion house is a very pleasant one, situated on the south bank of the Whiteadder, well sheltered by trees and with a wide view of grass parks and open country, with the Cheviot range in the distance.

Mr John William Stewart purchased Broadmeadows House and the home farm from Mr Watts in 1923. On his retiral from business Mr Stewart took a great interest in the breeding of race horses and owned a herd of prize Angus cattle. He died at Lausanne in September 1933. The present proprietrix of Broadmeadows is Miss E. Stewart.

Tweedhill House. Tweedhill House from its position is an ideal country residence facing south-east with a beautiful view of the river Tweed. It is well surrounded by trees. The grounds are not extensive, consisting of a few parks all in grass. The garden is productive, enclosed by a high wall and is well sheltered from strong winds. Tweedhill seems at one time to have formed part of the lands of Paxton and Fishwick. In recent years Tweedhill has had several proprietors. The present proprietor is Mr Charles Brackenbury.

Paxton House. When the Barony of Paxton became divided up the land passed into the possession of different well-known Merse families, the Ramsays of Foulden, the Homes of Ninewells and the Homes of Wedderburn. Eventually the greater portion of the land passed into the possession of the Homes of Wedderburn. Patrick Home, who succeeded to the Paxton-Wedderburn-Billie estate in 1766, built the present mansion houses of Paxton and Wedderburn. George Home became heir to the estate in 1812. His literary taste brought him into contact with many of the Edinburgh literati including Sir Walter Scott.

There is a glamour overhanging the whole of the fortunes of this famous Border family so intimately connected for centuries with the history of the Border land. I daresay the most interesting relic of the family's past will be the fragment of the banner borne by the Homes at the battle of Flodden. It is now preserved under glass and framed like a

[1]

Hutton Mill Hutton Mains	} –	Mr Arthur Bell
Fishwick	–	Mr William Murray
West Fishwick	–	Mr John Tait

picture. The banner was discovered in 1822 in a chest along with a number of old uniforms and dresses, not so old as the flag. The banner is made of silk and charged with a white saltire in the form of a St Andrew's cross on a green ground — white and green being the colours of the Home family.

The Homes of old were warriors bold
    As e'er auld Scotland ken'd, man
Their motto was Their Country's Cause
    And 'true unto the end', man
This is the banner which they raised
    On Flodden's battle field, man
There noble men, their name be praised
    They died ere they would yield, man.

It is recorded that the Wedderburn vassals and retainers were attached to the Royal Brigade at Flodden. Their leader, Sir David Home, with his eldest son George, was slain in defence of the King's person, and while the body of the hapless monarch fell into the enemy's hands, the bodies of Sir David and his son George were borne off the field wrapped, it is said, in the Wedderburn standard.

Spital House. Spital House is a neat little country residence, built of durable white freestone and snugly hidden among trees, well sheltered from all the strong winds that blow. It is built on the site that was once occupied by a hospital of St John.

In 1927 the Spital Estate was broken up. Spital House was sold to Mr Mackenzie, the Cedars, Sunderland, and resold to Colonel Machin. Clarabad Mill was sold to Mr Robinson, Annan, and latterly to Mr J. Smith, Edinburgh; Spital West Mains to Mr George Watt, Spital Mains to Mr J. Bell, Broadmeadows Farm. Clarabad farm was sold to Mr Alexander Wightman. The name Clarabad is derived from one Clarabald d'Esseby, a Huntingdonshire knight who received his lands about 1242 from Walter Olifard or Oliphant, Lord of Hutton before the Douglas family.[1] Clarabald d'Esseby evidently had greater possessions in the parish than the lands now designated by Clarabad farm.

It is pleasing to think that, in spite of economic pressure and the difficulty of staffing, the five country mansion houses are still being maintained in this rural parish. The great problem for the proprietors of these dwellings is to obtain servants to work in the house and to live in. The present staffing difficulties are in a measure being met by obtaining the help of married women who can spare a few hours daily from their own household duties.

Salmon fishings. On the portion of the Tweed forming the boundary of the parish, there are two fishing stations which pay teind to the Church of Scotland Trustees, New Fishings and Hornwell and Scots

[1] Coldingham Charters

New Water. The Berwick Salmon Fisheries Co. rent several of the fishing stations on the Tweed. For many years the catches of salmon have been normal, but at the beginning of the salmon netting season in 1952 a phenomenal quantity of fish was caught. The Tweed salmon are despatched by the Fisheries Co. to the London and Newcastle markets and command high prices. Several local men from Paxton village are employed by the Fisheries Co. for the fishing season from February to September.

WAY OF LIFE

In the villages of Hutton and Paxton the social life of the people has altered considerably during the last 50 years. With the better means of transport to the towns young people are attracted to seek employment in the larger centres of industry. Fifty years ago there were joiners, blacksmiths and shoemakers in Hutton and Paxton; now there are none. A few men are employed in salmon fishing on the Tweed during the spring and summer months. In the autumn and winter seasons the fishermen find employment with local contractors. Recently new dwelling houses have been erected in Hutton and Paxton villages by the County Council for the benefit of agricultural workers. These have now been let to suitable tenants. In the two villages, halls have been erected which are very serviceable as community centres for the social life of the parishioners. In the autumn and winter months Bowling and Badminton Clubs are well supported by the young people. Instructional classes under the auspices of the County Educational Committee are generally well attended. There are primary schools in Hutton and Paxton, with modern and comfortable residences for the schoolmasters. The community too is greatly helped by the County Library scheme by which up to date books suitable for all ages are supplied to willing readers. The books are distributed weekly by the schoolmasters and the system is well patronised by the parishioners. Dances, whist drives, and concerts are held from time to time, generally with the purpose of raising money for charitable purposes or in support of some local object requiring help.

The rapid system of motor transport from one place to another, in contrast with the horse-drawn vehicle, has brought a great change over the countryside during the last 50 years. Long ago, residents on the farms had very infrequent trips to town; generally the visit coincided with the 'Hirings' held at Berwick and Duns or with Berwick Fair held at the end of May. Fifty years ago holidays for farm workers were few and far between, probably consisting of only a weekend during the summer and before harvest. Now the farm worker has his fortnight's holiday with pay in addition to the Saturday afternoons. The efficient bus services enable farm workers to get to town centres more easily and to visit cinemas and places of entertainment whenever they wish.

A striking change that has taken place within the last few years is that young girls leaving school show no inclination for domestic service but prefer to be employed as clerkesses, typists or shop assistants. Young boys leaving school are inclined to apprentice themselves to some trade such as joinering, engineering or painting, in preference to working on the farm. It may be that in the near future farmers will find it increasingly difficult to find trained labour for their farms. The growing system of employing seasonal labour gangs is not conducive to getting the best out of the farming industry.

With regard to the people's attitude to the church and church-going, a considerable change has been noticeable since the First World War which has been intensified since the conclusion of the Second World War. The fellowship of worship does not make the same appeal to the present generation as it did to church members before 1914. It is difficult to attribute the decline to any specific cause, but there is a general spirit of indifference to things spiritual and to matters pertaining to religion. Materialism appears to be the engaging principle of life controlling the mind and energies of the majority of people. There is no doubt that the laxity shown by people to church matters and to the religious upbringing of their children is having an injurious effect upon the lives and manners of the rising generation.

1952

THE PARISH OF HUTTON

by Rev. W. G. Dunnett, M.B.E.

POPULATION

There has been a steady decline in the population of the parish in the last 30 years. The figures since 1801 are as follows: 1801, 955; 1841, 1133; 1851, 1102; 1901, 750; 1911, 682; 1921, 655; 1931, 614; 1951, 556; 1983, 350.

One of the major causes of this decline has been the mechanisation on the farms, so that where formerly many men were employed who had families living in the cottages, now there is seldom more than one family.

However, in the last few years there has been an upsurge of private house building in both Paxton and Hutton villages which should stabilise the population. In Paxton in particular houses have been built and people have come in from outside to live there, mainly from Berwick where they work. Some take a very active part in village and community affairs, but sadly many look only to Berwick and beyond for their social life.

ROADS AND TRANSPORT

There have been no new roads made, but existing roads are well maintained and on the whole suitable. However, there are more and more very heavy lorries using the parish roads, which were not engineered for such large vehicles.

Public transport still runs between Berwick, Paxton, Hutton, Swinton and Chirnside, but on a very limited scale. It is possible to go from Hutton to Chirnside by bus via Hutton Barns and Allanton, but only if you are prepared to turn round and come straight back. On the other hand the buses more often than not are travelling empty or nearly so, since the majority of people run their own cars.

FARMING

It is here that the biggest changes in the life of the parish have taken place. Agriculture is still the principal industry. There are now only 14 farm holdings since several have been combined into larger units, such as Fishwick and Nabdean, Paxton South Mains with North Mains and Hutton Mains. The main grain crops grown are winter barley, wheat and a limited amount of oats. Root crops are potatoes and turnips; sugar beet is no longer grown anywhere in the parish.

A new crop being grown is oil-seed rape, which in the last few years has expanded considerably throughout the Merse. Also there are peas grown for feed, and beans and cauliflower for freezing at the plant in Eyemouth.

As far as livestock is concerned, there are now no working horses, no dairy cattle and no pigs and poultry. Beef cattle and sheep are kept, both the traditional breeds and also many new breeds. There are Charolais and Limousin cattle and Mr Stobo at Fishwick has just added some French sheep to his flock.

Yields of grain have vastly increased over the past years through increased drainage and the greater use of fertilisers and pesticides. The machines on the farm, from tractors to combines, have become larger and more complicated, but capable of covering greater acreages more quickly and more thoroughly. This has however meant the enlarging of many fields and the loss of hedges, but fortunately this parish has not as yet succumbed to the prairie-like wide open expanses such as are to be found in other places.

Life for the worker on the farm is now greatly improved. The heavy work has largely been taken over by machines, and the farm worker now has to be a bit of a mechanic to keep the various machines going where before the horse was his main responsibility. The average weekly wage of a farm worker is now £100, with every possibility of that being increased by the overtime worked at busy times.

There are no longer foreign workers on the farms. Earlier difficulties in finding young men to work on the farms seem to have disappeared.

OTHER INDUSTRY

Although farming continues to be the main industry in the parish, several new industries have in the last 30 years been established which help to provide employment for the local people. In Hutton on the site of the old Hutton Croft Mr Rutherford set up a drainage contractor's business which has expanded greatly and now carries out work north and south of the Border. At Hutton Mains there has been a haulage business for some years and the Jeffrey family run an agricultural contractors' business in Hutton. Mr Greer, the owner of Spital House, runs an import-export business from the house, and a new potato sorting and bagging factory has been set up on the site of the old Winfield airfield camp.

There are however no longer any tradesmen's shops operating in the villages. The last joiner's shop closed in Paxton some years ago, and when our young men wish to learn a trade and work at it they have to go to Berwick or other places to do so. In similar fashion the young girls have to look to the cities for work, as locally there is very little opportunity.

SCHOOLS

There is now only one school in the parish, and that is in Hutton. The school in Paxton was closed in 1967 and the buildings sold. The future for the school in Hutton is very doubtful now since there are at present only seven pupils attending. This has partly happened through the decline in the population, but also through many children being sent to schools outside the parish for a variety of reasons.

Once the children have finished the primary school stage they go to Eyemouth to complete their education.

HUTTON CHURCH

The congregations of Hutton and Paxton were united in 1974 to form one congregation under the present minister, the Rev. W. Gavin Dunnett. In 1979 a further linking took place when Hutton was joined with Foulden and Mordington, with Mr Dunnett remaining as minister of the linked charge. This has proved a happy linking and of benefit to both parishes.

RECREATION AND PARISH ACTIVITIES

While television has damaged the old community get-togethers, there are still many organisations very active within the community to provide interest and enjoyment for a variety of people. Both village halls are used widely and the following are some of the organisations at present in being: Hutton Bowling Club; Hutton Badminton Club; Hutton Woman's Guild; The W.R.I.; Hutton and Paxton Horticultural Society; Paxton Onion Club; Paxton Guides and Brownies; The Over 60s Club; The Playgroup; The Mothers and Toddlers Group; Modern Dancing Club; Darts Club.

During the winter months there are whist drives held in both halls that are well patronised.

Finally there is a flourishing Youth Club which meets in Paxton Hall.

LOCAL GOVERNMENT

With the reorganisation of local government the parish no longer has direct representation on either district or regional councils. There is however a Community Council of eight members, four representing the Hutton and Fishwick area and four from Paxton. This Council has been active since its formation and has accomplished a few things and proved its worth. But like all such organisations it does not get the support it deserves, except in isolated cases such as the possible closure of the school when a public meeting called by the council was well attended.

COUNTRY HOUSES

Since the last revision there have been considerable changes in the occupancy and use of the large houses of the parish. After the removal of the Burrell Collection, Hutton Castle fell into disuse and was sold with the land to Mr Houston of Hutton Hall Barns. Since then the Castle has been vandalised and is slowly but surely becoming a ruin.

After the death of Miss Stewart, Broadmeadows House passed into the possession of Mr Aitken and then to Miss Bartholomew. It is now owned by Mr Crichton.

The main part of Paxton House is still occupied by Mr John Home Robertson, M.P. and his family, but the wings have been converted into flats. Spital House is both the residence and offices of Mr Greer, the owner, and Tweedhill, since the death of Mr Charles Brackenbury, has been in the ownership of Mr Murphy. The problems of staffing and maintaining these houses has become no easier in the past years.

1980s

THE PARISH OF LADYKIRK

by The Rev. Andrew Pringle

HISTORY OF THE LOCAL COMMUNITY

The parish of Ladykirk undoubtedly takes its name from its parish church, often referred to by its founder, James IV of Scotland, as 'The Ladie Kirk'.

Originally two parishes — Horndean and Upsetlington — it became one parish at the Reformation. While this is so these two place names are still in common use. This is quite natural for despite the fact that Ladykirk may be called a scattered rural parish made up of farms, farm cottages, and estate workers' cottages there is a certain grouping of these houses which makes this possible.

The name Horndean is Anglo-Saxon, deriving from Horn, meaning a curve or corner and Dene, meaning a wooded vale or valley, and this aptly describes the site of this part of the parish as it lies in a corner and in a valley sloping towards the river Tweed.

The lands of Horndean were once part of the lands of Coldingham Priory by gift from King Edgar. The same lands were granted to Kelso Abbey, by the Viponts or De Veripontes. How this Norman family came into possession of these lands is not known by the writer of this account. Vipont also gave the monks the Church of Horndean which must therefore have existed in the year 1156. It is said to have been dedicated as a Church of the Holy Rood and consecrated by David de Bernham, Bishop of St Andrews on 4th April 1243. Now, only the foundations remain in the middle of what was once the churchyard, about half a mile east of the present hamlet of Horndean.

Upsetlington: — It is certain that this place was connected with the monks. When St Cuthbert and other monks from Old Melrose travelled to Holy Island their favourite route was by the ford at Upsetlington and there is a tradition that they had, on the Scots side of Tweed, a cell or rest-house for their frequent journeyings between their two chief monasteries. The ancient Church of St Mary's, Upsetlington stood on high ground and the place is still known as the Chapel Round. One writer states that this church was built by King David, but he gives no authority for it. However, tradition does seem to corroborate this, as in 1598 a question arose as to the proper place of meeting for the Wardens of the East Marches, and Sir William Bowes, Governor of Norham Castle, writes to Cecil, 'I have heard (if I forget not) from the late worthy Lord Treasurer of an ancient privelege granted by both Princes to a monastery at or near the Ladie Kirk, now a good distance within reputed Scottish ground, supposed to be builded upon the ground of old, and till this day, called debatable ground, where from its peaceable motions the princes were content to meet on all occasions of interparlance and treaty.' Upsetlington, says Chalmers, took its name from the Kirktown which stood on the northern margin of Tweed and a little to the north and east of the English village of Norham, on the opposite bank of the river. The origin of the name is, however, obscure. The appelations New Ladykirk and Old Ladykirk are really farm names.

The parish is bounded on the north by the parish of Whitsome, on the south by the river Tweed, on the east by the parish of Hutton and Fishwick (now one parish) and on the west by the parishes of Coldstream and Swinton.

The area is approximately 3100 acres of flat country with a few rising grounds; situated in a haunted countryside and full of memories of Scottish Kings from Malcolm to Bruce and James IV; and of English monarchs from William the Conquerer to King John and Edward I, it is truly steeped in historical associations and Border folklore.

POPULATION

By return to Dr Webster in 1755 the population was 386; by census in 1801, 516; 1851, 561; 1861, 564 (max.); 1901, 316; 1911, 315; 1921, 338; 1931, 305. The census of 1951 showed the population as 261.

From the foregoing statistics it can be seen that the population of the parish has greatly decreased in the last 100 years in common with most rural parishes, and the reasons for this are many. Mechanisation on the farm is general and there are consequently fewer 'hands' needed to cultivate the soil and reap its fruits. The combine harvester is now widely used here, and where a farmer does not own one of these machines, he hires one for his grain harvest. Bad housing, lack of proper sanitation, few homes with water 'on tap' within the house, distance from school, poor transport facilities (two buses per day to Berwick or Kelso with little time between arrival and departure at each of these towns) and, of course, smaller families, must also be taken as causes.

While there were approximately 90 children at the village school in 1890 there are now only 20. The present day system of transferring children at the age of 11+ years to junior secondary or high school (according to I.Q. and ability) in the towns of Coldstream and Duns respectively will probably cause a further decrease in the future. In the past seven years all but eight young people, on leaving school, have either left the parish for other employment than the land, or travel to and from their work. Of these eight young people, five are farmers' sons, now working with their fathers, and two are farm workers' daughters employed, indirectly, in the farm house. The other one has since given up farm work to join H.M. forces.

PUBLIC AND SOCIAL SERVICES

There is still no general water supply, water having to be pumped either by engine, windmill or hand. A few homes have this pumped water led into their houses, others still have to carry it in pails. The position is still far from satisfactory, and what water we have has a great deal of lime in it and is consequently very 'hard'. It is hoped that the County Water Scheme and reservoir, at present under construction in the Watch Burn valley, a little above the village of Longformacus, is soon completed. There are, as yet, few houses with electricity installed, only three having a mains supply (mansion house, estate factor's house, and one farm house) and four farmhouses with private generating plants. Work has, however, started on the 'Grid system' for the parish and most of the houses have been 'wired', or are about to be 'wired'. The power is expected by late 1952 or early 1953. At present lighting, with the above mentioned exceptions, is by paraffin lamps. Some households have either 'calor' or 'rural' gas for cooking purposes. The others must depend on paraffin stoves or coal fires.

There are no inns or shops, but the parish is well served with motor vans which bring 'to the door' such necessities as bread, groceries, fish, meat, coal, and drapery goods. There is a sub-post office. The nearest police station is at Swinton, a neighbouring village four miles away.

The classified roads are well surfaced, but most farm roads are in a bad state of repair.

There is a primary school, staffed by one female teacher, appointed by the Education Authority. Pupils pass on for further education either to Coldstream Junior Secondary or Berwickshire High Schools according to their pass mark in a 'Grading Examination' which they sit at 11+ years of age. School meals (two courses) are served daily in school and are of great benefit to children who normally would have carried their lunch, especially in the winter months.

There are no resident doctors but the parish is served by several (at least five) from other districts. There is also a district nurse who resides in Coldstream, six miles away. The school children are examined, medically and dentally, periodically by school doctors and dentists. Recently a mass Radiography Unit visited the county and most of the children and a few adults took advantage of this new service. The general health of the people is good. There is a small cottage hospital at Coldstream (six miles) and an Infirmary at Berwick (nine miles), but most cases necessitating hospital treatment are sent to the Royal Infirmary, Edinburgh some 51 miles distant. There are maternity hospitals at Duns and at Berwick-on-Tweed, but most of the births take place either at Duns or at home. Pre-natal and ante-natal care are given usually by the doctor and district nurse.

The parish church was founded in the year 1500 by James IV of Scotland as a thank-offering for being saved from drowning in Tweed. He vowed that he would built a church which neither flood nor fire would destroy. It is a strongly built building of red sandstone with a roof of wrought ashlar. To support the weight of this stone roof 18 great buttresses support the walls. It is cruciform in shape, the transepts or transeptal chapels having semi-hexagonal terminations similar to the nave. The church has seating capacity for approximately 300. The manse, now in use, was built in the 1870s and is kept in good repair. It is not too large and once the amenities of water and electricity are laid on it should be a most comfortable house. The 'steading' or out-buildings, which are much older than the manse, are beginning to show their age. Several years ago the barn was converted into a hall suitable for Woman's Guild meetings etc. The Glebe, extending to some 11 acres, is at present let to local farmers as grazing lets.

Unfortunately many of the old records of the church have been lost.

There is a branch of the Woman's Guild of the Church of Scotland and also a branch of the Women's Rural Institute.

A Boy Scout Troop has been revived and a Young People's Fellowship started and led by the present incumbent. The Fellowship meets every alternate Sunday evening and every Tuesday evening during the winter session. These are run under the auspices of the church. There is also a Sunday School which is well attended and a Bible class which is not so well attended.

There is a Young Men's Club which caters for those interested in billiards, darts, table tennis, and carpet bowls. The club meets in the village hall. The hall was built after the 1914-18 war and accommodates about 150 people.

HOUSING

The houses are in good condition, mostly built of stone and lime. A great number have been reconstructed during the past 25 years and are brick roughcast. A great many still lack modern sanitation owing to the lack of a gravitation water supply, but a public supply is expected to be introduced in the near future and within a few years thereafter all the houses will have water laid on. In most cases lighting is by paraffin lamp. But with the introduction of electricity in the near future all houses should have electric light in the space of a few years.

There are 93 dwelling houses in the parish, mostly three and four rooms, with good gardens, and there are no cases of overcrowding. The cottagers are keen gardeners and therefore all the gardens are kept in good condition. There is great competition among them at the local

Flower Show. Mention should also be made of Ladykirk House Gardens which are still kept in very good condition despite a greatly reduced staff from pre-war days. The chief landowner is Major J. M. S. Askew of Ladykirk who succeeded to the estate about 1930. He resides at Ladykirk House, a mansion built in 1797.

AGRICULTURE, INDUSTRY AND COMMERCE

Occupations are mostly agricultural or incidental. Great changes have inevitably taken place in farming during the past 12 years. As has been said already, horses have been almost entirely replaced by tractors which naturally greatly expedited and eased the work on the farms during this period.

The main crops are oats, wheat, barley, turnips and potatoes. There are still about 300 acres of permanent grassland (approximately 100 years old), and with periodical liming and manuring, these are still first class grazing land.

Poultry farming is also being extensively practised. There is an accredited poultry station or farm in the parish, which has round about 3000 birds and hatches several thousand chicks annually. The other farmers also keep a fair number of hens. At Ladykirk Home there is a fine herd of Jersey cows.

The nearest market town is Berwick-on-Tweed, which serves both sides of the border. There is a grain market every Saturday where farmers show their goods to the grain merchants in the Corn Exchange wherein all farming business can be transacted. The nearest cattle markets are in Duns and Reston to which the farmers go to buy and sell their cattle, sheep and pigs.

There is one smithy in the parish, at Upsetlington, but as there are so few horses now to shoe the main work carried on there now is the general repair of farm machinery.

WAY OF LIFE

The way of family life is generally good at the present time. The people are friendly and willing to help in all religious and secular activities when asked to do so. For whatever reason, the days of the family pew are gone for the time being at least. There are of course the few exceptions which encourage every minister to greater efforts among his flock for its return. There is no antagonism to the church, as can be seen at all special and most communion services. There is, however, a certain indifference, the cause of which is difficult to trace.

There is little or no drunkenness and no serious crime. There is, however, a growing amount of betting and gambling especially in football pools and raffles.

As there is an extra bus which runs late in the evening on a Saturday many people go to the town of Berwick where there are two cinemas. All the farmers have motor cars and might be called prosperous. The farm workers and other workers have experienced many changes in the past 20 years and are much better paid. The minimum wage for a male farm worker today is £5 17s 6d, and that of a female worker £4 1s 6d.

It is doubtful if there is a single home without a daily newspaper and hardly any without a wireless set. There are no destitute poor in the parish and the few elderly people who live alone have many friends who visit them.

1952

THE PARISH OF LADYKIRK

by Rev. Alan C. D. Cartwright

The ancient kirk from which the parish of Ladykirk takes its name is worthy of some comment. An old tradition holds that King James IV built it in honour of the Blessed Virgin of the Steill, who had saved him from drowning in a 'steill', a deep pool in a river where salmon nets were placed. He vowed to build a church that could not be destroyed by either fire or flood, and thus the kirk has a very unusual stone roof and stands 120 feet above the River Tweed.

Built from a lovely pink stone from Swinton Quarry, three miles away, the kirk has a large and imposing appearance with its 20 large buttresses. These are necessary to support the weight of the roof which is covered with overlapping stones of wrought ashlar. The tower was completed in 1743, only the lower part, to just below the clock, being original. The upper portion was designed by William Adam, whilst the clock was inserted in 1882 by Lady Marjoribanks. In 1861 the kirk was reseated and the walls were cleaned, and it was probably then that wooden pews were first introduced. The kirk is cruciform in plan and consists of an aisleless nave, a chancel with a semi-hexagonal termination, and north and south transepts which are similar in form to the chancel. The walls above the arches leading into the transepts are carried vertically up above the roof outside, and form gables for the transept roofs — a very unusual, if not unique, feature.

The height of the roof is impressive, and there are only some transverse ribs to relieve its baldness. As the side windows are kept below the springing of the vault, the building is quite dark, but in 1987 new lights were installed which highlight the roof and also brighten up the kirk for the worshippers. The arrangement of the seating was altered at the same time, so that all the congregation now face east,

Plate 31. Paxton House.

towards the Communion Table and pulpit. The pews and pulpit came from St Andrew's, Berwick, which sadly had to be demolished due to subsidence. The new pews and lights give the kirk a brighter and lighter look and it is a delight to worship in or visit. Many people from the surrounding area were present to hear the Rt. Rev. Duncan Shaw, Moderator of the General Assembly of the Church of Scotland, rededicate the pews and furnishings and dedicate the new lights at a service on 10th January 1988. Much of the cost of the renovation and of the repairs to the roof was borne by the Historical Buildings Council, without which assistance the people of Ladykirk could not have afforded the necessary work, for there are far fewer people in the parish than at any time during the past few hundred years.

The population has decreased in every census from 1921, until by 1981 there were only 160 people in Ladykirk. According to the estimate of the present writer this had further decreased to 155 in 1987. The population has been reduced mainly due to the mechanisation of agriculture and to the better roads. Services which before were in the parish are now outside it (e.g. blacksmith, joiner, public house). The parish is now serviced from either Norham or Berwick-upon-Tweed.

The balance of population has altered too, with Ladykirk having a far smaller proportion of children than the national average (14 per cent under 16 as against 25 per cent in Scotland and 22 per cent in Berwickshire). It also has a higher proportion of old age pensioners (25 per cent against 17.7 per cent in the U.K. and 16.7 per cent in Scotland). The changes which have been brought about by mechanisation on the farms have resulted in not one farm in the parish having all its cottages filled, and many of those occupied are rented by retired people.

The Merse is a very attractive place to which to retire, because the weather is never very severe, as the land is low-lying and protected from the south-west by the Cheviots and from the north by the Lammermuirs. The shelter of these hills also means that the rainfall is not very high (about 22" — 560 mm — per annum), in fact one of the lowest in Scotland. The rain is sufficient, though, to help the crops and the grass grow, and most of the farms in Ladykirk (unlike other areas of Berwickshire) still have sheep and cattle as well as grain. There are, however, no dairy farms in the parish. In recent years the Ladykirk Estate (owners of most of the parish) have been replacing many of the old trees which were planted last century.

The fact that there are quite a few woods — both deciduous and coniferous — and plenty of hedges, ensures that there is an abundance of wild life. It is rare to drive along the quiet country roads without seeing rabbits, hares or hedgehogs, or the occasional stoat, weasel, fox or deer, as well as the numerous birds which nest either in the trees or beside the river. The river itself has many fish and on a pleasant summer evening fishermen can be seen lining both banks of the Tweed fishing for trout or salmon.

Sometimes, too, groups of people can be seen out shooting for pheasants. These are quite numerous in the area, and there are partridges too. There are no grouse, however, as the land is too fertile and too low. The highest point in the parish is only 235 feet (72 metres) above sea level, so although the snow can lie for weeks on end in the hills around the Merse (and sometimes for a while behind the hedges), it rarely blocks the roads for more than a day. Transport is mainly by car as public transport is virtually non-existent apart from the school buses.

Transport communication with the rest of the country is reasonable as there are regular trains from Berwick (only eight miles away) to Edinburgh, Glasgow and Aberdeen and down to London, Leeds and Birmingham, with connections to other inter-city stations. As Edinburgh and Newcastle are less than an hour away on the train, and just over the hour by car, people from the parish do not feel remote, and this has attracted many folk from both sides of the Border to retire here.

Mains water and electricity came in the early 1950s and since that time there has been a steady decline in the number of the population who actually live and work in the parish, and an increase in those who are retired or who commute to work (mainly in Berwick). At the time of writing there are only 30 people out of the 155 who live in the parish who also work in it, and there are only another two or three coming in from outside to work.

The more people travel out of the area to work the fewer amenities the area retains. It is obviously easier for someone working in Berwick also to shop in Berwick. The local school was closed in 1963 and the children now go to Swinton (two or three miles away) for primary education, and then on to Berwickshire High School in Duns (a further seven miles). If the school had been open in 1986 there would have been only eight children at it, with three of pre-school age.

There is a sub-post office at Upsettlington which serves the parish, which has fought off closure several times. As this is the only shop of any description in the parish everybody wishes it to remain open. There are still a few vans which travel the area, but even ten years ago there was a much greater variety of travelling shops.

There is now a resident doctor, although his surgery is across the border at Norham, and he serves most of the parish, although doctors from Coldstream and Chirnside have some patients here. Most patients in need of hospital care now go to the Borders General Hospital at Melrose, although some go south to Ashington. Some major cases go either to Edinburgh or Newcastle. There are cottage hospitals at Berwick, Coldstream and Duns which are used for minor operations and convalescing, as well as geriatric care. Most maternity cases now go to the Borders General. At the other end of life, the majority of funerals are burials in the kirkyard, with the occasional cremation at Edinburgh or Blyth. Up until 1957 the registration of Births, Deaths and Marriages took place in the parish, but since 1st January 1958 the registration district has been joined with Swinton, the Registry Office now being the vestry of Swinton Kirk.

With the improvement of farming techniques, it is possible that the decline in population and the consequent reduction in services will continue, with a further movement of younger people into the towns. Even in Ladykirk it is the population living on the farms, as against the two little hamlets, which has declined. When a house becomes vacant on a farm it may stand empty for years, whilst the houses at Horndean and Upsettlington will be filled reasonably quickly. People obviously prefer to have neighbours.

Horndean is a lovely little hamlet of ten houses and takes its name from the dean (small valley) by the horn (bend) of the Tweed. The area around the village is a pleasant little valley which slopes down to the Tweed. The name is Anglo-Saxon and there was probably a church there before the Norman Conquest. Certainly by 1156 there was a church in the parish, for in that year it was given to the monks of Kelso. It was dedicated in 1243 by David de Bernham (who dedicated or rededicated at least 140 churches through Scotland). The first mention of Horndean occurs in what is said to be the first decision recorded under Scots law. King Edgar had given to Coldingham Priory the lands between Horndean and Knapdene (three miles north-east), but the vagueness in respect of what the gift entailed led to a dispute, and the future King David I was called in to arbitrate. After James IV had built and endowed Ladykirk, Horndean Church was left to decay. The last record of Horndean as a separate parish is in 1576 and now only the foundations of the kirk remain — about half a mile east of the village.

In 1786 a Burgher Church (one of the factions of the Secession Church, which had separated from the Church of Scotland in 1733) was built in Horndean. This was to draw those who were dissatisfied with the established church's ministers in either Ladykirk or Hutton. The church was enlarged in 1812 to accommodate 450 people, and it continued fairly successfully for most of the 18th and 19th centuries. The membership of the church was 108 in 1899, which was about two-thirds the size of the membership of the Ladykirk. By this time the Burgher Church had become the United Presbyterian Church and in 1900 it became the United Free Church. Soon it was decided that a new church should be built in Paxton to serve the previous congregations of Horndean and Mordington, and both these buildings were closed. The Horndean church has now been demolished, but there are some people who can remember it. It is amazing that a little parish which is less than four miles long by one mile wide should have had at one time or another four different church buildings: Horndean, Upsettlington, and Horndean U.P. as well as the present Ladykirk. Ladykirk has now been designated a List A historic building and its future is thus assured.

There is a marvellous community spirit in the parish. Although there are not many people, they all know each other and are prepared to help and support each other. The village hall which was built after the First World War holds regular dances which are well supported, not only by local people but also by folk from all parts of the eastern Borders.

One of the great changes of the past 30 years has been increased mobility. Many will travel 20 or 30 miles for work or recreation. The percentage of households without a car was nearly 50 per cent in Scotland as a whole in 1981, but was only 33 per cent in Berwickshire and by 1987 Ladykirk had only 8 per cent of households without a car. This tells us a great deal about the way of life which has evolved in the parish over the past 30 years.

1988

THE PARISH OF LANGTON

by W. W. Elliot, Esq.

Langton parish is situated almost in the very centre of Berwickshire, and is partly Lammermuir and partly Merse. It is also cut in half by the Langton Burn which flows in an easterly direction and which came down like a raging torrent in the flood of 12th August 1948, carrying with it almost every bridge in its course; in fact not one bridge was left intact, and it was by the fall of one of the main bridges that the large breach in the Duns — St Boswells Branch Railway Line was caused. This branch has remained closed since that date, and it is very doubtful if it will ever be opened again.

Since the last report of 1845 much has happened in this lovely rural parish. In 1863, John, Marquis of Breadalbane, rebuilt in most magnificent style the mansion house of Langton, his main reason being to store the priceless collection of art treasures which were in his Perthshire home of Taymouth Castle. Taymouth had to pass to the direct male heir but he wished to leave the very valuable moveables to his sister, Lady Elizabeth Pringle, and felt it necessary to build a house worthy of their reception. Langton House was built for this purpose and remained in the family until 1924, when the entire estate, mansion house and valuables were sold. The farms were first offered to the tenants by the syndicate who purchased the estate, and failing acceptance by them, they were sold by public roup. This meant many changes in the parish and a consequent reduction in its population. Many record prices were obtained for the pictures, among them the Raeburn record of £25,000 for 'The McNab'. The wonderful collection of armour was also disposed of, and some of the finest specimens from the Langton Collection can now be seen in the Tower of London.

With this beautiful mansion now reduced to a ruin, the population of the parish has decreased but will tend to rise in the near future as a new housing scheme is nearing completion. The Free Church, built by a member of the Breadalbane family, has been closed, leaving the Old Parish Church at Gavinton which is one of the prettiest village churches in Scotland. The public school, which about 1904 had an average attendance of almost 100, has now an attendance of less than 20, and is only a one-teacher school taking children up to the age of ten years.

The animal life in the parish is much the same as recorded in the two previous accounts, but there has been a very marked increase in the number of rabbits and as in many other places they have become a menace to the countryside. At present the parish is alive with them and hundreds must be killed weekly by the cars passing through the parish. Even poisoning seems to have little effect and the damage to young crops caused by this pest is very extensive. The game can hardly be said to be up to the standard existing when there was a Laird of the Manor, and as Langton's extensive and lovely policies were used as a camp all through the Second World War it is hardly to be wondered that the amount of game in the parish has been very much reduced.

There is no doubt that the parishioners now enjoy much better living conditions, and since the population is mainly made up of farm workers, whose wages have never been so high, a certain amount of lavish spending takes place. Farm prices have soared to a height which they never before attained, and farmers too are in a much better condition financially than they have been for many years.

Farming conditions are better than they have ever been in the parish and the crops seen on the larger farms are as good as can be seen in any part of southern Scotland. These farmer owners of the parish have now more money in their hands, and they have been able to do extensive repairs to their farm buildings and houses and much better treatment of the land can be seen all around. Because the property is now their own, they are able to spend more on what belongs to themselves and this will be of great benefit to their heirs and those who come after.

Langton is truly one of the most beautifully wooded parishes in the County of Berwick, and as the land slopes down to the lower Merselands of Berwickshire it becomes most fertile in its southern parts. The view from the Hardens Hill, one of the highest points in the parish, is truly one of the best to be had in the length and breadth of Scotland. It was appreciated by the National Bard himself and inspired the poet to burst into verse as he neared the home of his great friend Douglas Ainslie of Berrywell, Duns, and looked down on the lovely scene which met his eyes from Hardens Hill. One does not, however, need to have the genius of Robert Burns to appreciate the beauties of the parish of Langton.

Time marches on and one generation succeeds another, but the parish of Langton still retains much of its old natural beauty, and all the grandeur of its hills and valleys where many a Border raid took place in the days of Border warfare. With so large a camp the parish still retains the marks of the recent war, but these are gradually disappearing and nature is again mellowing the scars suffered during that world-wide conflict. Life is very peaceful at present and let us all hope that the peace may continue for many a day to come.

1950

THE PARISH OF LANGTON

by Rev. James A. Hall, Th.B.

Since the 1950s much has changed within the parish of Langton. The railway line has disappeared completely, leaving only the shape of the cutting in some places, now reverting to nature and completely grassed over. The mansion of Langton House has also completely disappeared. Gavinton School, closed in the 1960s, has been a dwelling house since 1976 and the ten or so children of primary school age are taken by bus to Duns Primary School. Many children go away to the cities for further study when they leave Berwickshire High School and, as employment in the area is very limited, few return to work locally.

In 1950 Langton parish church in the village of Gavinton was linked to Polwarth Church and in 1983 was further linked to the hill parishes of Abbey St Bathans, Longformacus and Cranshaws under one minister who resides in the Manse at Cranshaws. Attendances average between 35 and 45 although the roll is considerably greater.

The population is a mixture of retired people and young people who work in Duns and further afield. The changes in the employment pattern have resulted in many new people coming to live in the area and also in frequent changes in sections of the population. Very little employment exists within the parish, the increase in mechanisation reducing the numbers needed to work the land. The piggery, blacksmiths and bakery which used to offer employment in the village of Gavinton no longer exist and the post office and general store employs only its owners.

The council estate in Gavinton has been slightly enlarged in recent years and many of the very small private houses have been combined to make larger housing units. Throughout the parish there has been a little private building. It is fortunate that the area has, so far, escaped the scourge of many holiday homes, which has so distorted other communities.

Gavinton village hall has been renovated and is used almost every night for leisure pursuits for adults and/or children. These do not perhaps draw the numbers they once did, but continue to flourish despite the attraction of television and help to foster the sense of community which the village enjoys. The amenities have been improved by additional electric street lighting.

The only public transport to visit the area is the courier bus, which will call at Gavinton if requested, and the sparse Eastern Scottish service which passes along the Duns to Greenlaw road occasionally.

Water now comes from the Watchwater Reservoir at Rathburn.

The rabbits recorded in the 1950s have been significantly reduced by myxomatosis, although in very recent years there has been an upward swing due to a developing immunity to the disease. A relatively new phenomenon is feral mink which do damage to wild life, being rapacious predators. Collared doves abound.

The reorganisation of local government, which saw Berwickshire County swallowed up in the Borders Region, brought into existence the Gavinton Community Council which has the care of the village and its environs.

1986

THE PARISH OF LAUDER

by A. G. Doughty, Solicitor and ex-Town Clerk

PHYSICAL

The parish, which includes the Royal Burgh of Lauder, extends through most of Upper Lauderdale into the heights of Lammermoor, from a little north of Crib Law (1570 ft.) and Siennes Law (1686 feet) in a southerly direction to the bounds of Blainslie and Melrose Parish. The descent is 1250 feet, the area being watered by the River Leader and its tributaries. The greatest length of the parish is ten miles from north to south and the greatest breadth is seven miles, from east to west.

ANTIQUITIES

There are numerous prehistoric hill forts and hut circles in the parish. The most prominent of these are the camp on Addinston Farm, the Blythe Harefaulds with a fine outlook to the Merse and Cheviots, the Barrow Stones on the moor to the east of the parish, and the hill fort at Tollis Hill in the extreme north of the parish. There are many other indications of former activity, as well as traces of the Roman Dere Street on the western slopes; and in the cultivated fields there, many flints and arrowheads are found from time to time.

Old Thirlestane Castle was the home of the Maitlands until the days of Chancellor Maitland (1537-1595), when they removed to Lauder Fort which, after many vicissitudes, is now the well-known Thirlestane Castle, the seat of the Earl of Lauderdale. Family feuds, mainly directed against the Lauders, led in 1598 to the destruction of the Tolbooth in Lauder Burgh and the death of the hereditary bailie Robert Lauder. These and other antiquities are described and illustrated in the *Report on the County of Berwick* (1915) of the Royal Commission on Ancient Monuments . . . of Scotland, pp. 106-123.

POETS AND POETRY

Lauderdale is the eastern rampart of the Ballad country, and one of the oldest ballads celebrates in 'Auld Maitland,' the prowess of Sir Richard Maitland in defending the castle of Leadertown (now Thirlestane Tower) in 1296, against an English attack. This ballad was sung to Sir Walter Scott by the Ettrick Shepherd's mother, Margaret Laidlaw.

There were several accomplished men of letter among the Maitlands, notably Sir Richard, the Blind Baron, whose house and lands of Blythe were harried by Liddesdale thieves. Blythe lies in the south-east of the parish and is now a typical Lammermoor farm, forming part of the Lauderdale Estates.

Another famous ballad was 'Leader Haughs and Yarrow', credited to Burne, the Violer (Minstrel Burne), who is thought to be the prototype of the minstrel of 'The Lay'. He is said to have played Scots tunes to Pepys, the diarist, who was one of Lord Lauderdale's visitors in 1666.

In modern times there was a minor poet, William Brockie, born of humble parents at East Mains, near Lauder. His 'Lauther East Mains' is full of homely nostalgic reference, and some sage remarks on education.

HISTORICAL

Apart from the literary Maitlands, the most noted were Sir Richard (Auld Maitland of the Ballad), William Maitland of Lethington, better known as Secretary Maitland, who was an astute politician in Queen Mary's time, and John Maitland, Duke of Lauderdale, remembered as one of the notorious Cabal, and for his zeal against the Covenanters; yet also for his kindness to Midside Maggie, the farmer's wife at Tollishill, who is reputed to have produced a snowball in June which saved the life of the Duke.

In 1482 the Scottish Nobles met in Lauder Kirk and plotted the destruction of James III's favourites. The King was leading an army in an endeavour to frustrate Edward IV's support of the Duke of Albany and incidentally to recover the town of Berwick. The story of 'Bell the Cat', when Cochrane and other favourites were hanged on Lauder Bridge, is well known even in these days.

In the year 1638, when the Rev. James Guthrie, the 'little man that could not bow' was called to Lauder Kirk, he signed the Covenant and in 1661 he was tried for high treason and executed. His last words were 'The Covenants, the Covenants shall yet be Scotland's reviving'. In 1745 Prince Charlie lodged at Thirlestane Castle on his way to invade England and in Lauder town there is a house known as Cope's House where Sir John is said to have lodged while fleeing from Prestonpans.

A tragic incident in connection with the Maitland family was the death by lightning of the 12th Earl of Lauderdale, at Broadshawrigg on his Estate, on 12th August, 1884.

POPULATION

For reasons common to agricultural parishes, the population shows a steady decline: 1801, 1760; 1841, 2198; 1851, 2154; 1861, 2198; 1891,

1588; 1901, 1461 (alteration to boundary during intercensal period); 1911, 1336; 1921, 1369; 1931, 1214; 1951, 1190.

AGRICULTURE

The agricultural statistics for the parish are:

Tillage	3502 acres
Rotation Grass	4423 acres
Permanent Grass	3505 acres
Rough Grazings	20314 acres

Agriculture and stock-rearing, with their ancillary occupations, form the main industry in the parish of Lauder. There are 35 full-time farms and eight part and spare-time. Sixteen are owner-occupied. The normal length of lease is ten to 15 years. Several sheep farms with rough grazing extend to 3000 or 4000 acres. The average sheep farm is about 2500 acres and the arable 350. The average rent of the former is 3s. per acre, of the latter 27s. 6d. Fifty-nine per cent of the land is devoted to stock-rearing and feeding.

There are no minerals, and no factories, in spite of the amount of water power available, although there were at one time numerous meal mills, as evident by such names as Carfraemill, Wyselawmill, Newmills, St Leonard's Mill and Burnmill at Lauder. Nearly all thrashing of corn is now done by travelling mills, which generally have a baling machine attached for baling the straw. Some farmers have oil or petrol engines in their steadings, fitted up for grinding, thrashing or any other necessary operation, and in this year, 1950, there are three 'Combine' harvesters in the parish which are proving of considerable help to the farmer. The chief white crops are oats, barley and in some parts wheat, and turnips and rape are largely grown for the feeding of stock.

Owing to the elevation, the district is not early, but the soil is good, being of the reddish brown soil of Berwickshire, and heavy crops are obtained in a good season. Even on the lower grounds, the slopes of the fields lend themselves to 'lodging' when there is heavy rain with wind. Cultivation is carried on in some farms up to 1200 feet above sea-level, but at this elevation crops are apt to be late. Cattle, outliers as well as court-fed, are in goodly numbers, and the breeding of half-bred sheep is extensively carried on in the lower grounds of the parish. The higher areas intersected by glens such as Earnscleugh, Glenburnie, Scorhope and Kelphope, that cut into the Lammermoor plateau, are mainly heather clad and form excellent pastures for black-faced sheep. The sheep produced in these glens are not surpassed by any in Scotland and at the annual ram sales good prices are obtained: up to and over £1000 are sometimes given for rams from these hills. The chief sales take place at Lanark and Peebles for black-faced, and at Kelso and St Boswells for other breeds. St Boswells and Edinburgh are the main regular marts for stock and the sales are easily attended now that mechanical transport has superseded the old-time foot travel.

The people of the landward part of the parish, i.e. outwith Lauder burgh, live in the farmhouse and in cottages near the steadings, but nowadays the size of a farm cannot be gauged from the number of 'pairs' of horses, as agriculture is extensively mechanised and few horses are required, hence fewer men. This reacts on the number of inhabited houses, as every man in charge of a pair of horses used to have a tied house, but now, unless he has learned to drive a tractor, the ploughman may find his occupation gone. Some of the women go to the fields for turnip singling and shawing and their numbers are in modern times increased at potato-lifting time by gangs of school children released for a 'back-end' holiday. The ubiquitous Irish labourers come in useful when extra jobs are on hand and they are to be found in goodly numbers throughout the parish. In the harvest field, few workers are now seen, so highly mechanised are the operations, and when for the ordinary 'binder' is substituted the 'combine harvester', of which type there are three in the parish, one realises that the farmer and his men are practically something between the farmer and the motor mechanic.

TRANSPORT

Two main roads run through the parish. The road from Edinburgh which surmounts Soutra Hill forks at Carfraemill Hotel, one branch leading direct to Kelso, the other western one passing through Lauder on its way to Earlston, St Boswells and the Border. Berwickshire roads are held in repute throughout Scotland, and are kept in first class condition. The farm service roads are fairly long, as many of the steadings are situated high above the dale.

The nearest town of any size is Galashiels, some 12 miles distant, and there is a good bus connection between Lauder and Galashiels. It possesses good shops and two picture houses which tempt the good folk of Lauder and the parish to spend their money further afield than previously.

Edinburgh also is easy of access, and there are few inhabitants of Lauder parish who are not familiar with its streets. Such jaunts are made possible by the shorter hours and half-holidays now enjoyed. Every farmer has his car, while most young farm workers have push bikes or motor bikes.

SOCIAL LIFE

The foregoing facilities make social life more active and isolation is not now the bugbear many town-dwellers imagine it to be. As a matter of fact, the isolated shepherd seldom realised that he was lonely, for in his cottage among the hills he had, and has, a social technique of his own.

He has the radio, the newspaper and a bicycle, and being a walker by occupation, he thinks nothing of the few miles between himself and a friend, and if he is young he will go many miles to enjoy a dance or a whist drive. The women have their Women's Rural Institute (108 members) with their home industry classes or demonstrations, which all help to pass the dark nights of winter. There are also in the parish two branches of the Woman's Guild for those more interested in the church (old church 53, west church 25). The crowning glory of social life, however, in the landward parts is the 'Kirn' or harvest-home 'Social', generally held in the barn or granary of some steading. Not even the much favoured whist drive is considered equal to this form of entertainment, but of course 'Kirns' are seasonal functions depending on the goodwill of the farmers.

There are church socials, too, at rare intervals, probably better attended than the church itself.

RELIGION

The parish now has two churches, both within the burgh and both of the Church of Scotland denomination. The Old Church has 604 members on its roll and the West Church 141. The former church, which takes the form of a Cross, was built in the 17th century, and stands in the old churchyard which is now practically closed for burials. The other church was erected about 100 years ago and is of modern design and has no outstanding features. The Berwickshire countryman has little use for sentimental or emotional religion. As a rule, he does not take the 'kirk' as seriously as his predecessors. Indeed, his attitude to it is a kindly tolerance seeing that it is so intimately connected with birth, marriage and death. There are, of course, staunch supporters of the church, but if, in the two churches of the parish, the attendance on a Sunday is as much as 20 per cent of the membership, that is considered gratifying. The minister's visits too have ceased to be 'visitations', and there is an element of good-natured familiarity in some households when the minister makes a call.

EDUCATION

There are two schools in Lauder parish, one at Cleekhimin (one teacher and 14 pupils) where primary subjects only are taught, and a larger one in Lauder (three teachers and 81 pupils), now de-graded. Beyond the age of 12 the scholars go either to Earlston Junior Secondary School or to the Berwickshire High School at Duns. School meals are provided at Lauder and the Cleekhimin children are driven to Oxton in Channelkirk parish for their midday meal, an innovation now established throughout Scotland.

THE ROYAL BURGH OF LAUDER

The administrative duties are conducted by the town council consisting of the Provost, two bailies and six councillors, their meetings being held in the old Town House, which is at the head of a row of houses called the Mid-Row, the wide Market Place at this point dividing into two streets. The House or Hall is a little more than 300 years old, having replaced the old building which was destroyed. The council sit in the Town House, familiarly known as 'up the steps' above the old Tolbooth prison, now disused. This old Tolbooth is referred to in a recent publication as 'the queerest of queer erections'. About half of the population of Lauder Parish live in the Ancient and Royal Burgh, the only Royal Burgh in the county of Berwick. This little plain-looking town of some 650 inhabitants is the shop-keeping centre of the parish and beyond, in spite of the facilities for modern transport that takes many of its people to the bigger centres. It has good shops and three hotels and there is a guest house in the landward vicinity. The railway is now out of use except for certain goods traffic, so transport is entirely by road. Many summer visitors take advantage of the bracing air that blows over 100 miles of hills from the west or from the 30 miles across Lammermoor. The town itself is 600 feet above sea-level, and yet seems to lie in a hollow when viewed from heights in the vicinity. An attraction of former years was the golf-course on the Chester Hill, meantime not being used, but visitors can enjoy bowls and tennis if they feel inclined. The breezy heights of Lauder Common attract many hikers, whose numbers might increase if a suitable hostel were near at hand. The road through the town is always busy, as cars, wagons, lorries and caravans make for the south or north in large numbers. There is no industry except the minor ancillaries to the agricultural interest of the district, unless one counts a small darning branch from one of the Galashiels Mills, which employs girls and probably deters them from migrating.

The town's water comes from springs on the burgh lands, but it is hoped that a county scheme to be installed in the near future will give a larger and more reliable supply.

BURGH LANDS

The chief pride of the townsfolk is the fact that they have retained their burgh lands extending to over 1700 acres in spite of all encroachments and this fact is celebrated in the annual Riding of the Marches, when a circuit of ten miles is followed by enthusiastic horsemen, the Cornet bearing the burgh Standard 'Safe oot and safe in'. The Cornet is follows by a retinue of riders of both sexes, the number being usually over the 100 mark.

Inseparably involved through history with the tenure of the Burgh lands is the Burgess sytem which to this day remains intact. In connection with the system, Burgesses hold certain rights on the Common, by virtue of their ownership of small portions of land called Burgess Acres, after explained.

BURGESS ACRES

A Burgess Acre may be a holding of from one and a half to three imperial acres, and when a Burgess has inherited his 'ticket' — the ownership of an acre being an essential — he has the right to graze sheep on the Common under certain conditions. The number of sheep he grazes depends on the number of Burgesses exercising the right, and as this number is gradually decreasing, the size of each individual's share is inversely increasing.

As the land belongs to the Burgh, subject to the grazing rights of the Burgesses, the latter pay to the Town an annual cess or grass mail of so much per sheep and so much per cow or stirk.

The stock is managed by a Sheep-Stock Company composed of the Burgesses, but the Town Council levy and collect the grass mail, thereby increasing the Common Good. There is a shepherd in charge of the sheep stock, together with any cattle, and his house, about a mile from the town, is on the edge of the open grazing. When a Burgess dies with no heir or widow who can carry on his acre and rights, the acre is usually sold, and many of the acres are now held by non-burgess proprietors who, along with the actual Burgesses, usually employ contractors to cultivate their land. Any one having bought an Acre may apply to the Town Council to be entered as a Burgess on payment of a fixed sum which entitles him to the Burgess rights. A Burgess, to enjoy his full rights, must reside within the Burgh.

This system of land holding is of very ancient date, having been in existence before the Burgh received its Charter, the extant copy of which dates from 1502 in the reign of James IV.

1950–51

THE PARISH OF LAUDER

by Rev. Duncan J. McGregor

The parish of Lauder is the largest in the county of Berwickshire and it is believed that the town of Lauder gave its name to the parish, through which the River Leader flows. At its greatest length, the parish is ten and a half miles, and eight miles at its broadest. To the west it lies adjacent to Channelkirk, south-west to Stow, and to the south, the parishes of Melrose and Earlston; while to the east lies Legerwood and northwards, Westruther.

About two-thirds of the parish is coarse moorland and much of the area is hilly, though the valley of the Leader is fairly flat, being two miles wide at its broadest, that area constituting the best farmland. The total acreage is about 35,000 of which 164 acres are occupied by roads, both public and private, and 83 acres are under the water of the Leader and its tributaries. It is bounded in the north by the Lammermuir Hills and from many vantage points in the hilly parish may be seen the Eildon Hills to the south. The parish extends through Westruther to the hilly area of Blyth from which the road over Carter Bar can be clearly seen.

The population is centred on the former Royal and Ancient Town of Lauder which was granted a Royal Charter by William the Lion, and this was renewed in 1502 by King James IV, who frequently held court in the town. The ancient town, known in the 12th century as a 'Kirk Town', received several visits from royalty: Edward I of England came twice and his son, Edward II, rebuilt the old Lauder fort which had been destroyed by the English. It is on this site that the present Thirlestane Castle has been built. The ancient town was governed by a Provost and seven councillors elected annually from the Burgesses of the town. Since the re-organisation of Local Government in Scotland, the government of the area has been by the Ettrick and Lauderdale District Council.

The highest point in the area is Lammerlaw which is about 1500 feet above sea level, Lauder being about 600 feet and about 25 miles from Edinburgh to which many commute daily on the A68 over Soutra Hill. Other distances are: 17 miles to Kelso, seven to Earlston, five to Stow and 12 to Galashiels. While the parish boundaries were not altered by Local Government re-organisation, the District is now in the Parliamentary constituency of Selkirk and Roxburgh and it is under consideration by Presbytery of Melrose and Peebles to alter slightly the parochial boundaries.

At its greatest, the population of the district was 2198 at the 1861 census, and while the population has decreased mainly because of the mechanisation of farming methods, the town of Lauder has steadily increased in size as former city dwellers sought to live in a rural community in a healthy though variable climate, and there has been a programme of building of new houses on the west and eastern edges. The population is now around one thousand.

The difficulty of traversing the heights of Soutra Hill has been reduced in recent years by improvements in the surfaces and a straightening and widening of the road. Gates across the road on the eastern and western slopes of the hill are operated in times of adverse wintry weather to ensure that no traffic is stranded. A team of roadmen, based in Lauder, ensure that the road is open for emergency services most of the time, there being no Fire Station or ambulance service in the town. The nearest for these are the neighbouring towns of Dalkeith,

Plate 32. Near Preston in the 1950s.

Plate 33. St. Abbs Harbour.

in Midlothian, and Galashiels.

The area has many sites of antiquity, there being numerous prehistoric forts, notably Addinston Farm, Blyth Harefaulds with its fine outlook to the Merse and the Cheviot Hills, the Barrow Stones on the moor east of the parish and the hill forts to the north at Tollis Hill. There are traces of Roman occupation in the area; the old Roman road of Dere Street traverses the parish from Newsteads, near Melrose and the old fort of Trimontium to the South, and passes near Blainslie and Lauder on the way to Oxton and eventually to the Roman camp at Cramond near Edinburgh. Many arrowheads and flints have been unearthed in the cultivated fields.

To the north of the town lies Thirlestane Castle, built on a solid rock foundation on the banks of the River Leader and on the site of the former fort. The original Thirlestane Castle (now in ruins) was occupied by the Maitland family until the days of Chancellor Maitland (1537-1595), when they removed to the present Castle. The present owner is Captain, the Honorable Gerald Maitland Carew who inherited the estate which had been disentailed by an earlier generation. The present Lord Lauderdale is resident in London and is the Hereditary Standard Bearer of Scotland. An ancestor, John Maitland, Duke of Lauderdale, was a member of the notorious CABAL and was an antagonist of the covenanters, yet he showed gratitude when he was saved from lengthy imprisonment when Margaret Hardie, known as 'Midside Maggie', and wife of one of his tenants, farming at Tollis Hill, made the long journey to Windsor where the Earl had been held captive for nine years. She gained entrance to the prison and gave him a bannock which she had baked, inside of which were enough gold coins to secure his freedom. The silver watch chain which the Earl later gave to her is now on display in the Museum of Antiquities in Edinburgh. Maggie had her own debt to pay, for during hard times she had pled with the Earl that prolonged snow in the high lands prevented the farm from being prosperous and it did not yield enough to pay the rent. His reply was that she provide him with a snowball in June as one year's rent. The following winter she packed tightly snow in one of the gullies on the farm and in due time she brought the desired snowball to Thirlestane Castle. It was accepted as one year's rent.

In 1482, the Scottish nobles met in the old Lauder Kirk, then situated within the grounds of Thirlestane Castle, and plotted the destruction of three favourites of King James III. Their chief antagonist, Archibald Douglas, Earl of Angus, saying that he would 'Bell the Cat', together with others, led the unfortunate men to the then Lauder Bridge, from which they were hanged and the bodies quickly interred nearby.

In 1643, John, Lord Lauderdale, afterwards Duke of Lauderdale, was one of the Commissioners of the General Assembly of the Church of Scotland who met at the Assembly of Westminster and formulated the Confession of Faith together with the Sum of Saving Knowledge on which the Episcopalian and Presbyterian Churches' government in based.

The Rev. James Guthrie, a former minister of Lauder, had signed the Covenant and later, in 1661, was tried for high treason and executed. His last words on the scaffold at Stirling were: 'The Covenants, the Covenants shall yet be Scotland's reviving.' In 1745 Prince Charles lodged at Thirlestane Castle on his way to invade England, and in Lauder there still stands 'Cope's House' in which some of his men were billeted.

A memorial to the 12th Earl of Lauderdale who was killed by lightning at that spot is on the hill at Broadshawrigg.

Lauderdale, the name originating from the Celtic word Lade, meaning the passage or course of a river, and formerly spelled, Laweder, is situated in the highest part of Berwickshire and is predominantly a farming community, there being some 35 farms, the majority of which are owned by the farmer, fewer now being tenanted. In recent years, several have been sold, the majority of the new purchasers coming from south of the Border where the price of land is considerably higher. The agricultural lease now is mainly one to three years.

Farming practice has altered greatly in recent years, mechanisation having reduced the necessity of employing many farm workers, the former houses of whom are now rented to non-farm workers or as holiday homes to visitors. All these cottages have been modernised and many have been sold, thus releasing capital for further farm expenditure. The recently applied European Economic Community farming regulations have resulted in the growing of different crops, mainly barley, of which quite a portion is sold for malting and distilling purposes. The former method of rotational farming has largely been abandoned following the increased use of fertilisers and improved seeding. Fewer shepherds are employed, though many farmers still have flocks of sheep. The increase in cereal crops has reduced cattle breeding and feeding in a land where the soil is mixed, richer earth being found in the south and east.

About 10,000 acres are tilled, rotational grass accounts for 4,400 acres; 3,500 are permanently under grass and about 13,800 are rough grazing. The average rent for arable land is between £25 and £30 per acre and for rough grazing the rent is about five pounds an acre. Most farms of any size have their own combine harvester and horses are no longer used. Grain is dried by the farmers themselves, farm machinery being electrically driven and the tractors diesel engined. Cattle are fed mainly on silage or hay and sheep on turnips, which are no longer sold outwith the area. The chief white-crops are barley and in lesser proportions oats and wheat. The lambing season extends to April on the high ground, and black-faced sheep are sold mainly at the sales in Lanark and Peebles, store stock are bought and sold at St Boswells and fat stock at the markets in Edinburgh, Hawick and Wooler.

To the south of Lauder lies the former Burgess land which the local burgesses used for sheep grazing. When a burgess died and his widow did not continue to exercise the right, that portion was sold and in recent years the whole area has been occupied by the sheep owned by a small local syndicate. During World War Two, the Lauder Common was used by the army for tank manoeuvres.

In 1984 the Heritage Trust assumed the responsibilities of Thirlestane Castle, and while the family of Maitland Carew continue to reside therein, the Castle is open to the public during the summer months, a team of local volunteers acting as guides. The family still own land and rent farms to local farmers. The Castle contains a superb collection of furniture, china, paintings and children's toys. It is well known for its magnificent plaster ceilings. There is also a Borders Country Life Museum at the Castle.

The riparian owners of the River Leader rely on the local Lauderdale Angling Association to manage and stock the river with brown trout, this being done on a regular basis, and permits are available locally.

The local primary school has a head teacher and six teachers for the 130 pupils who live in the area, those from any distance being brought by a school bus service, and the children are given lunch on the premises. On reaching secondary school age, children go to Earlston High School and are taken by a school bus service. Behind the school are situated 22 houses in the Kirk Care Residence for elderly people, who come mainly from the area. This establishment, under the supervision of a warden, was opened in 1984.

Although there are many retired people in Lauder, especially in the council houses to the south and south-west of the town, there are also many young people with families, who have bought new houses on the west and south-west periphery. Prior to the change from assessed rents of houses to the Community Tax, the lower cost of housing in the area, together with a climate which though cold is healthy, encouraged many from the cities to settle here. Many commute to nearby towns and to Edinburgh. There is little or no unemployment in the area, though there are only two light industries in the parish. The large hen factory employs a few men and the factory making small animal models mainly for export gives work to many women, both in the factory and in the home. Many indeed have secondary or part-time occupations. There are three general stores of varying sizes, two joiner's businesses, three electricians, a baker's shop, a newsagent, and a post office. Three clothes shops, two garages, a greengrocer and two cafes, as well as three hotels and one public house, give employment and supply the needs of the community. In addition there are two travelling general store shops, one from the nearby village of Oxton. Blainslie has no shops. There is a bank and a solicitor's office.

Houses are heated by coal which is brought from Duns or Hawick, and by gas. The Lauder Gas Company was established in 1842 but ceased to exist when the town was connected to British Gas, now supplied from the North Sea. Local water works supply water and electricity is on two circuits within the town and is from the National Grid system brought from the Lothian area by high pylons. The sewage works lies to the east of the town.

The Town Hall is used for certain civic functions, particularly at the end of the Common Riding of the town, which is held on the first Saturday in August each year. A young man, born and brought up in the area, having been elected to be Lauder Cornet for the year, receives the Burgh Standard (a blue flag depicting the Virgin Mary with the child Jesus in her arms), from a local lady who exhorts him to ride: 'Safe oot, safe in!' The Cornet then bears the Standard round the town and then the hills to the south and a ceremony of toasts to the Cornet takes place at the Waterin' Stone, the southern boundary of Berwickshire and Midlothian and Roxburghshire on the road from Lauder to Stow. This annual repetition of an ancient tradition was restarted in 1912 and with the exception of the war years, has been maintained to this day. As many as 400 horses and riders follow the Cornet, men, women and children. Prizes are given for the youngest and oldest riders. A brief ceremony of Remembrance at the War Memorial in Lauder is held before the Cornet returns the Standard at the Town Hall for safe-keeping. The Common Riding marks the most important part in the life of Lauder in the year, notwithstanding there being some 38 other activities ranging from sport — golf, tennis, angling, rifle-shooting — to Young Farmers meetings, church-based activities and local uniformed organisations such as Scouts, Cubs, Guides and Brownies, none of whom are now church-based.

There is also a thriving pre-school-age group which meets in the Scout Hall, the hall of the former U.F. Church which closed in 1951. There is a public hall which is used for local functions and a recently extended church centre in the grounds of the church which is used for smaller meetings by the general public.

The West Church congregation having disbanded, the members joined the Old Parish Church, the present congregation numbering 485 with a number of members living outwith the parish. The original building was situated within the grounds of Thirlestane Castle, but an Act of Parliament in 1617 authorised its removal to a new site in the town. The present building dates from 1673 and was designed by Sir William Bruce, then employed by the Duke of Lauderdale to enlarge the Castle. Many of the stones and timbers of the former building were used in its construction, which is in the form of a Greek Cross. It was further extended about 1790 and the present vestibules added in 1820. There is a central octagonal tower inside which is suspended the ancient bell which was cast in 1681 and recast in 1751 and 1834, timber to support it being taken from the former Lauder bridge. The church was renovated in 1973 and retains the old box pews and the four lofts over the north, south, east and west transepts. The church, which is unique in its architecture in Scotland, is open at all times and a recent trend, favourable to members and non-members alike, is to conduct funerals and marriages in the church. It can accommodate 850 people, considerably more than the present number of the Communion Roll. Through the years, church membership has ceased to be a priority; 200 years ago the members were described as 'not greedy for the Kirk', and this attitude, typical through the land, obtains to this day. Hope springs eternal, for there is a well-organised and supported Sunday School and the recently rejuvenated bible class and youth group make full use of the church centre. Some 90 members have died in the past seven years; most interments are in the cemetery which lies about a mile to the south, there being no interments now in the churchyard. The manse and glebe were sold in 1981 and a modern manse built on the west side of the town.

The older members of the community are catered for by several clubs, one of which organises a summer outing, the other being run by the enthusiastic Women's Voluntary Service. There is a well supported Women's Rural Institute, the Woman's Guild consists of about 30 members and there is a church-based Young Woman's Group. Meals on wheels are provided for the elderly and housebound, and such is the friendliness of the populace, no one in the older age group is unvisited by neighbours and friends. The small village of Blainslie also possesses a community spirit which is fostered by use of the local hall by young and old, for social and recreational activities.

Medical care is provided by a general practice based on the New Medical Centre, a former hotel, and those in need of greater care are referred to the Borders General Hospital at Melrose, or to one of the Edinburgh hospitals. Enthusiastic fund raising by residents has ensured that additional medical equipment could be purchased both for the medical centre and for the hospital.

The Registrar for Births, Marriages and Deaths operates from Melrose during the week and on Monday mornings in the church centre in Lauder. The local police station is open during office hours, and the Lothians and Borders Police force is centred in Galashiels and provides mobile cover of the area.

The A86 trunk road from Edinburgh to Jedburgh bisects the town from west to east, and has been widened and straightened through the parish in recent years in order to promote safety, though it also encourages excessive speed in places. The long mooted Lauder by-pass to the north of the town between it and Thirlestane Castle has not yet reached planning stage and traffic must still traverse the town. The original roads encircled the High Street, there being formerly a toll house at the eastern end. The old road known as 'Rue de Roi' (the road of the King) and now the Row, led from the west end and bounded the town on the north side between the gardens of the houses and the high wall of the Castle. This road, like the one on the other side of the town, was used in times of plague in the town, and is the route followed by the Cornet on his annual ride round the Marches. The central part of the town retains its medieval antiquity, with the Mid Row being the central area at the end of which, on the west side, stands the Tolbooth, formerly used as a gaol with courthouse above.

Private transport has assisted locals to travel easily to Galashiels, to which a number commute daily for employment and for social and recreational activities not provided in the town. The public library has long been closed but the Regional travelling library van makes weekly visits to the town. There are many social events, held mainly in the public hall, and the Lauder people are noted for their generosity when subscribing to 'good causes' within and outwith the town. The bus service from Kelso to Edinburgh passes through Lauder at regular intervals daily, but for evening visits to outlying areas, private transport must be used. Many offer 'lifts' to friends and neighbours to ensure that no one is ever isolated or lonely. The friendship which abounds in the locality means that there is a great deal of caring, especially for the elderly and housebound, a factor less evident in larger communities.

The Ettrick and Lauderdale Community Council is also very active in its work in the area. The Lauder Horticultural Society holds its annual show in August and is well supported, revealing the talents of local gardeners.

The programme of new houses being built on the west and south sides has now ended, no more being planned until the mid-nineties. Thus the population should remain fairly static, while Oxton and Blainslie will increase in size.

1989

THE PARISH OF LEGERWOOD

by R. Scott Aiton, Farmer in Legerwood and
Rev. J. Mercer Hunter, D.D.

THE PHYSICAL BASIS

The Parish of Legerwood lies in the extreme western district (or Lammermoor, as opposed to the Merse district) of the County of Berwick in the Presbytery of Melrose and the Synod of Merse and Teviotdale.

The boundaries of the parish remain exactly as they were fixed as far back as our oldest records go, and this is perhaps indicative of the quiet and peace which have prevailed for so many centuries in this lovely rural parish.

The boundary line is irregular and an idea of the area of the parish may be conveyed by stating that it is roughly four and a half miles wide from east to west and five miles from north to south. The greater part of the parish lies high and the whole area can be described as hilly or rolling, with heights up to 1200 feet at Boon Hill and 920 feet at Legerwood Hill.

The parish with certain excepted areas noted hereafter may be described geologically as of the New Red Sandstone, which, while not putting it in the top class as arable land, makes it eminently suitable for the raising of livestock. The exceptions referred to above are that the northern part of the parish shows exhibits of Greywacke filled in with clay, which reappears in the southern part of the parish in a modified or 'shivered' form much more granular than in the extreme north end. Again, a formation called Moorband (clay with imbedded stones indurated by iron) is found in several areas throughout the parish. Peat, reputed to be of great depth and excellent quality, is present but nowhere is it worked.

The cold and moisture in this district are considerably greater than in the Merse owing to the elevation of the land and want of shelter. The frosts in winter are often intense and the falls of snow usually lie longer on the ground. The crops in autumn are generally later by a week, and often more, than in the lower part of the county. There is nevertheless some factor that makes the parish most health-giving to its inhabitants, and it is well known that sheep and cattle bred in this parish have the reputation of being good 'shifters' to any other district.

HISTORY OF THE LOCAL COMMUNITY

The places names are all, or nearly all, purely Anglo-Saxon. 'Legerwood' means the hollow part of the wood (as it would certainly be when the whole area was covered in woods and scrub).

The name itself appears in a variety of forms in 13th century documents — Legerdwod, Legardwod, Lygardwod, Ligardwod, Lygadwod. In Dr Gordon's *Ecclesiastical Chronicles of Scotland*, there is mention of 'Orm, priest of Ledgareswade' who witnessed the signing of important documents in the year 1127. Among older people today the pronunciation 'Ligertwood' is often heard, and the generous donor who in 1898 made possible the restoration of the Norman chancel bears the name 'W. Van Vleck Lidgerwood'. It is said that there was formerly a loch of considerable extent on the lands of Corsbie, and that it surrounded a small wooded mount on which the ruins of an ancient tower form a most picturesque feature today. The Loch or Mere extended right down through Legerwood farm and Birkenside to the River Leader. The first field it passes through on Legerwood farm is called 'Geesepool' which explains itself. The attempt by some historians to call it the Gospel field owing to its proximity to the church, would seem to be ill-founded. It was on the rising ground above this loch or marsh that the Ancient Britons lived in their 'Barrows', maintaining themselves by shooting and fishing. Many a fine flint arrow-head or 'knife' has been picked up in the fields upturned by the ploughs or harrows, and to those interested in this lore there is to be seen a most representative collection of flints in the home of Mr Wm. Readman at Earlston. Those ancient Britons were far travelled, as many of the flints picked up have been identified as having come from the County of Durham, probably in exchange for skins and gut strings of wild animals. A most magnificent axe head was found about 50 years ago in the Herneyleas field on Legerwood farm, and can now be seen in the Scottish Museum of Antiquities in Edinburgh.

To proceed one cannot do better than quote from the Second Statistical Account, beginning 'Historical Notices'.

> The whole land in the parish, or at least Birkenside, Whitslaid, Legerwood, and the Morristons, belonged before the 12th century to the family of Stewart. About the year 1160, Malcolm IV granted to his Stewart, Walter, the son of Alan, Birchensyde and Legerdeswode, as they had been held by his grandfather, David, in his demesne. Walter, his grandson, and the third Stewart, gave the lands of Birchensyde in marriage with his daughter Euphemia to Patrick who succeeded as the Earl of Dunbar in 1232; and Robert the Stewart, who succeeded to the Throne, granted to Alan de Lauder, his tenant of Whitslaid, many memorial rights in Birchensyde, Legerdswode and Morristown, a grant which was confirmed by King Robert II on 13th June 1371.

The family of Lauder were still in possession of Whitslaid in 1635. It afterwards belonged to the Montgomeries of Mackbiehill*; and, along with Birkenside, came by purchase into the possession of Mr Innes of Stow. Morriston and Legerwood were, in 1635, in the possession of the ancient family of Ker who still hold it. The barony of Corsbie appears at an early period to have belonged to the Cranstouns of Oxenford, and in 1635 it was still in their possession. Dods afterwards passed to the Hays of Mordington, and then came by purchase to the family of Spottiswoode. The rest of the barony, comprehending the farms of Boon and Corsbie, belongs to the Most Noble the Marquis of Tweeddale.

East Morriston in 1635 belonged to Francis and John Wilkison. It was afterwards the property of Mr Peter of Chapel, and was purchased by the last Thomas Scott, Esq.

A part of Birkenside, which in 1635 belonged to Robert Hart of St John's Chapel, advocate, became in 1689 the property of Wm. Shillinglaws, elder and younger, of the elder in liferent; and is now in the possession of Colonel Wm. Shillinglaw, their lineal descendant. It is the opinion of Colonel Shillinglaw that his ancestor, whose entrance to the parish seems to have been connected with Mr Calderwood's return, and who was an elder and keeper for some time of the Session records, assumed the name of Shillinglaw in consequence of transactions in which he had been engaged during the previous troubles; and that his real name was the ancient, and in this quarter honourable, name of Ker.

Since the above was written each one of these farms has changed ownership, and six out of the nine farms now remaining are farmed by their owners. This somewhat bald statement constitutes the most momentous change that has taken place in this parish during the past 100 years. The changes in agricultural methods will be dealt with later.

ANTIQUITIES

Of the three ancient towers which are mentioned in the former Statistical Account, two only, those at Corsbie and Whitslaid, are now standing. The tower of Morriston has been pulled down, and has been nearly altogether removed in the course of agricultural improvements. Neither of the towers still standing bears any date or inscription; but they are supposed to have been erected in the reign of James II. The traces of two British camps, one on the top of Legerwood Hill, are still discernible but they have been much defaced by the plough; and on the farm of Boon, in the barony of Corsbie, there is a stone which is called the 'Dodds Corse Stone'. It is a shaft of sandstone sunk into a square block of the same material, and is said to have been the place where a market was at one time held for the vicinity.

* There is a tomb-stone in the churchyard to the memory of Wm. Montgomery of Mackbiehill, who died at Whitslaid in 1689, which was repaired by his grandson, the Rt. Hon. James Montgomery, Lord Chief Baron of the Exchequer, in 1798.

POPULATION

The population of the parish in 1801 was 495; 1851, 587; 1861, 599 (maximum ever recorded); 1901, 431; 1911, 401; 1921, 379; 1931, 332. The Register of Electors at qualifying date, 10th June 1949, contained 180 names. The number of births in the year 1949 was three, of marriages four, of deaths four.

ECCLESIASTICAL

The church is conveniently situated and kept in good order under the new conditions brought about by the Church of Scotland Act 1925. The date of its erection is unknown, but its outer walls bear record that it was 'repaired in 1717' and again in 1804.

The seating accommodation is ample. There are no seat rents, the pews being allocated to the various farmers and their employees. There is no other place of worship in the parish.

In the year 1898 the old Norman chancel adjoining the building used as the parish church, which had been used as a vault for many years, was restored and once more made a part of the House of God. By this restoration a beautiful Norman arch was revealed with a 'lepers' squint' and three ancient 'slit' windows.

The number of communicants in the year 1949 was 131, representing 40 per cent of the total population and over 73 per cent of the Electoral Register. The Kirk Session records reveal that the percentage of communicants to the total population was in 1838, 14, and in 1874, 30.

The manse was built in 1750 and enlarged in 1812. A further addition was made in 1928 and there are now three public rooms with seven bedrooms with the usual offices and outbuildings.

In the year 1911 an excellent church hall was built on the glebe by public subscription and is used for church and recreational purposes. The glebe is let to the neighbouring farmer at a yearly rental of £25. It is well fenced and drained.

The teind stipend, now standardised, amounts to £361. In the year 1627 the parish minister has this note:

> The Kirk of Legerwood is one of the kirkis of Paislay, the patronage thereof is now in the hands of Alexander Cranstoun of Rummiltounlaw; the present provision thereof is three chalders of aitt meal, and the vicarage, quilk extendis to twa hundredth merkis; the teindis of the said paroche, as according to the stent of the Abbay of Paislay, fyfteen chalders of victuall, quhauof the minister has three chalders. There is husband land parteining to the parsonage fued with guidman of Rummiltounlaw be the Abbot of Paislay whereof the minister has four akeris.

An augmentation was granted in 1635 by mutual agreement. The heritors were: John Cranstoun, titular of the teinds; John Cranstoun of

Corsbie; Andrew Ker of West Morristoun; Robert Hart of St John's Chapel, advocate, heritor of nine husbands land of Birkenside; Gilbert Lauder, heritable proprietor of Whitslaid and Bridgehaugh; John Brown of Kirkhill.

The total Christian liberality of the members of the church averages about £200. There are two or three small bequests which bring in a sum annually spent on the upkeep of certain specified lairs in the churchyard. One of the bequests allows use of any surplus for parochial purposes.

There was apparently a hospice with a leper colony in the parish in the Middle Ages, and there is a well on the farm of West Morriston still known as the Leper's Well. The well and the 'lepers' squint' in the church attract interested visitors.

INDUSTRY

Agriculture being the only industry in this parish, it is important that it should be dealt with in some detail.

Previous accounts have shown that around 1750 there were 17 farms in the parish and the farmers were almost exclusively graziers and shepherds, growing only patches of 'bread corn' for their own sustenance. This resulted in a serious scarcity of winter food for cattle and they had little with which to stem the pangs of hunger other than some brackens and bog hay. Springtime was frequently referred to as 'lifting time' when the poor, half starved animals had often to be lifted out of the miserable building or hovels in which they had spent the winter. The advent of the turnip crop changed all that, and not only led to the adoption of a rotation of crops which persists to this day, but also enabled the farmers to grow grain for sale and have a sufficiency of winter keep for both sheep and cattle. Towards the end of the eighteenth century there was a general want of enclosures in the parish. Those in existence chiefly consisted of turf dykes. Later on hedges were planted and wooden fences put up wherever required, but, alas, they are fast disappearing, the former owing to the lack of labourers to attend to them and the latter because of the great increase in the numbers of cattle which pay little respect to a wooden fence. Wire fences are everywhere to be found, usually with a barb on top. The electric fence, although not in general use, is thought by some to have 'possibilities'.

The most outstanding development of the last 100 years is undoubtedly to be found in the greatly improved pastures. They have not only vastly increased the stock-carrying capacity of the farms, but the discovery of wild white clover has so improved the humus content of the soil that the weight of the grain crops often becomes a sore embarrassment to farmers and farm workers alike. This stored-up fertility has stood the farmers, and the nation, in good stead during the past war.

To pass to more recent times, the last 25 years have seen spectacular strides made in the mechanisation of farm work. The arrival in the parish of some 26 tractors has caused the almost total disappearance of work horses. What horses are kept are used almost entirely for carting. What a different story from that of 25 years ago, when one farm alone could turn out 12 pairs of horses ready for the plough!

All other branches of farming have been mechanised more or less, except that much of the drudgery pertaining to the turnip crop is still with us. The corn harvest has probably been more mechanised than any other section of farming. The power driven binder, the combine harvester and pick-up baler, along with the threshing mill, which can be taken to any field where wanted, have all helped in the handling of great acreages of grain. All this mechanisation has enabled the farmers to carry on the cultivation of the arable land and the harvesting of the crops grown thereon despite a much reduced agricultural population. A careful study of the first two Statistical Accounts brings out the interesting fact that the 2,000 acres of grain grown in the parish during the peak years of the war does not exceed the common acreage under grain of 100 years ago by more than about 20 per cent. So much for the vaunted mechanisation of our farms with its enormous initial cost and subsequent charges for maintenance and replacement! It must be emphasised, however, that without it we could not attempt the cropping targets now asked for, owing to the heavy fall in our population, and, further, the yield of grain and straw per acre is now probably double what it used to be.

To turn now to stock farming, there are in the parish some 4,600 breeding ewes, all of the half bred and Cheviot type, the former being crossed with one of the Down breeds and the latter with Border Leicester rams.

A change in the method of handling cattle is that a herd of cows is kept by most farmers. These cows are kept for rearing beef calves, and are crossed for the most part with an Aberdeen Angus bull. They produce calves of the very finest type, which are either sold at St Boswells at the October sale or kept on to be sold fat off the grass at two and a half years old. One farm, East Morriston, carries a herd of dairy cows kept on the 'court' system, the first of its kind in the parish. This system is particularly useful in saving the building of new byres, where a switch over from beef to dairying is desired. The winter food required to maintain this great head of sheep and cattle remains substantially the same as for many years past, except that there is much less artificial feeding stuff now available, and the making of silage, while making very slow progress in the parish, has been adopted with advantage in two instances. A very successful poultry business has been established at West Morriston farm, where the hatcheries and rearing departments are among the most up-to-date in the country. The last war brought many innovations to the parish, among those that affected farmers being compulsory cropping regulations, a Standstill Order for agricultural workers and the establishment of a camp at Corsbie, built originally to house a searchlight unit for spotting enemy aeroplanes. This camp was subsequently used for housing workers on the land. Through it passed at one time and another Italians, Germans, European Voluntary Workers, displaced persons, along with their various cross-breeds and inter-breeds. It has to be freely admitted that of all these the Germans turned out to be by far the most satisfactory workers. The war saw the formation of the Women's Land Army and the arrival of those girls in the parish, many of them to be introduced to a hard day's work for the first time in their lives, brought a cheery note to hearten us on our way. Many of them after a time of training proved themselves to be game and efficient workers, and it seems a pity that this year of 1950 has to see their disbandment. Other innovations that are worthy of note are the formation of a National Farmers' Union and a Farm Servants' Union. These were steps in the right direction and the two unions frequently hold joint meetings to iron out points of difference regarding hours of work, and so on.

During the two wars the parish sent out its full quota of men and women to the forces; some, alas, did not return.

During the Second World War the Home Guard and A.R.P. occupied much of the men's spare time, while the minister's spare rooms were packed with iron rations against a 'siege'.

To deal shortly with the social side of life in the parish, the formation of a local branch of the Scottish Women's Rural Institute has proved itself a great success. Their motto, 'For home and country', gives an indication of their objects. Meeting once a month or oftener, they spend the evenings in a multitude of activities, and in summer competitions are held throughout the district for the best rural exhibits. The women of this parish can hardly be excelled for their skill in baking.

In the musical world there is much talent among the people. A fiddle hangs on the wall of many a cottage, and there was for some time a very fine orchestra with headquarters at Kirkhill and Birkenside. The chief amusements in the evenings are dances and whist drives held in winter at the church hall, while the young men are keen on carpet bowls and football. There is not now such a thing as a public house in the parish. Can there be any connection between this statement and the fact that this is the first Statistical Account in which it can also be said that 'there are no poor in the parish'?

PUBLIC SERVICES

There is no doubt whatever that a supply of electricity available to all at reasonable rates would be the greatest boon that could be bestowed upon the parish. This, along with a public water supply where required, would be valued by all. Roads are excellent.

EDUCATION

There is still a parish school, the roll of which stands at present at 22. This is a great decrease from 98, the highest recorded roll. This decrease is, of course, not wholly due to the fall in population. Those who attend the parish school are of primary age. The Junior and Secondary pupils go either to Earlston (Junior) or Duns (Senior). And the increased facilities for transport have made it much more convenient for children from Whitslaid, Boon, Birkenside and Dods farms to attend the nearest accessible school.

Twelve of the children in the parish attend private schools — boarding or day. The local schoolmistress is Registrar and Clerk in Charge of the Churchyard.

TRANSPORT

Although local railway services have been much curtailed, the advent of the motor bus has brought a new feature into the life of our rural parish, and what buses there are, are made full use of, not only for shopping expeditions to Galashiels, Lauder and Earlston, but for summer tours to all parts of Scotland and the north of England.

SPORT

The farms afford excellent shooting and some are visited in winter by huge flocks of wild geese which feed on the corn stubbles and young clovers. The parish lies in the centre of the country hunted by the Lauderdale Foxhounds, and such is the enthusiasm for the chase that all work seems to come to a standstill whenever the cry of hounds is heard.

SUMMARY

To sum up, it would appear that owing to the lack of minerals, and perhaps to a slight extent to its isolation, nothing should in the foreseeable future disturb the successful pursuit of agriculture in this parish. The contributors of this account feel, however, that they must end on a note of regret that there appears to be no clearly defined road along which farm workers can travel towards setting up in farming for themselves. Neither is the soil nor the climate of this parish particularly well adapted to the intensive type of farming which must be followed if a small holding is to be successful. They think that the existence of some workable scheme, whereby highly skilled farm workers could be assisted in setting themselves up in small holdings or small farms in areas where conditions are favourable, would be a valuable incentive.

1950

THE PARISH OF LEGERWOOD

by J. Scott Aiton

PHYSICAL

The parish boundaries are unchanged and the only difference in the conformation of the farms is that Boon farm has now been split into two separate holdings. This increases the number of principal farms in the parish to ten. All these farms have been purchased by their occupiers from the landlords; although one or two have since been sold, on a lease-back basis, to Union Pension Funds or insurance companies. There are also two holdings of about 60 acres each and three large residential houses with adjacent fields. There are two blacksmith's shops in the parish but both smiths are well past retiring age. There is a thriving garden centre at Legerwood farm which specialises in rock plants.

The farms of the parish are now totally enclosed by wire fences or stone walls. The old turf and whin dykes of the eighteenth century have disappeared and can only be traced by the odd whin bush; a descendant of those planted artifically 300-400 years ago. Large areas of moorland on the farms of Corsbie, Dodds and Boon have been drained and sown with good grasses and clovers. It is up to future generations to ensure that they do not revert to useless grazing.

An interesting publication is Dr R. Shirra Gibb's 'A Farmer's Fifty Years in Lauderdale' (Oliver & Boyd, 1927). This describes his farming of Boon from 1872 to 1922.

POLITICAL

At the time of local government changes about ten years ago, Legerwood Parish came under the jurisdiction of Ettrick and Lauderdale District Council which is a part of the Borders Region.

In this year (1983) the political voting constituency is being changed: no longer will Berwickshire and East Lothian form a constituency. Ettrick and Lauderdale will join with Roxburgh District to send a member to Westminster.

POPULATION

There are now only 150 people residing in the parish of whom 26 are children of school age. This reflects the huge reduction in farm staffs since the 1939-45 war. Most of the children attend either Earlston or Lauder schools, depending upon where they live within the parish. They are transported to and from these schools by minibus. Six children are educated privately. Legerwood School has now been closed and sold as a private residence.

ECCLESIASTICAL

A shortage of ministers of the Church of Scotland and the fall in the population of the parish created the necessity, in 1964, of linking Legerwood and Westruther churches. In the process Legerwood was transferred from Melrose to Duns Presbytery. In 1971 there was a further linking of these two parishes with Gordon. The minister now resides at Gordon manse and a service is held at Legerwood once a month. Legerwood manse became a private residence in 1971. There are now 67 communicants on the Legerwood Roll and 11 adherents. The sacrament of Holy Communion is observed regularly twice a year. The church building was extensively restored in 1977 during the ministry of the Rev. R. M. Fraser, M.A. This work was aided by a grant from the Historic Buildings Council; the church, especially the chancel with its Norman arch, being widely recognised as an architectural gem.

The church hall unfortunately has not stood the test of time. It was built on ground which subsided and had to be demolished in the interests of safety in 1978.

AGRICULTURE

Mechanisation has accelerated since 1950 and there is neither a Clydesdale horse nor a binder left in the parish. Even the turnip crop has been successfully mechanised. It is now astonishing to think that it is only 40 years since the travelling mill was to be seen trundling round the parish: steam engine — mill — baler — caravan, all in a great unwieldy train; belching smoke and accompanied by much shouting of instructions and a good deal of swearing. The only binders and threshing-mills to be found now are in agricultural museums. Electricity reached the parish in 1952 and grain is now all handled in bulk with potatoes, seed etc. put onto pallets. The days of humping 16 stone of barley have gone; completely unmourned!

Cropping. Grain acreages are similar to 30 years ago but there is a much greater emphasis on barley as opposed to oats. Yields of barley have increased since 1950, it now being usual to harvest two tonnes per acre and occasionally nearer three. Feeding barley now sells at harvest time in excess of £100 per ton and oats at about £90. It is interesting to read in the 1795 account that oats were then fetching £7 per ton! The acreage of oats has been drastically reduced, there being only 50 acres grown in the parish. The barley yields have been increased by an improvement in available varieties and an increased use of fertilisers.

Plate 34. St. Abbs from the north, 1950s or 1960s.

Stocking. Stocking rates with regard to cattle are heavier than they were in both 1835 and 1950. Beef suckler cows, put usually to a continental bull, and beef calves, either bred or bought-in at the calf sales in October or, more usually, finished off the farm under two years old. Silage is the main winter fodder for these cattle. With regard to health it should here be mentioned that since 1950 two large and costly eradication schemes have been completed among British cattle herds. The first was the elimination of bovine tuberculosis, and this was followed by the eradication of brucellosis in cattle. These schemes, although very expensive to the agricultural industry, have greatly improved the human health of the nation. Ewe flocks are much the same in numbers as in 1950, but the Scotch half-bred has lost ground to the Greyfaced ewe on several of the farms.

Social. Motor-cars and television sets, which are now owned by virtually every household, have together brought an end to organised functions within the parish; with the notable exception of fund-raising activities, in aid of church or charity, chiefly organised by the ladies of the parish. There is no longer a Woman's Guild or a Scottish Women's Rural Institute. Social life consists of visiting friends or attending sporting events and functions throughout the Borderland. What the bicycle did in the 19th century has been continued by the general ownership of motor-cars and there is now no danger of sib-breeding among the rural population. Farm workers can now truly say that the world is their oyster, and with paid holidays to a total of five weeks per annum they can make good use of this freedom. All farm cottages are now fully modernised and almost every household has a deep-freeze. No longer do tradesmen's vans visit the parish; most of the household shopping is done once a week in supermarkets in local towns. Roads in the town have been reduced by the Local Authority, no less than four and a half miles having become 'de-classified,' and they have quickly degenerated to the condition of farm tracks.

The changes mentioned above have all occurred during the last 30 years. People can still be heard referring to the 'good old days', but there would be few volunteers to return to them. Crime within the parish is minimal, but burglary and vandalism from outwith the parish must increasingly be guarded against.

In spite of agricultural mechanisation the population is becoming more educated as to the beauty of the parish and conservation in general. Litter is a constant and increasing unsightliness.

The climate of Legerwood Parish has not improved one bit since the reports of 1795 and 1835; indeed the winter of 1981-82 was particularly severe; for all the first half of January the temperature was down to -27 degrees centigrade. However, in spite of the cold winters and wet summers this remains one of the most beautiful parishes in the land.

1983

THE PARISH OF LONGFORMACUS

by the Rev. John A. Nisbet

NAME

The origin of the name still remains obscure. Since Longformacus was first mentioned in a charter of 1140, many attempts have been made to explain this unique name. It first comes to light as 'Langford Macchus' — 'the long ford on the lands of Macchus,' and throughout the years other renderings have been 'Longfordmakehous' (1384), 'Lochirmackehous' and 'Lochirmakehous' (1395), 'Lochirmacus' (1505), 'Lochrymacus' and 'Lockermaccus'. The present spelling appears to have been used since 1556, although Sir Walter Scott, in his novel 'The Heart of Midlothian' (1818), makes Jeanie Deans speak of 'Lockermachus in Lammermuir'. One interesting spelling not noted in either of the previous Statistical Accounts is that in the inscription on the two communion cups, which reads, 'Given by Sir Robert Sinclair of Lamformacus to the Kirk thereof 1674'. Others try to connect the name with 'Llan' or church as in so many Welsh names. Probably the first explanation comes nearest to the truth regarding the derivation, because Macchus (who is mentioned in a charter of 1116) became a powerful landowner in the reign of David I, with large possessions also in Roxburghshire, and the river Dye before the bridge was built certainly would present a long and wide ford just below the church.

PARISH

The parish has an area of 21,000 acres and is bounded on the north by Garvald, Whittinghame and Cranshaws; on the west by Greenlaw, Westruther and Lauder. It consisted of nine estates as follows [1953]: I. Longformacus — owner Miss Helen Margaret Brown — comprising the farms of Muirton (Tenant - Walter Coltherd); The Mill (Albert Paterson); Caldra (Alexander Craik); Calside (J. H. Elliot Scott); Dronshiel (John Davies): II. Whitchester — Mr S. E. A. Landale — III. Horseupcleugh — Mr William Paterson Pate: IV. Redpath — Mr Andrew Pate: V. Kettleshiel — Mr Andrew D. Elliot: VI. Byrecleugh — Duke of Roxburghe: VII. Rawburn — Duke of Roxburghe (Tenant — John Elliot): VIII. Part of Stobswood (Langton Parish) — Mr William Grieve: IX. Rathburne — Mr Ronald Gore Graham. It is interesting to note that Blakerstone, once in Longformacus parish, now forms part of the parish of Abbey St Bathans; Rawburn was once in Cranshaws parish; Ellemford, Smiddyhill and Craig Winshiel (part of Harehead farm), once in Longformacus, are now in Cranshaws parish. The Teind Roll was declared final in 1943, and the total stipend of the united parishes of Longformacus and Ellem (these being joined in 1712) fixed at £304.16.3d. Stipend is paid on all the above-mentioned land with the exception of Rathburne.

The main geographical features have been commented on in previous Statistical Accounts and nothing falls to be added here.

Fauna and Flora. No unusual animals are found although there are a considerable number of foxes and a few deer have been seen. Interesting flora have already been mentioned in the New Statistical Account, and to these might be added cowberry (on Dirrington), upright vetch and the climbing fumitory. Various other native plants have been gradually disappearing, mainly for two reasons: (a) extensive hill drainage, and (b) the ploughing up of much land formerly in pasture, the 1939-45 war making this necessary.

HISTORY OF THE LOCAL COMMUNITY

In 1140 that part of the estate known as Dronshiel was under the ownership of the monks of Kelso Abbey (Longformacus itself was never church property), and it and the surrounding district were used only for the summer grazing of sheep and cattle. The earliest feudal overlords of the barony and township of Longformacus of whom any information is available were the Morthingtons of Morthington. (Mordington parish was joined to Longformacus parish for about 400 years and was disunited in 1667, when Longformacus was erected to ecclesiastical independence.) The Morthingtons were succeeded as superiors of the barony by, in turn, the Earls of Moray and the Earls of March. However, no accurate information is obtainable as to the actual owners and occupiers of the manor until Sir Gregory Sinclair, third son of Sir William Sinclair of Roslin, head of the influential St Clair family, is mentioned as owner of the lands of Longformacus about 1300. Fifteen generations of Sinclairs in direct line succeeded to the estates until 1764, when Sir Harry Sinclair, who had become fifth baronet, as a declared bankrupt, sold all his possessions. The estate was then purchased by a certain Thomas Raitt, who in 1784 was succeeded as owner by Rear-Admiral Rodham Home. In 1820 the estate passed to his son Major John Home Home. In 1848 he sold it to David Wardlaw Brown, who was succeeded in 1864 by his brother, F. S. Brown (d.1874), and the latter's son, Colonel A. M. Brown. The present owner is Miss Helen Margaret Brown, who came into possession of the estate in 1921.

Mention has been made in the previous Statistical Accounts of the 'Mutiny Stones' (the 'Long Cairn') on Byrecleugh. These are known locally as the 'Mitten-' or 'Mitten fu'-stanes,' from the old legend that the devil, out on some nefarious exploit with these huge stones as ammunition, dropped them from his mitten or glove when pursued by good spirits. No satisfactory explanation can be given as to how these stones came to be there, although it has been suggested that they might form the burial cairn of some chieftain.

It is of interest to note that there is the well-defined site of a British fort on the southern shoulder of Wrunklaw (Redpath farm) on the bank of the Dye about a mile below Horseupcleugh.

A list and description of ancient monuments and constructions in the parish is given in the *Report and Inventory of Monuments etc. in the County of Berwick*, pp. 129-132. Reference should also be made to the proceedings of the Society of Antiquaries of Scotland and to the Berwickshire Naturalists' Club.

As in most parishes, the main source of local history is the records of the Kirk Session, which in Longformacus go back to 1684. Those up to 1800 have been deposited in the strong-room of the Church of Scotland in Edinburgh. The records of Longformacus Free Church (later U.F.) are also preserved in the library of the General Assembly and include Kirk Session Minutes, 1848-1930, Deacons' Court Minutes, 1853-1941 and Account Books and Baptismal Registers, 1885-1889 and 1910-1922. Duns Presbytery records (from 1659) and United Presbyterian and Free Church records are preserved in the same repository. The old parochial registers in the custody of the Registrar General, New Register House, Edinburgh, include baptisms and marriages from 1654 and deaths from 1716. Other records, which provide valuable material for local history, are the Heritors' Records for the parish from 1777 and acreage livestock and produce returns, 1866-1911, preserved in the Scottish Record Office, H.M. General Register House, Edinburgh. What local endowments there were for education have been taken over by the County Council Education Committee. There is one bequest — the Murray-Fair — for the poor of the parish and under the control of the minister.

POPULATION

1801, 406; 1811, 444; 1821, 402; 1831, 425; 1841, 390; 1851, 411; 1861, 448; 1871, 452; 1881, 385; 1891, 378; 1901, 281 (after a boundary change); 1911, 263; 1921, 250; 1931, 259; 1951, 320. The population of the parish dropped from 425 in 1831 to 263 in 1911, and it has remained at about that figure. The latest figure is somewhat inflated due to the presence of a number of workmen, mostly Irish labourers, engaged on the reservoir scheme which will be dealt with later in the report. This decline is certainly due in the main to the mechanisation of the farms. The horse has disappeared almost entirely from the fields, and the tractor has taken its place. There used to be two very active blacksmith's shops in the village; now there is none, and the visiting blacksmith has ceased to make even his weekly call. The large families of previous generations are seldom found now among the land workers, 'out-by' shepherds' cottages are standing empty or in ruins, and fewer people are 'thirled' to the land. Some of these outlying houses have no access road, water supply or sanitation, although some farmers are doing their best to improve conditions by building new cottages or reconstructing old ones, and installing what modern conveniences the circumstances permit. This has had the effect of stemming somewhat the threatened depopulation of the parish, but still the call of the city is heard and obeyed by some and there have been three cases of emigration to Australia.

PUBLIC AND SOCIAL SERVICES

While it is true to say that during the past 100 years Scotland has seen great changes and improvements in the services to the public of water, sanitation, transport, gas and electricity supplies, it cannot be said that all these changes and improvements were experienced in Longformacus. The water supply is fairly adequate and the quality good, most of the houses being connected with the main supply. But Berwickshire as a whole is very badly off for water, many villages being without water except from taps or pumps in the streets. On 20th April 1949 the then Member of Parliament for Berwick and East Lothian, Mr J. J. Robertson, cut the first sod of a water scheme that will eventually supply the whole of the eastern half of the County of Berwick. This was estimated to cost three-quarters of a million pounds, but the figure is likely to be well over the million pounds mark. The reservoir is situated in the Watch valley on Rawburn farm. With regard to sanitation, this too is adequate, although some of the houses have their own septic tanks. Transport presented a different picture, however. It was not until 1946 that any public service vehicle connected Longformacus with the county town, Duns, seven miles away. Three buses in each direction on Tuesdays and Saturdays now cater for the population of the village and district. These are well patronised and satisfy a definite need. The facilities for power and light are as far off as ever and are likely to remain so for a long time to come. In spite of petitions to the appropriate electricity authorities, no hope of an early remedy of the present situation is held out and most of the houses are lit by paraffin lamps, although practically all the farmers and a few others have installed private generating plants. There is no likelihood whatsoever of gas being brought to the village owing to the great distance from the source of supply. Cylinder gas is used in many homes and proves a great boon, especially for cooking.

The road from Duns to Gifford (14 miles distant) passes through Longformacus, and is good though very hilly. This hill road to Gifford provides a quick route to Edinburgh, but, owing to its elevation (1422 feet at its highest point) presents many difficulties to travellers in winter months, when it is frequently blocked by snow-drifts for long periods. The road to Rawburn and the Watch Water Scheme and that connecting Longformacus to the Whitadder valley by Whitchester are also good. Some of the farm roads could be greatly improved.

There is no street lighting in the villages. An automatic telephone exchange, with which Cranshaws is connected, makes the village independent of the Duns exchange for local calls. There is a kiosk in the village, and the General Post Office has a sub-office for nearly all classes of Post Office business. The postal services are satisfactory, there being one delivery and one despatch each day, with the exception of Sunday. The outlying farms and cottages are served by a postman whose round on foot is approximately 14 miles.

One primary school is adequate for the number of children resident in the parish. (Some of the children from the Whitchester estate houses attend Cranshaws School.) It has one teacher for all ages from five to 11, and the pupils in attendance number from 20 to 30. From the local school they pass to the Berwickshire High School in Duns, which is now an omnibus secondary school for all grades of pupils. (The children are provided with an excellent mid-day meal at reasonable cost and this is proving of great benefit, especially to those who come long distances to school. Medical and dental examination and treatment are carried out at intervals.) There is no resident doctor, but as there are four in Duns, the village and district are well looked after medically. A small cottage hospital and a maternity hospital in Duns serve a wide area.

Some 20 years ago the resident policeman was withdrawn from Longformacus and now police patrol cars make contact with the village from time to time and when necessary.

For many years, probably 50, the parish was 'dry,' but in 1949 a seven-day licence was granted to a private hotel. This does not seem to have disturbed the amenities of the village to any great extent.

The County Library service brings books to both shop and school, and a fine selection is changed once in two or three months. This service is much appreciated by young and old alike.

Attempts have been made in several ways to help the young folk of the village and district. The first was by the formation of a Bible Class to cater for their spiritual needs. The second was by the organisation of a youth club, so that a greater interest might be stimulated in cultural activities. But after two years these had to be abandoned due to lack of interest among all sections of the community. There is now no youth organisation in the village. It was attempted to form a discussion group, but that too ceased to function after a short life. There are, however, two active women's organisations — the congregational branch of the Church of Scotland Woman's Guild (founded 1911), with an average membership of 30; and a branch of the Women's Rural Institute, with probably a similar membership. Many of the women are members of both organisations and quite a number come some considerable distance to attend the meetings, both of which are monthly.

There is an indoor carpet bowling club affiliated to the Berwickshire Carpet Bowling League, and although outdoor curling has ceased in the village, a local team — 'Lammermuir' — engages in competitions at the indoor rink in Edinburgh. This club has held the World Championship and several national and local trophies.

There are no cultural societies, nor is there any group for the advancement of knowledge. A flourishing horticultural society did exist at one time, but for some reason was disbanded many years ago. The same fate befell the local rifle club. An attempt is being made to keep alive the local angling association, as the rivers Dye and Watch still provide good sport, although considerable damage was done to the fishing beds in the floods of August 1948, which also damaged river banks. A few of the men are keen bee-keepers, claiming membership of the Berwickshire Bee-Keepers Association, and excellent honey is produced. The Berwickshire Naturalists' Club, too, draws members from the parish. A village improvements committee is in being, which looks after local interests and passes on suggestions to the Middle District Council of the County Council. An excellent and well-equipped hall, built and presented to the village in 1913 by the late Mr Andrew Smith of Whitchester, is used for all functions.

There is one church — the Church of Scotland — in the parish and most families are members. There are a few Episcopalians and no Roman Catholics, except perhaps an occasional Irish farm labourer. The present church is built on the site of one dedicated by Bishop David de Bernham of St Andrew's on 11th March 1243. In 1667 the choir was in ruins, and the church itself 'very ruinous'. It was rebuilt on the old foundations in 1730 with obvious use of much of the old materials, and thoroughly renovated in 1892. The sundial on the old west gable (the church in its present form being extended beyond the lines of the previous building), and the remains of the 'jougs,' are interesting relics of bygone days. In 1847 there was built in the village a church to serve the needs of those who 'came out' in the Disruption of 1843. For the 79 years of its existence, first in the Free Church of Scotland, and then in the United Free Church of Scotland, it ministered to faithful souls from a wide area and from other parishes. In 1926 it was closed by the then United Free Church Presbytery of Duns and united with the Church of Scotland — three years before the national union of these two branches of the Church in Scotland. It was subsequently purchased and presented to the united congregation as a hall, for which purpose it was used till 1951 when it was sold to a farmer and converted into an implement store. The prohibitive cost of necessary repairs and upkeep, and the added burden which this would entail to a small congregation, made this step inevitable. In any case, the village hall already mentioned is admirable for all church functions. Within the last decade the membership of the congregation has averaged 120, with a usual Sunday attendance of 35, and at communion 70. The Sunday School children number about 18, while at Whitchester a small Sunday School functioned for a short time in one of the houses.

It is difficult to gauge locally the relative numerical strength of the two major political parties — probably a fairly even division. For the purpose of County Council and District Council elections the parishes of Longformacus and Cranshaws are united.

HOUSING

In the years before 1938 the housing problem in Longformacus was quite acute, only one new house having been built since long before 1918 and that for the now no longer resident policeman. Most of the houses in the row forming the main part of the village were condemned. Some are now empty, but others, owing to lack of suitable accommodation, are still occupied. These in the main are of two or three rooms, with 'box' beds, no water laid on and no inside sanitation. A row of three houses was demolished in 1949. In 1938 the County Council built four houses (two blocks of two houses each), to re-house those from the condemned properties, and in 1950 another six (three blocks of two 'Orlit' houses), mainly for agricultural workers. In 1949-50 the contractors on the Watch Water scheme built five houses of a temporary nature to house some of their employees. Some of the existing houses in better condition have been renovated and modern appliances installed. There is now little overcrowding, due to smaller families and the new three/four apartment houses. Most of the gardens are small and manageable, and are well tended. The mansion house and two others are the only owner-occupied houses in the village, while there are only three other owner-occupied in the parish, in addition to three farmhouses. Three of the farms (Horseupcleugh, Rawburn and Redpath) have had or are having new cottages built for workers, principally shepherds. A house is being built in connection with the water scheme, to accommodate the man in charge of the filter-beds. It is difficult in a rural parish for the people to realise a sense of community, but, apart from the village and the estate houses at Whitchester, which are the two obvious groups, each individual farm is a small community on its own, and to a certain extent exists as such.

AGRICULTURE, INDUSTRIES AND COMMERCE[1]

The last two can be immediately discarded, for the parish is purely agricultural, there being no industrial or commercial undertaking of

[1] *See* end of this section for agricultural statistics as at 4th June 1953.

any kind from the days when the parish boasted four tailors, six weavers, three wrights, three smiths, three masons, and one cooper. All commodities from these trades can be supplied from Duns. The land is divided into (i) the low-lying area (below 400 feet) to the south of the parish; (ii) marginal (400-800 feet) — immediately surrounding the village; (iii) hill (over 800 feet) — the remainder of the parish to the north. Naturally, most of the area is under rough grazing, 77 per cent to be exact, leaving only 23 per cent for tillage and grass. Only 6 per cent of the land in the parish comes under the category of 'improved,' this low figure 'being due to the increased height, thin soils and harsh climatic conditions'. (The Land Utilisation Survey Report — Berwickshire, p. 43). Sheep comprise the largest class of livestock reared in the parish, although here again the figure is remarkably low — 90 per 100 acres, or less than one sheep to every acre of ground. All the well-known breeds are grazed, each appropriate to elevation. Cattle are also reared, mainly for beef, with a small percentage for the dairy, from which the local needs are supplied, but no particular breed takes pride of place. Milk is not collected by the Milk Marketing Board, but eggs are sent to the packing station. Crops as found on most farms are grown both for home consumption and marketing. The hilly conditions are suitable for oats and barley, but not for wheat, although a special wheat has been successfully grown on land at 1000-1100 feet on one farm (Whitchester). Potatoes and turnips are grown extensively, the latter entirely for local winter feeding. The threshing of the harvest presents no problems in the parish, as the travelling mill visits those farms that do not possess their own threshing machines. There are no combine harvesters. The principal markets and sales centres attended by the farmers are Duns, Reston, Berwick-on-Tweed, St Boswells, Kelso and Lanark. The parish is well wooded, so that excellent shelter is provided for the sheep, but many of the woods suffered spoliation (and one disappeared) during the war of 1939-45.

There is only a small general store to serve the immediate needs of the villagers, but vans visit the village every day from the larger shops in Duns. One exponent of the rapidly disappearing art of dry-stone dyking is in great demand from every quarter. The last of three generations of men skilled in building dry-stone dykes, he is one of the very few master dykers in Berwickshire.

Agricultural Statistics — 4th June 1953 (supplied by the Department of Agriculture for Scotland)

Crops (acres)	
Wheat	—
Barley	25
Oats	483
Potatoes	11
Turnips and Swedes	187

Sugar Beet	—
Rape	90
Other crops	40
Rye grass and other Rotation Grasses and clover for mowing	146
Ryegrass and other Rotation Grasses and Clover not for mowing	926
Total Arable Acreage	1908
Permanent Grass for mowing (hay)	107
Permanent Grass not for mowing	1329
Total Acreage Crops and Grass	3344
Rough Grazings	16,525
Livestock (numbers)	
Horses	31
Cows in milk and cows and heifers in calf — Dairy	68
Other Dairy Cattle	46
Cows in milk and cows and heifers in calf — Beef	206
Other Beef Cattle	354
Sheep and Lambs	20,512
Pigs	87
Poultry	1048
Labour (numbers)	
Regular Workers	39
Casual Workers	5
Classification of Holdings	
Acreage (Crops and Grass)	No.
1+ to 5	2
5+ to 15	2
15 + to 15	2
15+ to 30	2
30+ to 50	—
50+ to 75	1
75+ to 100	1
100+ to 150	—
150+ to 300	5
Over 300	3
Total	16
No. rented	9

WAY OF LIFE

Longformacus long enjoyed comparative isolation owing to transport difficulties, for while the farmers and a few others owned cars and vans, the bulk of the people was cut off from the busier centres by miles of hill and moorland. A saying current many years ago — 'Out of the world and into Longformacus' — expressed the separateness of the community. The people largely had to make their own amusements and entertainments, but with the advent of public transport the tendency has been to seek these in Duns and even further afield. While that statement is true, it must be remarked that, especially in the winter months, social events organised in the village are widely patronised. But something of the old spirit of the countryside seems to have died. One seldom encounters that sturdy independence, that quiet pride and satisfaction over a task well done. Whether it is due to centralisation, or the almost complete disappearance of power vested in local authorities, or a general unsettling due to conditions brought about by the war, it is difficult to say. Certainly there seems to be a lack of initiative and willingness to accept public responsibilities. That is not the final comment, however — it would be unjust to leave it there. The farms are well-managed, and the farmers and farm servants hard-working and industrious. The best is done to raise farming to its highest level of productivity.

In common with most parishes throughout Scotland, the church is no longer the centre of the community life; it has not its former influence over the people committed to its care. From the figures given previously, it will be surmised that the church in Longformacus has its core of loyal and faithful members, whose value to church and community cannot be estimated. But on the whole the people are apathetic to the claims of religion. The ministrations of the church are sought when something is required — a baptism, marriage or funeral, a paper to be signed or a testimonial to be given. Many attend at the half-yearly Communion services only and some not even then. The family pew, practically without exception, has disappeared, and there is nothing to take its place. There is little or no marked and open antagonism to the church — just apathy!

The question of delinquency, juvenile and otherwise, does not really trouble Longformacus and crime among the permanent residenters is unknown. Betting and gambling are not unknown, however, and football pool betting seems to be on the increase. Few cases of drunkenness are reported.

The hopes and prospects of the people for the future must be confined to improvements in the existing conditions, particularly housing, electricity supplies and communications, for it is obvious that no marked alteration in the industrial life of the community can be looked for and certainly no new enterprise started.

1953

THE PARISH OF LONGFORMACUS

by John Elliot, Farmer

In the 33 years between the report in 1953 and its amendment in 1986 the economy of the parish of Longformacus has been profoundly affected by changes common to most high and outlying districts of Scotland.

In the period some of the amenities such as buses, the village shop, grocer's vans and the local snow plough have disappeared. However, others such as mains electricity, street lighting and water from the Watch Water Reservoir have been introduced. The postal service is now entirely on wheels and provides transport to Duns on some weekdays. Most households have a car. The loss of the local roadmen has meant that roads are less tidy than formerly, however more powerful and efficient snow clearing machinery has improved winter road conditions.

Depopulation, both in the village and on the surrounding farms, continues, for the same reasons as elsewhere. One such reason is the increased mechanisation of agriculture. Much more grain has been grown than formerly and even, on occasion, cash crops such as oil-seed rape. Profitability of grain has been relatively short-lived, however, and farms are being increasingly laid down to pasture once again. Numbers of suckled cows have increased considerably over the past 30 years; however, as with grain, erosion of profitability of beef suggests that numbers of cows may drop. As considerable capital investment has taken place in erecting sheds for cattle the probable drop in the cattle population will not be to the levels of the pre- and immediate post-war period. Sheep farming, with a considerably reduced labour force, will remain the main agricultural enterprise in the parish. A feature of local farming over the past two decades has been the increased planting of shelter-belts and provision of fodder in event of snow storms. Despite the reduction in number of shepherds, these factors, coupled with improved winter transport, have greatly improved the welfare of local flocks. Due to closure of some of the local markets much of the farm produce is sold outwith the county.

Despite increases in efficiency of agriculture locally, much apprehension is currently felt by farmers about decreasing profitability due to factors beyond their control. These factors are considerably accentuated in areas such as Longformacus which are climatically disadvantaged.

The local school continues to employ one resident teacher who receives assistance on occasion. The 12 pupils currently on the school role aré conveyed to Duns for physical education and swimming classes.

The church is now united with those of Cranshaws and Abbey St Bathans under the name 'The Kirk of Lammermuir' and is linked (shares a minister) with the churches of Langton and Polwarth. While many of the community do not regularly attend church, numbers have not noticeably declined in recent years.

The Southern Upland Way enters the parish north of the Twinlaw Cairns and leaves it south of Whitchester. Many more ramblers and hill walkers enjoy the countryside than ever before and a tearoom, which offers bed and breakfast accommodation, has been opened. Country sports continue to be practised and the Watch Water Reservoir has been stocked with trout.

While depopulation over the past 30 years has had a big effect on the community* there are signs that the population has stabilised. Increased efficiency of transport and snow clearance mean that travelling to work is easier, and television has provided a link with the outside world in the long winter months. For those that are left, the physical barriers between the world and Longformacus are growing less.

1986

* (it declined from 320 in 1951 to 176 in 1981).

THE PARISH OF MERTOUN

by The Earl Haig

TOPOGRAPHY AND NATURAL HISTORY

Name, boundaries etc. In the immediate vicinity where the old village stood there is a piece of marshy ground. Perhaps from this both the village and parish may have been designated Mire-town or Mertoun. The parish is situated in the south-west corner of Berwickshire. It is bounded on the south and west by the river Tweed, on the north by Earlston, and on the east by Smailholm and Makerstoun. In length the parish may be about six miles and in breadth from two to three. On the 15th May 1891, part of Bankhead Farm in the parish of Mertoun was transferred to the parish of St Boswells.

Topographical Appearances etc. The western part of the parish stands high and is extremely picturesque. From Bemersyde Hill, the property of Earl Haig, over which one of the most public roads in the parish passes, the traveller has a magnificent view — to the west across the horse-shoe bend of the river Tweed and the Eildon hills beyond, to the north to the Lammermoors and the Gala Water hills, and to the south across the Merse to Big Cheviot beyond. The rest of the parish gradually declining to the south is extremely pleasant, with a prospect of excellent enclosures and thriving plantations. The soil towards the Tweed, particularly the haughs, is sharp with a gravelly bottom. Towards the north, and indeed through the rest of the parish, there is a stiff clay with a till bottom.

Looking towards the ancient Peel Tower of Sandyknowe, a relic of Border warfare days, built about 1535, at the same time as the Tower of Bemersyde, one sees the waters of Bemersyde moss, the haunt of wild duck and the nesting place of black-headed gulls.

The farm steadings, built mostly during the prosperous days of the 19th century, have been the subject of extensive modernisation and enlargement over the years since the end of the 1939-45 War. Such undertakings, encouraged by the availability of financial support in the form of Government grants, have had as their principal objectives the creation of conditions more amenable to livestock and less labour-demanding, as well as the provision of facilities for the storage and drying on the farm of the increased production of grain now entirely separated at harvest time by ever-larger combine-harvesters. Sadly the old festival of the visit of the travelling threshing mill lives only in the memory. The modern harvesting technique has removed from the landscape the old-time beauty of the carefully built and often decorated stacks of sheaves. The simple beauty of the stackyards and steadings of bygone days has by sheer necessity given way to the less romantic but much more purposeful modern buildings now accepted as a natural part of the countryside.

The rocks are all greenstone and other trap-rocks, except on the banks of the Tweed, where they are deposits of old red sandstone. Many of the local buildings are made from this stone, including Mertoun, Bemersyde and Dryburgh Houses.

CIVIL HISTORY

Old Buildings and Antiquities

Dryburgh Abbey, the oldest building in the parish and a reminder of a past civilisation, dating from the 12th century and before, attracts many visitors. Its beautiful grounds are maintained by the Department of the Environment. The Abbey was renovated soon after it was presented to the nation by the late Lord Glenconner. Sir Walter Scott and Field Marshal Earl Haig are buried in their family burial-grounds in the abbey, and many visitors from all over the world come to pay tribute to the memory of these two distinguished sons of Scotland. Each June the Border Area of the British Legion holds a service to remember the birth of the Field Marshal, who was the Founder of the Movement.

The original house of *Mertoun*, designed in 1703 by Sir William Bruce for Lord Polwarth, had a wing added to either end, one in 1830 in the time of Lord Polwarth and the other in 1912 in the time of Lord Ellesmere. Both these wings were taken down by Lord Ellesmere's son, then Earl of Ellesmere, later Duke of Sutherland, in 1954. Its present aspect reveals an early 18th century country house of extreme beauty. The house and estate passed from the hands of the Polwarths to the Ellesmeres in 1910. Mertoun houses a large part of the Bridgewater House Collection of paintings.

Bemersyde House had a new west wing added to it about 1860 at a time when the owners, the Misses Barbara, Mary and Sophia Haig, were living in Italy, and when the house was being lived in by a tenant, Lord Jerviswood. The Misses Haig died without heir and the house was left to Colonel Arthur Balfour Haig. After the First World War a group of donors purchased the house from Colonel Haig and gave it to his cousin, the Field-Marshal, as a mark of gratitude for services rendered during that war. 1400 acres of farming land round Bemersyde were purchased by the second Earl Haig in 1940 from his cousin, Mr Nigel Haig, grandson of Colonel Arthur Balfour Haig. The collection of the late Field-Marshal's uniforms and other possessions previously on view in the Peel Tower is now at Huntly House, Edinburgh, where it is visited by many thousands of people, including a large percentage of ex-service men and women. The west wing was redesigned in 1960 by the architect Ian Lindsay. The Peel Tower now provides studio space for the second Earl, who is a painter.

Landowners. The principal land-owners in the parish are the Duke of Sutherland, Laird of Mertoun, the Earl Haig of Bemersyde, Mr John Cormack of Dryburgh and Lord Portarlington of Gledswood.

Modern Buildings. A new village hall has been built at Clintmains for the public meetings of parishioners. A new feature at Bemersyde West End is the transformation of a barn and horse grinding mill into a fine dwelling-house designed by Multi-Professional Architectural Practice, Edinburgh.

POPULATION

The figures for Mertoun are as follows: 1801, 535; 1841, 722; 1851, 692; 1861, 729; 1891, 622; 1901, 576 (Alteration to boundary during intercensal period); 1911, 532; 1921, 463; 1931, 522; 1951, 459; 1961, 398; 1971, 366; 1981, 268.

There is to be seen a reduction in population during the last 100 years. During that time the number of farm workers has been reduced, partly due to the introduction of machinery. Many farm workers have departed for the towns. Other factors causing reduced population are (1) contracting of timber operations and fencing to firms outside the parish; (2) reduction of indoor and outdoor staffs of land-owners. A contributory cause of the decline in rural population is the centralising of secondary education in bigger centres where the child is introduced to an urban way of life. This creates a dissatisfaction which he resolves to the disadvantage of the rural way of life.

PUBLIC AND SOCIAL SERVICES

Water supply. The parish has been given supplies of water from Earnscleugh Reservoir in recent years.

Electricity. All farms in the parish have been supplied with electricity.

Rates. The old Parish Council used to fix the rates in the parish. The rates were 2s. 4d. in the pound up till about 1928. During this time the parish was run by its own parish Council. In 1928 the County Council took over the administration of the parish affairs. In more recent times responsibilities have been shared by the Regional and District authorities and by the Community Council which is a joint Mertoun/Maxton effort.

There are no local authority *sewage disposal* schemes. Cess-pools are the responsibility of the land-owners under the supervision of the district council.

Plate 35. Fishing boats at Burnmouth.

Roads. The improvements to roads may be listed under the following headings:

(i) The improvement of the St Boswells-Kelso road to a double lane modern surfaced highway through the parish of Mertoun.

(ii) The improvement of all other roads in the parish in respect of bituminous surfaces, pipe drainage and adequate margins. The old water-bound roads are replaced with proper metal ones. Most of the material for road maintenance comes from Craighouse Quarry. This quarry, originally operated by the County Council, was re-opened in 1938 by Messrs Kings & Co. Ltd. with a view to supplying road-making materials, but in point of fact, the bulk of the output has gone to building and defence works and very little to roads. The output of crushed stone over a period of ten years has amounted to over half a million tons. The stone is of the Ophitic Olivine Basalt class.

(iii) The mileage of roads extends to 16.7 miles.

(iv) The road at Scott's View has been widened and a parking place built.

(v) The amenity of the area has not been affected by the various road improvements, thanks to the landlords who are ensuring that roadside trees, walling and such features as contribute to the appearance of the landscape are properly maintained. Dutch Elm Disease has almost eliminated the species and caused serious gaps in old woodlands and hedgerows.

Education. The children of the parish receive their education at Earlston or St Boswells. Earlston School caters for all ages from primary to Scottish Certificate of Education O Grade, H Grade and Certificate of Sixth Year Studies.

Mertoun School was built towards the end of the 18th century. In 1885 an infant classroom, cloakroom and shelter shed were added to the original buildings, and the sanitary accommodation was improved. In 1929 the large classroom was divided by a folding partition. Later improvements, completed since the passing of the Education (Scotland) Act, 1946, included the conversion of the former infant room and cloakroom into a dining-room and scullery for the service of school meals, the introduction of central heating, electric lighting, the erection of new sanitary accommodation, cloakrooms and staff-room and the provision of bitumen-surfaced playground.

In latter years the number of pupils on the roll varied between eight and 55. The senior pupils were taught by the headmaster or headmistress, the infants and juniors by a lady assistant teacher. Finally small numbers reduced the requirement to a one-teacher establishment till it was given up in 1980. Whereas at the time of the last Statistical Account the curriculum included mathematics, Greek and Latin for the senior pupils, the subjects taught latterly were arithmetic, English, history, geography, art, handcraft, music, nature study, physical education and religious education.

For all pupils in the parish conveyance to and from school is provided by bus free of charge by the education authority.

Shortly before the final closing of the Mertoun School an excellent exhibition was organised within the school demonstrating in graphical and pictorial form the history and progression of this centre of education from its early years.

VOLUNTARY SERVICES AND RECREATIONAL ACTIVITIES

In the parish there is a recreational hall which is governed by a committee of those who use it. It fills a large place in the community life.

The Women's Rural Institute. This is a flourishing body founded by the late Lady Haig, and with a present membership of about 21 ladies, who meet on the first Tuesday in every month for activities calculated to help housewives in improving their skills as well as providing an opportunity for social intercourse.

Men's Club. This is a strong organisation with 40 members who meet twice a week for recreational purposes such as carpet bowling and darts.

Dramatics. Occasional performances by parishioners were given in aid of local funds in the school-house or parish hall.

Fishing. Excellent trout fishing in the river Tweed gives enjoyment to many parishioners. The salmon fishing in the parish administered by Mertoun, Dryburgh, Bemersyde and Gledswood Estates has altered considerably during the last 100 years. In the old days, few salmon were caught before the month of August. Later the river had a spring run instead of an autumn run. In the 1970s the river reverted to an autumn cycle. The average spring fish weighs approximately eight pounds, and the autumn fish approximately 15 pounds. Improved methods of angling and the price of a pound of salmon have increased the opposition to the fish. Sport has been adversely affected since the late 1960s by salmon disease and by sea and river poaching. The use of nylon nets by sea fishermen has been a major factor in the reduction of salmon stocks. Letting of fishing is now an important part of the economy of estates.

Gardening. Certain parishioners are members of the St Boswells Horticultural Society and contribute to the Annual Show. Professional gardeners from the parish have achieved much fame and success from competing at shows all over the country. Indeed one has gained the distinction of earning an entry in the 'Guinness Book of Records' for having grown a gladiolus to the height of 8 feet 4 inches.

Other sports. Pigeon racing has for a long time had a keen following in the parish and many important national successes have 'homed in' to this area.

Of recent years a great many of the parishioners have taken up the sport of curling which is enjoyed at the nearby Ice Rink at Kelso.

Although no rugby pitch exists in the parish, a number of players from the parish have achieved distinction in this game at national, district and club level.

ECCLESIASTICAL

The church, built in 1241 and dedicated to St Ninian, was in the Norman style, and was situated in the churchyard by the banks of the Tweed some 700 yards east of the present building, which was built in 1658, and reconstructed and extended in 1820. It has remained unchanged since the untimely death of the Rev. George Buchanan Smith. The parish became linked with Maxton about 1960 when the Rev. Alec Sawyer was the incumbent. Later in 1981 the parish church became linked with St Boswells.

Out of an adult population of approximately 200, 124 claim to belong to the church. Attendances at morning service average about 30 and 70 take communion at least twice a year.

The attitude to religion is respectful, if often neutral. Towards the minister there is still great goodwill and friendliness. At times of crisis in their lives the people are eager to avail themselves of the ministration of the church though many do but little to maintain and help it. Many factors have contributed to this.

The considerable improvement in the wages and standards of living of the agricultural worker has caused him suddenly to be plunged into the prevailing tides of materialistic humanism, which tend to make him blind to the claims of the spiritual and to become benevolently superior to the claims of religion, though, as ever, friendly and respectful towards the ministry.

Being better off, many farm workers now own motor-cars or motor-bicycles, and this leads them to travel about much more at weekends visiting friends and relations, making regular church attendance difficult.

Wireless and television are now found in practically every home.

In spite of these factors, however, although they have led to a decline in church attendance, religion is in a healthy state. Whereas it was fashionable to go to church in former years, today it is not, and only those who really want to go do so, and through them the influence of the church on the life of the community is maintained.

During the past hundred years there have been minor changes in religious ceremonial. Many of the drab, dismal trappings connected with funerals have disappeared and, while there is still as much respect for the dead, the emphasis would seem to be more on the hope of a future life than on the dead past. Marriages are now celebrated almost invariably in church. This is doubtless due in part to the improved standard of living and also, perhaps, to the number of marriage ceremonies which are portrayed on the cinema. The vast majority of people still seek baptism for their children — mainly in church.

Library. The parish of Mertoun is served through a travelling library from St Boswells.

HOUSING

There have been great strides in the housing position in the parish. Water and sanitation are general and all the cottages have electricity. Almost without exception bad houses have been either reconditioned or replaced. The landlords have been assisted in their improvements by grants for each house. In order to obtain a grant a cottage has to fulfil certain provisions defining minimum height of rooms, precautions against damp, adequate windows, etc. Most of this work began about 1914. The late Lord Ellesmere was responsible for much good work in the early days on Mertoun Estate. Previously, during Lord Polwarth's time as Laird, there was little money available and tenants were made to carry out improvements for themselves. There is no overcrowding today.

AGRICULTURE

Cattle and sheep. Apart from one herd of pedigree Aberdeen Angus and two small herds of Simmentals, the cattle population of the parish is geared to commercial beef production. Some farms run herds of breeding cows producing suckled calves either for sale or for ultimate finishing for the butcher. Others rely on buying in suckled calves or store animals for finishing. The genetical make-up of both the breeding stock and the store stock is very varied. Of the indigenous breeds the Hereford has probably the greatest representation; while imported breeds (mainly from the Continent and chiefly of the Charolais and Simmental breeds) are making an ever-increasing impact.

Nevertheless, the traditional Aberdeen-Angus still makes a significant contribution — especially to the make-up of the breeding females.

On the whole the ewes are half-breds (a Border Leicester — Cheviot Cross), which are crossed mainly with the Suffolk ram to give lambs of excellent fleshing quality.

Marketing of stock is made very easy owing to the nearness of St Boswells Auction Mart which, in the hands of Messrs John Swan & Sons Ltd., is becoming one of the chief marts in Scotland.

Great technological advances have been made in the farming industry and this parish has never been slow to adopt new methods to improve the efficiency and financial health of the farming systems.

Rapid strides in mechanisation have enabled new methods to be employed — resulting in the more timeous conduct of farming operations along with the need for fewer employees.

Crops. Developments in fertiliser production and usage together with the breeding of new and higher yielding crop varieties have been responsible for spectacular increases in crop yields.

Potatoes are fairly widely grown in the parish and this crop is generally both planted and harvested mechanically. The traditional 'potato lifting squads' are fast disappearing — with the loss of the welcome revenue of pocket money for the school children during the 'tattie holidays' in the autumn.

Cereal production is now chiefly of barley for malting or feeding. The wheat acreage is on a slight increase while the oat crop is virtually disappearing. A recent significant change has been towards the winter sowing of barley — thereby spreading the work-load of seeding in the spring and also because the earlier ripening of winter barley affords a quicker start to the harvest.

The decline in the acreage of turnips and swedes as the conservation of the grass crop has increased has been partially halted due to the almost complete mechanisation of this one-time high labour demanding root crop. Additionally the technique of chemical weed control and the precision sowing of the seeds for the root crops has further helped to re-establish the popularity of this excellent source of animal feed.

Grass conservation in the form of silage has now a firmly established place in the farming of the parish, although some farms still depend on hay-making as their principal source of winter fodder.

Although at all times subject to the vagaries of the weather — ofttimes too wet, occasionally too dry — the farming industry of the parish, with some help from government support, is on average in a healthy economic position.

Farm rents, which remained for a long period at unrealistically low levels, are now generally subject to review every five years and have recently been subject to very sharp increases.

Hedges. The arts of hedge-laying and stone-dyking are dying out, and hedges are often left to grow and then cut so that there is only a line of stubby trunks left. Mechanical hedge cutters are generally used. Wire fences, which provide no cover for game, are prevalent.

Trees. Landlords have been helped to plant young trees by government grants which cover the cost of rabbit-netting. Though myxomatosis has now practically extinguished the entire population to the great advantage of the whole countryside, the landlord has been put to heavy expense in the past century combating the ever-increasing hordes of rabbits. The killing of rabbits involved a small industry; but the dissolution of that industry has produced overwhelming advantages.

The following statement gives the main details of crops, stock, etc. for the parish of Mertoun according to the Agricultural Returns for the year 1981-82:

Total number of holdings over one acre	14
Holdings 50 acres or less	1

Holdings over 50 acres		13
Total area rented	1952.80 ha.	
Total area owner farmed	596.40 ha.	
Areas of crops	1261.50 ha.	
Areas of grass	2549.20 ha.	
Livestock:		
Sheep	8610	
Cattle	1157	
Pigs	211	
Poultry	92	

Labour: Exact figures not available, but the total must be approximately half the number of employees in the 1950s, which was then approximately 80 (so the farm labour force would probably now be about 40).

WAY OF LIFE

The people of Mertoun are on the whole contented and hard-working. This is due in part to the general well-being of the rural worker, but it is also due in no small measure to the fact that employers are understanding. In many cases employer and worker have grown up together, and there is a mutual trust and understanding which is lacking in the more depersonalising relationships of the big towns and industrial areas. The parish relies a good deal upon the stability of the big houses. The people of Mertoun live a life which is in touch with the life of the countryside, the life of nature, of seeds and growth, of harvests and times of fallow and of cold winter. The people of Mertoun, who during their work-time enjoy growing things from the soil, enjoy looking after their flocks and bringing new life into the world, can also be people who foster country pursuits during their leisure. They can be people who enjoy watching bird-life, or who enjoy spending extra hours cutting and laying a hedge, or growing things in the garden.

The local organisations are alive to the danger of losing country people into the towns, and these organisations are trying to foster life in the country. They act as a counter-weight which stops the drift back to the town, back to the cinemas and bingo halls and so on. The activities enjoyed in the village hall help greatly to promote social life and communal feeling amongst parishioners.

The countryman in the past has always been known for his sturdy independence. He has often been very slow, but his slowness has gone hand-in-hand with sureness and deep thinking. He has often thought things out for himself and has often refused to lose himself in the herd. So the countryman is a very great source of strength to the country as a whole, and in politics and everyday views he acts as a sort of balance. More important than anything else is that the country people should preserve a love for the soil of Great Britain, and with this love for Great

Britain there should go a love for a particular locality. A community which dwells in a place it loves is a happy community, and if we have enough happy communities in the world there is less danger of having another war. Mertoun parishioners live in a very specially beautiful country, amidst a very beautiful landscape. Those people who have the inclination and are happy to spend a large part of their lives in the country, living quietly and peacefully without distractions, are creators in a very true sense.

The only crime of any significance which has occurred during the past 100 years was on 5th September 1952, when a kitchen porter employed at Dryburgh Abbey Hotel assaulted an assistant chef by stabbing him with a carving knife. The accused later appeared at the High Court, Jedburgh, when the charge was found not proven. In addition, there have been a few minor cases of unruly boys damaging local property. There is no police station in the parish, which comes under the jurisdiction of Newtown St Boswells and St Boswells.

On the whole, the people of Mertoun Parish are going through a stage of transition. They have lost the primitiveness and the settled peace of the country peasant. They have been greatly affected by improved transport and by the introduction of buses and motor-cars. So far, happily, the parish has maintained its independence, and although many thousands of charabancs and motor-cars carrying tourists from all over the world pass through the parish every month during the summer, the settledness of the inhabitants themselves is maintained to a marked degree.

The hotel at Dryburgh Abbey opened in 1931 by the Scottish Motor Traction Co. Ltd., provides much seasonal employment. It is interesting to recall that Mr James Amos, the manager of the Scottish Motor Traction in Edinburgh, who founded the hotel, was the first man to drive a bus from Melrose to St Boswells.

1980s

THE PARISH OF MORDINGTON*

by The Rev. Andrew Martin

PHYSICAL BASIS AND FEATURES

These features of this largely moorland parish are fully set out in the two previous Statistical Accounts. The boundaries are the same, namely: 'It is bounded on the north by the parish of Ayton; on the east, by the German Ocean, and the liberties of the town of Berwick on Tweed; on the south, by the river Whitadder; and on the west by the parishes of Hutton and Foulden. Its form is irregular, somewhat resembling a sand-glass, or the letter g — on the narrow part of which stand the church and manse; the parish is there only the breadth of the glebe. Its length from north to south is between three and four miles; its greatest breadth, which is towards the northern extremity, is above two miles.' Other features remain substantially the same. Nevertheless, there are two notable exceptions. The first is the running of the double railway line, the main line between Newcastle and Edinburgh, which runs through the whole northern boundary of the parish skirting the sea, constructed and opened in 1865. The other is the improvement of the Great North Road running between England and Scotland, making it suitable for the ever growing motor traffic. Otherwise the parish is still as described from this point of view in the two previous Accounts. The railway line suffered badly by the flood of 12th August 1948, when many bridges and culverts were destroyed. This damage has been completely and splendidly restored. Many burns and streams altered their courses, and these too have been made right. Stretches of woodlands and many trees have been cut down, and are in course of being replanted. Owing to the necessities of the Second World War, considerable stretches of moorland have been reclaimed and now produce arable root crops.

HISTORY

Many advances and changes have taken place especially in the last 40 years. These concern land tenure, agriculture, education, social habits and ways of living. All of these are now on an immeasurably higher standard. The only small village within the bounds is part of the fishing village of Ross (population 18) nestling at the foot of the rocky coast on

* *See* also Foulden

the edge of the sea, at an extreme northern end of the parish. It is situated in the ancient parish of Lamberton incorporated into the parish of Mordington in 1650. Several new houses of the county council type have been erected in recent years. The interesting little hamlet known as the Clappers (population 20) is situated inland at the extreme other end. A fairly modern school and schoolhouse is situated here, but owing to the centralisation policy of the County Education Authority was closed five years ago and its pupils transferred to Foulden school. The buildings are now used as a parish hall.

Clappers. This quaint name is attributed to James VI who, when about to revisit Scotland, was asked which road he wished to go by, and replied 'by the Clappers', referring to a previous journey when the people all came out and clapped their hands as he passed through.

ANTIQUITIES

The ancient toll house of Lamberton on the Great North Road, where marriages used to take place, is now a ruin. A portion of the Lamberton Tomb (the Campbell-Renton family) on the site of the ancient chapel of Kirk of Lamberton still remains. The witches' knowe can still be pointed out. The Mordington-Aisle with the name 'Lord Mordington' carved out on the arch, situated in the field in front of Mordington House, can still be seen. Of the famous Edrington Castle or Fortress on the northern bank of the Whitadder scarcely a trace remains. *See* the *Report on the County of Berwick* (1915) of the Royal Commission on the Ancient Monuments . . . of Scotland, pp. 152-5.

POPULATION

The population of this parish seems to be on the downward grade. One hundred years ago it stood at 427. In 1931 it was numbered at 319, and in 1951 at 247. This decline has taken place in spite of the fact that the land has been divided up into small holdings. This is to be regretted. The advent of the motor car has opened up this sparsely populated parish. There are few families who have had two or three generations within its bounds.

TRANSPORT AND RURAL ACTIVITIES

The excellent bus services now in force serve this parish well. The main route along the Great North Road between Berwick and Edinburgh has an almost hourly service; the Berwick-Duns service goes inland and just touches the bounds at the Starch-house. These services have made the district easily accessible, and have had an immense influence on the social life and activities of the inhabitants. Most rural activities are represented in the parish: the Women's Rural Institute (membership 50), the Woman's Guild of the Church of Scotland and the Young Farmers' Club, both joined with Foulden, and several Sports Clubs, such as football, tennis, darts and carpet bowls. There is now a constant intercourse and interplay with similar activities and clubs in other communities. Social life has been tremendously widened and travel made easy as well as possible.

AGRICULTURE

It is in this that a very big and notable change is to be observed. It was in this parish that probably the first large scale colony of small holdings was established. In 1920-22 the Scottish Department of Agriculture took over almost all the arable and moorlands from the Laird of Mordington and Lamberton, the late Mr R. C. Campbell-Renton (1867-1948). The farms were subdivided into holdings and suitable houses and steadings were built. In the Mordington area of the parish these numbered 14, in the Lamberton area, 26. They vary in acreage. During the Second World War much of the moorland was reclaimed and much grass ploughed up. Arable and roots took the place of sheep and cattle. Sugar beet, the one new root crop of the last century, became extensively grown.

Work is going on in connection with the supply of electricity and it is expected that it will be available next winter, 1951. The one main road through the parish is good. Water, especially at certain seasons of the year, is scarce, a great drawback, to be rectified by the completion of the Berwickshire water scheme now in construction.

Agriculture is enjoying a prosperity, such as never before. Other industries are fishing around the village of Ross, a small quarry on the north road, with joiners and blacksmiths.

LOCAL GOVERNMENT

The county council and the educational authority have taken the place of the old local bodies and the parish shares a joint representative with the neighbouring parish of Foulden.

ECCLESIASTICAL

In 1867 a new church was erected and gifted by the then Laird of Mordington, Major C. F. Campbell-Renton. It is situated on a small eminence overlooking the Berwick-Duns road midway between the Starch-house and Clappers. It is a very beautiful little church, and is perfectly appointed. In preparation for Union of the two greater Scottish Churches (1929), legislation displaced the Heritors and placed the responsibility for the upkeep of the property on the local congregation.

In 1927 the old Presbytery of Chirnside, just prior to the larger Union, by direction of Act of Assembly 1927, in the interests of readjustment decided to unite the two parishes of Foulden and Mordington into a joint charge. This was duly carried out towards the end of 1927. The manse and glebe of Mordington were sold. Services are held in each church on Sunday and the joint congregation is now under the Presbytery of Duns. The new churchyard to the south-east of the new church is now under the care of the County Council. The former churchyard is now closed.

LANDOWNERS

The mansion-house of Mordington and grounds are still in the hands of the Campbell-Renton family; the new 'Laird' is Miss Margaret Campbell-Renton, M.A. (1948). The estate of Edrington was recently acquired by Mr A. Lindsay-Edwards who is specialising in pedigree shorthorns. Cawderstanes is now owned by Misses Robertson, who are farming also in the most up-to-date methods. Thus much progress has been made in the last 100 years in the staple industry of agriculture, which is enjoying a prosperity never before known.

1951

THE PARISH OF MORDINGTON

by Rev. W. G. Dunnett, M.B.E.

HISTORY

There have been few changes since the last Account. Some of the old houses at the Clappers have been demolished and replaced by nice stone-built cottages occupied by elderly people. The old mansion house of Mordington was demolished as it had become riddled with rot and was beyond saving. The ground was bought by Mr Furness and a fine new house has been built on the site of the old mansion. This house has recently been sold by Mr Furness and the present occupant is Mr Dalgetty from Dumfriesshire.

POPULATION

The population is now in the region of 136, showing the previously reported decline to be continuing. This has been brought about by the lack of work opportunities for the young people, resulting in almost all of them having to move elsewhere, and to the joining together of several of the small holdings to make more economic units.

TRANSPORT AND RURAL ACTIVITIES

The bus services can no longer be described as excellent, but since most of the inhabitants run cars this is not as serious as it would otherwise be. However, the re-alignment of the A1 road in Lamberton and the fact that the buses are now even further from the holders' houses, have made it increasingly difficult for anyone without a car to get to Berwick or elsewhere.

AGRICULTURE

There are now in the Mordington area of this parish a total of six holdings where previously there were 14. The same situation exists in the Lamberton area of the parish where there are now 13 holdings out of a previous total of 26. This has been brought about by the deaths of some holders, and the need to enlarge holdings by joining together two or three to make a more economically viable unit.

A certain amount of the land is used for arable crops of grain and roots, but the greater proportion is used for feeding stock of cattle and sheep. There is no longer any dairying in the parish.

LOCAL GOVERNMENT

The old County Council has disappeared and local government is now exercised at regional and district level that is, Border Region, and Berwickshire District. The 'local' element is provided by the Foulden and Mordington Community Council which, with little power and less finance, seeks to promote the interests of the local populace.

ECCLESIASTICAL

The parish of Mordington is united with the Parish of Foulden. The church in Mordington is still in use, a service being held there every alternate Sunday, but the minister in addition to Foulden and Mordington has charge of the parish of Hutton, Fishwick and Paxton. Although membership of the church has remained fairly constant over the years, it is now ageing and fewer young people remain in the parish to bring new life to the Church. There are now two lady elders, members of the Kirk Session, of whom one is Session Clerk.

1980s

THE PARISH OF NENTHORN

by David Stark, B.Ed.

NAME

The origins of the name are not at all clear but probably the explanation given in the New Account of 1834 is the best: viz. that the name is recorded as 'Naithansthirn' in ancient documents, and is therefore likely to have nothing to do with thorn trees as the writer of the previous account remarked. The word 'thairn' is still in use as 'Little and Muckle Thairn', which are cliff-like outcrops of rock beside the Eden below Girrick farm.

BOUNDARIES AND GEOGRAPHICAL FEATURES

The parish is of hour-glass shape, lying in a north-west to south-west direction. At the waist of the hour-glass, at Nenthorn bridge, it is a mere quarter-mile wide. The area of the parish is about 3500 acres (1400 hectares). The Eden Water is a very significant feature of the parish. It forms the parish boundary partly on the north, west and south. Of a total boundary of 13 and a half miles, the Eden forms the boundary for seven miles.

A ridge of volcanic rock, rising to over 600 feet, runs roughly north-east to south-west, in the north of the parish, about one mile from the most northerly point. The land to the north of the ridge faces north and slopes down to the Eden Water. It has therefore a less favourable aspect than the rest of the parish which largely faces south. Here the land falls away to the south in a series of undulations. These also lie in a north-east to south-west direction and are the results of glaciation. The south of the parish is about 150 feet above sea level.

Where the rock of the ridge outcrops it is seen to be basalt with columnar jointing. This has been remarked on in the earlier accounts.

The River Eden has done considerable downcutting to form in places a very steep-sided valley. At the Little and Muckle Thairn, mentioned above, these sides are sheer. The valley here is not however narrow as the meandering river has formed a broad haugh enclosed by these steep sides. The only place where the river has failed to cut through the bedrock is at Stichill Linn on the north side of Newton Don estate. Here it falls about 30 feet over a ledge.

LAND USE

Of a total acreage of about 3500 acres, some 250-300 acres are forested. The main areas are Mellerstain Estate with 80 acres in the north and Newton Don Estate with 150 acres in the south. These are largely commercial plantations of pine and spruce, although Newton Don has also extensive plantings of hardwoods for landscape value. There are other smaller areas of commercial softwoods planted as shelter belts or in places where the land is of little use for anything else, as on the rocky land above Blinkbonny or the now-drained Lurgie Loch.

It is, however, the roadside and fieldside hardwood trees which characterise the beauty of the landscape. As these die or are felled there is very little planting being done to replace them. The red tape of the roads authority and modern farming's dislike for fieldside trees seem certain to make for a more barren landscape.

Only the hill ground and river haughs have never been under the plough. There is very little ground in the parish of which no productive use is made.

The soil is in places a heavy red clay but is much improved by liming and fertilising with dung. Over the larger area it is better drained, being more gravelly. This can however produce the problem of stones and boulders coming to the surface each year after ploughing and harrowing. These then have to be removed. It is however good farming land.

NATURAL HISTORY

Roe deer are found in the more isolated wooded areas. In winter they come into more inlying areas in search of food. There are no other unusual mammals.

It is the river with its two lakes at Nenthorn and Mellerstain and isolated reaches in between which contributes greatly to the wildlife, especially waterfowl. The reedy banks and islands provide an excellent habitat for such creatures.

There is a flock of Canada Geese. This year 15 have been noted, although several years ago there was as many as 28. There is at least one pair of heron as well as swans, coots and moorhens.

In the fields can be found curlews and lapwings, while in the hedgerows yellowhammers are the more exotic among the common species.

Brown trout is the common fish caught in this part of the river as salmon cannot come up the Eden beyond Stichill Linn.

HISTORY

A recent survey of archaeological sites has shown Nenthorn as a site of early settlement. Evidence has been found of 117 house sites and a farm grange dated as 700-900 A.D. There was also an early monastic settlement, established by monks from the royal priory at Coldingham before 1242. This is believed to have been sacked by the Danes. A few years ago a quantity of large oyster shells were found at Nenthorn stables. These may be from the rubbish tips of the medieval monastery.

As noted in the 1834 Account, Nenthorn was on the route of warring English armies making their way to and from Edinburgh. As a result the village was sacked and burnt at least twice.

In more recent peaceful times the estates of the parish have tended to be divided up into individual farms when the estates changed ownership. Nenthorn Estate now has only one farm on it, Burnbrae farm. It operates as the home farm.

The present distribution of land ownership is: Newton Don Estate (Harrietfield and Home Farm) — Balfour of Balgonie Estates; Nenthorn Estate (Burnbrae Farm) — Major N. Thomson; Blinkbonny Farm/Courthill Farm — each is leased from Roxburghe Estates. Only a part of Courthill Farm, including the house and steading, lies in Nenthorn parish; Girrick Farm — T. Sanderson; Whitehill Farm — W. Redpath; Mellerstain Estate — Lord Binning. Only a small part of this large estate lies in the north-west corner of Nenthorn parish. Here about half is in agriculture and half is forested.

POPULATION

The census figures for the parish show that since 1801 the population peak was 461 adults in 1861. Since then it has declined steadily to its present level of 117 adults, 54 male and 63 female. Adult population: 1861, 461; 1881, 454; 1901, 416 (there was a boundary change before this census); 1921, 363; 1951, 279; 1971, 178; 1981, 117. These figures are taken from volume 4 of the 1981 Census Report on the Borders Region. On an unofficial count there are 28 children under 16 in the parish at the present time.

INDUSTRY

Virtually the only work available within the parish is concerned with the land. Each farm employs only about three men now, usually including the farmer or manager himself. Not all farm workers live in the parish. At busy times in the farming year contractors or extra casual labour may be brought in to help. With sheep this could be at lambing and clipping times, and with arable work at muck-spreading and crop-spraying times. In places even sowing is done under contract. Only minor farm repairs are done by the farmer's own men. Hedge-clipping, dyke-building, and new fencing are usually contracted out.

All the farms are mixed, arable and stock. Only two, Blinkbonny and Newton Don Home Farm, now have dairy herds. Previously there was dairying at Whitehill and Burnbrae. The farms are about 400 acres each, with a typical field size of about 20 acres. In most cases the field boundaries have remained constant, there being little grubbing up of fences and hedges to produce much larger fields. The main market for livestock is Newtown St Boswells.

Other workers employed by the estates are two gardeners on Nenthorn Estate, a gamekeeper each on Mellerstain and Newton Don estates, and two foresters on Newton Don.

At Newton Don the estate market garden is now leased out and run as a private enterprise. At Nenthorn the market garden is run as part of the estate and sends produce to Kelso as well as occasionally to the market in Edinburgh.

The estate stables at Nenthorn — at one time housing horse and carriage like those at Newton Don — are now leased and run as a commercial riding and livery stables.

Mellerstain and the Roxburghe estates employ their own foresters but they live outwith the parish. Elsewhere thinning, felling and planting are carried out by contractors.

The only other industry in the parish in recent times has been the use of the former village school as a small factory producing toys and craft goods. This now appears to have declined.

A sizeable proportion of residents work outwith the parish in local towns such as Kelso and Earlston. Taking Nenthorn village as an example, of those in paid employment, ten work in the parish and 18 work outwith it. To some extent this is an extreme and is balanced by those working and living on the farms. Even on the farms, where there is a surplus of housing, the cottages may be occupied by those working elsewhere.

HOUSING

The 1981 Census from which the following figures are taken notes 38 households: Owner-occupied, 3; Council (local authority), 1; Others, 34. Although this distribution has changed slightly in the last two years it does show clearly that the great majority of housing is estate or farm owned. All however do possess that great measure of civilisation, the bathroom and W.C. The most common size of house is 4-6 rooms.

Sixteen houses are listed as vacant in the parish. Nowhere is the reduced labour force required on farms today shown more clearly than at Courthill Farm where, out of ten farm cottages, two are occupied by farm workers, one is occupied by a local worker, one is empty and six are holiday houses.

Elsewhere two cottages are combined into one house as at Blinkbonny, or redundant houses are sold off privately for modernisation as at Harrietfield.

Plate 36. An old photograph of Eyemouth Harbour.

There are two large mansionhouses in the parish. That at Newton Don, dating from 1818, is neo-classical in style and stands in an elevated south-facing position among extensive wooded policies. There is a large stable block close to the house arranged around a courtyard capable at one time of housing horses and carriages. The flats in the upper half are now empty.

Nenthorn House is built of red sandstones in a style typical of the late 19th century. It replaced an older house on an ancient site on low ground beside the Eden. Old Nenthorn House is now derelict. The walled garden close by is still in use but the adjacent graveyard has been superseded since 1930 by a new one opposite Burnbrae Farm. There are no visible signs of the chapel which once stood beside the old graveyard. The headstones here give an indication of the uncertainty of life in the 19th century — especially the unfortunate Roy family, one-time owners of Nenthorn Estate. Of the six children of William and Isabella Roy, only one survived more than 20 years and he died in 1836 aged 47, leaving the mother as the only surviving member.

In the last few years two new bungalows in Nenthorn village have been built and older property converted. These include the conversion of the derelict blacksmith's and joiner's shops into a house, and the disused parish church into a house.

SOCIAL ORGANISATION

Politically Nenthorn parish lies in the new Roxburgh and Berwick parliamentary constituency, and is served by a district councillor for Roxburgh District and a regional councillor for the Borders Region. There are also three community councillors serving the Nenthorn ward of Floors, Makerstoun, Nenthorn and Smailholm Community Council.

The only social centre the parish has is the village hall. It was the former United Free Church, gifted by the then laird in 1928 to be held in trust for the benefit of the parish. It is run by an annually elected committee.

The local branch of the S.W.R.I. holds monthly meetings during nine months of the year. There are 14 members at present. Nenthorn Recreation Club meets in the village hall during the winter and offers darts, carpet bowls and table-tennis. The support it receives is variable.

CHURCH

After the Disruption, Nenthorn had two churches, the United Free Church and the Church of Scotland. Such was the strength of feeling at this time that U.F. members from Smailholm would make a long detour via Mainberry and cross the Eden at Old Nenthorn House by a footbridge they built themselves in order to worship at Nenthorn. When the churches were reunited the U.F. church became the village hall.

In 1944/45 the parish church was united with Hume and Stichill under one minister, and in 1972 the building itself ceased to be used for worship due to falling attendance. This building is now being converted into a house. The two manses, each about the same size as the church it served, reverted to ownership by Nenthorn Estate.

EDUCATION

The village school, built in 1859 by the gift of Lady Balfour of Newton Don, was closed in 1972 due to a falling roll. Previously the Old Schoolhouse was the school and schoolmaster's house combined.

At the present time children in the north of the parish are taken by bus to Gordon Primary School and Earlston High School, while those in the south go to Edenside Primary and Kelso High School. There is some flexibility in these arrangements.

TRANSPORT

In the 1970s there was no public transport through the parish at all. However there is now a post-bus service to Kelso on weekdays. Also with fare-paying passengers being carried on school buses and the introduction of other services, the availablity of public transport is much improved.

On the other hand most households have access to a car and have become used to this convenient method of transport. The 1981 census shows that of 38 households only four had no car.

SERVICES

Mains electricity is available throughout the parish and is the principal fuel used for cooking. Other households use bottled gas, oil or solid fuel stoves. Piped gas is not available. Nenthorn House now has its own hydro-electric power scheme with a turbine generator using the water power of the dammed lake at Nenthorn.

Coal and wood fires are the most common ways of heating the houses. Central heating, using solid fuel or oil, is becoming more common, but mainly in owner-occupied houses. There are now many more of such houses than the 1981 census shows. In Nenthorn village itself there are now seven owner-occupancies.

All houses have piped water, most of it supplied by the public water authority. Until a few years ago the supply to Nenthorn village was from a cistern on the Green Hill. The water in this had been pumped up from a spring beside the Eden. This water was very hard, leaving a scale deposit on boiling.

There is no main drainage scheme in the parish. In new or improved property septic tanks are required, but elsewhere effluent may be discharged into ditches.

Nenthorn Post Office is the only 'shop' in the parish and operates as a sub-post office only.

Although a fish merchant and bakers still travel round the houses with vans there is now no general grocery van. Most people get milk delivered by van from Kelso.

Kelso is also the shopping centre travelled to by most people at least once a week for groceries etc. This is usually by car. Other shopping centres such as Berwick and Galashiels are also used. Edinburgh and Newcastle may be used on special occasions.

Many households have a telephone. In Nenthorn village, out of 14 houses, 11 have a telephone. On the other hand few farm cottages have one and most rely on the farmhouse to take messages. There is one public call box in the parish.

MISCELLANEOUS

There is a strange piece of architecture on a ridge west of Girrick Farm. This is known as Hundy Mundy. From a distance it looks like a gateway flanked by two towers. On closer inspection it is a mere folly, the gateway being only about four feet wide and built of rough whinstone. It was built on this ridge due south of Mellerstain House to provide an item of interest on the horizon for that house.

1983

THE PARISH OF POLWARTH

by Sir John McEwen of Marchmont, Bart.

PHYSICAL BASIS

The Parish of Polwarth lies approximately in the middle of the county of Berwick and is triangular in shape. It is bounded on the east and west by the parishes of Fogo and Greenlaw and to the north by that of Langton. It has a total acreage of 3013 acres, of which 13 acres are water. A small loch, much overgrown by rushes and weeds, lies on the north-western border. The highest point in the parish is Kyleshill (923 ft.), at the top of which is a quarry which is worked for roadmetal. Of the rest of the area 1162 acres are moorland, 930 acres are arable, 573 acres are grass parks and 334 acres are woodlands, etc.

THE PARISH OF POLWARTH

Polwarth village — the Polwarth-on-the-green of the song — was once a flourishing hamlet boasting an annual fair which King James V is reputed once to have attended. The Thorn, likewise mentioned in Allan Ramsay's lines, still stands (there are in fact two of them) enclosed in an iron fence in the centre of the village. The statistical account of 1793 states that there were then some 50 families living in Polwarth; since then the population has dwindled at an accelerating pace until today it amounts to no more than a bare handful of individuals. The cottages are for the most part thatched and innocent of all modern conveniences — including damp-courses — and have been for many years past invariably condemned by the county authorities whenever they fell vacant at the death of the last survivor of the family inhabiting them. This has necessitated a process of gradual destruction which the high costs and difficulties of building — both of which have vastly increased in late years — have made it well-nigh impossible to reverse. No houses have been built by the local authority since 1918. The 'Polwarth acres' which were two-acre strips of cultivated land rented severally by the families living in the village, have, within the last year or two, been handed over to the adjacent farm of Polwarth Mill owing to lack of villagers to work them. There is a single-teacher school with a roll at this date (May 1951) of 20 children. Polwarth lies in a hollow and the ground is apt to be swampy, which probably accounts for a tendency to rheumatics among the inhabitants who, nevertheless, are remarkable for their longevity, the ripe age of 80 being of common attainment.

There are no trades followed in the parish today. There is a public telephone in the village but no shop or post office. Up till a year or so ago representatives of certain families long resident in Polwarth — Smiths, Watsons, Denholms and Andersons — were still resident in the village. Now, however, they have all died or removed to other parts of the county.

PARISH HISTORY

Polwarth Kirk stands upon a spur overlooking the Swarden Burn about half a mile south of Polwarth village. The existing building, standing on the site of many previous ones, was erected in 1703 by Sir Patrick Hume of Polwarth (later 1st Earl of Marchmont) and bears his coat of arms on a stone panel over the door, and a crowed orange—an augmentation to his arms granted by William III—on the gable-top at the east end. Underneath the church, and of a much earlier date, is a vault which was a burying place of the Hume family. It was in this vault that Sir Patrick lay hid for four weeks in 1683, he then being under suspicion for complicity in the Rye House Plot, during which time he was supplied with food nightly by his daughter Grizel from the house at Redbraes.

On the death of the Rev. W. E. Grimwood in 1944 the question of joining together the two parishes of Polwarth and Langton was mooted. However, the congregation showing themselves unwilling to lose their status as an independent parish, the Rev. J. F. Anderson was inducted as minister for a period of three years (1945-49). At his departure, however, the decision to unit was arrived at, and accordingly in 1950 the Rev. Alastair Robertson became minister of the combined parishes, himself residing in the manse pertaining to the Langton Parish Church in Gavinton, and preaching in both churches every Sunday. The Manse of Polwarth, a handsome Georgian house, was subsequently advertised for sale by the Church Trustees and sold in 1951, the purchaser being a Mr Bennet, son of the Earl of Tankerville. Meanwhile the glebe, consisting of 17 acres, was retained in the possession of the Church authorities.

In October 1949, H.R.H. Princess Margaret, being then on a private visit to the McEwen family at Marchmont House, attended Sunday morning service in Polwarth Kirk, Mr Anderson preaching. The weekly attendance at Sunday School is now 20. Apart from a private chapel (R.C.) in Marchmont House where mass is celebrated once a week by the priest from Duns when the family is in residence, there is no other place of worship in the parish.

AGRICULTURE

There are four farms in the parish, viz. Polwarth Rhodes (or Roads), Cothill, Polwarth South Crofts and Polwarth Mill. The farmers of three of these farms are tenants of Marchmont estate. The following are the rents per acre of the farms and the name of the sitting tenant. (Polwarth Mill was bought in 1953 by Mr George Tait of Choislee who now farms it himself.)

Cothill	—	James Dickson	—	19/2
Polwarth Rhodes	—	James Wightman	—	24/-
Polwarth S. Crofts	—	John Kinghorn	—	26/8
Polwarth Mill	—		—	14/-

The normal length of lease is 14 years. There are no farm horses working in the parish at the present time.

The only change in farming methods that has appeared in the last hundred years is the substitution of mechanical for horse and man-power. Dairy farming is another innovation in recent decades in the county as a whole. This came about partly owing to increased demand and government-fixed prices for milk and partly through the taking on of farms by men from the south-west and west where dairy herds were, and are (owing to better facilities for winter grazing) a favourite form of enterprise. In Polwarth parish one farm (Polwarth Crofts) is run as a dairy farm, not unsuccessfully. There has also been a certain tendency in recent years on the part of farmers to cut down hedge-row trees as being inimical to growing crops. In many parts of the county wide-spread devastation from the point of view of amenity has been caused by this practice which has, however, not been carried very far in this parish owing to the fact that the proprietor has always set his face against it.

MARCHMONT ESTATE

The whole of the parish except the moorland part is on Marchmont estate which is owned, since 1913, by the family of McEwen of Marchmont and Bardrochat. Sir John McEwan, Bart., sometime Member of Parliament for the County and Parliamentary Under-Secretary of State for Scotland 1939-40, is the present laird. Marchmont House, built in 1750 by Hugh, 3rd and last Earl of Marchmont, and embellished in 1913 under Mr R. F. McEwen of Marchmont by Sir Robert Lorimer, is a large house of noble proportions containing a number of superb examples of XVIII century French and Italian Plaster work.

POPULATION AND THE WAY OF LIFE

The total population of the parish is now 115, including 25 children under the age of 15.

There only remain, besides the schoolhouse (a modern building adjoining the school and presently inhabited by the Director of Education for the County) four habitable houses in Polwarth village, of which two are occupied, one by a roadman and the other by a farm servant.

The houses have neither light nor water, which latter commodity is obtained from the Black Well which has been the village water supply from time immemorial. This also is the supply, by a piped system, of three of the farms and the manse. There is in the village a renovated cottage built in 1919 by the then laird of Marchmont, Mr R. F. McEwen, and given to the people of Polwarth as a hall. It is used spasdmodically for social occasions such as whist-drives with special objects in view, wedding breakfasts, presentations of various kinds and so on. But it is no longer, as it once was, used nightly for carpet bowls and as a club. This is partly attributable to the reduction of the population in Polwarth itself, and partly to increased facilities for getting into Duns — four miles away — where there is a cinema and other attractions. A larger and more important social centre than the village is at Marchmont where the estate workers and their families are housed. But here again, with ever increasing wages and crippling taxation, the numbers tend to decrease rather than increase. In the gardens, for example, where six men used to be employed there are now only three and a boy; foresters number six instead of 16, and there is only one gamekeeper where there used to be three. A great deal of the depopulation of the countryside about which so much is written these days is due, not to lack of amenities or amusement, but to a scarcity of employment owing to the gradual destruction of the landed estates. In this respect, Polwarth parish, which is largely comprised in one large estate, is a striking example.

1951–54

THE PARISH OF POLWARTH

by Lady McEwen of Marchmont

Since the third account written by my father in law, Sir John McEwen of Marchmont, in 1954, there have been a number of changes in the parish of Polwarth District which I will enumerate as follows.

HISTORY

Polwarth in the Presbytery of Duns and the Synod of the Merse of Teviotdale is now linked with Longformacus, Cranshaws and Abbey St Bathans as well as Gavinton, and is served by the very hard-working minister, the Reverend Alexander Slorach. There is a service at Polwarth Kirk every other Sunday attended by about 10 people. There is no Sunday School. The bequest, sometimes called the Marchmont Bounty and amounting to £27 per annum, which was left by Sir William Purves Hume Campbell for the poor of the parish, is now paid with the Gavinton Common Good Fund.

AGRICULTURE

The Cothill and Polwarth Rhodes land was sold in the seventies. In the early eighties the remaining Marchmont farm land, amounting to about 1400 acres, was entirely reorganised with a heavy injection of capital and use of the EEC grant scheme for fencing and drainage. Despite, or rather, perhaps, because of this expenditure, Marchmont farms went into liquidation and the land was bought by a Mr Oliver Burge and his company. The rents are now between £30 and £40 per acre. Having reached a pitch of intensive and modern farming methods (autumn sowing, use of fertilisers and fungicides, the installation of a grain dryer and weighbridge, the growing of oil-seed rape and new strains of wheat), the land is now being 'set aside', thus attracting a grant of £80 per acre for growing no crops, the new owners having the commercial possibilities in mind of Marchmont as a shooting estate.

MARCHMONT ESTATE

In 1954 there was no electricity in the houses at Polwarth and all the water came from springs and wells. Marchmont itself, from having its own generator, moved on to the grid before the war. Its water system, a lot being of 18th and 19th date, was entirely on spring water. This however, though excellent for children's teeth and for the digestion and having quenched the thirst of generations, did not meet EEC requirements and was replaced in 1986/7 by the mains which the local authorities brought to within a few hundred yards of the house. A lot of cooking is done on bottle gas, the mains not being available though the big gas pipeline from Cockenzie runs underground through the parish. Its presence can be identified by the gap in the tree sky-line along the Greenlaw-Polwarth road because no large trees may be planted over it. There is no household without television, some have videos and practically all have telephones.

The site of the old village of Polwarth has been bought by Mr Peter Leggate who, after encountering considerable problems in the drainage required by the local authorities, has got planning permission to build or re-build seven houses around the Polwarth thorn (The old thorn is beginning to die back but a younger scion is flourishing.) It is not insignificant that 'Polwarth' is said to come from 'Pol' (Gaelic) or 'Pul' (Cambro-British) meaning muddy stream and 'Warth' (Saxon) meaning dwellings or homestead, and the village has always been known for its dampness. At Polwarth Crofts, owned by the present Sir John McEwen, a spring has just been discovered rising immediately behind the house.

Both schoolhouses are still occupied, and in the case of the more recent one, its adjoining school is now inhabited. The area has recently become more secluded due to a road improvement straightening out the Blackburn bend which was an accident black spot. It is a very quiet, green and pleasant place full of bird-song and wild life. The distinguished etymologist Dr Albert Long, used to spend much time here 'treacling the trees for moths', and only recently 93 bats were counted by Mr Boyle of the schoolhouse emerging from under his roof.

Marchmont itself was bought, after the deaths of Sir Robert McEwen in 1980 and his elder son Sir James in 1983, by Lady Ryder of Warsaw as a Sue Ryder Home for the Sick and Disabled. It is due to open in August 1989 and will house more than 40 patients of whom 20 will be sufferers from Huntingdon's Chorea. The main rooms of the house, however, with the fine 18th century plaster work and the Music Room with the organ and the concert grand piano, will be open to the public for concerts, plays, exhibitions, wedding parties, dinners, etc. which will generate revenue for the Sue Ryder Foundation which is a charity.

The Roman Catholic chapel where mass is said every week will also be used for inter-denominational services. Besides caring for the sick and catering for the public Marchmont will be a source of employment in the neighbourhood (the renovation work on the house, costing over one million pounds, has been done mostly by Henry Steel & Sons of Greenlaw), as well as a focus, as it already has become, of local generosity and goodwill.

Necessarily when the house is filled with patients and staff this will affect the population of the parish of Polwarth which currently is as follows:

Polwarth village, 4 houses,	3 couples, 1 widow	7
Polwarth Rhodes,	1 couple	2
Polwarth Rhodes cottage,	1 couple, 2 children	4
Cheviot View (holiday cottage)		
Polwarth Manse	1 couple, 2 children	4
Cothill farmhouse,	1 couple, 2 children	4
Cothill Cottage	1 couple, 2 children	4
Cothill farm cottages 1 & 2	2 couples	4
Marchmont Station	1 couple, 2 children	4
Redbraes	1 couple, 4 children	6
Marchmont cottages	1 couple, 1 son, 1 widow	4
Marchmont House	1	1
Marchmont Kennels	1 couple, 2 children	4
		48

There may not be as many people, even when Marchmont is full, in the parish of Polwarth as there were in 1954 (115 including 25 children), and, in a short space of time, there has been a radical alteration in a way of life which had remained constant in principle for several hundred years. There is a Greenlaw man still living whose first job as an apprentice painter in the early 1930s was to paint the sign of the Polwarth sweetie shop, now long vanished with so much else. But despite the changes and the depredations of the past few years it does seem as if life, albeit a different sort of life, is beginning to return.

1989

THE PARISH OF SWINTON AND SIMPRIM

by The Rev. J. B. Longmuir, T.D., M.A., B.L.

PHYSICAL BASIS AND GEOGRAPHICAL BACKGROUND

The parish, situated in the Merse district of south-east Berwickshire, extends some four miles east to west and some three miles north to south. It consists of a series of gentle ridges running from east to west and descending to the River Tweed. The soil is for the most part red clay soil and between the ridges it was marshy and may still be, where the drains are poor or not functioning.

There is one small stream, the Leet, which passes through Swinton and ultimately reaches the Tweed near Coldstream.

Both red and white sandstone have been quarried at the border of Whitsome parish, and marl was at one time dug for tiles and bricks.

The soil is fertile, if heavy, and suitable for growing grain, but in places is too heavy for sugar beet. There are a few plantations. Oak, ash and beech grow well, but generally the ground is too good to be thus used.

Since the union of the two parishes of Swinton and Simprim in 1761 there has been no change in the boundaries of the united parish. It is bounded north by Edrom and Whitsome, east and south-east by Ladykirk, south by Coldstream, west by Eccles and north-west by Fogo.

Both the previous Statistical Accounts suggest that the name Swinton is derived from the word Swine. However, it has been noted that the early form of the word — Sueneston — of date 1098 — makes it appear more probable that it is derived from Suen's or Swegen's Town. In other words, the village of Suen.

There is little more knowledge of the derivation of Simprim. But it has been suggested that it might be so called after the name of a person whose settlement it was originally, after the example of Sempringham in Lincolnshire.

CIVIL HISTORY

The history of the parish has been fully dealt with in the previous accounts. The family of Swinton is still in possession of Swinton House and of part of the estate at least. The farms, which are no longer in the possession of the Swinton family, are owned by their occupiers or by neighbouring proprietors.

The administration of civil affairs is now vested in the County Council and Middle District Council, to each of which the parish returns one councillor. There is a local advisory parish committee which assists the councillors by advising on local needs.

The schoolmaster is Registrar and Clerk to the Burial Committee and there is no Justice of the Peace resident in the parish.

AGRICULTURE

Agriculture is still the main occupation of the people and there is no industry of any kind. For a great many years the farms in the parish were taken by farmers from the west of Scotland and many of their descendents still occupy these farms, but in the last 35 years, as in the days of the First Account, there has been an influx of Northumbrian farmers and today Swintonhill, Little Swinton, Butterlaw, Ruthven, Longbank, Bridgend, Morningbank and Simprim are all farmed by men from across the border. The farms of Little Swinton, Butterlaw, Simprim, Ruthven, Swintonhill and Swinton Quarter are farmed by owner occupiers.

Due to the recent demands and needs of the Government, the parish is mainly arable. Between the wars it was mainly pasture. Probably three quarters of the parish is now under the plough. The main crops in order of acreage are barley, oats, wheat, beans and a small acreage of linseed; with considerable acreages of roots — swedes, turnips, kale and rape for stock feed. Because the soil is on the whole heavy, only a moderate acreage of potatoes is grown and the same applies to sugar beet. All these in this parish are up to or above the average yield. The whole parish is highly mechanised, with few horses in use now. Mechanisation ranges from tractor power lifts to grain dryers, and includes several combine harvesters.

The farm of Simprim is the only farm in the parish which has a dairy herd. The stock on the other farms is either beef cattle or commercial breeding herds. Some are fed in courts in winter and more on grass in summer. There has, in the last 15 years, been a gradual departure from the court system of feeding. Nearly every farm has a flock of half-bred ewes and most of the lambs are fed off the farms. Most pigs are fed for home consumption only. All prices are now controlled for farm produce.

The old four or five year rotation of crops has largely disappeared owing to the demand for grain crops during and since the last War, and there is no longer the normal rotation of grass, oats, green crop and barley, with sometimes an extra year of grass. Fences are gradually taking the place of hedges, though the old double hedge or traces of it are still in existence.

Farm workers' wages are now much higher and there has been considerable improvement in the amenities. Most of the farm cottages have inside water and lavatories and many have electric light either from a local plant on the farm or from the Grid. At some farms there has been a complete re-building of cottages, notably those belonging at some time to Ladykirk Estate — Simprim and Simprim Mains. New cottages have been built also at Swinton Quarter. At Mountfair and Little Swinton the cottages have been renovated and water etc. installed.

The tenants and rents of the farms on Swinton Estate are as follows:

Harcarsehill	—	W. R. Ketchin	—	£400
Bridgend	—	A. Buglass	—	£225
Longbank	—	J. Trotter	—	£140
Crowfootbank	—	G. Brown	—	£230
Morningbank	—	J. Moscrop	—	£155

The farm of Simprim Mains is owned by Ladykirk Estates, tenanted by W. Fleming, and the rental is £629.

The farm of Mountfair is owned by Lord Brocket, tenanted by W. A. Stirling, and the rental is £405.

The farm of Swinton Mill is owned by Major H. R. Trotter, tenanted by John Fleming, and the rental is £467.

The following farms are owner-occupied and the rents are as follows:

Swintonmill	—	W. R. Little	—	£770
Swinton Quarter	—	W. B. Prentice	—	£522
Swinton Greenrigs	—	G. H. Mills	—	£436
Little Swinton	—	T. W. Brewis & Son	—	£720
Butterlaw	—	James Robertson	—	£260
Simprim	—	R. L. Johnston	—	£390

The rent for the grazing of the North Glebe is £16 and for the South Glebe, which is cultivated, £28.

Apart from agriculture the main occupations are those of roadman, rabbit catcher, mason, estate worker and lorry driver.

There are the following businesses with the numbers employed:

Butcher, 5; Garage, 6; Blacksmith, 1; Timber Merchants, 3 and 6; Cobbler, 1; Plumber, 1; Joiner, 5; Threshing Mill, 2; Builder, 6; Contractor, 2.

There are the following shops:

Teashop; Stationer; Post Office and Grocery; Nurseryman; Butcher; Baker; Grocery.

EDUCATION

Originally, there was a parish school only but after 1843 a Free Church School was formed and prior to 1874 both schools were used — called the North and South schools, the South being the infant department under an infant mistress. However, the building of a new school in 1874 brought all pupils under one roof. That is the school still in use today, having three classrooms and one room with woodwork benches. Recently, central heating has taken the place of open fires and after two years of electricity made from the Schoolmaster's plant, it is now connected (1951) with the Grid.

Until recently, too, pupils remained at Swinton School till the age of 14, but now all children at the age of twelve attend either Coldstream or Duns Secondary Schools. They are transported by school bus or hired cars. The number of pupils at Swinton School in May 1951 was 72.

Evening classes are conducted in the school and in different years there have been classes in Woodwork, Basket-making, Embroidery, Tailoring, Beekeeping, Dressmaking etc.

CHURCH

The parish church is now the sole church in the parish. The earliest reference known is that of Hugh, Parson of Swinton, in 1209. In 1271 Alan of Swinton granted the Kirk Croft to the monks of Coldingham Priory. The Bell is dated 1499, with the inscription on it: *Maria est nomen meum* — Mary is my name. In 1542 the church was defended against the English and a man was killed in it. It is said that the original building was rebuilt in 1593 and of the present building the lower parts of the east, south and west walls are considered to be original. A stone over the west doorway has the inscription: Mak no delay to turn to the Lord, Anno 1593. The triangular stone over the gallery door is said to be one of the oldest armorial carvings in Scotland. In the east wall there is a coat of arms with the date 1635. The church underwent considerable renovation, additions and repair in 1729. In 1782 the Feuars' Aisle was built and in 1800 there were further additions and repairs. In 1830, the then minister, Mr Hunter, had a plan made for enlarging and making the church more commodious, but it was not till 1837 that this was done under Mr Logan, writer of the Second Account. It was given seating for 366, there being 110 in Feuars' Aisle and 256 in the rest of the church. The population of the parish then was 971 and the number of communicants 420. The total cost was £150.1.7 1/2.

In 1900 the Rev. D. D. F. Macdonald raised the question of the renovation of the church, and after an action against the Heritors in the Court of Session, Lord Guthrie ordained that the renovation should be executed 'on the sight and to the satisfaction of Mr R. S. Lorimer' (later Sir Robert S. Lorimer). The work was finished in 1910 at a cost of £2,000. In 1949 the church was wired for electricity and lit from a plant which also supplied the manse. At the end of 1951 it was connected to the Grid supply.

In 1932 a union was effected between the parish church congregartion and the United Free Church congregation. The result has been most happy and has led to the strengthening of the church in Swinton. The membership in 1951 was 292, with eight elders. The Christian liberality was £652. The stipend in that year was £500 made up of Teind Stipend, Glebe Rent, Endowments, and augmentation by the congregation of £50.

The manse is too large for modern days — with four staircases and many corridors it is too difficult to work without domestic help. It has had many additions since 1700 when it seems to have suffered from fire. In 1750 it was largely rebuilt and slated. It may be that a new part was built in 1771. In 1815 a new wing was added with staircase. In 1842 the kitchen, pantries etc. were flagged, the roofs stripped and re-slated. At this time the gighouse, coal house and piggery were detached from the manse and these were also re-roofed. This at a cost of £82.0.9. In 1892 once again there was considerable renovation and repair. Water was pumped by hand from a well in the Glebe, which still supplies the water for all purposes, though now it is pumped by engine.

POPULATION

The population fell from 971 in 1831 to 676 in 1931. The latest figure in 1951 was 571. The Census gave the distribution as 267 males and 304 females.

There is no change in the number of houses but the families are smaller. Mechanisation has made it possible to work the farms with fewer workers but the cause of depopulation lies deeper. Once there was a brewery and two mills. There was a saddler and many tailors etc. Factory-produced articles have caused these local trades to disappear. There are now no weavers, no bakers, no carrier and no dancing master. There is no demand for domestic servants and many of the girls on leaving school find work in factories, shops or offices in neighbouring towns.

Around the middle of last century there was a brick and tile works in the parish but all that remains now are the water filled pits on Morningbank and Crowfootbank farms showing where the clay for the tiles and bricks was dug. The name of the company was The Tweeddale Patent Tile and Brick Company. It was assessed in the years 1843 to 1846 for Poor Relief and Road Money.

A quarry of white sandstone, actually in Whitsome parish, provided work for many in earlier years but for long has been in disuse. Lately, work was restarted there to supply stone for the building of the new dam at Longformacus designed to supply water to the County, though no local men are employed.

There is now no industry to absorb workers, and men who do not wish to work on the land have to seek employment in the city.

There are few amenities for those who would stay. Transport is inadequate. There is no other form of transport than by bus. It would be an improvement if more buses were run. There is no resident doctor, and practically every baby is born in the Knoll Hospital in Duns.

VOLUNTARY ORGANISATIONS

There is a Scout Troop formed in 1938 and Youth Club with over 40 members. A Women's Rural Institute with over 80 members is balanced by a Men's Club with a similar membership.

A wooden hut, erected after the 1914-18 War as a public hall, is now used by the Women's Rural Institute — and for school meals. The former Free Church is let to the Men's Club and is available for public functions.

The Men's Club is organised for carpet bowling and billiards and takes part in the County Carpet Bowling League. There is a Quoiting Club and a Curling Club, though most of the curling is now done at Edinburgh. There was a Tennis Club but like the Football Club it is now defunct. In earlier days there was the Box Meeting which derived from the ceremonial opening of the Box which contained contributions to a kind of insurance fund, and this was followed on the same day by sports which developed into the Swinton Games. The place of the Games was taken during the War of 1939-45 by Sheep Dog Trials which raised many hundreds of pounds for Red Cross and other charities, but recently no games of any kind have been held.

SWINTON VILLAGE TRUST

By the Will of Alan Swinton of Swinton, dated 8th June 1888, a sum of £2000 was left to Trustees. The interest on this sum was to be used for the upkeep of a library in a building — also bequeathed — in which a house was set apart for a Biblewoman. A soup kitchen was to be opened on Christmas Day and warm clothes and coals distributed to the poor.

For the last two years there has been no soup kitchen for lack of any desiring it, but some 20 years ago there would be 20 to 30 obtaining soup, bread and meat three times a week. The library contains many old volumes which were either gifted by Alan Swinton or bought by the Trustees in the early years of the Trust. The library is now supplemented by a regular supply of books from the County Library at Duns and the income is now used for the upkeep of the building and for the supply of coals to the poor. By decision of the Court of Session permanent Trustees were the Chairman of the Parish Council, the minister of the United Free Church congregation and the minister of the

Plate 37. The village of Whitsome in the 1950s.

Plate 38. At Earlston in the 1950s.

Parish Church congregation. Of these only the minister of the united congregation remains as sole Trustee.

HOUSING

There are 104 houses, of which 49 are owner-occupied and the rest rented or occupied by virtue of office, e.g. manse, schoolhouse, police. There had been only one house built since 1930, but a start has been made with new houses built for the County. There are still houses roofed with pantiles but most are slated, and the last thatched roof was on an old cottage used as an armoury by the Territorials up to 1914, but now it has disappeared. Clay floors have been cemented and many houses have modern fireplaces. Box beds have disappeared. There is still no water except from wells, and only a few houses have water inside. There is no system of sanitation in the village but pipes for water have been laid and drains are also being laid for sewage. It is expected that by the end of 1952 water and drainage should be available. Meantime, only a few houses are still lit by oil lamps. Rents are low and vary from £3 per annum to £22. The manse is assessed at £30 and this assessment is the highest in the village. Gardens are usually large and most houses have stables and outhouses, relics of a time when there were many carters and carriers in the village. There is one hotel in the village but there are seldom any residents. There is a telephone kiosk and a police station with a resident policeman.

WAR MEMORIAL

At the east end of the village a War Memorial was built in the form of a Border Cairn with a granite panel containing the names of the fallen in the 1914-18 War, to which have been added the names of those who died in the 1939-45 War. There are 24 names on the Memorial of the 1914-18 War and two names for the 1939-45 War. The Memorial has been taken over by the Middle District Council and is maintained by them.

WAY OF LIFE

There is practically no crime in the parish and the people are generous and kindly. They are much better off than ever before, financially, and there are no destitute poor such as existed even 20 years ago. Every home has its daily paper and most have wireless. The furnishings of the cottages have improved greatly since farm workers' wages were increased. There is considerable football pool coupon gambling and a little horse-racing gambling, but apart from these nothing else worthy of censure. Drunkenness is almost unknown.

Not many go from home for holidays but there are numerous bus day trips to places as far afield as Whitley Bay and the Highland Show. This year the school-children visited the pantomime in Edinburgh.

The long awaited water and drainage will — with the electric light — transform the village and be an immense benefit to everyone.

1952

THE PARISH OF SWINTON AND SIMPRIM

by Rev. Alan C. D. Cartwright

Over the years since the writing of the previous Statistical Account there have been dramatic changes in the parish of Swinton. The biggest has been the coming of water, drainage and electricity into every home, but there have been many changes in agricultural practice too. The change in agriculture firstly created more jobs and thus produced a higher population, and then this century mechanisation reversed the trend. In 1755 there were 494 people in Swinton parish; this increased through the late 18th and early 19th centuries to reach a high point in 1871 of 996 people, but steadily dropped from then to 369 in the 1981 census.

The balance of the population has changed over the years as well, and now Swinton — like all other country areas — has a high proportion of people of pensionable age. (This may be caused by the better nutrition and cleaner air in the country). The Great Britain average in 1981 for the proportion of the population of pensionable age was 17.7 per cent; Scotland's was 16.7 per cent; whereas the Borders Region had 21.5 per cent, Berwickshire had 22.0 per cent, and Swinton Parish, in 1985, by my reckoning has 22.5 per cent with the village itself having 24.2 per cent. The proportion over 75 years of age is 5.9 per cent (compared to the G.B. average of 5.7 per cent and Scotland's of 4.2 per cent). This figure is very high considering that there is no sheltered housing or old people's home in the parish.

Strangely, though, the proportion of children under 16 is, at 21.5 per cent, not much lower than the national average of 22.3 per cent. This figure for children gives a bright outlook for the future, and it may be that the population of Swinton, after falling for so long (every census since 1871 showed a decrease), is beginning to increase. By 1985 there were 427 people in the united parishes of Swinton and Simprim.

The population has not only decreased over the years but has also moved from the farms to the villages and towns; by 1985 nearly two-thirds of the population of Swinton parish lived in the village itself, where all the houses have been renovated and the local council has built 22 houses at the east end of the village and nine others on the site of two derelict cottages.

Even in the 1950s many people lived and worked on the farms, but now, in the 1980s, there is not one farm in the parish with all its cottages filled with farm workers. Most of the people now living in farm cottages are either retired from the farm or have come from the Central Belt of Scotland or the Newcastle area.

Berwickshire, in generally, and the Merse in particular, is a very pleasant area in which to live, and there are now many 'incomers' — people who were born and brought up outside the Merse but who now have settled happily in this lovely area, and who have brought their skills and talents with them. Some of them have come to work in the area, whilst others have retired here.

Some incomers find strange expressions of speech which are peculiar to this area. For instance: 'hard-up' is an expression used to describe not someone in financial difficulty but a person who is very ill (sometimes a piece of machinery which has reached the end of its useful life); 'shabby' is also used for an ill person — not for someone who is poorly dressed; 'starving' means feeling cold and has nothing to do with hunger; 'puggled oot' means very tired; and a 'baigie' is a turnip. Some of the old words are still used, as in 'marches', meaning 'borders with', and people from Northumberland are from 'across the water' (the Tweed).

Another feature of life in the Merse is the number of cross-border marriages. Partly this is explained by Berwick-upon-Tweed being the nearest big town, and, with the closure of the local railways in the 1960s, also the nearest railway station. Many people now go into Berwick for their shopping which has, of course, meant the closure of local shops and the stopping of the delivery vans. In the 1950s there were seven shops in Swinton; now only a grocer/newsagent and the sub post-office remain. However there has been a new shop opened by a potter who makes his goods behind his shop in what used to be the bakehouse. Over the years the number of vans coming to the parish has reduced from two or three per day to only a baker, two butchers, a fishman and the library van.

The library van comes to the village once a fortnight. These visits replace the Swinton Village Library which had been set up from the bequest of Alan Swinton in 1888. The library house was handed over to the County Council (now the District Council) and was converted into two small houses for older people, whilst the library itself was placed at the disposal of the County Library Service. The one remaining item from the Alan Swinton Bequest is that each child on leaving Swinton School receives a Bible.

The school, which celebrated its centenary in 1978, is now a three-teacher school whose number of pupils stabilised in the mid 1950s. This school, which serves the parishes of Ladykirk and Swinton, and also takes some pupils from Whitsome, takes the pupils up to the age of 12 when they all transfer to the Berwickshire High School in Duns.

The evening classes which were held in the school and were a great success in the 1950s, have now all ceased except for a piping class organised by a local man, Tim Ainslie. If people wish to attend evening classes — and many still do wish to further their education — they now travel to Duns or Coldstream (six miles away).

This centralisation of activities and interests, and also the gradual disappearance of the delivery vans, reflects the fact that most people now have cars and many households have more than one car. (Berwickshire has only 35 per cent of households with no car; the Great Britain average is 40 per cent; whilst in Swinton parish only 19 per cent of the households have no car, and all of these have the use of one, with a close relative living close by). Similarly, where most of the homes had a wireless in 1951, now nearly all have a coloured television, many have video recorders, and the vast majority have a telephone. All of the houses have been modernised and there are now no derelict houses in the village of Swinton; Berwickshire County Council designated the area round the Green a Conservation Area in the early 1970s. The way of life has changed because of the general affluence and whereas few people went on holiday in the 1950s, most families now go away at least once per year and many of these holidays are abroad.

This higher standard of living meant for a while that people were less concerned with their local community and travelled to Edinburgh or Newcastle for entertainment, but in the past few years there has been an upsurge in local interests. The former Free Church in the middle of the village was taken over in the late 1950s by the County Council and let out as a village hall, and was used by the Women's Rural Institute, Men's Club and some other organisations. It had a very handsome spire which had to be removed in the interests of safety, and many people still regret its passing: the Free Church had been built in 1860, and its spire could be seen from all around the Merse. In 1978, the District Council asked local people to take over and run the hall and the Swinton Village Hall Committee was formed. Over the years they have made tremendous improvements to the hall. It is now used far more than before — by the Badminton Club, the Men's Club, the Rural, the Toddlers' Group, and also for dances and wedding receptions. It has now become one of the best halls in Berwickshire and in 1985 there was a very successful exhibition on Swinton of Yesteryear, called 'Looking Back', in which many people showed off their treasures of the past and everyone got a glimpse of what life had been like in Swinton many years ago.

The Village Hall Committee also revived the 'Queen o' the Merse' Festival — a Gala day held on the village Green. At this now annual event there are various activities and one of the young girls from the school is crowned 'Queen o' the Merse' a title traditionally bestowed on the village itself. The 1984 'Queen o' the Merse' (Lesley Spence from Ladykirk) had the privilege and honour of handing over a bouquet of flowers to Her Majesty the Queen, when she stopped in Swinton on the 5th July 1984. It is not known if a member of the Royal Family had ever previously stopped in Swinton since the days before the Union of the Crowns. Her Majesty was welcomed to Swinton by a large crowd of people on a beautiful day, and a banner proclaimed 'The Queen o' the Merse Welcomes The Queen o' the Scots'.

Simprim has changed even more than Swinton over the years. In 1751 there were 143 people in the parish, and in spite of an increase in the late eighteenth and early nineteenth centuries, by 1985 the population had decreased to 46, including eight children. Simprim must have been one of the smallest parishes in Scotland, as it is less than three miles long and not one mile wide. The kirk at Simprim was only 45 feet long by 13 feet wide. It existed in the reign of David I (1124-1153), but is now little more than a ruin.

The kirk at Swinton has undergone many changes in its long life. It is first mentioned in 1098, and stands in the middle of the triangle joining the Holy Island with Coldingham and Melrose; it is possible that there was a kirk in Swinton over 1000 years ago. Originally it would have been a long narrow east-west building, and then after the addition of the 'Feuars' Aisle' in 1782, it became the traditional T-shape of many country kirks (Fogo, Edrom, Polwarth, Whitsome, Chirnside, Greenlaw, Legerwood etc.). This extension was necessitated by the union of the parishes of Simprim and Swinton in 1761, but although the 'Feuars' Aisle' probably doubled the number of seats, that was still not sufficient for the increase in population in the early 1800s, so in 1837 another extension was put on, making Swinton an L-shaped building. In 1910 it was renovated under the direction of Mr Robert Lorimer. This renovation entailed raising the roof by two feet, renewing the pews and the furnishings, and introducing a parquet floor. The pulpit was a gift from the Swinton family and was carved at the Kensington School of Art. A small pipe organ was also installed about this time. One of the organists, Robert S. Robertson, served his God and the church by playing the organ from 1903-1961, which must be one of the longest spans of service at the organ of any church.

Since the renovation the kirk has been well maintained and is a credit to the Kirk Session and the various ladies who have kept it clean and tidy over the years. At the present time the walls are a light shade of pink and together with the diffused light coming in through the small tinted squares of green, pink and yellow glass, this creates a warm, welcoming atmosphere. In 1985 Swinton Kirk welcomed the Moderator of the General Assembly of the Church of Scotland, the Very Reverend John M. K. Paterson, and the kirk was full of people from all over the Merse and from other parts of the presbytery. Swinton itself had a minister who in later years became Moderator — Rev. James B. Longmuir. He was minister of Swinton from 1934-1952 and he wrote the 1951 Statistical Account.

The present minister — Rev. Alan C. D. Cartwright — is minister of five kirks: Fogo, Ladykirk, Leitholm and Whitsome as well as Swinton. In 1967 Swinton was linked with Fogo under the ministry of the Rev. Robert Martin, and when he left in 1975 Fogo and Swinton were united and a further linkage took place with Leitholm under the ministry of the present minister. Then in 1978 the minister of Ladykirk with Whitsome (Rev. W. Graham Bailey) left, and these two parishes were linked with the three others, with the minister staying at Swinton. This was the first quintuple linkage in Scotland and seems to be working reasonably well, although obviously five separate ministers could manage more easily. The reason for this linkage and most others in the country areas is depopulation; whereas in 1851 there were over 3400 people in the area covered by the minister, there are now about 1100.

The Kirk itself has some interesting features, some of which have been mentioned in previous Statistical Accounts. There is only one stained glass window — in the west gable end — which records that Archibald Adam Swinton, B.C.S. and Captain George Herbert Taylor Swinton brought about the repurchase of the Swinton Estate into the Swinton family. This window represents the Entry into the Promised Land, and has in the background a view of the Cheviot Hills. Within and outside the church there are a number of plaques and tablets commemorating members of the Swinton family.

In the east end of the north wall there is an aumbry — near to where the altar stood in pre-Reformation times. This aumbry is an open cupboard which was used to store the sacred vessels for the Mass. In the middle of the south wall there is an effigy of Sir Alan Swinton, who died about the year 1200, and above the gallery door is a carving of the Swinton family arms which is reckoned to be one of the oldest carvings of heraldic arms in Scotland. This carving could be from the same era as the effigy, as the boars in both are similarly carved. Also from pre-Reformation days in the bell, which is certainly the oldest in regular use in the area and may be the oldest in Scotland.

This bell, so the legend goes, was rung after Flodden to sound the death not only of the King but also of a whole nation's hopes. Although the bell is actually called 'Mary' it is affectionately known as the 'Flodden Bell'. The bell from Simprim was returned to the Swinton family when the kirk closed its doors in 1761 (only five years after the bell had been bought), and on the building of Christ's Church in Duns they presented it with the Simprim Bell. This forged a link between the staunch Presbyterians of Simprim and the Episcopalianism of Duns, and maybe between the descendants of those who fought on the Scots side at Flodden and those who were on the English side.

There are other links between Swinton and the national life of Scotland. The Lord Lyon King of Arms from 1927-1929 was George Sitwell Campbell Swinton and his life is commemorated in the kirk. When Sir Robert Lorimer was given the task of building the Scottish

National Shrine in Edinburgh Castle, he remembered the Swinton stone and used stone from the Swinton Quarry for the inner walls of the Shrine. This quarry is now disused (it closed down just before the Second World War) but there are many buildings in the area built with Swinton stone — either the gray sandstone or the pink (for there were two separate quarries, one on each side of the Berwick road just at the boundary with Whitsome parish). One of the landmarks of the Merse — Ladykirk — is a lovely shade of pink from the Swinton quarry.

Apart from the Scottish National Shrine there is another link between Swinton and Edinburgh Castle. Mons Meg — the famous cannon — rests on timber from the Swinton estate. This is appropriate, as on the retreat from the siege of Norham Castle one of the ammunition wagons sank in a marshy piece of ground in Swinton and had to be abandoned. Nearly 400 years later the remains of the wagon and six cannonballs were found, one of which now rests at the home of Sir John Swinton, the present laird, at Kimmerghame, and another, a marvellous granite specimen 19 inches in diameter, at the manse, the rest being sent back to Edinburgh Castle.

The manse, which was thought over-large in the 1950s, having been altered and re-organised seems ideal to the present incumbent and very comfortable, as its design allows the centre of the building to be kept warm using open fires. The garden is quite large but manageable and is a haven for birds. Over 40 different species of bird can be seen regularly in the manse garden or glebe, and there are occasional sightings of a further 20 species. Many of the smaller birds nest in the manse garden, and it is a delight to see them.

One of the reasons for the number and variety of birds is that near the manse and kirk is one of the few remaining deciduous woods in the parish. Many trees planted in the mid to late 1800s, are now coming to the end of their life and are being cut down. Sadly few of these trees are being replaced and those which are, are being replaced by conifers. The conifers are quicker growing but they do not have the attendant wild-life. Even so there is quite a bit of wild-life in the parish of Swinton, apart from the birds. There are plenty of mice, voles, shrews, moles, rabbits, hedgehogs, stoats and weasels and the odd fox, badger and mink. Occasionally we get visits from roe deer.

Many people in Swinton parish now travel to work in Duns, Coldstream, Kelso or Berwick, few being now employed in the village or on the farms. Even the biggest farms are now only employing two or three workers, with a few others being brought in at the busy seasons. In the village itself there are two builders employing nine and four people respectively; a joiner employing five; a haulage contractor nine; timber merchant — husband and wife; the garage, three. There is also the Wheatsheaf Hotel, which apart from the husband-and-wife team who run it employs one other full-time and a few part-time staff.

As was said at the beginning of this account, it seems as if Swinton is now a much more stable community and the future looks bright as there are quite a few young families. It is a pleasant place in which to live and has a very happy community spirit which makes it the envy of many a larger place. Swinton can be proud to be called 'The Queen o' the Merse'.

1986

THE PARISH OF WESTRUTHER

by Rev. Edward Mackay

PHYSICAL BASIS

The parish contains Westruther and Houndslow villages. The parish formed part of Hume till the Reformation and then of Gordon till 1647. It is bounded north and north-east by Longformacus, east by Greenlaw, south-east by Gordon, south-west by Legerwood, west and north-west by Lauder. The utmost length from north to south is six and a quarter miles. The utmost breadth from east to west is five miles. The area is 22 and three quarter square miles or 14,643 and three quarter acres, of which 13 and three quarter acres are water.

Eden Water flows two miles east-north-eastward along the Gordon boundary; Blackadder Water, formed by several headstreams that rise in the north of the parish, winds two and one eighth miles south-south-eastward along the Greenlaw boundary.

The surface sinks in the south-east to 590 feet above sea level and rises to 785 feet near Hyndberry, 856 near Weddlie, 1242 at Flass Hill, 1255 at Raecleugh Hill and 1466 at Twinlaw Cairns near the northern border — bleak, cheerless uplands these last, but commanding brilliant and extensive prospects of the Merse and Teviotdale. There is a quarry for building purposes, no longer used. Nearly 1000 acres of the parish are under wood, about 180 in a state of moss and the rest is arable or pastoral.

The parish is in the Presbytery of Duns and the Synod of Merse and Teviotdale.

FOLKLORE

The parish of Westruther was originally called Wolfstruther. It seems that in the dim past it was overrun by wolves; the original name was then altered to Westruther. There is, however, still evidence of the origin in as much as there exists on the Farm of Cammerlaws a tree at which, according to folklore, the last wolf in Scotland was killed. There is ground for such a belief for until up to the time of her death Lady John Scott of Spottiswoode (afterwards mentioned), who was intensely interested in the antiquities of the district, caused this tree to be fenced round in case of damage.

CUSTOMS

Although this hill parish in common with many others is gradually losing much of its individuality, possibly due to easier transport facilities, one custom still exists which we feel merits mention, namely 'The Running of the Braes'. This custom is carried through at marriage. After the marriage service and the assembly of the guests for the marriage reception, the bride and bridegroom make their way to the nearest suitable piece of land and officiate at a flat-race, the male guests running to the bride and the female guests to the bridegroom. The male winner kisses the bride and the female the bridegroom. The winners are also rewarded with a silk handkerchief from the bride and the bridegroom respectively.

MONUMENTS AND CIVIL HISTORY

Mention should be made here of the two cairns referred to in the account of 1834. These are still in existence as the 'Twin Law Cairns' but in a much dilapidated condition. During World War II the hill ground on which these cairns stand was a tank training region and inadvertently or otherwise both cairns were shot at. The late Andrew Grieve, Esq., of the Flass Farm on whose ground the cairns are built, and who was interested in antiquities, raised the question of the restoration of these cairns with the proper authorities and it is understood, though this restoration is not yet carried through, that money has been set aside for this purpose. Lady John Scott of Spottiswoode has been already referred to in this account as taking an interest in antiquities. Farms in the district still exhibit stones and cairns which she wished preserved for historical or sentimental reasons. On the walls of one of Spottiswoode Estate lodges we find to this day painted clock faces which face either way along the main trunk road. These faces exhibit different times, those at which the up and down Edinburgh to London stage coaches passed the lodge. The wall of the same lodge has a tablet on which the mileages shown are those to Edinburgh, Dalkeith and also to London. Mention might also be made of the 'Popping Stone' on Raecleuch Farm from where it is said Lady John Scott received a proposal of marriage from the gentleman who became her husband. This lady will be remembered as the authoress of the words of 'Annie Laurie'.

CHURCH HISTORY

In the last 100 years Westruther has not lacked stirring times in matters of church history. In that time the parish was prominent in the Disruption. From the Annals of that name we read of some of the difficulties which were experienced by those who struggled for spiritual independence. The Heritors of Westruther refused to give the necessary facilities toward the building of a place of worship for the newly organised Free Church. The Earl of Lauderdale, Spottiswoode, Kerr Seymour of Cattle Shiels, Lord Blantyre of Wedderlie, Curle of Evelaw, and Home of Bassendean would have prevented the Free Church men from obtaining a site on which to build. But such action was forestalled by the leader of the new body, a Mr Wood, by his securing a portion of a feu in the village, sufficient for the purpose. But every quarry and every sandpit in the neighbourhood was closed to them. Timber and lime they could procure, but the other necessities were not within their reach. Mr Wood however applied to a friend named J. Cunningham of Coldstream, at that time residing at Greenlaw, and asked his counsel in the matter, and it was agreed to build a structure of timber. But once again the plan was changed. Mr Wood received a visitor who had to hide his identity but who turned out to be a member of the village who told Mr Wood that sand was hidden under the top surface of his feu, and in the end a church building partly made of wood and partly made of stone was erected. This church building lasted for ten years and by that time hostility to the Free Church members had ceased to manifest itself in the same outrageous manner, and this building was replaced by a solid and comfortable building of stone which was finally opened on 1st November 1854. There is one church in use today for public worship, the old Parish Church which was built in 1841, so it would appear that the Heritors had just completed their church at the time of the Disruption. Happily in 1929 these two congregations, the old Parish Church and the Free Church, were united, which union has been most successful, and today one congregation worships in Westruther. One of the outstanding ministers who served in the parish of Westruther was the Rev. J. Veitch. Although working a considerable time before 'The Disruption', his outstanding personality caused many to flock to his services, and the undernoted Memorial pays due tribute to his memory. His work has previously been referred to in the Statistical Account of 1834. The Memorial mentioned is in the Free Church building in Westruther and reads:

> To the memory of John Veitch
> For 54 years Minister of this Parish
> He was Ordained 1649, was twice forced
> To leave his home because he would not
> Receive Ordinances, the Commandments of men
> And died on his returning from the General Assembly
> On December, 1703, at Dalkeith where he was buried.
> The people of Westruther again departing from the
> Parish Church because they cannot own other than
> Christ's authority within Christ's Kingdom and
> Remembering the example of one who being dead
> Yet speaketh . . . Erected this stone
> In the Year of Grace .... 1843.

— showing how strong were the convictions of those staunch God-fearing people.

PUBLIC AND SOCIAL SERVICES

Very little new building has taken place over the past 40 years. There are six new semi-fabricated houses built by the council. The parish in the main enjoys a good water supply and the drainage system is adequate. The water is obtained from springs from within the parish, and was laid on to the main village as a result of Parish Council activities. This scheme is now fully paid up and financially independent. There is no public electricity or gas supplied in any part of the parish, although a considerable number of farms own their own electric lighting plant, and many of the houses have installed one of the several types of rural gas. Where these amenities are not present, lighting is by paraffin oil, and cooking by oil or open fire.

Lying at the foot of the Lammermuirs, the main roads all tend to run roughly parallel to the line of hills, i.e. east to west. Roads, whether main or secondary, are in good condition. Evidence of the old drove road used when Dalkeith was the only market frequented by the crofters is still in existence in the east-west Green Road from Wedderlie Farm to Raecleugh Farm.

There is now one primary school in the village with a roll of approximately 40 pupils. There is a headmaster and one assistant teacher. Because of the outlying nature of many of the farms, upwards of 30 per cent of the children are conveyed to school. At Pyatshaw, on the western parish boundary, there is also a one-teacher school with approximately 12 pupils. The village school has independent school meals, the kitchen being started about seven years ago, and in a parish such as this this is possibly one of the biggest advances made in education over the past half-century. Both schools run a branch Lending Library from the County Library Scheme.

There is no resident doctor or nurse in the parish. While the health of the pre-school children and school children is very well looked after, there are times during stormy winters when difficulties have been encountered in obtaining the services of doctor or ambulance.

HOUSING

Most of the farms are owner occupied now: in the past 50 years more tenant farmers have had the opportunity of purchasing their farms from the large estate owners, as a complete farming community. Therefore the majority of the houses fall into the category of tied cottages. Almost without exception advantage has been taken of the various opportunities in the past for the improvement of these cottages. There are six local authority owned houses. In general it might be said that the housing falls into the following categories: There are the larger houses on the farms normally occupied by the landlord farmer. The workers' cottages (tied cottages) are also situated on the various farms. The council houses are occupied in the main by free-lance agricultural workers, e.g. workers who move about from farm to farm for seasonal occupations such as lambing and harvesting, but who are not hired to any one particular master. A great many of the owned cottages are owned and occupied by retired or semi-retired people. There is one shop which acts as a sub-Post Office and general store. There is also a quiet country hotel.

Year	*Houses Inhabited*	*Houses uninhabited*	*Male*	*Female*	*Total*
1801	165	7	361	418	779
1861	152	12	377	409	786
1951	116	7	163	132	295

POPULATION

From this table it will be noted that over the past 100 years there has been a fall of approximately 50 per cent in population. This might be accounted for by three social changes: there has been a drift from country to town; families must obviously be considerably smaller now, as the drop in houses is not commensurate with the population drop, being in the region of 20 per cent; and the largest estate in this parish no longer exists as such. A large number of people in the parish had always been employed as servants and workers on Spottiswoode Estate, which even in the closing years of last century was in its heyday. After the death of Lady Anne Spottiswoode in 1900 the estate gradually dwindled away. Farms were sold, in many cases to the occupying tenant, and finally the house of the estate was demolished. Shades of the past arise when it has to be stated that the stones of that very fine house now form the foundation of an adjacent aerodrome! Locally Lady Spottiswoode is also remembered for an endowment of £2,000 to the moral and respectable poor of the district. The interest from this endowment is disbursed quarterly to deserving cases. The present population is mainly engaged in rural pursuits. Only approximately 10 per cent of the working adults might be said to have no direct contact with agriculture, e.g. minister and schoolmaster.

AGRICULTURE

The parish is devoted entirely to agriculture. As most of the land is marginal in character the hill sheep industry predominates. Root crops where grown are not usually grown for sale but for cattle fodder. Mention might be made of the large expanse of heather on the northern boundaries of the parish, one of the happy hunting grounds of the apiarist in the month of August. Since sheep rearing is the main agricultural industry the shepherd must be the mainstay of the farm. The old type of hill-herd lives on, and it is remarkable to notice how often sons follow fathers. In this district, for example, three sons are following their fathers' calling, herding the hills. In another family, a son and grandson are shepherding, while the grandfather has only within recent years gone into honourable retirement.

The lack of population has forced the farming fraternity to change from the horse-drawn implements to the more modern method of tractors etc. for tilling, preparing the ground and reaping the harvest. Jobs which cannot be done by mechanical methods are usually accomplished with Irish labour. These Irish workers are classified as casual workers, remaining only for six to nine months during the growing season and returning to their homes for the winter.

THE WAY OF LIFE

There is a village hall, annexe of the 1914-18 War hut, which has been considerably improved by public effort. While not by any means ideal as a community centre, nevertheless it acts as such. On the recreational side perhaps the two most active associations are the Women's Rural Institute and an Indoor Bowling Club. Associations not purely recreational have also sprung up or have been resuscitated within the past ten years. The Church Woman's Guild has become an active factor in church life, while the Youth Fellowship is also doing a good work both for mind and body.

The simple facts about the parish of Westruther: over the past 100 years there has been a steady decline in population which would appear to be alarming. Such a state of affairs can be stayed by the local authorities' providing better facilities such as light industry, lighting and transport services. These facilities would entice people, especially young people, to remain in the area of their birth, who in the main seek employment in the larger cities either in Scotland or over the border. There is little evidence that many venture further than these islands, but those who do find homes and employment away from their native heath always return for a holiday at some time.

The circumstances of the farm worker have changed considerably over the past 20 years. Higher wages and set hours of work make for a greater number of leisure hours which are utilised to the full in such hobbies as gardening, bee-keeping, shooting and fishing. The transport facilities in this area are very inadequate. The one-time enterprising private bus owner, who operated a local bus service, has now disappeared in favour of the bigger combines of transport. Today there is only a bus on Friday, Saturday and Sunday; the remainder of the week the village is more or less isolated. These bus services are as follows: on each of the three days to Edinburgh, on Friday and Saturday to Kelso, and on Saturday and Sunday to Berwick.

In religious matters there has been a decided change from the Disruption days. Yet there is still to be found among the older people (which is altogether lacking in the younger generation) the strong convictions of their forebears who put their Church first and all other things second.

Nevertheless even without all these needed facilities, which would lighten the burden and consequently the heart, the people in the parish are a friendly and considerate people, and on the whole are quite content with their lot, but always hoping that in the near future these needed facilities will come their way, which they feel will help at least to restore the village of Westruther to its former status of a progressive Scottish village.

1953

THE PARISH OF WESTRUTHER

by G. R. Dickson

The parish boundaries remain unaltered, the area being 22 and three quarter square miles or 5926.1 hectares.

Over the past 30 year period, the area under timber has remained fairly constant, and now extends to 404.7 hectares. At this point of time, trees planted by the Forestry Commission from 1940 onwards are reaching maturity. In some sections, controlled felling for wood pulp production has commenced.

Through extensive grant-aided drainage schemes much more of the permanent pasture or bog land in the parish has been reclaimed for cropping and rotational grassland. At present, one large project involves the reclamation of 100 hectares on the Lammermoor foothills. About 75 per cent of all the cropping area, in any one year, consists of grain — principally barley, the remainder being fodder crops for stock feeding purposes.

As a result of the regeneration of grassland, the stock-carrying capacity of farms has increased considerably. The traditional method of in-wintering cattle on turnips and hay has largely been replaced by that of using grass silage and ground barley. Hay is still used extensively in feeding out-wintered cattle and sheep. In recent years, the use of manufactured high protein 'cob' has been introduced as a 'balancer' for cattle being fed on a diet of barley straw and other high fibre fodders.

Since the previous survey, no new houses have been built in Westruther or Houndslow villages, whereas, on surrounding farms, 11 new houses have been completed. There are some 18 farm cottages which are either unoccupied or have been allowed to become derelict. Many of the remaining cottages, being surplus to requirements, have been leased as holiday homes. The traditional type stone and slated farm steadings have almost completely been replaced by modern wide-span sheds of brick or concrete construction roofed with asbestos or similar materials. All farms now have mains electricity supply and some also have mains water for domestic and commercial use.

The advanced state of mechanisation on farms and the rising costs have had the effect of reducing the labour force to a minimum. Some farmers find it more economical to hire in contractors to assist during busy periods. Consequently, these factors have accelerated depopulation in the parish. The population figure at present is 252. This represents a decrease of 15 per cent since 1953.

The school roll is now 12 and the school reduced to a one-teacher unit. It can be foreseen that, at some future date, the school may be closed down with the remaining pupils being transported to a neighbouring centre.

Likewise, church membership has declined, the number of communicant members now being 84.

In 1963, Westruther became a 'linked' charge with Legerwood and in 1970 with Gordon. In 1985 the three parishes were linked with Greenlaw where the present minister lives. Westruther Manse was sold at the time of the first linkage. In common with other congregations, church attendance has declined, with only some 25 per cent making a regular appearance at Sunday services. A joint Woman's Guild meets regularly in Gordon.

Public transport is non-existent apart from a thrice weekly 'Courier' bus service linking Houndslow and Westruther with Lauder, Galashiels, and Peel Hospital. Most families in the parish find it essential to own private cars and, although running costs are high, there is no alternative means of transport for business or social purposes.

There is a shop in Westruther village which incorporates the local post office. Although residents find it convenient to obtain daily supplies there, many choose to travel further afield to buy at supermarkets, etc., where prices are naturally lower. Since the advent of domestic deep-freeze storage cabinets, perishable commodities can also be bought in bulk quantities and at keener prices.

The farm worker of today could be considered more versatile than his counterpart of previous generations. This is explained by the fact that advanced technical equipment is being used, in controlled environmental conditions, to replace traditional systems of rearing and feeding livestock. Field machinery and equipment are also more technically advanced. To keep pace with these developments, young workers are encouraged to attend agricultural centres where day release and longer courses are provided in a wide range of subjects.

In recent years, farm workers' incomes have risen more rapidly, and, to some extent, commensurate with their increased responsibility. Wages are now comparable to those of other industries and currently average £100 per week. Due to the overall decrease in work opportunities, some younger people have to move elsewhere to find employment. As a result, the balance now swings towards a higher percentage of older residents in the parish.

There is one small non-agricultural industry in Westruther village. In what was the original U.F. Church building, a small work force of some four people manufacture labels for use in the clothing trade.

The village hall continues to be used as a centre for social activity. During the winter months, the carpet bowling club and W.R.I. meet there regularly.

Since the advent of television, more people tend to favour that source of entertainment. It is of particular benefit to the elderly and housebound who, through this medium, can maintain contact with the world outside.

Since the previous account, a higher tier of local government has been introduced, viz. the Borders Regional Council. While this has, in effect, increased the number of clerical and administrative job opportunities, few of the electorate consider that any advantage has accrued from the system. The former County Councils appeared to be equally, or even more efficient, in their approach to dealing with local matters.

Since its inception the National Health Service has, in the main, provided adequate facilities. One exception is that, in all but acute cases of illness, patients are obliged to attend surgeries for treatment. This naturally makes some residents in remote areas, dependent on neighbours and others for transport. In such circumstances, it is envisaged that perhaps someone could suffer harm from neglecting to seek timely medical attention.

In rural areas, crime was formerly infrequent and of a minor nature. In 1966 the community was deeply shocked by the murder of the local postmistress by an itinerant Irish worker. Occurrencies of this nature alert everyone to the dangers of living in this 'modern' society which, unfortunately, has become less law-abiding during the course of one life span. Should this deterioration in moral standards continue, one indeed feels apprehensive of what the future and the 21st century may hold for our children and grandchildren.

1983

THE PARISH OF WHITSOME

by the Rev. R. Y. Cairns, M.A.

The extent of the parish is about five miles from east to west and about two miles in breadth, the whole containing about eight square miles. This includes the parish of Hilton which was joined to Whitsome in the year 1735. The united parish is now always referred to as Whitsome Parish. The ruins of Hilton Church may still be seen near the farm-house of Hilton but there are only a few pieces of crumbling masonry left to mark the spot. The contiguous parishes are Hutton on the east, Ladykirk and Swinton on the south, and Edrom on the west and north.

The parish of Whitsome is in the Presbytery of Duns. In former years the Presbytery used to meet in Chirnside but it now has its meetings in Duns, the county town of Berwickshire. The Presbytery of Duns is in the Synod of Merse and Teviotdale, meeting twice a year, in April and October, at Melrose or Kelso or as may be appointed. Occasionally it meets in Hawick.

The land throughout the parish is undulating, rising not more than 250 or 300 feet at any point. French Law, a slight eminence to the east of the village on the Berwick road, has a local tradition or superstition. It is regarded as belonging to France and should it be interfered with dire international repercussions would result. The soil is regarded as being very fertile and many farmers from the west and other districts of Scotland have settled in this south-eastern corner attracted by the suitability and productivity of the land.

COMMON LAND

The Loaning, as it is called, situated at the western end of the village, is of no great extent, possibly not more than two acres. Part of it is used by the blacksmith to graze a few cattle. The new housing scheme occupies another part. This is a good site in the village. The school and schoolhouse occupy a prominent position at the western end of the village and immediately thereafter the road trends sharply downwards passing the manse. About halfway down this brae, called Hardie's Hill, stands the church on the south side of the road.

The church is pleasantly situated and commands wide prospects of rich agricultural lands on all sides. The building itself has ample accommodation for all who care to attend. It is a pleasant building with wide lancet windows glazed with clear glass. The church is consequently well lighted, there being not a dark corner in it. Some 50 years ago the seating accommodation was changed round. This greatly improved the internal appearance of the church. There is a fine little chancel where stands the Communion Table, and at one side a baptismal font in memory of Lord Lowe who resided at Laws House. This font was designed by the late Sir Robert Lorimer. On the south side of the chancel is the pulpit. The church seats about 200. Recently a new boiler was installed which adds considerably to the comfort of the worshippers. Oil lamps are still used but as there is just one service at 11.30 a.m. this is no great inconvenience. The church bell starts to ring for about two minutes *after* the congregation has assembled for worship. There are two Communion Cups of silver. On the outside of each near the top is the inscription: 'Gifted by Countess of Home, to the Kirk of Whitsome, 1704'.

The new cemetery lies between the school and the church on the south side of Hardie's Hill. There are perhaps about a couple of dozen people buried there and a number of headstones have been set up. At the end of a road running between the eastern end of the new cemetery and the school lies the old burying place. This graveyard is now closed for further burials except in a few remaining lairs where certain people have the right of burial.

The stipend of Whitsome in former years before standardisation, especially during the 1914-18 period, must have been considerable. It is now just the minimum, which at present is £520. There are two glebes, one of about ten acres bordering the manse grounds, and another of about 18 acres forming part of the lands of Hilton farm. The income from these two glebes is about £46 but this amount is included in the total amount of stipend, viz £520. The minister is technically responsible for the upkeep of fencing of his glebe, or glebes, but owing to the high cost of fencing and other repairs there is a tendency to dispose of glebes.

The manse is a fine substantial building but much too large and expensive to keep up on present-day stipends, especially where a minister has to run a car which takes on an average about £100 of his slender emoluments. The manse garden is also on the same scale, much too large for one man to keep even in reasonably good condition. But it is a good garden and the soil is fertile — the difficulty is the expense of upkeep. The date of the building of the manse is difficult to ascertain but it must be over 200 years old. It is very damp and cold, due, no doubt, to the old fashioned foundations which did not allow for sufficient ventilation underneath. This would appear to be a condition difficult to remedy. Whitsome is an old *quoad omnia* parish and there is the usual range of outbuildings consisting of two-stalled stable, byre for two cows and calf, a large thrashing-room with machinery which is slowly deteriorating, a fairly large cattle shed, harness room now used as a garage, a fine airy loft running above the stable and byre, two other small places and a stack-yard.

The only stream in the parish is the Leet which rises somewhat north of the village in the lands of Leetside Farm. It flows westwards towards the farm of Ravelaw and increases somewhat in volume as it approaches the neighbouring village of Swinton.

The parish of Whitsome is entirely agricultural and there are 12 farms within its bounds, viz. Whitsome Hill, Ravelaw (or Langrig) (the present owner who acquired the property some years ago, changed the name from Langrig to Ravelaw, Ravelaw being the older name of the farm lands); East Newton, West Newton, Whitsome Laws, South Laws, Jardinefield, Hilton, Dykegatehead, Heriotbank, Winfield and Leetside. The acreage of these farms runs from about 100 acres (Heriotbank) to about 600 acres (Whitsome Hill). All forms of farming operations are carried on, raising crops, cattle and sheep; and dairy farming is carried on at Jardinefield and to a greater extent at the farms of Ravelaw and South Laws. Farming operations including milking are now almost entirely carried on by mechanical means. There are also other mechanical devices for work in the fields. One seldom sees a horse either in field or road but in one or two farms an 'orra beast' is kept for occasional work. All the farms are excellently well managed and the drainage and fencing of the fields leave little to be desired.

Within recent years, as well as the rise in wages, the housing conditions of the farm worker have been greatly improved. Most of the farm cottages have been completely modernised with up-to-date kitchens, bathrooms, toilets, hot and cold water and electricity. Until a few months ago the sanitary arrangements were primitive, dry closets, water from pump or pipe in the village and open drainage for slops, etc. The Watch Water Scheme (County) has now reached Whitsome and most of the houses have water connections and sewage disposal pipes. Electricity, too, has been led in. More than half the houses are supplied with electricity. In the meantime, however, the power does not go farther than the school and schoolhouse at the top of Hardie's Hill. This still leaves the church, manse and four other houses outwith the scope of the electrical supply; also some few farms which, however, have their own power plants. This also applies to water supply. In some cases the water is pumped from a well by windmill or diesel engine. Well water is much preferred by the people to the new scheme water which in the meantime is much discoloured and, so it is said, does not make good tea. Consequently most folk still continue to use water from the wells to make this beverage. The scheme water, however, is excellent for all other domestic purposes, especially for washing, being much softer than the water from the wells which is heavily charged with lime and is consequently very hard and leaves a thick deposit in a very short time on domestic utensils. It is expected that the filter beds will be in operation in a month or two and this will give a service of good clear water. A number of the houses have cookers burning calor or rural gas but no house in the parish is lit by this means, although there are one or two families outwith the bounds who use this form of illumination. It would appear to be quite a satisfactory type of lighting and an excellent substitute for electricity until power reaches these points.

County Council houses are built on the common land called the Loaning. These consist of three and four apartments with kitchenette, etc., and are replete with all modern improvements — eight houses in all. Excluding the council houses there are about 20 small houses in the village, two shops and a blacksmith's smithy. One of the shops is a baker's with a bakery attached. The other shop is the post office which also carries a good selection of general merchandise. Miss Agnes Ferguson has carried on business in the post office for upwards of 50 years, and she is also the Registrar of Births, Marriages and Deaths and in many other ways is a most useful and respected member of the community. The blacksmith has only an occasional shoeing but is kept busy with many other jobs in ironwork and the repair of tractors and large lorries.

POPULATION

The total population of Whitsome amounted in 1951 to 30, 152 males and 152 females.

RELIGION

There are no complications in the religious life of Whitsome. The parish church is the only church and all are Protestants with the exception of one family who have recently settled in the village. There are three Communions in the year and about 50 to 60 per cent of those on the Communion Roll attend, otherwise attendances are small. There is, generally speaking, widespread indifference to religious ordinances although there is good feeling towards the Church. The services of the parish minister are always sought for baptisms, marriages and funerals. Even those who seldom darken the door of the sanctuary seem eager to have their children received into the Church by the Sacrament of Baptism, to be joined in Holy Matrimony by the minister and to have Christian burial. By the generosity of former generations of pious men and women the church is well-endowed, yet in spite of this good help every penny of available money which reaches the coffers of the church, whether by plate or other means, is required to square accounts at the close of each year's working. Those who come to church join heartily in the singing and although they do not apparently show any outward sign of interest in the sermon, nevertheless they follow it closely.

There are on, an average, 12 scholars in the Sunday School and attendance is commendably regular in spite of fairly long distances to be covered on foot by the children, weather conditions permitting. It is noticeable that those children who attend are eager to do so. Numbers might be greater and one cannot help thinking that this is due in no small measure to indifference on the part of parents.

Saturday night entertainments have some influence in non-church attendance by the younger folk. If there is nothing special to attract them at the local hall, they make their way by bus to Berwick-upon-Tweed. There they may go to a cinema show and afterwards to a dance hall, arriving home after midnight and in no way inclined to rise and get ready for church on Sunday forenoon. This practice is general throughout Scotland and it is a problem which has been facing the Church for years. In these circumstances it is next to impossible to induce young people to join a Bible Class. Even the visit of a fine choir on a Sunday evening to give a feast of sacred song attracts few. In this connection it seems hardly necessary to mention that family worship is a thing of the past. The radio services take the place of this former Sunday evening custom to some extent. A number listen in to the forenoon service in lieu of attending church.

Health services are fully available. Ambulances take patients as far afield as Edinburgh and where necessary take them back to their homes the same day. Maternity cases have the full resources of the service at their disposal and a qualified Queen's nurse attends regularly on all necessary cases. The health of the community generally is good, but it would appear that children are kept off school for rather trifling ailments and even grown-up folk take to their beds more easily than in days of yore.

There is only one school in Whitsome, a primary, the two teachers being husband and wife. There are about 45 to 50 scholars. Those who pass the leaving certificate on the higher scale go to Duns High School and the others to Chirnside, a Junior Secondary School. Transport for these scholars, both to Duns and Chirnside, is provided by the Education Authority. There are the usual evening classes which are fairly well attended. Woodwork, which is taught at Chirnside, seems to be a popular subject with the young men.

Within the last eighteen months a village hall has been completed. It was opened by Lord Blades, Q.C., who is a native of the district. He is the son of a former minister of Allanton who died a few years ago at the advanced age of 93 while still exercising the duties of his sacred calling. The village hall is a great acquisition to Whitsome and neighbourhood and supplies a long felt want in the social life of the community. In it meet the Youth Club, the Men's Recreation Club, Badminton Club and the Women's Rural Institute. Sales of work are also held and there are frequent whist drives and dances. Dramatic displays are occasionally staged by local players and visiting dramatic societies, and concert parties add to the variety of entertainment.

Bus services are fairly good for a place like Whitsome which is not on a main highway. Buses ply three times daily between Berwick-on-Tweed and Kelso, taking Whitsome on the way both going and returning. Communication with Duns is awkward, change of transport having to be made at the village of Swinton. This takes up most of the day as there is just one opportunity, about 4 p.m., of returning to Whitsome and that by a circuitous route. This is the school bus, as it is called, dropping children at various points within a wide area. For this reason, as far as Whitsome is concerned, Duns as a shopping centre is somewhat inconvenient. The village and neighbourhood is, however, well served by vans for provisions. The railway does not touch Whitsome, the nearest points being Duns, Edrom and Berwick-on-Tweed, and these places have first to be reached by some form of transport. Edrom, we understand, has been discontinued as a passenger station within recent weeks, only goods traffic being handled from this point. Although Whitsome is none too good a centre for transport, many of the farm workers have transport of their own. Some have motor bicycles and a few have cars of their own. Less than a quarter of a century ago it was a common sight to see the farmers cycling in to the market at Berwick-on-Tweed in all weathers. Now they roll into Berwick in their luxury cars in under 20 minutes.

It is recognised and appreciated by people round about the mid years that owing to increased transport facilities they enjoy greater and more frequent freedom of movement. They remember the days not so long ago when a journey to Berwick-on-Tweed, Coldstream or even Duns was only undertaken at long intervals and at considerable expense and inconvenience. In these circumstances the bus services, though infrequent as compared with other places on main roads, are fully taken advantage of, not only to places 'near hand' but also to destinations much farther afield.

WAY OF LIFE

The moral condition of the people is moderately good and with a few exceptions indulgence in alcohol is moderate. There is no public house in Whitsome, the nearest licensed premises being at the neighbouring village of Allanton about one and a half miles distant.

The people are industrious and moderately contented with their lot. They are intelligent and hold tenaciously to their own point of view. With all the modern improvements round about them which make life easier and more comfortable, especially for their women folk, many are traditionalists and hold strongly to customs and practices of the past. Some read good literature but most confine themselves to the daily press and the weeklies. In politics one would say there is a strong Labour strain among all classes. The handsome aid given to farming, generally, by the Socialists, such as subsidies, cannot very well be ignored no matter how it may be deplored in other quarters. Yet there are some who hold other views. Many send their contributions to the pools and no occasion for raising money is complete without a raffle, indeed raffling is rife. On the whole the people are friendly though somewhat reserved.

Even with more comfortable and modernised houses there is considerable movement among the farm workers. This is no doubt due to the monthly hiring system which allows a man to seek employment elsewhere if he is not satisfied with conditions after he has settled down in his new job. This system may be satisfactory to the employer as well, although at times it may be awkward. On the whole it may be said that both parties are well enough satisfied with the working of this system.

Throughout the parish the farmhouses are mostly large substantial buildings fully modernised and equipped with the latest conveniences and labour-saving devices. Outbuildings such as byres, hay sheds and old stables have received similar treatment. In two farms at least large modern byres have been built almost, one would think, regardless of expense. This is all to the good and goes a long way to ensure a plentiful supply of good and pure milk.

The only mansion house in the parish is Laws House, presently occupied by a retired lawyer.

There are some expressions peculiar to this part of the Borders: hard up, clever, rael handy. We understand that the first signifies that a person is not too weel — 'he has been very hard up this while back'; the second has a somewhat similar meaning — 'she is no very clever the day'; and real handy — 'you can tak a cauld rael handy'.

In regard to work on the land much is heard in the press about the scarcity of workers and the migration of the younger folk to the big industrial centres. While this is true generally, one would say that as regards the Whitsome area, excluding the frequent moving around of the farm worker and his family, not many of the young men of the district desert the country for the town. Nevertheless, it is a general complaint that wages in Scotland lag behind the English standard.

1952

THE PARISH OF WHITSOME

by Mr and Mrs J. M. McDonald

Since 1952 when the last report on Whitsome was prepared, the parish has continued to change in line with national trends and local needs. One of the most important of these changes is the diminished importance of the parish as a recognisable unit of social or administrative importance. The Church obviously still recognises the parish but only as one part of a wider grouping of churches and not a unit on its own. It is significant that even this wider grouping has changed since 1952 —

the parish sharing a minister with Ladykirk until a further reorganisation resulted in Whitsome becoming part of a group of parishes consisting of Whitsome, Ladykirk, Swinton, Leitholm and Fogo. Although the primary school still serves the old parish area there have been two attempts to close the school and send the pupils to either Swinton or Chirnside. After the reorganisation of local government in 1975 a community council was set up covering Whitsome, Edrom and Allanton — yet another grouping of old communities and parishes. There is no doubt that much of this amalgamation of interests is the direct result of the continued loss of rural population and the need to make better use of scarce resources, but the inability to see larger groupings in a consistent way has tended to lead to a lack of identity and thereby a lack of interest in such things as the Community Council.

POPULATION

Since 1952 there has been a further drop in population, there being in 1981 94 males and 88 females within the parish. This total of 182 compares with a total of 304 in 1952. To a large extent this is the result of the continuing mechanisation of farming and the changing types of crop to reduce labour costs; many of the former farm cottages have been abandoned, demolished or left empty. Some are used for summer holiday accommodation or are let to retired people. Farms which had on average five farm cottages now employ at most three full-time workers. Many farmers employ a minimum of full-time employees and rely on seasonal contract labour to assist in sowing, spraying and harvesting crops. Employment within the village of Whitsome has also changed over the past 30 years. There is now only one shop — a combined sub-post office and general merchant. There is no longer a blacksmith in the village, and it is true to say that, with the exception of the shop keeper, school teacher and those working on farms, nobody else obtains their income from within this parish. There are of course several retired people in the village, but all the non-farming actively employed people have to work outwith the parish — in Duns, Berwick-upon-Tweed or even abroad.

The population appears to be an ageing one with many people coming into the parish to retire. Private and local authority houses within the village are sought after by retired people — but lack of public transport must weigh against the low cost housing and comparative quiet of the area. The reduction in the number of young people within the parish has put great strains on the school; and concern has been expressed on two occasions that the numbers attending the school cannot justify its retention. This has been strongly resisted on both occasions by parents and many villagers. There is every reason to believe that the loss of the school would adversely affect the population and lead to further decline.

It is worth noting that there is a much more mobile population than in the past. Those born and bred and still working in the parish are in a minority and the close family ties and intimate knowledge of all and everything that happened in the parish in the past are fast disappearing. This dilution of local knowledge and tradition leads to confusion over such things as the rights of commoners and the status and location of ancient rights of way.

EMPLOYMENT

As has already been stated the major change in local employment is related to agriculture. This employment, although always subject to change, was the mainstay of the local population. The rural area and the village were dependant on the intensive cultivation of the rich farming lands and this employment resulted in a density of population which supported local public transport, shops, local tradesmen and craftsmen, the local school and church. The mechanisation of farming and the introduction of new crops have resulted in a great reduction in farm labour and a correspondingly lower density of population in the parish. There is now only one teacher (who may well not be kept on): there is no resident minister, only one shopkeeper/sub-postmaster; there are no local blacksmiths or joiners, all such services being located in larger villages such as Chirnside, Allanton, Swinton and Duns. One of the largest farms does employ a motor mechanic, primarily to service the farm's own machinery and grain lorries, but other non-farmwork is also carried out. Non-agricultural employment is provided in the neighbouring centres of Duns, Chirnside and Berwick-upon-Tweed but there is no public transport suitable for normal working hours to any of these places.

Employment in agriculture continues to decline as farmers take advantage of more sophisticated machinery and methods of culture. The popularity of winter-sown crops and a greater variety of crops spreads the periods of sowing and harvesting, thereby making better use of manpower and machinery. This trend in declining agricultural employment is furthered by the growth of contracted labour for ploughing, sowing, harvesting, draining, fencing and hedge-cutting. There is therefore not the need to retain labour in the quiet periods to carry out these trades.

AGRICULTURE

A little has already been said about agriculture in considering the population and employment. With the exception of the Heritage all the farms which existed in 1950 still retain their separate identity. The two farms of Hilton and Dykegatehead are managed as one unit by father and son. Jardinefield is still predominatly a dairy farm. What has changed dramatically since 1950 is the type of crop being grown. Winter sown cereals are now common and the bright yellow flower of oil-seed rape is a feature of the countryside in May and June, Most farmers have rationalised their field boundaries and there has also been a considerable loss of hedgerows within the parish. Those hedgerows which remain are mostly in a poor state of health because of the universal maintenance of the hedges by mechanised means. No repairs, layering or replanting are being carried out and where new drainage or road works are carried out the hedging is not replaced. The loss of hedgerow trees over the past 20 years is even more noticeable and again no new trees are being planted. Whitsome parish seems to have been particularly denuded of hedgerow trees whether by reason of soil conditions, age of the original plantings, exposure or the intensity of the farming.

Most of the traditional farm buildings have been replaced, with only the farm house and some storage buildings of traditional design and materials being retained. Large modern cattle buildings of concrete block and asbestos have replaced the stone and slated buildings and every major farmstead is marked by the siting of a group of silage towers. The appearance of the countryside has therefore been radically changed in the last 20 years by the replacement of most of the traditional rural buildings and this change has been made more obvious by the removal of hedgerow trees.

TRANSPORT

The revolution in transport is directly related to the prosperity of agriculture. With improved wage levels and the availability of private transport the vast majority of households have a private car and many households have the use of two cars or more. Such a revolution in private transport makes rural living more acceptable for many but the effect on public transport has been disastrous. There is now only one scheduled service per day into Berwick and back. There is no service to Kelso or Duns and the timing of the one service makes it unpopular with old people. A local authority organised courier bus has been organised to help provide transport to hospitals, doctor's surgeries and other necessary services, but it still remains true that those people outwith private transport have been greatly disadvantaged by the reduction in public services.

The other notable change in transport is the arrival of large agricultural service lorries. These are of course necessary to transport the crops to the large grain centres, but the roads within the parish have not been improved to take the increased lorry traffic into account. Road verges have consistently to be driven on and narrow rural roads can soon become unpleasantly fringed by churned-up mud.

EDUCATION AND OTHER SERVICES

There still remains a primary school within the parish, secondary education being provided at Duns. In recent years the education authority has proposed the closure of the school because of the drop in numbers of pupils and the lack of educational opportunity. This closure has been strongly resisted by the majority of people in the parish, the main reasons being the lack of an identifiable alternative with public transport links and the strong feeling of identity with the existing Whitsome school. Further education is provided in Duns, Chirnside, Eyemouth and Berwick.

The Church remains part of the life of the parish but it is no longer possible to know the religious beliefs of all the residents, mainly because it is no longer of such great importance in the social life of the community. There is no longer a resident minister for the parish church, the one clergyman living in Swinton and looking after the parishes of Whitsome, Ladykirk, Swinton, Fogo and part of Leitholm. Services are held in Whitsome Parish Church on the 1st and 2nd Sundays of each month at 10.15 a.m. The church is beautifully maintained but it may now be regretted that the 18th century layout was changed, as the building is more architecturally interesting from the outside rather than for the internal fittings and arrangements. The two glebes are still let and the old graveyards at Whitsome and Hilton are still of interest to historians of the area. The graveyard at Whitsome is especially attractive, containing a Mort house and some interesting old gravestones. The area is well maintained by the District Council, even if the over-enthusiastic grass and yew cutting diminishes the wildlife and wildflowers.

The village hall is now maintained by the community. Having originally been provided by local people it was handed over to Berwickshire County Council to maintain until once again the responsibility was assumed by a local committee. The main source of financing the running of the village hall is a club which runs a monthly lottery. This club has approximately 90 members, including representatives of most of the families in the parish. Recent improvements to the toilets, lighting and decoration reflect the renewed interest which is borne out in the use of the hall by the men's club, the Church Guild, the S.W.R.I. and the Badminton Club. Recently a monthly Old People's Club was formed and this club also uses the village hall. From time to time the hall is used for entertainments and wedding receptions.

There is support for most of the long-established organisations but with the reduction in population levels and the advent of television and more affluence, a lot of the social and recreational activities are now based on the larger villages and towns. Young farmers' clubs, art clubs and sporting activities therefore oblige more and more people to find their recreation outwith the parish. The centralisation of schools, the dispersal of employment and the availability of private transport make it more difficult to foster local community spirit, but the retention of the village hall and the fight to save the village school testify to the latent loyalty of local people to the old community framework.

There are no health facilities in the parish, the local doctors being situated in Duns, Chirnside and Norham. Hospital treatment is based in Duns and Peel Hospital in the Borders, and Berwick and Ashington in Northumberland. Many special treatments can only be catered for in Edinburgh and Newcastle. There are no public transport services linking the medical facilities and patients and their visitors must rely on private transport or the service specially provided by the Regional Council. There is no doubt that the distance from hospital facilities puts a great strain on patients and visitors alike.

There remains in the village one shop which serves as a post office and general merchant's. In recent years there has been a great reduction in the number of travelling shops in the parish and many of the older residents find it difficult to shop for their needs locally. The only public bus service is to Berwick-upon-Tweed which is an expanding shopping centre — the only problem being that the timing of the buses means that too long has to be spent in the town. The changing patterns of retail food shopping mean that more and more people are taking advantage of the large supermarkets and the shops in the rural areas are being made less viable.

THE FABRIC OF THE PARISH

The Parish of Whitsome is typical of the lowland area of Berwickshire. Although at one time ill-drained and regarded as unhealthy, the farmland, though of heavy clay soil, has now been well drained and is of the finest agricultural value. The parish may not be well treed but it has an attractive landscape with extensive views to the north to the Lammermuirs and to the south to the Cheviots. The large flat plain in which the parish is situated enhances these distant views and makes up for the lack of special features or trees within the parish. There is still in existence the remains of a wartime airfield at Winfield and the runways are still used by light aircraft. The village of Whitsome is not regarded as picturesque, being situated on a windswept ridge with the houses set out plainly on either side of a public road. Most of the houses are of old traditional design but there is a group of four blocks of semi-detached council houses and three modern bungalows have been built within the last 15 years. All the property is in reasonable condition with the exception of one block of old houses which although capable of being modernised have remained unoccupied for at least 10 years. All houses have main drainage to a septic tank and works situated to the west of the Heritage land. There is a public water supply and electricity to all houses. The electricity service has recently been augmented to overcome local faults but the overhead lines still appear vulnerable to winter blizzards.

The school and schoolhouse are substantial stone buildings situated in a commanding position at the west end of the village. For so small a parish it is interesting to note that there is a telephone exchange, which at least ensures that Whitsome appears in the telephone directory. The only other landscape features are the disused quarries at Heriot Bank and East Newton, and the Leet burn which was regraded 10 years ago to improve the farm drainage but in the process lost all its character.

There is still a field at the west end of the village which is regarded as common land and people still recall the use made of the land by villagers who kept livestock. This tradition has recently been revived and the field has been used for the grazing of horses and sheep. The village hall is also built on common land. There are no signposted rights of way, and old footpaths used as shortcuts by school children and workers to get from the farms to the village have all but disappeared. The most openly recognised are the footpaths from the village to Blackadder by way of Leetside and from West Newton by way of East Newton. There are also footpaths in the Hilton area which once linked farms which have been incorporated in larger farm units.

CONCLUSION

Although Whitsome is not a well-known parish it is part of the larger area of well farmed lowland Berwickshire — the Merse — which has been noted for its rich agricultural traditions. The legends, local expressions and dialects of the parish are those of Berwickshire. In the past the parish has boasted a Law Lord as a resident of Laws House, but today the name of Whitsome is probably most often mentioned in connection with Andrew Cowan, a noted rally driver who still makes the headlines in international car events.

1983

BIBLIOGRAPHICAL NOTE

Neither a bibliography of material relating to Berwickshire nor any general history of the county is in existence. Readers seeking further information on Berwickshire and its history are therefore advised to consult the following more general works:

Arthur Mitchell and C. G. Cash, *A Contribution to the Bibliography of Scottish Topography*, 2 Vols, Scottish History Society, 1917.

P. D. Hancock, *A Bibliography of Works Relating to Scotland, 1916-50*, Edinburgh University Press, 1959.

National Library of Scotland, *Bibliography of Scotland, 1976*—, published annually from 1978 by the N.L.S.

Materials on Berwickshire, published in the years between 1950 and 1976, are listed in a bibliography kept by the National Library of Scotland on typewritten slips, which are available for public consultation on request.

GENERAL INDEX

INDEX OF PLACES

Casual and passing references are not included